The First Four Notes

The First Four Notes

*Beethoven's Fifth
and the Human Imagination*

Matthew Guerrieri

ALFRED A. KNOPF   NEW YORK   2012

784.2184
Due

THIS IS A BORZOI BOOK
PUBLISHED BY ALFRED A. KNOPF

Copyright © 2012 by Matthew Guerrieri
All rights reserved. Published in the United States by
Alfred A. Knopf, a division of Random House, Inc., New York,
and in Canada by Random House of Canada Limited, Toronto.
www.aaknopf.com

Knopf, Borzoi Books, and the colophon are registered trade-
marks of Random House, Inc.

Library of Congress Cataloging-in-Publication Data
Guerrieri, Matthew.
The first four notes : Beethoven's fifth and the human imagination /
by Matthew Guerrieri.
p. cm.
Includes bibliographical references.
ISBN 978-0-307-59328-3
1. Beethoven, Ludwig van, 1770–1827. Symphonies, no. 5,
op. 67, C minor. 2. Beethoven, Ludwig van, 1770–1827—
Appreciation. I. Title.
ML410.B42G94 2012
784.2'184—dc23   2012019886

Jacket design by Peter Mendelsund
Manufactured in the United States of America
First Edition

For my father,

who let me steal his books and records

Contents

FORD: . . . here, how about this . . . "Da da da dum!"
Doesn't that stir anything in you?

f/x airlock door opens

VOGON GUARD: 'Bye, I'll mention what you said to my
aunt.

f/x airlock door closes

FORD: Potentially bright lad I thought.

ARTHUR: We're trapped now, aren't we?

FORD: Errrrr . . . yes, we're trapped.

—DOUGLAS ADAMS
The Hitchhiker's Guide to the Galaxy (radio series)

Preface

MARTEN: What about you? Do you have any big nostalgia-inducing songs?

HANNELORE: Beethoven's Fifth reminds me of Canada. I don't know why. I've never been to Canada.

—JEPH JACQUES, *Questionable Content*[1]

In his best seller *Beethoven: The Man Who Freed Music,* first published in 1929, the poet and essayist Robert Haven Schauffler polled a parade of opinions of Beethoven's Fifth from a pool of straw men:

To Brown it may signify a fierce conflict with a sexual obsession. To Jones a desperate campaign against an inferiority complex. To Robinson an old-fashioned pitched battle *à la* "Paradise Lost," between the forces of good and evil. To a victim of hysteria it may depict a war between sanity and bedlam. To a neurasthenic a struggle between those two mutually exclusive objectives: "To be, or not to be?" To an evolutionist it may bring up the primordial conflict of fire and water, of man with beast, of civilization with savagery, of land with sea.[2]

Such mutable celebrity had already long surrounded the symphony. Beethoven's Fifth, the Symphony in C minor, op. 67, might not be the greatest piece of music ever written—even Beethoven himself preferred his Third Symphony, the *Eroica*[3]— but it must be the greatest "great piece" ever written, a figure on which successive mantles of greatness have, ever more inevitably, fit with tailored precision. And its iconic opening is a large part of that: short enough to remember and portentous enough to be memorable, seeming to unlock the symphony's meaning but leaving its mysteries temptingly out of reach, saying *something* but admitting nothing.

This is a book about Beethoven's Fifth Symphony. More specifically, it is a book about the opening notes of that symphony; and more specifically than that, it is a book about what people have heard in those notes throughout history, and how history itself has affected what was heard. It is, then, history viewed through the forced perspective of one piece of music; though, to be fair, there is only a handful of pieces of music that could yield a comparable view, and most of them are by Beethoven. And, even within the subject's limited parameters, it is hardly a comprehensive history. Any writing on Beethoven is an exercise in selection, and the selection says at least as much, if not more, about the writer's obsessions as it does about Beethoven. This is only one possible path through the biography of the Fifth Symphony; there could be many others.

To say a piece of music has meaning is to say that it is susceptible to discussions of meaning; by that standard, Beethoven's Fifth is easily one of the most meaningful pieces of music ever written. The number and variety of the interpretations assigned to the Fifth, the creativity with which the piece has been invoked in support of countless, often contradictory, causes—artistic, philosophical, political—all this is a tribute to its amorphous power. It is also, on the side of the interpreters, a testament to human creativity, ingenuity—and folly. The vaunted universality of Beethoven's achievement encompasses the sublime and the ridiculous.

Not that he didn't try to warn us. In 1855, an unknown writer felt compelled to make a handwritten addition to a copy of Anton Schindler's biography of Beethoven:

Something about the beginning of the C minor Symph-[ony]. Many men were disturbed over the beginning of the Fifth. One of them ask[ed] Beethoven about the reason for the unusual opening and its meaning. Beethoven answered: "The beginning sounds and means: *You are too dumb.*"[4]

The First Four Notes

Revolutions

The first thing to do on arriving at a symphony concert is
to express the wish that the orchestra will play Beethoven's
Fifth. If your companion then says "Fifth what?" you are safe
with him for the rest of the evening; no metal can touch you.
If, however, he says "So do I"—this is a danger signal and he
may require careful handling.

—DONALD OGDEN STEWART, *Perfect Behavior* (1922)

JEAN-FRANÇOIS LE SUEUR was not quite sure what to make of
Beethoven's Fifth. Le Sueur was a dramatic composer, a specialist in oratorios and operas, and the Parisian taste for such fare
(along with Le Sueur's career) had persisted from the reign of
Louis XVI through the Revolution, through Napoléon, through
the Restoration. For audiences suddenly to be whipped into a
frenzy by *instrumental* music—as they were in 1828, when a new
series of orchestral concerts brought Paris its first sustained
dose of Beethoven's symphonies—was something curious. Le
Sueur, nearing seventy, was too refined to fulminate, but he
kept a respectful distance from the novelties—that is, until one

of his students, an up-and-coming enfant terrible named Hector Berlioz, dragged his teacher to a performance of the Fifth.
Berlioz later recalled Le Sueur's postconcert reaction: "Ouf! I'm
going outside, I need some air. It's unbelievable, wonderful! It so
moved and disturbed me and turned me upside down that when
I came out of my box and went to put on my hat, for a moment I
didn't know where my head was."

Alas, in retrospect, it was too much of a shock: at his lesson
the next day, Le Sueur cautioned Berlioz that "All the same, that
sort of music should not be written."[1]

IN 1920, Stefan Wolpe, then an eighteen-year-old student at the
Berlin Hochschule für Musik, organized a Dadaist provocation.
He put eight phonographs on a stage, each bearing a recording
of Beethoven's Fifth Symphony. He then played all eight, simultaneously, with each record turning at a different speed.

A socialist and a Jew, Wolpe would flee Nazi Germany; he
eventually ended up in America, cobbling together a career as
an avant-garde composer and as a teacher whose importance
and influence belied his lack of fame. (The jazz saxophonist
Charlie Parker, shortly before he died, approached Wolpe about
lessons and a possible commissioned piece.)[2] In a 1962 lecture,
Wolpe recalled his Dada years, revisiting his Beethoven collage;
in a bow to technological change, this performance used only
two phonographs, set at the once-familiar 33 and 78 r.p.m.
Wolpe then spoke of "one of the early Dada obsessions, or interests, namely, the concept of unforeseeability":

> That means that every moment events are so freshly
>   invented,
> so newly born,
> that it has almost no history in the piece itself
> but its own actual presence.[3]

. . .

IF TODAY we regard Le Sueur's frazzled confusion as quaint, it is at least in part because of the subsequent ubiquity of the Fifth Symphony. The music's immediacy has been forever dented by its celebrity. Wolpe's eightfold distortion can be heard as a particularly outrageous attempt to re-create Le Sueur's experience of the Fifth, to conjure up a time when the work's course was still unforeseeable. It is an uphill battle—in the two centuries since its 1808 premiere, Beethoven's Fifth has become so familiar that it is next to impossible to re-create the disorientation that it could cause when it was newly born.

The disorientation is built right into the symphony's opening. Or even, maybe, *before* the opening: the symphony begins, literally, with silence, an eighth rest slipped in before the first note. A rest on the downbeat, a bit of quiet, seems an inauspicious start. Of course, every symphony is surrounded by at least theoretical silence. Though, in reality, preconcert ambient noise, or at least its echoes—overlapping conversations, shifting bodies, rustling programs, air-conditioning, and so on—may in fact bleed into the music being performed, we nonetheless create a perceptive line between nonmusic and music, enter into a conspiracy between performers and listeners that the composer's statement is self-contained, that there is a sonic buffer zone between everyday life and music. (Like most conspiracies, it thrives on partial truths.) The obvious interpretation is that silence functions as a frame for the musical object.[4] The less obvious (and groovier) interpretation is that the music we hear is but one facet of the silence it comes out of.[5]

This is almost certainly not what Beethoven was thinking about when he put a rest in the first measure of the Fifth Symphony. But, were Beethoven really trying to mess around with the boundary between his symphony and everything outside of it, he would have been anticipating the French philosopher Jacques Derrida, the guru of deconstruction, by nearly two hundred years. Derrida talks about frames in his book *The Truth in Painting*, noting that when we look at a painting, the frame seems part of the wall, but when we look at the wall, the frame seems part of the painting. Derrida terms this slipstream between the work and outside the work a *parergon*: "a form which has as its traditional determination not that it stands out, but that it disappears, buries itself, effaces itself, melts away at the moment it deploys its greatest energy."[6]

Our minds dissolve the frame as we cross the Rubicon into Art. But Beethoven drags the edge of the frame into the painting itself, stylizing it to the point that, for anyone reading the score, at least, this parergon refuses to go quietly, as it were. Beethoven waits until we're ready, then gruffly asks if we're ready yet.

We can *see* the silence on the page, in the form of the rest. But do we hear it in performance? The rest completes the meter of 2/4—two beats per measure, with the quarter note getting the beat—which, normally, would mean that the second of the three following eighth notes would get a little extra emphasis. But most readings give heavy emphasis to all three eighth notes, steamrolling the meter (which is really only one beat to a bar anyway—more on that in a minute). Paleobotanist, artist, and sometime composer Wesley Wehr recalled one consequence of such steamrolling:

> Student composer Hubbard Miller, as the story goes, had once been beachcombing at Agate Beach. He paused on the beach to trace some musical staves in the sand, and then added the opening notes of Beethoven's *Fifth Symphony*. Hub had, however, made a slight mistake. Instead of using eighth notes for the famous "da, da, da, *dum!*," Hub had written a triplet. He had the right notes, but the wrong rhythm—an easy enough mistake for a young lad to make. Hub looked up to find an elderly man standing beside him, studying the musical misnotation. The mysteri-

ous man erased the mistake with one foot, bent down, and
wrote the correct rhythmic notation in the sand. With that,
he smiled at Hub and continued walking down the beach.
Only later did Hub learn that he had just had a "music lesson" from Ernest Bloch.[7]

Knowledge of the rest is like a secret handshake, admission
into the guild. (Bloch, best known for his 1916 cello-and-
orchestra "Rhapsodie hébraïque" *Schelomo*, was also a dedicated
photographer who liked to name his images of trees after composers: "Bloch sees 'Beethoven' invariably as a single massive
tree appearing to twist and struggle out of the soil."[8])

Indeed, one practical reason for the rest is to reassure the
performers of the composer's professionalism. Beethoven knew
that any conductor would signal the downbeat anyway, so he put
in the rest as a placeholder for the conductor's gesture. And it's
liable to be a fairly dramatic gesture at that. The meter indicates
two beats to the bar, but no conductor actually indicates both
beats, as it would tend to bog down music that needs speed and
forward momentum. Instead, the movement is conducted "in
one," indicating only the downbeat of every bar.

So the conductor has one snap of the baton to get the orchestra up to full speed. And the longer the Fifth Symphony has
retained its canonical status, the more that task has come to be
seen as perilous. For the two leading pre–World War I pundits of
conducting, Richard Wagner and Felix Weingartner, starting the
Fifth was no big deal. Wagner takes ignition for granted, being
far more concerned with the lengths of the subsequent holds,[9]
while Weingartner scoffs at his colleague Hans von Bülow's cau-
tion: "Bülow's practice of giving one or several bars beforehand
is quite unnecessary."[10] But jump ahead to the modern era, and
one finds the British conductor Norman Del Mar warning of
"would-be adopters of the baton" suffering "the humiliation of
being unable to start the first movement at all."[11] Gunther Schul-

ler, American composer and conductor, is equally dire, calling the opening "one of the most feared conducting challenges in the entire classical literature."[12] Del Mar reaches this conclusion: "It is useless to try and formulate the way this is done in terms of conventional stick technique. It is direction by pure force of gesture and depends entirely on the will-power and total conviction of the conductor."[13]

It is only a coincidence that the eighth rest resembles the trigger of a starter's pistol:

Beethoven was known for being moody and intolerant long before he began to lose his hearing. Apparently he was just as pissed off by what he could hear as by what he could not.

—PAULA POUNDSTONE,
There's Nothing in This Book That I Meant to Say

IF ONLY for the blink of an eye, the eighth rest leaves the symphony hanging in fraught silence, a condition that, even at the time of the Fifth's premiere, was already becoming attached to the Beethoven mythos. The fame of the Fifth Symphony has its biographical match in Beethoven's deafness.

Beethoven first noticed a deterioration in his hearing sometime in his twenties; when, in 1801, he first broached the subject in letters to close friends ("I beg you to treat what I have told you about my hearing as a great secret," he wrote to the violinist Karl Amenda, underlining the request for emphasis[14]), he had already been seeing physicians about it for at least a year. The initial symptoms were those of tinnitus—buzzing and ringing in the ears, a sensitivity to loud noises. ("[I]f anybody shouts, I can't bear it," he complained.[15])

It would be difficult to overestimate how disconcerting the onset of such a condition must have been to the young Beethoven, especially at that point in his career, having moved to the cultural metropolis of Vienna, on the precarious cusp between notoriety and lasting success. But it is also important to note that—contrary to much popular opinion—even at the time he was composing the Fifth Symphony (1804 to 1808, on and off), Beethoven could still hear fairly well, at least well enough to conduct the 1808 premieres of the Fifth and Sixth Symphonies and then write his publisher about correcting the score: "When I gave these works to you, I had not yet heard either of them performed—and one should not be so like a god as not to have to correct something here and there in one's created works."[16] His fellow composer-pianist Carl Czerny reported that Beethoven "still heard speech and music perfectly well until at least 1812."[17] While that optimistic characterization is more likely a testament to Beethoven's adjustment to his infirmity, it's clear that the Fifth Symphony was not born out of an absolute pathological silence.

Tracing the progression of Beethoven's deafness is difficult not just because of Beethoven's own tendency to overdramatize his affliction, but also because of the tendency of his friends and acquaintances to attribute to deafness symptoms that might just as easily be traced to another underlying condition: that of, well, being Beethoven. In 1804, Stephan von Breuning writes to a mutual friend that as a result of Beethoven's "waning of hearing . . . [h]e has become very withdrawn and often mistrustful of his best friends, and irresolute in many things!"[18] But, as biographer Maynard Solomon reminds us, the withdrawal, mistrust, and retreat from everyday concerns were there all along: "During his childhood, Beethoven often wrapped himself in a cloak of silence as a shield against both the vicissitudes of external reality and the traumatic events within his family constellation."[19] Pushed forward as a Mozart-like prodigy by his alcoholic, dissolute, abusive father, Beethoven retreated into solitude and daydreaming, the defense of a figurative deafness, well before any literal manifestation.

If the onset of hearing loss fed into Beethoven's penchant for isolation, his penchant for isolation may have, in turn, fed an exaggerated sense of the extent of his deafness. Recent proposed guidelines for tinnitus diagnosis include the reminder that "it has become clear in recent years that the 'problem' of tinnitus relates far more to the individual's psychological response to the abnormal tinnitus signal than to the signal itself. . . . [I]n some cases the altered mood state predates tinnitus onset . . . making it difficult to know whether tinnitus causes psychological disturbance, or whether psychological disturbance facilitates the emergence of tinnitus."[20]

Nevertheless, the adaptability of so much of Beethoven's middle-period "heroic" output to narratives of crisis and triumph has contributed to a popular sense that his deafness was sudden and total, rather than gradual. One finds it in an entry from an American music-lover's diary, published in *Dwight's Journal of Music* in 1853: "[Beethoven] was deaf, poor man, when he wrote the 3d, 4th, 5th, 6th, 7th, and 8th Symphonies. Deaf when he composed 'Fidelio,' 'The Ruins of Athens,' the two Masses, &c."[21]

The unidentified diarist was actually Alexander Wheelock Thayer, who would later undertake extensive research in Germany and Austria and produce a pioneering Beethoven biography, the first volume of which appeared in 1866; based on Thayer's findings, most critics and scholars would adopt a more nuanced view of Beethoven's deafness. But the story of a stone-deaf Beethoven and his dauntless musical response was too good, too inspirational, not to survive. The American composer Frances McCollin, for example, blind from the age of five, took powerful inspiration from the story, starting when she attended a dress rehearsal for the Philadelphia Orchestra's inaugural concert in 1900: "[S]he heard the slow movement of Beethoven's Fifth Symphony, which made her think of the deaf Beethoven and she burst into tears."[22] McCollin's story echoes one from the six-year-old Clara Schumann—who, for reasons similar to Beethoven's, was so withdrawn as a child that her parents thought she, too, might be deaf—noting in her diary, "I heard a grand symphony by Beethoven which excited me greatly."[23]

The image of a young, completely deaf Beethoven gained a foothold in children's literature, offering an educational example of human perseverance (and, maybe, playing on a child's delight in paradox: a composer who can't hear). *McGuffey's Fifth Eclectic Reader* included an excerpt from Harriet Martineau's *The Crofton Boys*, in which young Hugh Proctor's mother tries to console him after he has had his foot amputated:

> "Did you ever hear of Beethoven? He was one of the greatest musical composers that ever lived. His great, his sole delight was in music. It was the passion of his life. When all his time and all his mind were given to music, he suddenly became deaf, perfectly deaf; so that he never more heard one single note from the loudest orchestra. While crowds were moved and delighted with his compositions, it was all silence to him." Hugh said nothing.[24]

Even today, one can still find the myth perpetuated here and there.[25]

As an up-and-coming composer and performer, Beethoven probably feared that common knowledge of his encroaching deafness would have hindered his career prospects. The opposite occurred, as it turned out: within his own lifetime, Beethoven's deafness became a celebrated element in the reputations of both the composer and his music. A snippet of that celebrity is preserved in the conversation books, the trove of one-sided table talk from Beethoven's later years, when guests would jot down their share of the discussion on paper. During one chat, Beethoven's nephew Karl informs his uncle of popular perception: "Precisely because of [your deafness] you are famous. Everyone is astonished, not just that you can compose so well, but particularly that you can do it in spite of this affliction. If you ask me, I believe that it even contributes to the originality of your compositions."[26]

On this occasion, Beethoven seems to have taken his nephew slightly to task for overdetermining the nature of his genius, but there is some evidence that it was Beethoven himself who planted the seed of that astonishment and fame. By the time of the Fifth's premiere, Beethoven had come to terms with his deafness enough to stop concealing it and to start even subtly advertising it, writing a note to himself in one of his sketchbooks to "let your deafness no longer be a secret—even in art." The musicologist Owen Jander went so far as to reinterpret the Fifth Symphony in light of this self-admonition, making it not just a metaphorical struggle with infirmity, but, at least in the slow march that permeates the third and part of the fourth movements—a march built out of the symphony's opening motive—a musical re-creation of the experience of deafness. The third movement's translation of its theme into a desaturated skeleton of pizzicato strings, Jander suggested, was meant to simulate the composer's increasingly hazy sense of hearing.[27]

If the Fifth Symphony is about Beethoven's deafness, then what could we read into its opening rest? A brief jolt of the experience of deafness, perhaps—a deployment of great energy that remains bereft of sound. Or maybe a remembrance and a reminder: a moment of silence for Beethoven's hearing.

THE PITCHES of the opening phrase produce their own ambiguity, albeit one that, given the symphony's familiarity, is, again, well-nigh impossible to recapture. The Fifth is in C minor, a key forever associated with Beethoven in his most heaven-storming moods. But, strictly speaking, C minor is not actually *established* until the seventh measure of the first movement. Beethoven exploits a quirk of music theory concerning the triad, one of the basic building blocks of Western music: a stack of three notes, the first, third, and fifth notes of the major or minor scale. If you take away one of the notes of a triad, it starts to, in effect, gesture in two directions at once. So the first two pitches of the Fifth Symphony, G and E-flat, might be two-thirds of a C-minor triad, or they might be two-thirds of an E-flat major triad. The *second* pair of pitches, F and D, could be part of a dominant-seventh chord built on G (the most basic harmonic antecedent of C minor), or part of one built on B-flat (the most basic harmonic antecedent of E-flat major). From a music theory standpoint, the opening passage is playing fast and loose with the symphony's key: until the cellos and bassoons anchor the motive with a sustained middle C in the seventh bar, there's no way to tell whether the piece is in a major or minor key.

Modern ears might reflexively assign more dramatic weight to minor keys than to major, but that wasn't necessarily the case in Beethoven's time. Italian theorist Francesco Galeazzi, writing in 1796, called E-flat major "a heroic key, extremely majestic, grave and serious."[28] Not so for C minor. In 1713, German composer and theorist Johann Mattheson wrote, "An extremely lovely, but also sad key. Because the first quality is too prevalent and one can easily get tired of too much sweetness, no harm is done when the attempt is made to enliven the key a little by a somewhat cheerful or regular tempo."[29]

Jean-Jacques Rousseau's 1749 *Encyclopédie* opined that C minor "brings tenderness into the soul." Writing in 1783, Johann J. H. Ribock, an accomplished amateur flutist, compared the key "to the colour of a pale rose and also to the aroma of the same."[30] Late-eighteenth-century composers created a somewhat more Gothic atmosphere with C minor—as in Mozart's K. 491 Piano

Concerto, a brooding piece that Beethoven particularly admired. ("We shall never be able to do anything like that!" he once told a friend.[31]) But for heroism, Mozart opted for E-flat major—in the opening scene of *Die Zauberflöte*, Prince Tamino finds himself set upon by a slithery C-minor monster that the Three Ladies vanquish with a timely modulation to E-flat: "Triumph!"

In the concert hall, though, the sheer gravity of the Fifth's opening makes the vague tonality moot. The major-minor uncertainty in the opening of the Fifth Symphony engendered next to no contemporary comment—only E. T. A. Hoffmann mentioned it, in his seminal 1810 review of the symphony ("the listener surmises E-flat major," he surmised[32]), and he was working from the score, not from a performance. And, harmonically rooted or not, the *sound* of the Fifth's opening was actually somewhat traditional for C minor: many C-minor works of Haydn and Mozart (K. 491 included) also start out with passages in bare unisons or octaves.[33] Beethoven adopted that stylistic tic; his largest C-minor essay prior to the Fifth, the Third Piano Concerto, opens in ominous octaves (and with a theme strongly foreshadowing the Fifth Symphony's Finale), as does his Violin Sonata op. 30, no. 2.

But those openings were all quiet in their foreboding. The Fifth imbues the C-minor dialect with rhetorical force. Beethoven's orchestration of the opening is optimized toward weight: all the strings, in their lowest, heaviest registers, plus clarinets, which round and burnish the strings' tone. In the original manuscript, Beethoven initially had the flutes doubling the opening line an octave higher, then thought better of it and scratched those notes out. No double reeds—oboes, bassoons—and no brass: any hint of instrumental brightness has been banished. In place of an all-for-one *tutti* opening, Beethoven opts for only those instruments that can combine power with overcast gloom. The feminine overtones of contemporary C-minor impressions are absent—Leonard Bernstein heard the orchestration as gender-specific: "Beethoven clearly wanted these notes to be a strong, masculine utterance, and he therefore orchestrated entirely with instruments that play normally in the register of the male singing voice."[34] At the very least, Beethoven deliberately avoided Mattheson's advice to leaven C minor with a bit of cheer.

Beethoven's appropriation of E-flat major's dark majesty for his favored C minor was a success, to judge by a subsequent spate of revised key impressions. While some writings, still reliant on older traditions, continued the theme of gentle lament, an 1827 musical dictionary by J. A. Schrader assigned to C minor "rigid, numb grief," "fear and horror," "bitter lamenting," and "despair." In 1830, the German organist G. F. Ebhardt heard in C minor "extreme misery, sometimes raving nonsense."[35] Part of the shift no doubt came from the Romantic era's louder dramatic volume; descriptions of other keys also move toward more emotional extremes. But Beethoven's own stormy reputation drove much of that Romantic amplification—and his stormiest key was C minor. The Fifth Symphony endured as a ready-made example of the new association.

NO OTHER COMPOSER'S working habits have been analyzed as closely as Beethoven's. It helped that Beethoven's sketches survived to be analyzed. Most of Mozart's sketches, by comparison, were destroyed after he died, which contributed to the popular impression that he worked out everything in his head before putting pen to paper.[36] Whereas Beethoven's sketchbooks, in all their messy, indecipherable glory, seemed tailor-made for his Romantic admirers, a chance to witness the familiar themes twist and struggle their way to the surface like Bloch's Beethovenian trees. Unlike many of Beethoven's themes, however, the opening of the Fifth seems to have sprung nearly fully grown from his head.

The earliest sketches for the Fifth are found in a manuscript referred to as Landsberg 6, or, sometimes, the *Eroica* sketchbook—the bulk of the leaves are filled with workings-out of Beethoven's Third Symphony. Much of the rest is taken up with early work on Beethoven's only completed opera, *Leonore* (later retitled *Fidelio*).[37] Located at the creative locus of three of Beethoven's most celebrated works—the Third and Fifth Symphonies and *Fidelio*—Landsberg 6 might be the most famous of Beethoven's sketchbooks.

Amazingly, it was lost for much of the twentieth century, having vanished from the Preussische Staatsbibliothek in Berlin at the end of World War II. The library had acquired it in 1861 from the estate of Ludwig Landsberg, a Prussian-born violinist and singer who ended up living in Rome. Landsberg amassed manuscripts and early editions of Renaissance and Baroque music during his more than twenty years in Italy; on trips between Rome and his native Breslau, he was apparently in the habit of stopping to buy manuscripts from Viennese dealers as well. When a catalog of his collection was published after his death (in preparation for its sale), Landsberg's Beethoven trove—including eight of the sketchbooks—was listed first, the most obvious treasures.[38] Breslau, now Wrocław, became part of Poland after World War II. Landsberg, who died and was buried in Rome, didn't make it back home, but the highlight of his collection did: after disappearing from Berlin, Landsberg 6 eventually turned up in the Biblioteka Jagiellońska in Kraków—a souvenir of Beethoven's heroic period appropriately transformed into a trophy of war.

Sometime in early 1804, at the bottom of page 157, tucked into three extra staves under some scribbled ideas for *Fidelio*, Beethoven sketched out the opening section of the Fifth, in unusually well-developed embryo:

Sinfonia

The transcription—a bit of heroism in itself, given the illegibility of Beethoven's handwriting—is by Gustav Nottebohm, a German academic who did the first serious work on Beethoven's sketchbooks.[39] (Johannes Brahms, a longtime friend, once pranked Nottebohm by fashioning a fake Beethoven sketch and then bribing Nottebohm's favorite grocer to wrap up the scholar's cheese and sausage in it.[40]) The structure and contour of the opening sentences are already there; the only difference is in those places where Beethoven softens the three-note repetition of the opening motive by walking the melody down the scale. Beethoven, perhaps, was already considering how the motive would make connections between the symphony's movements; on pages just prior to this, he was jotting down ideas for the Fifth's third movement, in which the motive returns in march form, and the three-note figure does break into a step-by-step melodic descent. In the context of the opening, though, such filling-in was far too fussy, the musical equivalent of making a bold claim and then immediately qualifying it with a lot of hemming and hawing. By the time the Fifth was completed, Beethoven had decided that the repeated notes made a better effect, that the motive's rhythmic profile alone would be strong enough to tie the various movements together.

The rhythmic foot the Fifth lays out—short-short-short-long—was known in Classical antiquity as a *quartus paeon*. (Any combination of one long syllable with three short ones is a paeon; putting the long syllable at the end makes it the fourth, or *quartus,* paeon.) Beethoven, who revered the Greek poet Homer, would have read of the paeon's namesake, the Olympian physician, in Book V of the *Iliad:* "Thereon Hades went to the house of Jove on great Olympus, angry and full of pain; and the arrow in his brawny shoulder caused him great anguish till Pæëon healed him by spreading soothing herbs on the wound, for Hades was not of mortal mould."[41]

As the divine power of healing gravitated to Apollo, so did

the name, and paeans became hymns to Apollo. Later, the paean also acquired a martial connotation, a name applied to songs sung by armies heading into battle or, afterward, giving thanks for victory. (Conveniently, paeans often used the paeon for a metrical basis.)

Beethoven read Homer only in translation, and any connection he might have made between the Homeric healer and the rhythmic pattern he liberally applied to his most famous symphony is pure conjecture. But if the *quartus paeon* was a conscious choice on Beethoven's part, he couldn't have picked a more appropriate confirmation of the symphony's popular perception: a battle cry and a plea for healing, all wrapped up in a concise motive.

The ancient Greeks would have appreciated the *quartus paeon* as a source of the Fifth Symphony's oft-cited rhetorical power. Aristotle didn't discuss the paeon in his *Poetics,* but included it in the toolbox of his *Rhetoric.* After dismissing a host of poetic feet as unsuitable to oratory ("prose must be rhythmical, but not metrical, otherwise it will be a poem"), Aristotle allows for an exception:

> There remains the paeon, used by rhetoricians from the time of Thrasymachus, although they could not define it.
>
> The paeon is a third kind of rhythm closely related to those already mentioned; for its proportion is 3 to 2, that of the others 1 to 1 and 2 to 1, with both of which the paeon, whose proportion is 1½ to 1, is connected.

In other words, the slightly off-balance three-versus-two of the paeon (three short syllables plus a double-length long syllable) relieves the singsong nature of other poetic rhythms. Thus "the paeon should be retained, because it is the only one of the rhythms mentioned which is not adapted to a metrical system, so that it is most likely to be undetected."[42] The paeon gives prose the dramatic force of epic poetry without its sounding like poetry. The vague sense of rhetorical *meaning* that contemporary listeners found so novel about the Fifth may have been the by-product of an ancient Greek toastmasters' trick. (The Roman rhetorician Quintilian was, in fact, downright snobbish about the paeon: "Why it pleased [other] writers so much I do not understand; but possibly most of those who liked it were men that fixed their attention rather on the language of common life than on that of oratory."[43])

The trick still works. In the 1970s, the music education researcher Edwin Gordon was trying to sort basic building blocks of music by how easy or hard they were for students to learn. For one study, Gordon developed a taxonomy of 533 different rhythmic cells, then had more than four thousand fourth-, fifth-, and sixth-graders listen to tapes of the cells.[44] Each cell was played, then repeated, and the students were tested as to whether or not they perceived the repetition as identical with the original. Gordon then sorted the cells by both difficulty (the more the students identified the repetition of a cell, the "easier" that cell was considered to be) and progression—whether a given cell was "easier" for older students.

The perception of the 2/4, three-eighth-note pickup of the Fifth Symphony's opening was classified as both "Difficult" (fewer than half the listeners heard the motive's repetition as a repetition) and "Static-Regressive" (the age of the student made no difference in their perception).[45] It was, in fact, the only rhythmic cell in Gordon's "Usual Duple" category—symmetrical divisions of individual beats and measures—to rank as *both* difficult to perceive and age-neutral. By design or by accident, Beethoven made an ideal choice for an all-pervasive motive, one whose obsessive repetition doesn't come across as repetition—the exact intended effect of the paeon.

.   .   .

THE SIMILARITY of the Fifth's earliest sketches to its final iteration—one of the few instances in the sketchbooks where a bolt-of-inspiration interpretation could apply—lends at least passing credence to the earliest musical creation story of Beethoven and his four notes: a little bird told him.

The most-cited source for this story is Beethoven's student, the pianist and composer Carl Czerny. Beethoven heard the ten-year-old Czerny play in 1801 and was impressed enough to give the child lessons. Czerny in turn would become perhaps the nineteenth century's greatest piano teacher, training a host of performers and pedagogues more important than famous—Sigismond Thalberg, Stephen Heller, Theodor Leschetizky—as well as one whose importance *and* fame seemingly knew no bounds: Franz Liszt. Unlike almost everyone else who ever knew the composer, the sober and industrious Czerny never sought to cash in on his relationship with Beethoven; in turn, Beethoven stayed friends with Czerny, trusting him to edit proofs of his works for publication, recruiting him to give lessons to his nephew Karl.

"Many of Beethoven's motives resulted from passing outside impressions and events," Czerny recalled. "The song of a forest-bird (the yellowhammer) gave him the theme of the C-minor symphony, and those who heard him fantasize on it know what he was able to develop from the most insignificant few tones."[46] (Czerny reported that the theme of the Scherzo from the Ninth Symphony was also inspired by a bird.)

Beethoven, a lover of nature, probably would not have considered such a source trivial. It might have carried an echo of *Naturphilosophie*, a then-popular concept that the natural world was the manifestation of a single, ideal, dynamic process, an order that would be revealed once all of creation was arranged in a sufficiently intricate hierarchy. A foreshadowing of *Naturphilosophie* can be found in a book Beethoven particularly enjoyed, Christoph Christian Sturm's 1784 *Betrachtungen über die Werke*

Gottes im Reiche der Natur (Reflections on the Works of God in the Realm of Nature):

> How bountifully has God provided for the gratification of our *senses*! For instance, he has chosen the softest and most proper colours to please and refresh the sight. Experience proves that *blue* and *green* surfaces reflect those rays only which are least injurious to the eyes, and which they can contemplate the longest without being fatigued. Hence it is the Divine goodness has clothed the heavens with *blue*, and the earth with *green*. . . . The *ear* also is not unemployed: it is delighted with the songs of birds, which fill the air with their melodious concerts.[47]

Naturphilosophie would become more sophisticated after it was taken up by one of the era's leading philosophical celebrities, Friedrich Wilhelm Joseph Schelling. A later exponent of the style, Lorenz Oken (whose work Beethoven had at least a passing familiarity with[48]), would place the senses at the center of his conception, a fanciful taxonomy of nested five-part divisions; at its highest level, birds, representing hearing, ranked just behind mammals, representing sight.[49]

The tale of the yellowhammer and the Fifth seems to have been current during Beethoven's lifetime; Wilhelm Christian Müller, a music teacher and acquaintance of Beethoven, mentioned it in a remembrance he wrote shortly after Beethoven's death: "During [Beethoven's] walks he composed and often took his themes from birds, for example, the G-G-G-E-flat, F-F-F-D in the Fifth Symphony."[50] And the yellowhammer's song does bear at least some resemblance to the motive, a rapid-fire repetition of short notes followed by one or two longer tones.[51]

In other words, this is an unusually well-sourced and plausible Beethoven myth, and yet, its provenance notwithstanding, the yellowhammer's authorship gradually became a footnote, usually mentioned only in passing alongside more-well-known stories—including one that will occupy the entire next chapter of this book, the characterization of the Fifth's opening as "fate knocking at the door." In English-speaking countries, the bird story suffered a bit of guilt by association after Anton Schindler, Beethoven's onetime secretary and, later, his notoriously inaccurate biographer, related that Beethoven had told *him* that a completely different figure in the Sixth Symphony, a quick upward arpeggio, was also inspired by a yellowhammer. The discrepancy cast doubt on all Beethovenian birdcalls; most thought that the composer was merely pulling Schindler's leg. (Schindler may actually have been right for once, the victim of German-English dictionaries that translated his *Goldammer* and Czerny's *Ammerling* as the same bird, but Schindler was referring to a goldfinch, not a yellowhammer.)[52]

Mostly, Czerny's story faded to footnote status because the symphony's accumulating philosophical baggage crowded it out—a chance avian dictation of the famous theme came to be considered too insignificant a source for the Fifth's increasingly portentous reputation. Harvey Grace, an English organist and writer, put it thus in 1920:

> But how many hearers think of the yellow-hammer? They are all Werthers for a brief spell, and invest the music with a significance far more profound than the composer ever gave it. What verbal commonplace can ever come to mean so much as this trivial birdcall? It is as if such an expression as "I'll trouble you for the salt" suddenly became so charged with tremendous and shattering import that on hearing it people would fall into an agony of remorse.[53]

THE OPENING EIGHTH-REST IS BEETHOVEN'S first bit of misdirection—combined with the quick, in-one 2/4 meter, it produces the triplet-or-straight-eighth rhythmic uncertainty of the first three notes. The C-minor/E-flat major ambiguity is Beethoven's second bit of misdirection. Either uncertainty would be so brief as to be unworthy of mention, except that they're compounded by Beethoven's *third* bit of misdirection: fermatas over the fourth and eighth notes of the symphony, dramatic pauses punctuating the two statements of the four-note motive.

Throwing up such rhythmic roadblocks, holding the notes out for as long as the conductor sees fit, might seem like an avant-garde touch—a Beckettesque frustration, stopping the clock just as it's getting started. But beginning a piece with dramatic pauses had become something of a commonplace toward the end of the eighteenth century. Mozart's *Die Zauberflöte*, a piece Beethoven especially admired, opens with three grand chords interspersed with temporally generous space, fermatas over the intervening rests. And Beethoven's onetime teacher Haydn, as his career went on, was more and more likely to start his symphonies with similarly grand fermatas.[54]

The Classical-era music theorist Heinrich Koch had equated the fermata with an "expression of surprise or astonishment, a feeling whereby the movements of the spirit itself appear to come to a brief standstill."[55] Fermatas right at the start were an attempt to create that surprise and astonishment immediately, a proto-Romantic goal of jolting the audience into a heightened emotional state.

Mozart and Haydn, though, placed their fermatas in slow introductions (*Adagio* markings in both cases), set off from the thematic argument of the piece. Beethoven pushes the envelope by starting off at the movement's main, fast pace, then dropping his fermatas, in quick succession, into his main theme. (After the premiere, Beethoven added an extra bar before the second fermata, making it slightly longer than the first, and the whole opening that much more off-balance and edgy.)

In performance, the fermatas rather quickly became repositories of applied importance, with conductors stretching the emphases into extravagant flourishes. The most immoderate of such conductors was Richard Wagner, who, in a famous passage, prescribed overwrought fermatas, in prose to match:

> Now let us suppose the voice of Beethoven to have cried from the grave to a conductor: "Hold thou my fermata long and terribly! I wrote no fermata for jest or from bepuzzlement, haply to think out my further move; but the same full tone I mean to be squeezed dry in my Adagio for utterance of sweltering emotion, I cast among the rushing figures of my passionate Allegro, if need be, a paroxysm of joy or horror. Then shall its life be drained to the last blood-drop; then do I part the waters of my ocean, and bare the depths of its abyss. . . ."[56]

That image of conductors casting down the fermatas like Charlton Heston as Moses contributed to an increasingly DeMille-like aura around the Fifth as the Romantic era hit its stride, the sort of reputation that marginalized Czerny's yellow-hammer source as simply too trifling.

But Beethoven might have intended the fermatas to exaggerate a feeling of forward motion. The symphony shows off its power by only hinting at its speed—a couple of fearsome revs of the engine before Beethoven finally lets out the clutch—but the trip is already under way, leaving the listener scrambling to catch up. And almost from the beginning, Beethoven's combination of rebellion and haste rather fittingly engendered the question of whether it was *too* fast.

Nearly a decade after the Fifth's premiere, Beethoven augmented the first movement's *Allegro con brio* tempo with a metronome marking: 108 half notes per minute. Beethoven hadn't initially indicated a metronome marking for the Fifth for the simple reason that, in 1808, the metronome didn't exist yet. It was only in 1812 that Dietrich Winkel invented the device; not until 1816 that Johann Mälzel, having stolen Winkel's invention, began to manufacture it.

Mälzel and Beethoven were friends—Mälzel provided the composer with custom ear trumpets[57] and, having built a massive mechanical organ called a panharmonicon, commissioned for it Beethoven's op. 91 novelty *Wellington's Victory* (a commission that led to a characteristically Beethovenian falling-out over money). Beethoven became the metronome's most famous early adopter. With his nephew Karl, Beethoven went back over his catalog, retroactively quantifying his tempo markings with the new gadget, then published a table of such markings, covering the first eight symphonies, in a leading German music magazine, the *Allgemeine musikalische Zeitung*, in December 1817.

And, since December 1817, conductors and performers have been ignoring those markings. Anecdotal evidence hints that nineteenth-century performances customarily eased Beethoven's 108 marking to something a bit more manageable. The ever-unreliable Anton Schindler even insisted that Beethoven took the opening five bars (up until the second fermata) at a tempo of *quarter*-note-equals-126, or half-note-equals-63—almost twice as slow as indicated.[58] That was too much liberty for at least one famous colleague; Felix Weingartner tells the story: "Liszt told me that the 'ignorant' and furthermore 'mischievous fellow' Schindler turned up one fine day at Mendelssohn's and tried to stuff him that Beethoven wished the opening to be *andante*—pom, pom, pom, pom. 'Mendelssohn, who was usually so amiable,' said Liszt laughingly, 'got so enraged that he threw Schindler out—pom, pom, pom, *pom!*'"[59] (But even Weingartner, an early stickler for textual fidelity, advised dialing back the first movement to 100 beats per minute.[60])

With the advent of the gramophone, parameters of performance practice—at least those inherited from late

Romanticism—could be pinned down exactly. Conductor Arthur Nikisch and the Berlin Philharmonic made a complete recording of the Fifth in 1913; Nikisch's reading of the first movement coalesces around 88, albeit through a heightened haze of flexible speed. Weingartner lived long enough to record the Fifth four times in the 1920s and '30s, by which time his tempo had slowed from his earlier recommendation (his 1933 recording with the London Philharmonic settles in at around 92, for instance). In 1998, Gunther Schuller tabulated tempi for sixty-six different recordings of the Fifth; the average speed was just under 92 bpm.[61]

Nikisch's is sometimes cited as the first complete Fifth on record, but Friedrich Kark, a German conductor whose range extended from opera to popular dance music, had already led a cheerfully rough-and-ready recording with the Odeon-Orchester, a studio group, in 1910—with a first movement that does, indeed, reach the 108 mark here and there, albeit in somewhat runaway fashion. Kark aside, for many years, the only conductor to match Beethoven's markings (and not always) was the fiery taskmaster Arturo Toscanini. But Toscanini's fleetness was at least as much a sign of its own time as an effort to re-create the sound of Beethoven's era. Composer Lazare Saminsky called Toscanini "entirely a musician of our day. . . . His very aversion to adorning music, for inflating it with meaning, with extra-musical content, emotionalizing what is but pure line and form, is the aversion of today's musician."[62]

Even this approach was subject to its own modernist reaction, as when the quintessential avant-gardist, Pierre Boulez, conducted a recording of the Fifth in which the first movement clocked in at an astonishingly deliberate 74 beats per minute. "At the time it seemed to me people generally took off like bats out of hell in the first movement," he later explained. "I probably overcompensated. Certain things set one off."[63] (Another provocateur, Leopold Stokowski, even managed to out-Schindler

Schindler in one recording, taking the opening at a geologic 40 beats per minute.) Alternately obeying and ignoring Beethoven's tempi has created its own historical rhythm, the present's undulating dance with the past. (The controversy has even crossed over into other planes of existence. Attending a table-rapping séance, Robert Schumann asked the spirit to knock the first two bars of the Fifth. After a pause, the familiar rhythm commenced—"only slightly too slow," as Schumann told it. "The tempo is faster, dear table," Schumann chided; the table duly sped up.[64])

Those rare performances that adopt Beethoven's metronome marking can still sound almost cartoonishly fast. Such a reaction demonstrates either a) the extent to which two centuries of overdoses of injected Romantic gravitas have distorted Beethoven's original conception, or, b) that somehow or other Beethoven got his own tempo wrong. But the seemingly simple task of confirming Beethoven's metronome markings can quickly turn into a game of point/counterpoint. The Vienna of Beethoven's time apparently favored faster tempi—Carl Czerny, for instance, published tables of metronome markings for works by Mozart, Haydn, and Beethoven indicating such.[65] On the other hand, both Czerny and Beethoven were setting tempi at the piano, not in rehearsal with a full orchestra, and the sharper attack and quicker decay of the piano might have encouraged faster tempi.[66]

And then, there is the tricky business of Beethoven's advancing deafness. A Beethoven relying more on the *sight* of the metronome's swinging pendulum than its *sound* might have experienced a psychological phenomenon called saccadic chronostasis: watching a clock tick can produce the illusion that it's ticking ever so slightly slower than it actually is.[67] Another toss-up: musical training improves accurate tempo perception, but deafness inhibits it.[68]

Possibly the first person to notice that the ears were better than the eyes at judging intervals of time was a German physician named Karl von Vierordt, whose main claim to fame was figuring out how to measure blood pressure; he invented the forerunner of the modern sphygmomanometer. He was also curious about how the brain makes sense of time, publishing a book about it in 1868. Out of his experiments (performed mainly on himself), he formulated Vierordt's Law, a fairly robust rule of thumb that says that humans almost universally underestimate long periods of time, while overestimating short ones. This logically implied the existence of an "indifference point," where our perception crosses the line between under- and overestimation: one spot on the continuum where our perception of an interval of time is exact.[69]

The indifference point is not an uncontroversial subject (experimental parameters seem to affect it to a somewhat unruly degree, scientifically speaking), but—and here's where it gets interesting vis-à-vis Beethoven—the most commonly cited figures for the indifference point are between 625 and 700 milliseconds.[70] On a metronome, that would correspond to between 86 and 96 beats per minute—almost exactly the range of Romantic and post-Romantic performances of the first movement of the Fifth. Also, the 550-millisecond beat that Beethoven's 108-bpm marking prescribes is right in the middle of the range in which people are most sensitive to tempo discrimination.[71] In other words, in psychological terms, Beethoven's marking for the Fifth *is* too fast—perhaps *deliberately* too fast. Based on Vierordt's Law, 108 bpm will always feel like it's running away from us, the next beat always falling just before our overestimation wants to place it; and, what's more, 108 is right where that's liable to discombobulate us the most. All those plodding conductors might have been in search of rhetorical importance—or they might merely have been instinctively nudging the Fifth's tempo back toward the indifference point, each successive downbeat coming where they expect. Consciously or not, Beethoven gave the Fifth a tempo marking that exacerbated the symphony's sense of disorientation; consciously or not, ever since they got their hands on it, conductors have been trying to ameliorate it.

The 108 threshold reentered the musical world with the early-music movement, once its practitioners gained the confidence to classify Beethoven as a candidate for historically informed performance.[72] The early-music philosophy, with its focus on period instruments, textual fidelity, and "letting the music speak for itself" (as one sometime skeptic put it),[73] nonetheless, like Toscanini's machine-like clarity, reflected contemporary needs as much as Beethoven's; it was both a construct made possible by modern scholarship and an assertion of authenticity in an increasingly manufactured, consumerist culture.

The whole concept of "authenticity" fascinated the existentialists, especially Jean-Paul Sartre, as a symptom of modernity and its discontent; Sartre wrote of "that deep desire, that fear and anguish at the heart of all authenticity—which are apprehensions *before life*. . . . This fear is due to the fact that the situations envisaged are on the horizon, out of reach[.]"[74]

One is almost tempted to plot the fluctuations in the speed of performances of the Fifth as a kind of index of alienation over time, with instances of Beethoven's perceptually out-of-reach 108 beats per minute indicating, paradoxically, the most insistent need for an authentic experience.

SARTRE ONCE LIKENED Beethoven's music to a historical moment of unusual possibility:

Rhetorical, moving, sometimes verbose, the art of Beethoven gives us, with some delay, the musical image of the Assemblies of the French Revolution. It is Barnave, Mirabeau, sometimes, alas, Lally-Tollendal. And I am not thinking here of the meanings he himself occasionally liked to give his works, but of their meaning which ultimately expressed his way of hurling himself into a chaotic and eloquent world.[75]

For Sartre, Beethoven's exhortations were all too easily adaptable to revolution and reaction alike. (Hence the mention of Gérard de Lally-Tollendal, the Irish-born deputy to the Estates-General who defended Louis XVI and sought to preserve the ancien régime; whom the great French historian Jules Michelet described as "lachrymose Lally, who wrote only with tears, and lived with a handkerchief to his eyes."[76]) No stranger to the discord between the personal pursuit of intellectual freedom and the more restricted menu of political positions available in the public sphere, Sartre might have envied Beethoven's comparatively frictionless revolutionary reputation: energetically radical but politically elusive, embodying the passions of revolution without ever firmly coming down on any one side.

The French Revolution ended up being the great politico-intellectual winnowing of the subsequent century, as the boundaries of the European political and philosophical landscape were reconfigured around the poles of support for the Revolution's rights-of-man intentions and horror at its reign-of-terror consequences. The young Beethoven's sympathies with the ideals of the Revolution were sincere, as far as they went ("Liberty and fraternity—but not equality" is how Maynard Solomon aptly sums it up,[77] a formula that could be applied to the German Enlightenment as a whole), but his advertisement of them was selective.

The most famous of Beethoven's political statements would be his use of Friedrich von Schiller's "Ode to Joy" in the finale of the Ninth Symphony, premiered in 1824. But he was planning a setting as early as 1793.[78] That would have been just about the radical-chic zenith for Schiller, who had been arrested by the Duke of Württemberg after the sensational 1781 premiere of his play *Die Räuber,* and whose tragedies of authoritarianism and snuffed-out flames of freedom were enough to warrant the author a grant of honorary French citizenship from the National Assembly in 1792. But Schiller had already begun to sour on the French Revolution, its violence and chaos. In 1793, he would begin writing his *On the Aesthetic Education of Man in a Series of Letters,* in which he postulated art as a more reliable source of freedom:

> The dynamic State can merely make society possible, by letting one nature be curbed by another; the ethical State can merely make it (morally) necessary, by subjecting the individual will to the general; the aesthetic State alone can make it real, because it consummates the will of the whole through the nature of the individual.[79]

"[I]t is the aesthetic mode of the psyche which first gives rise to freedom," Schiller concluded.[80] By the time news of his French citizenship reached him, in 1798, Schiller considered the honor a postcard "from the empire of the dead,"[81] as he told his now-friend, the conservative Goethe. In 1802, ten years after the Assembly offered him symbolic fraternity, he accepted the nobiliary particle, becoming Friedrich von Schiller. (True, he accepted it from the comparatively liberal Charles Augustus, Duke of Saxe-Weimar, but still.)

The young Beethoven was enough of a Schiller fan that he and his friends could trade quotes from *Don Carlos* in their auto-graph books. But soon after Beethoven's arrival in Vienna, Louis XVI was guillotined in Paris, Schiller's plays were banned by the Hapsburg monarchy, and Beethoven's revolutionary enthu-siasms became more circumspect. He continued to work on a setting of *"An die Freude"*—perhaps even finishing it—but ulti-mately decided to keep it under wraps.[82] By the time Beethoven returned to the "Ode" in the Ninth Symphony, some three decades later, both the delay and Schiller's post-"Ode" moderation had somewhat dulled the connection with the Revolution.

Beethoven's politics are tricky to unravel, not just because of the novel political landscape he inhabited, but because his personal intersection with politics, fame, and necessary livelihood was largely unprecedented. One oft-repeated story of Beethoven and politics concerns the Third Symphony, the *Eroica*, which Beethoven originally planned to dedicate to—and name after—Napoléon. As Ferdinand Ries told it:

> I was the first to tell him the news that Bonaparte had declared himself Emperor, whereupon he flew into a rage and shouted: "So he too is nothing more than an ordinary man! mortal! Now he also will trample all human rights underfoot, and only pander to his own ambition; he will place himself above everyone else and become a tyrant!" Beethoven went to the table, took hold of the title page at the top, ripped it all the way through, and flung it to the floor.[83]

Beethoven scratched Bonaparte's name off the title page of the original manuscript with such vehemence that he wore a hole in the paper, and ensured his future reputation as a champion of individual freedom. Except that, as late as 1810, some six years later, Beethoven was considering dedicating another work to the former First Consul.[84] Napoléon had abandoned democratic ideals, occupied Vienna—twice—and yet Beethoven kept circling back. While working on the Fifth, he received a job offer from Jérôme Bonaparte, Napoléon's youngest brother, recently made King of Westphalia, a Napoleonic attempt at German unification; only an intervention of Viennese patronage kept Beethoven from leaving. Several years later, in 1815, Beethoven entertained dignitaries gathered to dispose of the

Napoleonic Era at the Congress of Vienna. In the wake of Waterloo, he must have felt as if his career had dodged a bullet—and yet, after Napoléon left the stage, Beethoven largely abandoned his heroic style, the style that had made him famous, the style of the Fifth.[85]

For all his paper-mutilating rage, Beethoven surely sensed that he and Napoléon were more alike than not: both coming up from modest backgrounds, both disdainful of the limitations of traditional class structure and privilege while leveraging tradition to their own ends. Napoléon paved the way for Beethoven, setting a pattern of innovative fame—one based as much on a cultivated force of personality as on achievement—that Beethoven exploited to the hilt. Leo Braudy, preeminent critic of fame, described the Emperor in terms that could easily apply to Beethoven: "He was at once the man of destiny—melancholic, brooding, striving alone—and the man of classic order, ensuring the survival of all those institutions . . . at whose center he stood."[86] Every anecdote of Beethoven's disheveled dress, his oblivious demeanor, his contempt of social ceremony, his reverence for the classics (literary *and* musical: toward the end of his life, Beethoven even bruited about the idea of an overture on the B-A-C-H theme), proved to be canny moves in a game Napoléon had pioneered.

It wasn't that the young and the restless hadn't pursued fame before, but that fame had been a means to a cushy end. As historian Henri Brunschwig put it, referring to young writers in late-eighteenth-century Prussia: "To become famous is a short cut to the heights of a career in politics or the civil service. It means gaining an embassy or a university chair without the heat of the fray; it means invitations from princes aspiring to be Maecenases."[87] But as the repercussions of revolution dried up those channels, ambition became diffuse and unfocused. Napoléon offered a case study in a new career path, one in which fame became an end in itself.

In Beethoven's case, the fame of both the composer and his music reinforced each other. The *Eroica* story burnished Beethoven's antiauthoritarian credentials, which in turn encouraged democratically "spun" interpretations of the rest of his music, which in turn further solidified the composer's radical reputation, and so on. The Landsberg 6 triumvirate—*Eroica, Fidelio,* the Fifth—had the biographical effect of making tales of Beethoven more believable the more they seemed to reveal a sympathy with revolutionary ideals.

And in Beethoven's relationship with Bettina Brentano—and Bettina's subsequent reportage of that relationship—one can clearly see the image being built.

In her own life, Bettina Brentano—later Bettina von Arnim—showed how the new rules of fame could be leveraged for feminine empowerment. Beethoven fell into the circle of the Brentanos sometime after the family moved into the wonderfully cluttered Vienna house of Joseph Melchior von Birkenstock, Bettina's half brother Franz having married Birkenstock's daughter Antonie. The Brentano sisters—Sophie, one-eyed and doomed to an untimely death; Antonie, the link between old and new Viennese aristocracy; and Bettina, confident and self-assured—were everything that Beethoven found attractive: lovely, intelligent, talented, and, for all practical purposes, maritally unattainable. At one time or another Beethoven found himself pulled toward all three. (Antonie, her marriage notwithstanding, has been not implausibly suggested as the mysterious "Immortal Beloved" to whom Beethoven wrote a series of impassioned love letters.[88])

It was in May 1810 that Bettina stole up behind Beethoven at his pianoforte and put her hands on his shoulders; when the misanthropic composer realized it was a pretty girl, and a Brentano to boot, he softened and sang to her a newly written setting of Goethe's *"Kennst du das Land?"* That, at least, is how Bettina told the story—and Bettina was quite a storyteller. The young woman had already made the acquaintance of Goethe himself, but when, later in life, she published her letters to Goethe, they were embellished, recombined, and otherwise literarily enhanced. Bettina was an unusually skillful mythologist, lively-minded and keenly observant, and the stories she is suspected of having invented nonetheless feel like they *ought* to be true. She had a knack for taking an anecdote and lightly fictionalizing it into something considerably more memorable.

So it was that one of Bettina's tales became Exhibit A in the transformation of Beethoven into a democratic hero. A kind of impresario of celebrity, she encouraged Goethe and Beethoven to meet in person; by the time they did meet, at Teplice in the summer of 1812, Bettina had been banished from the Goethe circle over a disparaging comment she made to Goethe's wife.[89] Nevertheless, Bettina recorded a letter from Beethoven describing a stroll taken by the two great men:

> Yesterday, on our way home, we met the whole Imperial family; we saw them coming some way off, when Goethe withdrew his arm from mine, in order to stand aside, and say what I would, I could not prevail on him to make another step in advance. I pressed down my hat more firmly on my head, buttoned up my great coat, and, crossing my arms behind me, I made my way through the thickest portion of the crowd. Princes and courtiers formed a lane for me; Archduke Rudolph took off his hat, and the Empress bowed to me first. These great ones of the earth *know me.* To my infinite amusement, I saw the procession defile past Goethe, who stood aside with his hat off, bowing profoundly.[90]

The letter is almost certainly an invention by Bettina. (The same week the letter is purportedly dated, Beethoven also displayed his own talents as a courtier in a letter to Archduke

Rudolph: "Your Imperial Highness!" he begins, "It has long been my duty to recall myself to your memory, but partly my occupations in behalf of my health and partly my insignificance made me hesitate. . . ."[91]) But the story became permanently enshrined in Beethovenian lore, along with the *Eroica* story, along with the letter Beethoven supposedly wrote to a patron, Prince Lichnowsky, admonishing: "Prince, what you are you are by accident of birth; what I am I am through myself. There have been and will be thousands of princes; there is only one Beethoven."[92]

Deliberately or instinctively, Beethoven (and his celebrants) again and again went out of the way to advertise his singular nature: an outsider, divorced from the hierarchical role-playing of class and status. In the wake of both the Revolution and Napoléon, that pose fueled his fame and his republican aura: a thoroughly nineteenth-century modern man.

A YELLOWHAMMER might have seemed too bucolic for the Fifth's revolutionary airs, but another bird puts Beethoven back in more weighty company: Coco the parrot, the ad hoc mascot of the Commodore Hotel in West Beirut during the Lebanese Civil War of the 1970s and '80s. The seven-story dive (by all accounts) was the primary home for Western journalists covering the conflict, a hub for sources and spin. The Commodore remained relatively unscathed by the conflict for fifteen years, but in February 1987, Druze and Shiite militias staged a seven-hour gun battle throughout the hotel, leaving it a looted shell. In the melee, Coco the parrot was kidnapped. Coco's owner, British journalist Chris Drake, had fled to Cyprus to avoid the increasingly common fate of journalist abductions in Beirut, but left the bird, at the insistence of hotel staff. "I have to accept that Coco may have been killed, but if he was, I'm sure he went down fighting," Drake eulogized. "He has a vicious beak,

and it wouldn't be too difficult to recognize the gunman who stole him. He'll be the one with his trigger finger missing."[93]
Coco could do uncanny re-creations of the sound of incoming artillery shells. He could also whistle "La Marseillaise," the French national anthem—and the opening of the Fifth Symphony.

The similarities between the two songs in Coco's repertoire raises the question of whether Beethoven was consciously alluding to "La Marseillaise" when he wrote the Fifth. Like the Fifth, "La Marseillaise" opens with a prominent, repeated-note *quartus paeon*. The Revolution rang with the meter, in fact: both of its rhetorical features—its blending of a prosaic air of conversational directness with the rhythmic force of poetry, and its ability to withstand repetition—served the Revolution's propagandists well. The triple-note upbeat into a strong downbeat—

short-short-short | **long**

—turns up often enough in French revolutionary *chansons* that a listener might consider it a stylistic feature. *"Les Voyages du bonnet rouge"* ("The Voyages of the Red Cap," referring to the official headgear of the revolution), a 1792 chanson, starts with a three-note pickup:

Le bonnet | **de** *la liber- | té*
The bonnet of liberty . . .

As does *"L'Heureuse décade"* ("The Happy Decade"), from *1793*:

Pour terras- | **ses** *nos enne- | mis*
To block off our enemies . . .

Similarly, an abolitionist plea from *1794*, *"La Liberté des Nègres"* ("The Freedom of the Negroes"):

Le savez- | **vous,** *Républi-* | *cains*
You know, Republicans . . .

The national anthem of the First Empire, *"Le Chant du départ"* ("Song of Departure"), also dates from 1794; the chorus starts in familiar rhythm:

La Répub- | **lique** *nous ap-* | *pelle*
The Republic is calling us . . .

A 1795 anti-Jacobin chanson, *"Le Réveil du peuple"* ("The awakening of the people"):

Peuple fran- | **çais,** *peuple de* | *frères*
French people, fraternal people . . .

And, lest we forget, Coco's favorite, Charles Joseph Rouget de Lisle's *1792* hit, originally called *"Chant de guerre pour l'armée du Rhin, dédié au maréchal Lukner":*

Allons en- | **fants** *de Patri-* | *e*
Come, children of the Fatherland . . .[94]

Indeed, like "La Marseillaise," both *"Le Chant du départ"* and *"Le Réveil du peuple"* were sung to specifically composed tunes, making the three-note pickup a deliberate revolutionary touch, not just a conveniently borrowed one. (The music for *"Le Réveil du peuple"* was by Pierre Gaveaux, who also composed the 1798 opera *Léonore, ou L'amour conjugal;* the libretto, by Jean-Louis Bouilly, would later serve as the basis for Beethoven's *Fidelio*.)

"La Marseillaise" alone would almost guarantee that any subsequent triple upbeat would carry a revolutionary echo. Gaveaux's was probably intentional. Was Beethoven's? The Finale of the Fifth Symphony has often been linked to both specific revolutionary songs and the general French Revolutionary musical style—martial, strongly rhythmic, almost aggressively major-mode triadic. But the Fifth's opening movement, especially the omnipresence of its opening motive—terse, direct, and incessant—could have just as easily found a place in the great *Fêtes* of the Revolution, those giant celebrations, part political rally and part revue, designed to periodically fire the public's republican enthusiasm.

Beethoven almost certainly was familiar with the musical portion of those celebrations. A series of volumes dedicated to music composed for the *Fêtes* was part of the library of Jean-Baptiste Bernadotte, then the French ambassador to Vienna, whom Beethoven frequently visited; Rodolphe Kreutzer, whose name became attached to one of Beethoven's violin sonatas, was part of Bernadotte's retinue, and had music of his own published in the *Fêtes* collection.[95] (Bernadotte's ambassadorship ended abruptly, after a riot sparked by his raising of the tricolor over the embassy; years later, unlikely political maneuvering made the French-born Bernadotte King Carl XIV Johan of Sweden and Norway.) In 1927, German musicologist Arnold Schmitz pointed out a passage in Luigi Cherubini's 1794 *L'Hymne du Panthéon* strikingly reminiscent of the Fifth's first movement, with short-short-short-long fragments cascading through the chorus.[96] An even better candidate for Beethoven's inspiration might be a massive, four-choir-and-orchestra piece written for the celebration of September 23, 1800, the Revolutionary calendar's New Year's Day. *"Chant du 1er Vendémiaire An IX"* ("Song for the First of Vendémiaire, Year Nine") bears an uncanny resemblance to the Fifth, a C-minor canvas that becomes positively saturated with the familiar rhythm once the touchstone of Classical antiquity is summoned:

Jour glori- | **eux** . . . jour de mé- | **moi**re . . .
(O Rome an- | **tique** . . . sors du tom- | **beau**!)

(Glorious day, day of memory,

O ancient Rome, leave the tomb!) [97]

The *"Chant"* was commissioned by the Minister of the Interior, Lucien Bonaparte—Napoléon's younger brother, who later fell out with the Emperor. [98] The words were by Joseph Esménard, who, some years later, provided the libretto for Gaspare Spontini's opera *Fernand Cortez,* portraying the title character as a heroic, decidedly Napoleonic figure. And the music was by none other than Jean-François Le Sueur, Berlioz's future teacher, who would be so discomfited by the Fifth. So we can see how the shifts from Republic to Consulate to Empire complicated the Revolution's legacy, and made any association with that legacy an equivocal matter.

And nowhere is the line between musical and political influence more blurry than in the case of a symphony obviously indebted to the Revolutionary musical tradition, full of the sort of instrumental effects common to the *Fêtes,* and fetishizing the three-note pickup that rhythmically propelled the songs of the Revolution—not the Fifth, but the Symphony no. 1 in G minor by Étienne-Nicolas Méhul. Even the timing is parallel: Méhul's Symphony was first performed no later than March of 1809, and some vague references in the French press indicate a possible performance in November 1808, making the premiere nearly simultaneous with that of the Fifth. [99]

Méhul, for a time Napoléon's favorite composer, had made his name in opera just as the Revolution took hold; though his intense musical energy and audacious orchestration were ideally suited to the Revolutionary style—he wrote the tune for the national anthem, *"Le Chant du départ"*—it was still too wild for some. (Le Sueur, for instance, hated him.) Something of that audacity carried over into Méhul's G-minor Symphony. The Minuet, like the Scherzo of Beethoven's Fifth, includes an arresting passage of pizzicato strings, and its *Allegro agitato* Finale seems to echo the Fifth's opening, riveted with repeated eighth notes, working a *quartus paeon* into nearly every bar.

When Méhul's First was performed in Leipzig in 1838 (under the baton of Mendelssohn), its resemblance to the Fifth was immediately noted by Robert Schumann: he thought it "so striking, that there can be no doubt of a reminiscence on one side or the other."[100] Schumann's suspicions notwithstanding, there is no evidence that either composer was aware of the other's latest project. But Beethoven did know and admire Méhul's operas. Méhul, in turn, was inspired by Beethoven's earlier efforts to try his own hand at symphonic composition; French conductor François-Antoine Habeneck recalled reading through Beethoven's first two symphonies at the Conservatoire in the early 1800s: "Of all the artists who heard us perform these works, only Méhul really liked them. It was actually these symphonies that encouraged Méhul to write similar ones of his own."[101] Similarities between Méhul's First and Beethoven's Fifth were in all likelihood the product of mutual and common influence, not plagiarism.

If anything, the Fifth's ubiquitous short-short-short-long tattoo was something Beethoven borrowed from his French colleague. Méhul uses the rhythm all the time. It turns up on the second page of his first performed opera,[102] *Euphrosine* (1790), and at least somewhere in just about everything he wrote. In 1799's *Ariodant* (Méhul's favorite among his operas), the accompaniment to the title character's first-act aria—

*Plus de doute, plus de souffra*nce	More doubt, more pain
Ah, tout mon coeur est enivré	Ah, my heart is intoxicated

—is built almost entirely from the motive.[103] In *Uthal* (1806), a chorus of soldiers uses the rhythm to swear vengeance against the eponymous Ossianic hero:[104]

perfide U- | **thal**
perfidious Uthal

Uthal, with its violin-less orchestra (the better to conjure an atmosphere of rustic shadow), illustrates Méhul's love of orchestral effect, another stylistic feature Beethoven borrowed. *Euphrosine* opens with strings, oboes, and clarinets in ominous octaves—not far from the Fifth's string-and-clarinet inception. Again anticipating the Fifth, Méhul frequently beefed up his orchestra with trombones, as in 1792's *Stratonice,*[105] and extreme *forte-piano* (loud-soft) juxtapositions are common.

Beethoven would adapt the Revolutionary style—the cutting-edge musical features developed by Méhul, Cherubini, Le Sueur—into the music of the future. In France, though, the style was falling out of favor. While the *Journal de Paris* waxed patriotic over the G-minor Symphony's 1809 premiere ("M. Méhul has desired to reconquer for France a branch of music that she had entirely lost"[106]), others disparaged the connection between Beethoven's symphonies and Méhul's: "The contagion of Teutonic harmony seems to win over the modern school of composition which has formed at the Conservatoire," scolded one critic. "They believe in producing an effect with prodigal use of the most barbaric dissonances and by making a din with all the instruments of the orchestra."[107] Even as Méhul's biblical opera *Joseph* became a hit in Germany, his career in France started to wane.

Napoléon's betrayal of democracy enraged Beethoven but depressed Méhul. His entry in the French *Encyclopédie de la musique* is blunt: "With the establishment of the Empire, when the revolutionary movement was completely crushed, Méhul's fecundity ceased."[108] Musicologist Alexander Ringer directly connected Méhul's symphonies to this disillusionment: "[R]ather than court the unpredictable taste of a public that only yesterday had consisted of ardent republicans but today shouted

'Vive l'Empereur!', the same composer who once argued that public opinion be accepted as an artistic guidepost now decided to write exclusively in obedience to his own conscience."[109]

When Beethoven's Fifth is heard as a Revolutionary call to arms while Méhul's very similar First can be heard as the Revolution's elegy, one wonders just how much specific republican sentiment Beethoven would have intended audiences to hear in his own instrumental *Fête*. Maybe Beethoven simply recognized in the Revolutionary style a musical force and drive missing in Viennese concerts. Then again, maybe Beethoven, a circumspect republican, intended the Fifth as a musical sleeper cell: a passive-aggressive dose of Revolutionary music slipped into the Austrian Empire under the guise of an abstract symphony, on the off chance that it would seed an upheaval of its own.

FRENCH URBAN PLANNER and philosopher Paul Virilio writes of "dromocratic" society, controlled not by power or money, but speed (*dromo-* from the Greek δρόμος, "road"). The final arbiter of government action is the ever-increasing velocity of military action. Under such consideration, the stop-and-go of the Fifth's opening, its hurtling pace and its braking fermatas, becomes the source of the symphony's variable politics. Movement is facilitated while being restricted: for the rest of the symphony, our attention is shifted from the note on the downbeat to the point at which that note *moves,* to the unstable rhythmic point between the first and second beats. Beethoven fuels the momentum of the motive by initially stopping it in its tracks; the energy it takes to overcome that stasis is renewed every subsequent time, an illusion of perpetual acceleration. Through Virilio's dromocratic lens, the opening becomes both the barricade and the irresistible advance. No wonder it seems so revolutionary.

But, as Virilio observes, "revolution is movement, but movement is not a revolution."[110] Power is no longer in resisting movement, but in channeling it. Virilio notes how the Jacobins, the architects of the Reign of Terror, encouraged the disaffected to keep on the move: "[T]he new organization of traffic flows that we arbitrarily call the 'French Revolution' . . . is nothing other than the rational organization of a social abduction. The 'mass uprising' of 1793 is *the removal of the masses.*"[111] Similarly, a reviewer of an 1830 performance of the Fifth wrote of its "restless forward motion made up of self-consuming longing."[112] A repository of political energies could also function as a corral.

In his autobiography, Igor Stravinsky ruefully quoted an observation from the Soviet daily *Izvestia*:

> Beethoven is the friend and contemporary of the French Revolution, and he remained faithful to it even at the time when, during the Jacobin dictatorship, humanitarians with weak nerves of the Schiller type turned from it, preferring to destroy tyrants on the theatrical stage with the help of cardboard swords.

"I should like to know," Stravinsky critiqued, "in what this mentality differs from the platitudes and commonplace utterances of the publicity-mongers of liberalism in all the bourgeois democracies long before the social revolution in Russia." Only in its directness. But Stravinsky's wish that Beethoven would be appreciated solely for his compositional achievement—"It is only the music that matters"—is equally utopian.[113] Beethoven hitched the Fifth to enough revolutionary stars that the connection was inevitable; and the connection, in turn, lent the Fifth a measure of historic significance that helped secure its impregnable canonic status. Even in purely musical terms, the Fifth was a product of its time: its disorienting, even subversive opening almost inevitably echoes the upheavals of the French Revolution and its Napoleonic aftershocks. But the zeal was shorn of a specific agenda. Beethoven became the prototypical revolutionary composer, while the true Revolutionaries, the composers of the *Fêtes*, for the most part, faded into obscurity. (Only Cherubini maintained a foothold in the repertoire.)

Eighteen forty-eight finally brought what everyone had been anticipating or fearing for more than fifty years, a French revolution that spread throughout Europe. It was triggered by the cancellation of a dinner; after the French King, Louis-Philippe, had banned political meetings, the various opposition factions had continued to meet under the guise of increasingly large feasts, the *Campagne des banquets* of 1847–48. Threats of a massacre quashed a Parisian banquet scheduled for February 22, 1848; within two days, Louis-Philippe had abdicated. (The old *chansons* should have tipped the king off; as one landlady noted, you could tell a revolution was imminent because of all the singing.[114])

The 1848 revolution in France would inspire Karl Marx's famous formulation of history repeating itself, "the first time as tragedy, the second as farce";[115] by December, the Empire was back up and running. But in the first days of the Second Republic, on March 5, 1848, the Paris Conservatoire hosted a benefit concert for those wounded in the previous month's uprising. The program validated the transfer of Revolutionary musical authority: "La Marseillaise" was followed by Beethoven's Fifth.[116] In *Le Monde musical*, Auguste Morel approved of the juxtaposition, but in terms that projected the Fifth's Revolutionary trappings onto a blank slate: though "Beethoven's Symphony in C minor does not, of course, express any specific idea . . . it conveys an eminently martial tone, and when it comes to celebrating a triumph one could not find anything better."[117]

2

Fates

"I'm not so much for Beethoven qua Beethoven," Gustav
argues, "but as he represents the German dialectic."

—Thomas Pynchon, *Gravity's Rainbow*

THE TITLE CHARACTER of Kurt Münzer's 1919 "erotic novella"
Mademoiselle is a young governess languishing in a "big, cold German town," teaching a lawyer's children. The eldest son, thirteen-year-old Eduard, has his piano lesson, his thin, pale fingers stalking the keyboard "like giant spider's legs"; from the next room, his mother finds the exercises "simply intolerable," and suggests a duet—"That thing by Beethoven . . . a symphony, isn't it?"

Mademoiselle reached for the Beethoven volume. She
opened to the symphony, put the music on the rack and
settled herself next to Eduard.

"One-and two-and three—and—," she began, and played.
But Eduard suddenly dropped his hands and said, without
looking at the girl:

"Today," he said quietly, "today Brunner from the *Obersekunda,* who wants to be a pianist, was talking with me. I
told him that we played this symphony, and he called it the
Fate-Symphony. These first notes, he said, mean: *so klopft
das Schicksal an die Pforte*—thus fate knocks at the door."

And he struck the notes while softly humming along:
So klopft das Schick-
sal an die Pfor—te.
"Naturally," said Mademoiselle, thoughtlessly.   God
knows where her thoughts were.[1]

Eduard's clumsy conversion into lyrics does no small violence to the tune, but the connection between sentiment and
symphony would have been familiar even to readers of erotic
novellas. That poetic image—fate knocking at the door—first
saw the (public) light of day in 1840, and immediately became
ineluctably attached to the Fifth's opening. The timing was aus-
picious: driven by some of the nineteenth century's most formidable thinkers—Hegel, Marx, Nietzsche—the very idea of Fate
was about to experience a momentous intellectual growth spurt,
expanding from a personal lot to an all-encompassing one. Riding Fate's philosophical coattails, the symphony—and its first
four notes—would become more famous than ever.

THE STORY linking the Fifth to fate comes from Beethoven's
biographer, Anton Schindler. In the first edition of his biography, published in 1840, Schindler connects the image only to
the opening: "Beethoven expressed himself in something like
vehement animation, when describing to me his idea:—'It is
thus that Fate knocks at the door.' "[2]

By the time of the third edition, 1860, mission creep is starting to set in, and Fate, it is hinted, is asking after the whole
symphony:

What a life of poetry this work unfolds before our senses,
allowing us to see into its depths! The composer himself
provided the key to those depths when one day, in this
author's presence, he pointed to the beginning of the first

movement and expressed in these words the fundamental idea of his work: "Thus Fate knocks at the door!"[3]

Schindler spent the last five years of Beethoven's life as the composer's amanuensis, and then parlayed that association into a long career (he died in 1864) as a purveyor of Beethoveniana. He was possessive and prickly regarding his musical hero. Conductor Felix Weingartner sarcastically summed up Schindler's reputation when he noted that "the key to [his] character, I think, is sufficiently given by the fact that after the master's death he had visiting cards printed with the title 'Ami de Beethoven' "[4]—though, in all fairness, maintaining a friendship with Beethoven may have seemed rather like a full-time vocation. Margaret Fuller, the New England Transcendentalist, called Schindler "one of those devout Germans who can cling for so many years to a single flower, nor feel they have rifled all its sweets."[5] Another American, composer and pianist William Mason, got to know Schindler while studying music in Germany. "He worshiped his idol's memory," Mason remembered, "and was so familiar with his music that the slightest mistake in interpretation or departure from Beethoven's invention or design jarred upon his nerves—or possibly he made a pretense of this."[6]

At a concert in Frankfurt, Mason witnessed Schindler typically advertising his own superior sensitivity to Beethoven's intentions:

> The concerts took place in a very old stone building called the "Museum," and on the occasion here referred to the symphony was Beethoven's "No. 5, C Minor." It so happened that, owing to long-continued rains and extreme humidity, the stone walls of the old hall were saturated with dampness, in fact, were actually wet. This excess of moisture affected the pitch of the wood wind-instruments to such a degree that the other instruments had to be adjusted to

accommodate them. Schindler, it was noticed, left the hall at the close of the first movement. This seemed a strange proceeding on the part of the "Ami de Beethoven," and when later in the evening he was seen at the Bürger Verein and asked why he had gone away so suddenly, he replied gruffly, "I don't care to hear Beethoven's 'C Minor Symphony' played in the key of B minor."[7]

Schindler's biography ended up erecting a rather large wing of the house of Beethoven scholarship on a foundation of sand. His account is, thanks to his years of daily contact with the composer, a primary source, and, indeed, the sole source for many of the more famous Beethoven stories (fate knocking at the door included). He was also prone to getting things wrong, making things up, and even concocting outright forgeries, be they marginal notes in Beethoven's scores,[8] minor pieces of music,[9] or, most seriously, the conversation books, the conduits for communication once Beethoven's deafness had advanced past the point of chitchat; coming into possession of the books after Beethoven's death, Schindler added and altered entries to exaggerate his relationship with the composer and thus his authority over Beethoven's legacy—that is, in those conversation books he didn't simply destroy.[10] (Interestingly, many of the forged additions were in the service of justifying Schindler's preference for performing Beethoven's music slower than Beethoven's metronome markings would indicate.)

So, like so many of Schindler's anecdotes, the Fate/Door characterization of the Fifth and its opening lives on in an indistinct limbo, neither confirmed nor contradicted. The historical haze, actually, was a boon to the image's popularity: instead of a confirmed fact, fixed in time and circumstance, Schindler's story became a fluid, adaptable trope. What may have been simply after-the-fact table talk—Schindler could only have heard the anecdote well over a decade after the Fifth's premiere—could be made into a precompositional inspiration. What may have even been a bit of mockery on Beethoven's part—Philip Hale, the venerable Boston music critic, was of the opinion that "Ferdinand Ries was the author of this explanation, and that Beethoven was grimly sarcastic when Ries, his pupil, made it known to him"[11]—thus becomes an earnest encapsulation of the state of the composer's soul.

And even if it was an out-and-out fiction, give Schindler credit for at least knowing what would make a plausible story. Beethoven talked about fate all the time.

IN NOVEMBER OF 1801, Beethoven sent a letter to his friend Franz Wegeler, discussing the miseries of a quack cure that Beethoven had been prescribed to combat his advancing deafness, as well as the hopeful prospects of new, different quack cures. ("People talk about miraculous cures by *galvanism;* what is your opinion?") But in the end, Beethoven gives himself a pep talk: "You will find me as happy as I am fated to be on this earth, not unhappy—no, that I could not bear—I will seize Fate by the throat; it shall certainly not bend and crush me completely—"[12]

Skip forward eleven years, and Beethoven begins a journal (*Tagebuch*), in which he makes entries on and off from 1812 until 1816. The opening entry finds a less defiant Beethoven:

> Submission, deepest submission to your fate, only this can give you the sacrifices—for this matter of service. O hard struggle![13]

Beethoven probably started the journal just after his intense but doomed affair with the infamous "Immortal Beloved," so one can understand the dramatic self-pity. Still, fate is a recurring theme in the *Tagebuch*. Beethoven jots down a line from Shakespeare's *Twelfth Night* (act 1, scene 5): "Fate, show thy force:

ourselves we do not owe; / What is decreed must be, and be this so."[14] A quote from Homer's *Iliad* ("But now Fate catches me! / Let me not sink into the dust unresisting and inglorious, / But first accomplish great things, of which future generations too shall hear!"[15]) includes indications of the poetic scansion, a sign that Beethoven was considering setting it to music. Throughout the *Tagebuch*, as throughout his life, Beethoven's fatalism varies with his mood. But though Beethoven can still muster determination, the sheer defiance of his 1801 self is gone.

And somewhere in between these two poles came the 1808 premiere of the Fifth Symphony, as well as Beethoven's most well-known statement on fate, the letter now known as the Heiligenstadt Testament, dated October 6, 1802, addressed to his brothers but never delivered, and only discovered after his death. (Well into the twentieth century, Beethoven's stays in Heiligenstadt were still a relatively fresh bit of local lore. The house where he wrote the Testament had stayed in the same family, and the old woman of the house recalled stories her grandmother had told her of the composer's "almost savage" irascibility. "[H]e must have been terrible," she concluded.[16])

The Heiligenstadt Testament was Beethoven's most emotionally raw effort to come to terms with his advancing deafness. To read it is almost like eavesdropping on Beethoven pulling himself together—what starts off like a suicide note ("Oh, how could I possibly admit an infirmity in the one sense which ought to be more perfect in me than others") ends up as an austere manifesto: "I hope my determination will remain firm to endure until it pleases the inexorable Parcae to break the thread." At the same time, the Testament might be the most self-consciously literary thing Beethoven ever wrote. It seasons the stream-of-consciousness style of his most personal letters with phrases that jut out from the prevailing tone like learned quotations, even though they're not. For example, the line toward the end of the Testament, "With joy I go to meet death" (*mit Freuden eil ich dem Tode entgegen*), calls to mind the faith of martyrs, and certainly may have been intended to echo something like this poetic evocation of Christ on the way to Golgotha, by the Swiss writer, physiognomist, and sometime friend of Goethe, Johann Kaspar Lavater:

> *Du gehst auf deinen dunkeln Wegen dem Tode freudiger entgegen,*
> *weil du des Sünders Hoffnung bist.*[17]
> (You go to meet dark death more joyfully, because you are the sinners' hope.)

On the other hand, it could have just as easily come from the secular heroism of, say, the poems of Ossian (as translated/forged by James Macpherson), which Beethoven read and admired in translation:

> *Er wandte sich nicht der spreissende Krieger. Er drängte Vorwärts*
> *dem Tode voll Muthes entgegen!*[18]
> (The young warrior did not fly; but met death as he went forward in his strength!)

Take even the Testament's striking opening, seeming to announce the document's at least partially public nature: "O you men," or "O ye mankind"—the original German, "O ihr Menschen," sounds biblical enough, but actually appears nowhere in Martin Luther's translation of the Bible. Where it does turn up is in the Koran. Friedrich Eberhard Boysen's German translation, first published in 1775, uses "O ihr Menschen" for the Arabic phrase *yaa ay-yuhan naasu,* as in Sura 27:

> *O ihr Menschen! Wir sind in der Wissenschaft unterrichtet*
> *worden, den Gesang der Vögel zu verstehn . . .*[19]
> (O men, we have been taught the speech of birds, and are endued with everything . . .)

While there is no hard evidence Beethoven ever read the Koran (either in Boysen's translation or the less-popular but favored-by-Goethe 1772 translation by David Friedrich Megerlin), there is more than enough evidence to say that it would not be at all surprising if he had. When he first came to Vienna, for instance, Beethoven made the acquaintance of Joseph von Hammer-Purgstall, an Austrian diplomat who would become a prolific Orientalist, translator of numerous Arabic and Persian texts, and author of a five-act "historical drama" called *Mohammed, or the Conquest of Mecca* (1823).

German-speaking intellectual life during Beethoven's time was permeated with a fashion for all things Eastern, near and far. European scholarship on the subject had been primed by imperialism—the British in India, France in the Middle East—but the German vogue carried with it the prospect of self-invention: against a backdrop of political division and French occupation, a lot of German writing about ancient India or Persia can read like a subtle pep talk, a dropped hint that the scattered states of the former Holy Roman Empire could be a cradle of civilization, too. August Wilhelm von Schlegel put it plainly: "If the regeneration of the human species started in the East, Germany must be considered the Orient of Europe."[20]

In his later years, Beethoven kept a framed quotation on his desk, the inscription that Plutarch recorded as having been on the statue of Isis at the Egyptian city of Sais: "I am all that has been, and is, and shall be, and my robe no mortal has yet uncovered." Beethoven had read the quotation in Schiller's essay *"Die Sendung Moses"* ("The Mission of Moses"), an analysis of that prophet's unique qualifications for engineering the renaissance of a race. The Israelites—like Schiller's fellow Germans, perhaps—were too downtrodden to muster the energy to free themselves; what was needed was an injection of new intellectual blood:

A native Egyptian was not inspired by the national sympathy necessary to become the saviour of the Hebrews. A mere Hebrew was deficient in power and mind for this purpose. What expedient did destiny [*Schicksals*] resort to? It snatched a Hebrew at an early age from the bosom of his brutalized nation, and placed him in possession of Egyptian wisdom; thus it was that a Hebrew, reared by Egyptians, became the instrument, by means of which his nation was freed from bondage.[21]

Beethoven remained fascinated by Eastern thought, and his *Tagebuch* contains numerous quotations taken from Eastern sources, Hindu scriptures and Sanskrit Vedas in particular. (Such proclivities might even have inspired a rueful jest from his onetime teacher Haydn; once he had outlived his usefulness to Beethoven's career, Beethoven largely ceased visiting the elder master, and Haydn took to asking mutual acquaintances: "How goes it with our Great Mogul?"[22])

Beethoven also, throughout his life, maintained close connections with Freemasonry, a milieu saturated with Eastern images and ideas. The composer apparently never joined a lodge, but so many of his friends and acquaintances were Masons—Beethoven's composition teacher, Christoph Gottlieb Neefe; friend-of-the-family Franz Anton Ries (Ferdinand's father); Franz Wegeler, in whom Beethoven confided regarding his advancing deafness—that one wonders why Beethoven never took the step himself. (Politics, probably—Beethoven arrived in Vienna just as the Hapsburg emperor was outlawing the societies, an authoritarian prophylactic in the wake of the French Revolution.) Maynard Solomon has speculated that the *Tagebuch* was actually a sort of self-study journal in preparation for initiation.[23]

In making the case for Beethoven's Masonic leanings, it is

almost too tempting to hear in the Fifth's opening—or at least its popular interpretation—an echo of such an initiation, especially when confronted with this detail of the elevation of an Entered Apprentice to the Fellow Craft Degree, from Malcolm Duncan's 1866 *Masonic Ritual and Monitor:*

> [Senior Deacon]—Worshipful Master (making the sign of a Fellow Craft), there is an alarm at the inner door of our Lodge.
>
> W. M.—You will attend to the alarm, and ascertain the cause.
>
> The Deacon gives three raps, which are responded to by the Junior Deacon, and answered to by one rap from the Senior Deacon inside, who opens the door, and says:
>
> S. D.—Who comes here?[24]

It should be emphasized that such a connection with the Fifth is without any biographical basis (though still less far-fetched than much of the conspiratorial speculation that Freemasonry has attracted over the years).

Accepting that Beethoven and/or Schindler may have come up with the fate/door image as an ex post facto interpretation allows another possible Masonic source: August von Kotzebue's 1818 one-act comedy *Der Freimaurer* (*The Freemasons*). The play's Count von Pecht is obsessed with Freemasonry, sending his hapless servant to spy on lodge meetings, and finally trying to get himself initiated just to satisfy his curiosity. But the Baron, the head of the local lodge, is suspicious:

> *Gemeine Neubegier kommt nie dem Lichte nah.*
> *Nur wer die Wahrheit sucht, darf an die Pforte pochen.*[25]
> (Vulgar Curiosity never comes close to the light.
> Only he who seeks Truth may knock on the door.)

Kotzebue, a cheerfully arrogant man of letters, was far and away the most successful German playwright of his time. That was enough to interest Beethoven; in 1812, he approached Kotzebue about writing an opera libretto, something "romantic, serious, heroic-comic, or sentimental, as you please," showing that he was familiar with Kotzebue's wide (if not particularly deep) range.[26] Nothing came of the opera (Attila the Hun had been a suggested subject), but Beethoven did compose incidental music for two of Kotzebue's plays, *King Stephen* and *The Ruins of Athens*. The latter yielded the famous "Turkish March," the familiar tune of which is, upon closer examination, a cousin of the Fifth's opening, flipped around: a drop of a third, *then* three repeated notes. The march supplied exotic color for the plot: Minerva, put to sleep by Jupiter for two millennia for letting Socrates die, wakes up to find Athens under Islamic rule.

GIVEN BEETHOVEN'S fascination with all things Eastern, it is not surprising that Schindler's tale would have gained immediate currency as an expression of individual fate, one not dissimilar from Eastern ideas of kismet or karma. Indeed, it is at the very least a pointed coincidence that what is quite possibly the first piece to purposefully quote the Fifth's germinal motive carries the unmistakably Eastern title of *Nirwana*, Hans von Bülow's op. 20 tone poem. Though today an obscure curiosity (and Bülow now largely remembered as a conducting pioneer, famous for his championing of Richard Wagner), *Nirwana* was the best known of Bülow's compositions during his lifetime. The piece unfolds with full Romantic drama (some of *Nirwana*'s harmonies would influence Wagner's *Tristan und Isolde*) until, just before the piece reaches its close, the strings suddenly unleash a barrage, *sempre forte e distaccato*, of Beethovenian short-short-short-long rhythmic volleys, the bassoons and timpani soon joining in, driving the orchestra to a *con tutta la forza* climax.

The title, *Nirwana,* was a late change; originally Bülow called the piece an *Overture to Byron's "Cain."* [27] Byron had published his three-act play-for-reading in 1821, portraying the biblical fratricide as motivated less by jealousy than by existential despair: Cain finds himself unable to worship a God who has burdened him with the knowledge of his own mortality.

> And this is
> Life. Toil! and wherefore should I toil? Because
> My father could not keep his place in Eden?
> What had *I* done in this? I was unborn;
> I sought not to be born; nor love the state
> To which that birth has brought me.[28]

Cain's fate is to survive, after an angel marks "upon thy brow / Exemption from such deeds as thou hast done"[29]—history's first murderer, cursed with the knowledge of his act and cast into the wilderness.

Bülow's change of title might indicate a change of heart about the nature and acceptance of one's fate. Had the Byronic context survived, Bülow's use of the Fate motive would have seemed more fatalistic: humans as actors in immutable, divinely ordered plays of which they can only perceive dim outlines. But under the title of *Nirwana,* the same quotation becomes, maybe, an individual fate that enlightenment reveals to be merely transient. And Bülow's individual fate during the gestation of *Nirwana* was sufficiently scandalous that he may well have wished to regard it as fleeting.

Bülow had already written the piece in 1854, to judge from a letter from Wagner in which he discusses it.[30] By the time *Nirwana* was published, in 1866, Bülow's wife Cosima had become Wagner's mistress, and had already given birth to one of Wagner's children. Even after an eventual divorce, Bülow's admiration for Wagner's music persisted, but one can imagine how an abandonment of the world and a peaceful indifference to its ups and downs of pride and fall, need and frustration, must have interested him. Ironically, the same 1854 letter in which Wagner talks of the then-untitled *Nirwana* also finds Wagner enthusiastically recommending to Bülow the works of the philosopher Arthur Schopenhauer. It was from Schopenhauer that Bülow learned the Buddhist concepts of Samsara and Nirvana: the cycle of birth and death and the understanding that allows one to escape its oppression. (As we shall see, Schopenhauer's philosophy would also shade Wagner's own relationship to Beethoven.)

Bülow would liken Beethoven's op. 111 Piano Sonata, another C-minor work that begins in struggle and ends in transcendence, to the Samsara-Nirvana dialectic. But Bülow's own *Nirwana* is hardly triumphant, forcefully recapitulating the same gloomy B minor in which it starts. Bülow admitted it was a conclusion "which optimism might regard as a so-called tragical one, but the last sigh of the vanishing 'Nirvána' is not intended by the author in this sense."[31] Bülow, like so many after him, was expanding Schindler's poetic morsel into a larger web of meaning: emerging from its stew of Cain and Buddha and Beethoven and Bülow himself, *Nirwana*'s quotation of the Fifth leaves one wondering just whose fate it is doing the knocking.

EVEN AS Bülow was writing *Nirwana*, the European conception of Fate was metastasizing from something individual to something more external and cosmic. The process finds its origin in a single sentence in the *Philosophy of Right* by that most formidable of nineteenth-century German thinkers, Georg Wilhelm Friedrich Hegel:

> What is rational is real;
> And what is real is rational.[32]

Hegel wrote this in 1820, but he had been espousing variations of the idea for a while. Hegel's correspondence between the actual and the rational—an unusually direct formulation for him—would actually muddy the interpretive waters around another of his ideas, that of historical progress. Hegel believed that history learned from its mistakes, continually evolving toward more freedom, fairness, and philosophical soundness.

Hegel insisted on regarding anything in existence as not just *being*, but constantly *becoming*, evolving, changing. Hegel's favorite Greek philosopher was another connoisseur of change, Heraclitus. ("Here we see land," Hegel complimented.[33]) The surviving fragments of Heraclitus's writings sound like the aphorist Hegel never became:

You cannot step twice into the same river. . . .

Out of discord comes the fairest harmony.

The way up [the road] and the way down is one and the same.[34]

Such statements hint at how a dynamic, change-encompassing point of view could relieve another of Hegel's philosophical hallmarks, his horror of contradiction. (If one recognizes the whole road, the divergence in travel direction goes from an inconsistency to a totality.) But what Heraclitus merely observed, Hegel would attempt to demonstrate logically. Hegel gave history a direction, and with it, a dose of Fate. And as the idea of Fate became more broad and all-encompassing, the perceived importance of the Fifth Symphony and its opening—now permanently labeled "Fate"—followed suit.

Born in 1770, the same year as Beethoven, Hegel was a late bloomer: studious and bookish almost from the start, but taking some time to find his place. Having graduated from the

Stüttgart *Gymnasium* at the top of his class (he gave a graduation address critiquing educational opportunities in Turkey), Hegel's initial thought was to study theology and then become a "popular" philosopher, using his learning and the authority of his degree to explain up-to-date, Enlightenment philosophical ideas for a general audience—a little bit ironic, given his eventual reputation for near incomprehensibility.

Hegel drew a line in the sand with his first published work, a long essay called *The Difference Between Fichte's and Schelling's Systems of Philosophy.*[35] Fichte was the leading disciple of the great Enlightenment sage Immanuel Kant; Schelling had become the undisputed star of the younger generation of German philosophers. Both had taken on one of the leading chin-scratchers of the day—what happened when the human intellect took *itself* as a subject? If the mechanisms of the intellect were consistent, the result would be a rabbit hole of self-regard—but Enlightenment thinkers were loath to conclude that the mind had different mechanisms depending on what it was pondering. Fichte had decided that self-consciousness cannot be realized without at the same time discovering that the self is finite, that there is a limit to the intellect. (You can only notice your own distinct identity, for example, if you allow for the existence of other rational subjects who are not you.)

For Hegel, any such limit verged on blasphemy. The solution, as he saw it, was to move forward from *reflective* philosophy—stuck in the mind's perception of itself, and in the limitations of language—into *speculative* philosophy. Speculation makes philosophy into a mirror (a *speculum*) of the Absolute by jumping over the boundary that Fichte ran up against: "Only by recognizing this boundary and being able to suspend itself and the boundary—and that, too, scientifically—does [philosophy] raise itself to the science of the Absolute."[36] If that sounds like a leap of faith, it's because it is. The Absolute is another in a long line of philosophical terms—Unity, the One, the Prime

Mover—that philosophers have used to talk about God without calling him/her/it God. Hegel was less coy about its divinity than some.

Hegel's goal was to philosophically clear a path all the way to the divine. His method was the dialectic, resolving contradictions by expanding understanding—zooming out from individual lanes to the whole road. Hegel's dialectic, the progressive leaps past the boundaries that philosophies and political systems carry within themselves, would be the engine driving his conception of history. Time might reveal the inherent contradictions within any endeavor—the "glorious mental dawn"[37] of the French Revolution, for example, giving way to the dark night of the Reign of Terror, the historical situation still too burdened with mistrust and corruption. But rational thought could reconceptualize the world so that such conflicts were rendered meaningless. One dissolved contradiction at a time, Hegel's dialectic would get us to the Absolute.

Like most philosophers at the time, Hegel made a distinction between logic and aesthetics, between the discipline of discourse and the realm of art. Music appeared in Hegel's logic (as opposed to his aesthetics) only in analogies. Actually trying to put music through Hegel's logical paces is more problematic. If we try to follow a bit of musical information—the Fifth's first four notes, for example—through Hegel's outline of logic, we can get a better sense of why, in his aesthetics, Hegel was suspicious of music. We can also start to understand why the subsequent Hegelization of Beethoven and his music, perhaps, short-circuited the progress of musical history as much as it advanced it.

The mechanism by which Hegel imagined an idea becoming an Idea is a three-step process: Being, Essence, and the Notion. It's the second step, Essence, where musical ideas seem to go off the rails. Hegel's discussion of Essence is one of those places where he really earns his reputation for obscurity. (When Hegel warns that "The theory of Essence is the most difficult branch of Logic,"[38] it's kind of like hearing Evel Knievel say that the ride is about to get particularly bumpy.) But one can think about it this way: if Being is all about recognizing that the first four notes of Beethoven's Fifth *are*, Essence is all about the discussion of what they *mean*—how we start to relate those first four notes to other concepts.

Hegel subdivides the realization of Essence into (of course) another three parts. *Reflection* is where everybody, say, tries out different interpretive concepts for the first four notes—Fate, or birds, or the French Revolution, or whatever. This will, inevitably, produce contradictory interpretations of the opening motive—differing opinions as to just who is knocking at the door. *Appearance* is the complement of Reflection; if Reflection is about clearing away unnecessary differences *between* interpretations of the first four notes, Appearance is about finding the interpretation best able to clear away differences *within* it. For the particular interpretation of the opening motive as a representation of Fate, for instance, the stage of Appearance is when both what we hear in the motive and what we think about Fate will adjust and grow to encompass each other. The Essence of the motive will begin to "shine forth" at this point.

But musical ideas hit a barrier with the final step of the realization of Essence, *Actuality,* a dialectic between Reflection and Appearance. "The utterance of the actual is the actual itself."[39] In other words: We are no longer talking about what we, individually or even collectively, think the meaning of the first four notes might be. We are talking about what the meaning actually *is*.

Can any interpretation of the opening of Beethoven's Fifth—or, indeed, of *any* piece of music—rise to that level of certainty? The sheer contradictory profusion of images and agendas surrounding the first four notes alone would indicate otherwise. In Hegelian terms, the protean nature of such interpretations is an indication that music and art are still historically stuck in a process of determining Essence, as the rest of society runs ahead in Hegel's logical process. Hegel made this point explicitly all the way back in his inaugural *Difference* essay: "The entire system of relations constituting life has become detached from art, and thus the concept of art's all-embracing coherence has been lost, and transformed into the concept either of superstition or of entertainment."[40] It's hard to think of *any* nontrivial statement one could make about the Fifth that would make it all the way to the stage of Actuality, always tripping over the barrier between subjective opinion and objective statement.

It's at this point that it becomes obvious just how contrived a target the opening of Beethoven's Fifth is for Hegel's logic, a square peg being crammed into a round philosophical hole. But it was the ill fit, perhaps, that encouraged Hegel's ambivalence about music in his aesthetic thinking. At various points, Hegel seems to be trying to have it both ways about music's capacity for meaning.[41] On the one hand, "[T]he real region of [musical] compositions remains a rather formal inwardness, pure sound";[42] on the other hand, without "spiritual content and expression," music is not true art, is "empty and meaningless."[43]

At times, Hegel's definitions of music verge on self-negation. "The meaning to be expressed in a musical theme," he writes, "is already exhausted in the theme."[44] The composer's subject matter is "a retreat into the inner life's own freedom, a self-enjoyment, and, in many departments of music, even an assurance that as artist he is free from subject-matter altogether."[45] Such inherent subjectivity, historically speaking, stalled music's advance toward the Absolute in the interpretive free-for-all of Reflection.

Could speculative philosophy ever push our understanding of music past its current Reflective shambles, past each individual listener privileging their own interpretive imagination? Hegel thought not—only literature or, even better, philosophy could get past such subjective "formal inwardness," get past one's personal "feeling" to engage the objective world and, eventually, reach the Absolute Idea, the ultimate unity, the end-all of Hegel's historical progress. Hegel admitted the Romantic idea that art and music could give a *glimpse* of the Absolute, but considered that a symptom of immature systems of religious thought. "As regards the close connection of art with the various religions it may be specially noted that *beautiful* art can only belong to those religions in which the spiritual principle, though concrete and intrinsically free, is not yet absolute," he wrote; art's vision of the divine is only as clear as an imperfect religion can make it. In the long run, though, art becomes unnecessary:

> [E]ven fine art is only a grade of liberation, not the supreme liberation itself. The genuine objectivity, which is only in the medium of thought—the medium in which alone the pure spirit is for the spirit, and where the liberation is accompanied with reverence—is still absent in the sensuous beauty of the work of art, still more in that external, unbeautiful sensuousness.[46]

The limited, irreverent liberation of art is better than nothing, but only a poor substitute for the Idea. If Beethoven affords a better-than-average view of the promised land, it's only because he can't cross over.

Nevertheless, other commentators were only too happy to give Beethoven a privileged place in Hegel-like intellectual hierarchies. American poet Sidney Lanier portrayed the "satisfying symphonies" as something like dialectic syntheses, soothing those "thoughts that fray the restless soul," including "The yea-nay of Freewill and Fate, / Whereof both cannot be, yet are."[47]And already by 1867, Ludwig Nohl, in his biography of Beethoven, was opening out the Fifth's philosophical playing field toward an encompassed Absolute, extending the expanded Fate of the first four notes over the whole work:

In his heart of hearts, Beethoven feels that fate has knocked at his door, only because in his following the dictates of force and action, he has sinned against nature, and that all will is only transitoriness and self-deception. . . . [T]he song of jubilation in the finale which tells not of the joy and sorrow of one heart only; it lifts the freedom which has been praised and sought for into the higher region of moral will. Thus the symphony in C minor has a significance greater than any mere "work of art." Like the production of religious art, *it is a representation of those secret forces which hold the world together.*[48]

But the most lasting incursion of Hegelian concepts into Beethoven's reputation concerned the composer himself: Beethoven's career and music, the very fact of his existence, was interpreted as an unprecedented watershed in a progressive view of music history. One of the most influential and subtle exponents of this idea was a Berlin-based lawyer-turned-music-critic named Adolph Bernhard Marx.

IN 1830, the year before he died, Hegel was appointed Rector of the University of Berlin. The same year, the university offered a chair in music to A. B. Marx, who promptly put into pedagogical practice what he had already been preaching through journalism: championing the evident greatness of Austro-German music—Bach, Mozart, Beethoven—in Hegelian terms. As musicologist Scott Burnham has written, it was a matter "of transforming the southern currency of the Viennese musical masters into a more fiercely northern intellectual and political capital."[49]

Marx is today primarily remembered for codifying and naming what we now call sonata-allegro (or just sonata) form, a structural pattern common to works of the mid- to late-eighteenth and early nineteenth centuries. The pattern goes like this:

A movement starts with a **first theme** in the overall key of the piece—the *tonic*.

Followed by a **second theme** in a contrasting key, usually the interval of a perfect fifth up from the tonic—the *dominant,* if the movement is in a major key—or a third away—the *relative major,* if it is in a minor key.

A **third theme** brings the opening section to a close in either the dominant key or its relative major.

There follows a freer **development** section.

After which there comes a **recapitulation** of the three themes; this time all in the tonic key.

The opening movement of Beethoven's Fifth fits this pattern to a tee. As it should: sonata form was explicitly modeled on Beethoven's practice, an after-the-fact attempt to systematize what the next generation regarded as the apex of Classical composition. But it also, deliberately, put Beethoven's music in a privileged position vis-à-vis history.

Marx took pains to present sonata form as the culmination of a Hegelian process. In his 1856 essay "Form in Music," Marx starts at the formal level of the motive ("Only the succession of two or more tones . . . shows the spirit persisting in the musical element"[50]) and works his way up through a series of dialectical oppositions to the "greater whole" of the sonata. "The evolution of this series of forms," he summarizes, "has been the historical task of all artists faithful to their calling." Unlike Hegel, however, Marx's ladder never runs out of rungs, for music is inseparable from the human spirit: "[T]he series of forms may be deemed *infinite*; at least no one can point to an end, or cut-off point, of the series, as long as music maintains its place in the realm of human affairs—that is, forever. For that which the human spirit has begotten in accordance with the necessity of its essence is created forever."[51] The difficulty of Hegel's theory of Essence is (perhaps dialectically) also an opportunity, a vacuum that Marx fills with a more exalted view of music than Hegel himself ever took—a vacuum that (as we shall see) the Romantics would fill with similar enthusiasm.

Marx's most complete exegesis of sonata form came in the third volume of his four-volume *Practical and Theoretical Method of Musical Composition*. Again, Hegelian hints abound, with Marx seeing a fundamental process of theme-digression-return rising through five levels of rondo form to arrive at sonata form, where the multiplicity of themes is fodder for synthesis: "the *whole* in its inner *unity* . . . becomes the main concern."[52]

Marx formulated his definition of sonata form primarily from Beethoven, yet he spends even more space exploring all those instances where Beethoven seems to push the definition to its breaking point. Marx is, in fact, engaged in an exercise more subtle than just demonstrating Beethoven's music to be a Hegelian culmination; he is defining sonata form as something that Beethoven has already surpassed. The laws are set down in order that Marx can show how Beethoven rendered the laws obsolete. Sonata form is a concept through which Beethoven's essence can shine forth. The implicit lesson for any composition students who happened to be reading: surpass the previous generation and keep history on the move.

But Marx's Hegelian definition of sonata form forever closed it off from the possibility of Hegelian progress. "When sonata form did not yet exist, it had a history," Charles Rosen once noted. "Once it had been called into existence by early nineteenth-century theory, history was no longer possible for it; it was defined, fixed, and unalterable."[53] But that was, perhaps, the point all along. Early on in his career, Marx had already cast the Fifth as "the first [symphony] to advance beyond the Mozartian point of view."[54] In Marx's analysis, sonata form changed from a basic, flexible framework into a historical boundary for Beethoven's genius to vault over.

There is a bit of a full-circle aspect to Marx's formulation. Beethoven thought in terms of a personal Fate to be surmounted: in his *Tagebuch* Beethoven copied down lengthy excerpts from Zacharias Werner's dramatic poem *Die Söhne des Thals* (*The Sons of the Valley*). Like much of the rest of Beethoven's journal, the drama is steeped in Masonic atmosphere—it retells one of the more popular legends of Freemasonry's origins, tracing the order to the fourteenth-century suppression of the Knights Templar. And it also poeticizes a Hegelian transcendence of Fate:

> The hero bravely presents to Fate the harp
> Which the Creator placed in his bosom.
> It might rage through the strings;
> But it cannot destroy the marvelous inner accord
> And the dissonances soon dissolve into pure harmony,
> Because God's peace rustles through the strings.[55]

A generation later, with Hegel as an enabler, Marx portrayed Beethoven as surmounting *historical,* rather than personal, Fate.

But such projecting of the Fifth's narrative onto the whole of human society raises a question, one that parallels the subsequent nineteenth-century rumpus over Hegel's concept of history: Is the Fifth's fateful struggle and eventual exultation a mirror of civilization, or its unrealized blueprint? Both explanations came into play as Hegel's legacy bifurcated; Hegel's rational-is-real formulation produced competing claimants to Hegel's mantle. The teams even acquired their own names, at least in hindsight: the Right-, or Old Hegelians versus the Left-, or Young Hegelians. (Both terms proved more useful to historians than to the players themselves: the Right-Hegelians never used the name themselves, and the Young Hegelians, like many

intellectual blocs, spent as much time arguing amongst themselves as they did taking on their Old counterparts.)

Putting it somewhat simply, a Right-Hegelian could argue
that if the real is rational, then the way things are, right now,
falls somewhere along Hegel's path to the absolute, the impli-
cation being that the way things are—economically, socially,
politically—is as good, and as moral, as it could possibly be. But
a radical Left-Hegelian could counter that the continuing existence of societal divisions was clear evidence that Hegel's Absolute remained unfulfilled, that change is always necessary, that
the work goes on.

IN 1839, eighteen-year-old Friedrich Engels was working as an
unpaid clerk for a linen exporter in Bremen. Bored and antsy,
he passed the time by writing letters to his sister. In one letter,
he showed off his burgeoning composing skills with a two-part
harmonization of Luther's chorale *"Ein feste Burg ist unser Gott"*;
Marie Engels must have given her brother some grief over it.
"Listen," Friedrich protests, "composing is hard work; you have
to pay attention to so many things—the harmony of the chords
and the right progression, and that gives a lot of trouble."[56]

Two years later, Friedrich's restlessness had only gotten worse.
"Thank God that I too am leaving this dreary hole where there
is nothing to do but fence, eat, drink, sleep and drudge, *voilà
tout*," he informs Marie. Still, he is proud of his moustache: "It
is now in full flower again and growing and when I have the
pleasure—as I don't doubt I shall—of boozing with you in
Mannheim in the spring, you will be amazed at its glory." And
Bremen still has its charms. "There is one thing in which you are
less fortunate than I. You cannot hear Beethoven's Symphony
in C Minor today . . . while I can," Friedrich boasts. And, continuing the letter the next day: "What a symphony it was last

night! . . . What despairing discord in the first movement, what elegiac melancholy, what a tender lover's lament in the adagio, what a tremendous, youthful, jubilant celebration of freedom by the trombone in the third and fourth movements!"[57]

In his teenage letters, Friedrich Engels comes across as very much the bourgeois scion he was: an indifferent apprentice, a bit of a dilettante, a devotee of beer, cigars, and music. But the letters also hint at an intellectual double life. Metternich's Carlsbad Decrees had made subversion prevalent by making just about everything subversive; even facial hair could be regarded as a dangerous republican provocation.[58] (Hence the moustache.) His taste in music carried rebellious overtones, not just the Fifth's "celebration of freedom," but also *"Ein feste Burg,"* its opening a distant mirror of Beethoven's (three repeated notes, followed by a downward leap), a chorale Engels, in later life, would characterize as "the *Marseillaise* of the Peasant War,"[59] the sixteenth-century German uprising that was the largest European rebellion prior to 1789.

And Engels was abandoning the "dreary hole" of Bremen for Berlin, where—while ostensibly fulfilling his military service—he would sit in on Schelling's lectures, pitting his youthful idolization of Hegel against Schelling's learned deprecations. (His fellow auditors included both the Danish philosopher Søren Kierkegaard and the anarchist Mikhail Bakunin.)[60] At the same time his family was grooming him to take over the family's textile business, Engels was fashioning himself into a political radical.

In true Hegelian fashion, Engels's road up to working-class liberation and down to capitalist exploitation was the same road. Sent to Manchester to learn the family trade, Engels turned what he saw into a book, *The Condition of the Working Class in England*, a groundbreaking exposé of the Industrial Revolution. One of the book's many admirers was another Young Hegelian, a peripatetic and perpetually impoverished journalist, polemicist, and dialectician named Karl Marx.

Marx and Engels formed one of history's most influential symbiotic friendships. They dropped an all-time intellectual bombshell by co-writing *The Communist Manifesto,* then chased the 1848–49 revolutions around Europe, hoping to get in on the action. (Marx, who was deported from Prussia in the midst of the revolutions, never quite caught up with an uprising, but Engels did, manning the front lines in the south of Germany before escaping back to London.) In order to have the funds to support Marx, whom he always regarded as the more brilliant thinker, Engels reluctantly returned to the family firm, assuming the role of a proper Victorian businessman. After Marx's death in 1883, Engels kept the faith, defending Marx's reputation, expanding and promoting Marxist thought, and having a go at finishing the last volume of *Capital.* The bond between the two was enduring; for all their later activity and notoriety, they never quite abandoned their identity as enthusiastic students, arguing Hegel and history over copious amounts of beer.

In fact, it was a pub crawl from later in his life that gave us one of the few glimpses of Marx's musical taste. Sometime in the 1850s, when London was seemingly flooded with revolutionaries-in-exile, Marx took Edgar Bauer and Wilhelm Liebknecht, a pair of old Young Hegelian associates, on a quest "to 'take something' in every saloon between Oxford Street and Hampstead Road," as Liebknecht remembered it, a fairly daunting prospect in that particular district. (Bauer, a frank advocate of terrorism, had apparently remained a drinking buddy even after being intellectually savaged by Marx and Engels in their "Critique of Critical Criticism" *The Holy Family*; Liebknecht would go on to be a founder of Germany's Social Democratic party. The Young Hegelians were always a confederation of strange bedfellows.)

At the end of this inebriated tour, Bauer took offense at the patriotic deprecations of a group of Englishmen, and Marx joined in the drunken defense of German culture. Liebknecht again:

[N]o other country, he said, would have been capable of producing such masters of music as Beethoven, Mozart, Haendel and Haydn, and the Englishmen who had no music were in reality far below the Germans who had been prevented hitherto only by the miserable political and economical conditions from accomplishing any great practical work, but who would yet outclass all other nations. So fluently I have never heard him speaking English.[61]

Marx never advanced anything close to a comprehensive philosophy of art; nevertheless, dosed with liquid courage, Marx defended not the German intellectual heritage—not Goethe, not Kant, not Hegel—but its composers, in a progression culminating with Beethoven.

Nowadays, Marx and Engels are still inextricably associated with—and blamed for—Communism and all its disgraces. Their most lasting contribution, though, was the materialist conception of history, a redesign of Hegel's historical engine to run on less mystical fuel. Marx: "My inquiry led me to the conclusion that neither legal relations nor political forms could be comprehended whether by themselves or on the basis of a so-called general development of the human mind, but that on the contrary they originate in the material conditions of life."[62]

For Marx, the best use of the dialectic was not to overcome contradictions, as Hegel preached, but to reveal and focus them: to clarify the content, not reveal a speculative form. History doesn't resolve conflict, advancing toward an Absolute stand-in for transcendental unity; history happens because of conflicts that are fundamentally unresolvable. If you can dialectically boil your analysis down to these fundamental conflicts—capital versus labor, say, or collective control versus anarchic individualism—you can grasp the levers of history.

Historical materialism even informed Marx's pub-crawl music

critique: to note Beethoven's achievement in the face of "miserable political and economical conditions" was high praise indeed. Hegel thought that it was the Idea that creates political, social, and economic conditions. Marx thought that Hegel had things completely back-to-front. Marx often thought that way—it was a critical trick he had picked up from one of the leading lights of the Left-Hegelians, a lapsed theologian named Ludwig Feuerbach, who liked to bring metaphysical flights of fancy down to earth by flipping around subject and predicate. For Marx, the Idea doesn't project circumstances onto people; people project onto their circumstances the illusion of an Idea. True greatness was not, as Hegel might have put it, the realization of an ideal Fate; true greatness—Beethoven's greatness—was to triumph in spite of it.[63]

But what does the materialist conception of history—and its colonization of the modern worldview—have to do with the Fifth's subsequent biography? A lot, perhaps; at the very least, a renewed focus on the first movement and its omnipresent motive. Once the motive's assigned meaning—Fate—became a matter of worldly friction instead of Ideal accord, the sharper contrasts of the opening movement were bound to sound more "real" and immediate than the relentless victory of the end. Initially, the Fifth was particularly celebrated for its Finale, the troublesome scherzo exploding into triumphant, major-key synthesis, a musical Hegelian in-and-of-itself. But as the perception of history shifted toward materialism, the first movement—and its epochal opening—gradually became the symphony's most famous feature: a dramatic showdown between history and the individual, irreconcilably defiant. The fact that more people know the Fifth's beginning than its end could be read as evidence that Marx's historical-materialistic inversion of Hegel, with its embrace of contradiction and struggle, is the more deeply woven into the fabric of society.

Then again, it could just be shorter attention spans. But it is worth noting that it was Engels, the onetime prospective composer, who initially formulated historical materialism—and who later forever complicated Marxist thought by insisting that the dialectic was not just an intellectual tool: "[D]ialectical laws are really laws of development of nature."[64] If the dialectic is inherent in creation itself, the struggle and triumph of the Fifth Symphony's narrative could be applied to the whole of existence.

AS MARXISM shifted into Marxism-Leninism, the materialist interpretation of history took a detour, one reminiscent of how the revolutionary impression of Beethoven's music was interpreted. Karl Kautsky, an evangelist for "traditional" Marxism, had criticized the Bolshevik Revolution, arguing that the Russian proletariat wasn't ready for Communism, that the revolution had, in effect, happened too early—beating history to the punch, as it were. As a result, he predicted, the conditions were ripe for another Reign of Terror. "If the morality of the communists has not formed itself before the beginning of socialisation," Kautsky warned, "it will be too late to develop it after expropriation has taken place."[65] Leon Trotsky ridiculed Kautsky's critique: "[T]he Soviet regime, which is more closely, straightly, honestly bound up with the toiling majority of the people, does achieve meaning, not in statically reflecting a majority, but in *dynamically creating it*"[66] (emphasis added). The Slovenian Hegelian-Marxist-Lacanian philosopher Slavoj Žižek has noted how Trotsky's formulation has a parallel in modern attitudes toward innovation and cultural history. He quotes T. S. Eliot: "The existing order is complete before the new work arrives; for order to persist after the supervention of novelty, the *whole* existing order must be, if ever so slightly, altered; and so the relations, proportions, values of each work of art toward the whole are readjusted; and this is the conformity between old and new."[67]

It's an expanded perspective on the idea that truly revolutionary works of art create their own audience—except in this view, such works actually create (and re-create) their own history. It is not hard to find notions like this applied to Beethoven and his symphonic style: one need look no further than the other Marx, Adolph Bernhard, who even during Beethoven's lifetime was already justifying a progressive view of his hero's music in terms similar to Eliot's:

> The preliminary works of philosophers of art are useful to us, and we find the way paved that they first had to prepare laboriously. Above all, however, we make reference to the fact that art first had to reach the stage of perfection where it provided material for a higher point of view.[68]

Of course, hanging that expectation on Beethoven's symphonies practically ensured that they would be continually reinterpreted to justify each newer "higher point of view"—which is exactly what happened. The idea of Beethoven's Fifth—or any other piece of music—being "timeless" originates with this (largely successful) effort to portray Beethoven as a figure in the vanguard of a progressive view of history.

In attempting to control that progression, the Soviet state ironically gradually came to rely on Beethoven's being a specifically historical figure. At the outset of the Bolshevik regime, the Commissar for Culture, Anatoly Lunacharsky, wrote of how "Beethoven . . . not only expressed the complexities of his own personality, but reflected most forcefully the storms of the Great Revolution."[69] Lunacharsky was using Beethoven as a yardstick for demonstrating that the Russian avant-gardists of the time—Scriabin, Prokofiev—were also expressing socialist ideals. By the time of the 1927 Beethoven centennial, however, things had changed: Lenin was dead, Stalin was tightening his grip on power, and socialist ideals were better expressed by

Beethoven's music, Lunacharsky pronounced, than by any contemporary "futurists and hooligan opponents of the classics."[70]

The straitjacket can be sensed in another momentous Fifth Symphony, that of Dmitri Shostakovich. Written in 1937, it was the composer's response to his own Stalinist difficulties, the frightening shift in his official reputation after his opera *Lady Macbeth of the Mtsensk District* was judged to be contrary to the tenets of socialist realism. Shostakovich's Fifth shadows Beethoven's both in its minor-to-major struggle-to-triumph trajectory, and in its obsessive use and reuse of short motives. And, like Beethoven, Shostakovich produced a work whose greatness is in no small part due to the ambiguity of its powerful rhetoric, creating a template for enduring reinterpretation: "a richly coded utterance," as Richard Taruskin has put it, "but one whose meaning can never be wholly encompassed or definitively paraphrased."[71] Shostakovich's Fifth mixed triumph and uneasiness enough for both Soviet officialdom and its discontents to claim its narrative.

But the symphony's opening theme hints at the increasingly suffocating presence of the Beethovenian paragon. Shostakovich jump-starts with a series of angular, dotted-rhythm leaps, up and down, but the vaults are herded into a mutter: by the fourth bar, the bravado has been abraded into a single note, rapped three times, staccato. In Shostakovich's version, Beethoven's repeated-note opening becomes a hesitant cessation: an ominous, unanswered tapping, quashing the defiance of those impulsive leaps. It is as if Beethoven's Fifth were run backward and the finale's dotted-rhythm outbursts subsumed back into the opening's grim announcement. (In Stalin's Russia, after all, a knock on the door could be all too literally fatal.)

The open-ended nature of the interpretation of Beethoven's Fifth complicated its status in Communist regimes, even as the Party relied on Beethoven's Fifth to fire up revolutionary fervor. Functionaries of the *Freie Deutsche Jugend*, the official East Ger man socialist youth group, noted the music's usefulness to a journalist in the 1950s: "What I like about Beethoven is the militant element. We recently heard his Fifth Symphony . . . 'and now the eyes of the youth friends light up.' "[72] Militant Beethoven could, however, become dangerous once revolutions turned monolithic: Beethoven's *Egmont* Overture (which plays like a potent distillation of the Fifth's struggle) became the soundtrack of the 1956 uprising in Communist Hungary; during the similar 1968 rebellion in Czechoslovakia, "as tension and expectations rose, Radio Free Prague played over and over Beethoven's Fifth Symphony."[73]

In Communist China, the vague knocking of the first four notes made Beethoven's Fifth a pawn in the Cultural Revolution. Western classical music in China had been drastically undermined by the Revolution—the faculty of the Shanghai Conservatory was decimated as professors were arrested or driven to suicide[74]—and Beethoven was officially eschewed in favor of ideologically pure operas and ballets created under the direction of Jiang Qing, Mao Zedong's wife. The power struggle between Jiang and Premier Zhou Enlai turned symphonic as rapprochement with the United States (the prospect of which Jiang despised) moved forward. For one of Henry Kissinger's trips to Beijing to plan Richard Nixon's 1972 visit, Zhou had the idea of marking the occasion with a concert by China's Central Philharmonic. "Kissinger's German," Zhou instructed Li Delun, the Philharmonic's conductor. "You should play Beethoven."[75]

But which Beethoven? Prior to the Cultural Revolution, the Central Philharmonic had often performed the symphonies; called into a meeting with Jiang Qing and Yu Huiyong, the minister of culture and Jiang's chief musical consultant, Li expressed a preference for the Fifth, as it was the piece the Philharmonic performed best. But Yu insisted that the Fifth was contrary to the spirit of Communist China, since—post hoc the first four notes—it was about fatalism.

Li had stepped into a Byzantine intellectual power struggle, one of Jiang Qing's perennial propaganda battles against those who would try to reverse the course of revolutionary history in favor of the status quo.[76] It was the Old and Young Hegelians all over again: the Fifth lacked sufficient specificity as to just which kind of fate it was in favor of. Jiang and Yu substituted Beethoven's Sixth, Beethoven's nature pictures presumably being less open to troublesome interpretation. (Jiang Qing pulled the same switch on Eugene Ormandy and the Philadelphia Orchestra on their 1973 visit, leading to a certain amount of last-minute scrambling, as the group had only brought parts for the Fifth, not the Sixth.[77])

After Mao's death, Yu Huiyong would commit suicide by drinking a bottle of sulfuric acid. The Cultural Revolution was over, the milestone having been marked, in part, by Li Delun and the Central Philharmonic returning to the symphony they played best, Beethoven's Fifth, a performance broadcast throughout China in March of 1977. Xu Ximing, head of the Shanghai Music Lovers' Association, recognized the significance. "It is about the light that comes after a period of great difficulty," he recalled, "so it was very appropriate."[78] (Then again, in 1997, during the ceremonial transfer of sovereignty over Hong Kong from Britain to China, Chinese police drowned out protesters with a PA broadcast of the Fifth.[79])

Elsewhere in the Communist world, Trotsky's dynamically created majority had long since ossified into a bureaucracy of oppression, with a cynicism toward progress to rival Metternich's. The order failed to make room for Trotsky himself, who was forced out of party and country. Asylum in Norway turned into house arrest, an internment slightly alleviated by a radio: "Beethoven was a great help to us, but the music was a rarity"—drowned out by propaganda broadcasts from both Stalin and Hitler.[80] Trotsky was shipped from Norway to Mexico, where he was assassinated in 1940. Even in exile, though, Trotsky had kept the historical-materialist faith, the same tenets that elaborated the perception of the Fifth's opening into a tolling of the fate of all mankind:

> And what of your personal fate?—I hear a question, in which curiosity is mixed with irony. . . . I do not measure the historical process by the yardstick of one's personal fate. On the contrary, I appraise my fate objectively and live it subjectively, only as it is inextricably bound up with the course of social development.[81]

> "Mankind" does not advance, it does not even exist.
>
> —FRIEDRICH NIETZSCHE, *The Will to Power*

ALL ALONG, there had been another lane on the Fifth's journey to canonic greatness, running parallel to Hegel and Marx, but surpassing both of them in its conception of Fate. Its surveyor was the era's great iconoclast, promoting a worldview fiercely generous and exuberantly desolate: Friedrich Nietzsche. In 1888, in the months preceding his sudden mental breakdown, Nietzsche wrote his own version of an autobiography: *Ecce Homo,* a breezy, cocky tour of his own works and thought processes. At the close of a chapter entitled "Why I Am So Clever," Nietzsche offered this prescription: "My formula for greatness in a human being is *amor fati:* that one wants nothing to be different, not forward, not backward, not in all eternity. Not merely bear what is necessary, still less conceal it—all idealism is mendaciousness in the face of what is necessary—but *love* it."[82]

Nietzsche's *amor fati,* his love of Fate, was the final mutation in the nineteenth-century evolution of concepts of Fate and History. Quite simply, after Nietzsche, there was no place left for Fate to go: in a way, it became philosophically indistinguishable from the whole of creation. Schindler's investing of the Fifth with a single share of Fate had unwittingly proved one of the canniest metaphysical investments possible. And yet Nietzsche himself would warn against the dividend.

Amor fati grew out of Nietzsche's contemplation of the old idea of eternal recurrence, the idea that, contrary to Hegel, history was not progressive but constantly cycled through the same patterns over and over again. It's as if Hegel's idea of everything perpetually *becoming* had no Absolute endpoint—becoming is all there is. Nietzsche famously posed the question in his 1882 book *The Gay Science:*

> What, if some day or night a demon were to steal after you into your loneliest loneliness and say to you: "This life as you now live it and have lived it, you will have to live once more and innumerable times more; and there will be nothing new in it, but every pain and every joy and every thought and sigh and everything unutterably small or great in your life will have to return to you, all in the same succession and sequence . . ."

"Would you not throw yourself down and gnash your teeth and curse the demon who spoke thus?" Nietzsche posits. "Or have you once experienced a tremendous moment when you would have answered him: 'You are a god and never have I heard anything more divine.' "[83] The latter response is the quintessence of *amor fati.*

Nietzsche had the eponymous hero of his *Thus Spoke Zarathustra*—an allegory saturated with *amor fati*—illustrate Fate as a deceptive gateway. "This long lane behind us: it goes on for an eternity. And that long lane ahead of us—that is another eternity," Zarathustra notes. "They are in opposition to one another, these paths; they abut on one another: and it is here at this gateway that they come together. The name of the gateway is written above it: 'Moment.'

"[A]ll things that *can* run have already run along this lane"[84]—up to and including the current moment; what's more, "all things [are] bound fast together" such that, in turn, the moment symmetrically *draws the future toward it.* As an example, the Canadian philosopher Peter Hallward provides another of history's great heroes of fate:

> Caesar's only real task is to become worthy of the events he has been created to embody. *Amor fati.* What Caesar actually does adds nothing to what he virtually is. When Caesar actually crosses the Rubicon this involves no deliberation or choice since it is simply part of the entire, immediate expression of Caesarness, it simply unrolls or "unfolds something that was encompassed for all times in the notion of Caesar"—and a world in which Caesar did not cross the Rubicon would thus have to be an entirely different world.[85]

Hallward's formulation clashes with every bit of our intuition about causality and agency, but also brings to the fore two of the more important facets of Nietzsche's thought: his bias against free will, and his emphasis on affirmation, on embracing one's becoming.

Amor fati is not just a cosmic version of playing the hand you're dealt; it defines the game itself as inescapably all-encompassing. The universe is a perpetual state of becoming; and nothing exists outside of that becoming—including what Nietzsche regards as the irrationally egotistic idea of free will. One of Nietzsche's favorite words is *Verhängnis,* which can be translated in multiple directions: literally "hanging together," but also meaning "fate" or even "calamity." It's all the same thing, and it's only the distorting habit of regarding ourselves as self-mastered individuals that keeps us from that realization: "[O]ne is a piece of fate, one belongs to the whole, one *is* in the whole."[86] There's no way of getting off the roller coaster of Fate: we're built into it. If you're enjoying the ride, you've achieved greatness.

No wonder Nietzsche doesn't go in for the Fifth Symphony's defiance. He prefers to praise "Beethoven's noble hermit's resignation."[87] Love your fate.

EARLY IN his career, Nietzsche worked on both philosophy and music, pursuing the latter with more raw talent than skill, a deficit that earned him a fair amount of scorn after the twenty-four-year-old professor of philology inserted himself into Richard Wagner's circle in the late 1860s. Nietzsche and Wagner talked over what became Nietzsche's first book, *The Birth of Tragedy*; Wagner defended the book when it came under attack from Nietzsche's more hidebound colleagues. But Wagner also made a point of left-handedly complimenting Nietzsche's piano improvisations, telling him "you play too well for a professor."[88] Nietzsche fared no better with his written compositions, having never mastered forms beyond miniatures; Hans von Bülow criticized one as "the most extreme piece of fantastic extravagance, the most undelightful and the most antimusical drafts on musical paper that I have faced in a long time. Frequently I had to ask myself: is the whole thing a joke, perhaps you intended a parody of the so-called music of the future?"[89]

Nietzsche, intellectually tougher than his enthusiastic-professor mien may have let on, went from lauding Wagner and his artwork (*Kunstwerk*) of the future to denouncing him, accusing him of being corrupted by Christianity, and enthusiastically proclaiming the superiority of Offenbach and Bizet. (Nevertheless, even after breaking with Wagner, in person and in print, Nietzsche recognized the importance of their discussions to his own intellectual journey: "I'd let go cheap the whole rest of my human relationships."[90])

The "fantastic extravagance" that Bülow faulted in Nietzsche's music was the touchstone of his prose; and as with much of his philosophy, Nietzsche's views on art and music are fluid, pungently aphoristic, and, over time, somewhat self-contradictory. The constant is Nietzsche's skepticism of art, a skepticism so deep that it can only have grown from an irresistible love: he is forever flying too close to the flame and then musing on just how and why it burns.

In Nietzsche's estimation, all artists were actors—benevolent liars, usually themselves unaware of their own make-believe. The deception is not in art's scope but in its importance: art is as meaningful as life itself, but—in the light of the consequences of *amor fati*—life is not nearly as meaningful as we would like to think. Nietzsche dismissed an artist's biography, his or her individual fate, as an irrelevant illusion. To interpret the Fifth and its opening motive in a way that emphasizes Beethoven's own emotional life—his struggle with deafness or loneliness, take your pick—is to fall into the same trap that artists always set, however unwittingly. "Artists are by no means men of great passion," Nietzsche wrote, "but they often *pretend* to be, in the unconscious feeling that their painted passions will seem more believable if their own life speaks for their experience in this field."[91]

Perhaps because he knew it so well, Nietzsche regarded music as particularly fertile ground for this sort of con game; music's "primeval union with poetry has deposited so much symbolism into rhythmic movement, into the varying strength and volume of musical sounds, that we now *suppose* it to speak directly *to* the inner world and to come *from* the inner world." Listening "for the *reason*" in music is a modern habit; music "does not speak of the 'will' or of the 'thing in itself'; the intellect could suppose such a thing only in an age which had conquered for musical symbolism the entire compass of the inner life."[92] That is, an age that has distorted music from a sensual pleasure into a repository for the Absolute—which is exactly what had happened to Beethoven's music, the Fifth Symphony especially.

Unusually susceptible to music's power, Nietzsche was also unusually sensitive to how explanations of its "meaning" could deflect that power. It was a pattern he sensed in other areas of human endeavor as well. One of Nietzsche's essays in his collection *Untimely Meditations* was a discussion of history and how it is written, a polemic he called *On the Uses and Disadvantages of History for Life*. Nietzsche's main target in his *History* essay is alleged historical objectivity, "a condition in the historian which permits him to observe an event in all its motivations and consequences so purely that it has no effect at all on his own subjectivity"[93]—which had become the goal of "scientific" historians in the nineteenth century, taking their cue from the German historian Leopold von Ranke and his famous (if somewhat ambiguous) call for a history that "wants only to show what actually happened."[94]

Nietzsche calls such objectivity "mythology, and bad mythology at that"[95]—not only impossible but also liable to distort history into something closer to the artificiality of drama, the competing needs of narrative cohesion and disinterested viewpoint finding patterns in historical events where no patterns exist. Such patterns, Nietzsche makes clear, are usually more than a little Hegelian, be it Right or Left: "But what is one to make of this assertion, hovering as it does between tautology and nonsense, by one celebrated historical virtuoso: 'the fact of the matter is that all human actions are subject to the mighty and irresistible direction of the course of things, though it may often not be apparent'?"[96]

The "virtuoso" in question is none other than Leopold von Ranke,[97] but the target is Hegel's Spirit of History, all its subsequent elaborations and/or simplifications, and its oppressive pressure on the individual will. "If every success is a rational necessity, if every event is a victory of the logical or the 'idea,'" Nietzsche mocks, "then down on your knees quickly and do reverence to the whole stepladder of 'success'!"[98]

The problem, as Nietzsche sees it, is that "history is held in greater honour than life"—dominating and enervating everything that makes life worth living, music included. It is "an injustice against the most vigorous part of our culture" that "such men as Mozart and Beethoven [are] already engulfed by all the learned dust of biography and compelled by the torture-instruments of historical criticism to answer a thousand impertinent questions."[99] Maybe this is why, when Nietzsche does get around to prescribing his ideal history, the description sounds more than a little like Beethoven's Fifth: "[I]ts value will be seen to consist in its taking a familiar, perhaps commonplace theme, an everyday melody, and composing inspired variations on it, enhancing it, elevating it to a comprehensive symbol, and thus disclosing in the original theme a whole world of profundity, power and beauty."[100]

IN *Human, All Too Human,* Nietzsche imagined exhuming Beethoven and asking what he thought of how subsequent generations had used his music:

> [H]e would probably for a long time stay dumb, undecided whether to raise his hand in a blessing or a curse, but at length say perhaps: "Well, yes! That is neither I nor not-I but some third thing—and if it is not exactly right, it is nonetheless right in its own way. But you had better take care what you're doing, since it's you who have to listen to it—and, as our Schiller says, the living are always in the right. So be in the right and let me depart again."[101]

The story of Fate knocking at the door, which might charitably be described as neither Beethoven nor not-Beethoven, but some third thing, only became more so as the century went on. Whatever the origin of Schindler's anecdote—a Beethovenian jest, a garbled memory, an out-and-out fiction—it ended up enhancing the Fifth's stature probably even more than the "friend of Beethoven" could have anticipated. From a personal destiny, malleable with enough effort, the notion of Fate would gradually acquire greater and greater significance: Hegel's historical engine, Marx's revolutionary sustenance, Nietzsche's all-pervasive force. Originally interpreted as a vivid portrait of an individual trajectory, by the end of the nineteenth century, the Fifth Symphony could plausibly be said to be about, well, everything.

Back to Münzer's *Mademoiselle:* having, in the meantime, caught a glimpse of his governess naked, young Eduard is understandably more pale and nervous—and less pianistically accurate—than usual when instructed to again join her for their duet; Eduard's mother wants to impress her husband with Beethoven's symphony, which, in her estimation, "seems so modern" with its "spicy effects":

Once again sounded the mysterious, stern, threatening motif. Unwritten dissonance increased its foreboding. . . .

"I don't know," said her innocuous husband. "To me, it sounds more *wrong* than spicy, so to speak."

"Adolf," cried his wife indignantly, "that's just the misfortune of your one-dimensional legal training. You've never done anything for your musical education. Now comes the payback: you cannot follow the artistic insight of your family."

The conclusion of the first phrase surpassed the middle in its considerable unresolved dissonance, because, while this time the young lady played correctly, Eduard was suddenly in F-sharp major.

The lawyer twitched sensitively and moaned audibly, but

his wife squirmed, as it were, with delight, and said in a tone of contemptuous profundity:

"Richard Strauss!!"[102]

The scandalous modernity of Richard Strauss—who did, after all, compose a tone poem on *Zarathustra*—might well have sounded to contemporaries like Beethoven's C-minor tonality overlaid with Eduard's F-sharp major, a tritone away, the height of dissonance. But the nineteenth-century shape of history, an inexorable movement toward some inherently better future, demanded it: composers were deemed profound only inasmuch as they pushed the envelope. Such escalation is nowadays taken for granted, to judge by persistent vocabularies of "advance" and "progress" from descendants of Left and Right alike; Beethoven was present at the creation. The grafting of "fate knocking at the door" onto the Fifth's iconic opening might have been nothing more than a romanticized anecdote, but it did its part to keep goal-oriented civilizations focused on destiny.

Perhaps inevitably, *Mademoiselle* ends with the governess paying a late-night visit to Eduard. No need to knock—Beethoven has taken care of that already:

She smiled and, graciously and lovingly, quietly opened the unlocked door of the boy's room . . .[103]

3

Infinities

"The modern school of music, Janet, is like the romantic drama," I added, with a forced attempt at continuing the conversation, for I felt my sadness increasing beyond my control. "I mean the music commencing with Beethoven; not the gay, joy-loving, Athenian Mozart, but from Beethoven, the sad old giant, up to poor Schubert and Schumann and Chopin. There is a whole lifetime of woe, sometimes, in one of their shortest creations. I wonder, Janet, if the Greeks ever suffered and sorrowed as we moderns do? They seem to have been exempt from our curse; they worshipped the beautiful, and raised it to their altars,—made of it God."

"Their drama, my friend, was the voice of their ideal, not of their real life. The moderns have indeed bowed down before sorrow and pain, lifted them up to their most holy of holies, and there they will remain so long as the quick pulse of anguish throbs in man's and woman's heart."

—ANNE M. H. BREWSTER, *St. Martin's Summer* (1866)

AS A YOUNG MAN just out of the University of Berlin, years before the materialist conception of history crossed paths with Fate and the Fifth, Karl Marx had been briefly pulled into the orbit of none other than Bettina von Arnim, the mythopoeicist of Goethe and Beethoven, then nearing sixty and as provocative as ever. But her spirit apparently proved too indefinable for Marx's skeptical taste. He wrote a poem mocking her:

> The child, who, as you know, once wrote to Goethe,
> In order to point out that he might love her,
>> The child was at the theater one day;
>> A Uniform advanced her way
> And, with a smile, his eye on her did rest.
> "Sir, Bettina wishes to suggest
>> Her curly head to lean upon
>> That choice supply of wondrous brawn."
> The Uniform, quite dryly, then replied:
> "Bettina, let desire be your guide!"
>> "Fine," she said, "you know, my little mouse,
>> On my head there's not a single louse!"

The poem was called "Newfangled Romanticism."[1] Marx's doggerel, perhaps, marks the point where Romanticism became a fad, but, by that point, Romanticism had already left its indelible mark. The Romantics were dedicated to bringing back into art the inexplicably sublime, which they thought had been bled out by the Enlightenment's excessive rationality. They were anything but timid: for a musical exemplar, the Romantics drafted the most singular and dynamic thing around—Beethoven's Fifth. Both symphony and school would benefit from the association, their fame and influence boosted to ever new heights.

The Romantics heard in Beethoven's music a representation of a limitless beyond; a result, paradoxically, of Beethoven being in exactly the right place at exactly the right time. Beethoven was already the greatest composer of an era in which it was suddenly decided that composers were eligible for greatness; he was specializing in instrumental music just when instrumental music made a worst-to-first leap in the aesthetic standings. And, unusually for such shifts of intellectual ground, Beethoven's transformation from an heir of the Classical tradition to a godfather of the Romantic tradition can be traced to a single source: a review of the Fifth Symphony in the July 4 and 10, 1810, issues of the leading German-language music magazine of the time, the *Allgemeine musikalische Zeitung.* If Beethoven's Fifth marks the birth of music as philosophical artifact, the midwife was the reviewer, E. T. A. Hoffmann.

To reconnoiter the Romantic era, its progenitors and propagandists, its crusaders and discontents, is not just an idle historical exercise; the Romantic era never really ended. The free-for-all of individualism, mysticism, and nationalism we loosely gather under the banner of the Romantic aesthetic became so ingrained in Western civilization's everyday assumptions about the relationship between art, creator, performer, and audience, that we don't even notice it anymore. Every time a singer-songwriter is praised for projecting autobiographical authenticity; every time a movie star expresses the desire for a project that's "more personal"; every time a flop is subsequently recategorized as a before-its-time masterpiece—all these are reverberations of the bombshell of Romanticism, and one of its preeminent delivery systems was Beethoven's Fifth.

BEETHOVEN'S CURIOSITY kept him current with the Romantics, with the likes of Schiller and Schlegel and Fichte and Herder, but in his *Tagebuch,* alongside passages from Romantic literary efforts, the only contemporary philosophy Beethoven saw fit to copy down was of the previous generation, that of Immanuel Kant: "It is not the chance confluence of . . . atoms that has formed the world; innate powers and laws that have their source in wisest Reason are the unchangeable basis of that order."[2]

To be sure, Beethoven was quoting Kant the forerunner of *Naturphilosophie,* not Kant the defender of rationalism, but it's still a reminder that Beethoven was adopted by Romanticism, and not the other way around. Beethoven's reference was, maybe, partly nostalgic: Kant's *Critique of Pure Reason,* the high point of the *Aufklärung,* the German Enlightenment, came out when Beethoven was eleven, and Beethoven's early education in Bonn included a healthy serving of Enlightenment zwieback.

Kant revamped his life and personality in order to write his trio of *Critiques,* turning from a gregarious wit (and sometime card sharp) to a man whose habits were so particular and fixed that Königsberg housewives, it was said, set their clocks by his daily walk. The *Critiques* made Kant famous, and an in-demand teacher, but by the time he died, in 1804—the same year Beethoven sketched his first ideas for the Fifth Symphony—his philosophy was already being autopsied by the next generation, the Romantics. Nevertheless, Kant made the Romantic movement possible by his sheer competence; the *Critiques* pushed the rationalist program as far as it could go, and it was at that boundary that the Romantics found their intellectual focus. Where Kant ran out of road was exactly where Hoffmann and the rest of the Romantics would locate the greatness of Beethoven's Fifth.

Kant ran out of road trying to critique aesthetics. His *Critique of Judgement* followed the more well-known *Critiques* of pure reason and practical reason (i.e., ethics). The half of the *Critique of Judgement* dealing with aesthetics is not exactly the watertight freighter you might expect from the author of the *Critique of Pure Reason.* Kant expends a lot of effort distinguishing between "free beauty," that is, beauty that is perceived without any intermediary concepts, and "dependent beauty," beauty based on comparison with some preexisting concept in the subject's mind. Only a perception of free beauty qualifies as a true aesthetic judgment; if there's an intervening concept, then the subject is merely judging what is agreeable or functionally good. In Kant's definition: "The beautiful is that which, apart from a concept, pleases universally."[3]

But, of course, only the perceiving subject could know

whether their judgment is concept free and therefore aesthetically valid, and Kant admits that the perceiving subject is an
unreliable witness, often unaware that a perception of beauty
is based on a concept. That makes it difficult to tell whether an
aesthetic judgment can be *universally* valid, which is Kant's ultimate goal. We can all too easily fool ourselves into mistakenly
believing that dependent beauty is free, as when Kant takes in a
seemingly spontaneous concert:

> Even a bird's song, which we can reduce to no musical rule,
> seems to have more freedom in it, and thus to be richer for
> taste, than the human voice singing in accordance with all
> the rules that the art of music prescribes. . . . Yet here most
> likely our sympathy with the mirth of a dear little creature
> is confused with the beauty of its song, for if exactly imi
> tated by man (as has been sometimes done with the notes
> of the nightingale) it would strike our ear as wholly desti
> tute of taste.[4]

In other words, we could consider what one thought to be a
yellowhammer's song and consider it free beauty, only to have
to backpedal furiously to dependent beauty once we realized it
was only the opening of Beethoven's Fifth Symphony. In Kant's
opinion, we were simply misleading ourselves from the get-go
("our sympathy" confused with the song's beauty). Nonetheless,
Kant goes on to claim that aesthetic judgments can, actually,
be universally valid, basically by engaging in a little rhetorical
second-dealing and hoping his sleight of hand is good enough
that you don't really notice. And it is pretty good:

> The judgement of taste exacts agreement from every one;
> and a person who describes something as beautiful insists
> that every one ought to give the object in question his
> approval and follow suit in describing it as beautiful. . . .

We are suitors for agreement from every one else, because we are fortified with a ground common to all. Further, we would be able to count on this agreement, provided we were always assured of the correct subsumption of the case under that ground as the rule of approval.[5]

To wit: whenever anybody makes an aesthetic judgment, they are also asserting that their judgment *should* be accepted by everybody. So the fact that we all make aesthetic judgments means we all believe that such judgments *should* be universal. Which means (and here's where you need to keep an eye on those cards) such judgments *can* be universal, even if the judging individual can never be sure if a given judgment is even valid. Kant may not be able to pinpoint it, but, like fifty million Beethoven fans that can't be wrong, if we all assume the *possibility* of a universally valid aesthetic judgment, it must be out there somewhere.

For Kant, an aesthetic judgment is not something you do, it's something that *happens to you,* and the philosophical circle to be squared is in knowing that such a judgment is, in fact, happening.[6] And that's because Kant needs to preserve the human ability to judge even if it goes against one's emotions or senses. At its heart, Kant's philosophy is all about freedom, the freedom of the individual to decide his own path. For Kant, the ultimate expression of freedom was in choosing duty over desire, in acting against mere stimulus in favor of rectitude. From the Romantic point of view, he may have been a killjoy, but he was at least right to emphasize the freedom that allows joy to be killed.

As much as Kant ingeniously dresses it up, however, his analysis of beauty is still a weak logical link: it's no wonder that aesthetics was a primary front along which the Romantics would assault the Enlightenment. Kant's basic aesthetic insight hints at a path the Romantics would practically pave. Aesthetics, for Kant, doesn't originate with the subject, but it isn't anything intrinsic in the object perceived, either—it is, instead, the mind's reaction to an influx of sense-data that's *too much to think about all at once.* Therein lies the difference between the Enlightenment and the Romantics: Kant pools that sublime excess into the concept-stocked pond of dependent beauty, but the Romantics let it overflow all the way to the mind's horizon, where, if you look hard enough, you might catch a glimpse of the Divine.

ONE OF THE first to catch that glimpse, the intellectual progenitor of the *Sturm und Drang* movement, and in turn, the Romantics, was a combative, baby-faced zealot named Johann Georg Hamann. Born in 1730, Hamann started out as a loyal *Aufklärer,* but in 1757, sent on a diplomatic mission to London that ultimately failed, he proceeded to indulge in a round of debauchery and dissipation. The discovery that a friend and companion was also the boy toy of a rich Englishman shocked Hamann to the core, although it is unclear whether Hamann's shock was sparked by revulsion or jealousy.[7] In any event, the experience drove Hamann to a spiritual crisis. He claimed to have had a vision, he converted to a mystical Christianity, and he spent the rest of his life attacking the prevailing rationalist philosophy for having the presumptive gall to analyze religious faith. (Hamann's rationalist employer, Christoph Berens, tried to reconvert him to the Enlightenment cause with the assistance of a forty-five-year-old, still-largely-unknown Immanuel Kant. Hamann and Kant managed to remain at least casual friends, even as they mocked each other in print.)

Hamann's writings sometimes seem to be testing the surfeit-of-sense-data model of aesthetics by example, in a torrent of dense polemic. His most focused statement on creativity and genius comes in a 1762 essay, *Aesthetica in nuce* ("Aesthetics in a Nutshell"). Hamann called the essay a "rhapsody in cabbalistic prose," a fair warning of his style: bouncing from idea to idea, dotted with allusions both obvious and obscure as they bob to the surface of Hamann's consciousness, the text peppered with footnotes both explanatory and tangentially digressive. Like a weirdly compelling cross between a haranguing street preacher and David Foster Wallace, Hamann's prose makes a bid to break free of normal discourse and take flight on pure linguistic power. "What for others is style," he once wrote, "for me is soul."[8]

And that is, in a nutshell, Hamann's aesthetics. To analyze art is to emasculate it; to separate sense from understanding is to put asunder what God has joined. "Oh for a muse like a refiner's fire, and like a fuller's soap!" Hamann proclaims (in a Hamann-esque mash-up of Shakespeare and the Old Testament). "She will dare to purify the natural use of the senses from the unnatural use of abstractions, which distorts our concept of things, even as it suppresses the name of the Creator and blasphemes against Him."[9]

Hamann's essay is concerned with poetry, mainly, but within the cabalism is the seed of Romanticism's elevation of instrumental music to the summit of art. Beneath Hamann's baroque ramblings is a kernel of linguistic insight. "To speak is to translate," he writes, "from the tongue of angels into the tongue of men, that is, to translate thoughts into words—things into names—images into signs; which can be poetic or cyriological, historic or symbolic or hieroglyphic—and philosophical or characteristic."[10] This was one of Hamann's main objections to the rationalist philosophy of Kant and his ilk—a failure to realize that the mere act of formulating a philosophical system in words dimmed the divine spark, a generational loss as action was recorded into language. The idea that music expresses what language can't—and the idea of holding that up as a virtue—follows directly from Hamann's gist.

For Hamann, the more that art is codified under rules and concepts, the more it corrupts itself by separating it from a Nature that puts such artifice to shame. In *Leser und Kunstrichter*

(*Reader and Critic*), written the same year as *Aesthetica in nuce*, Hamann calls Nature a beloved old grandmother. "[T]o commit incest with this grandmother is the most important commandment the Koran of the Arts preaches," he insists, "and it is not obeyed."[11] In a reversal that the Romantics would take to the extreme, the audience is excluded from this loving artist-nature family circle like a third wheel.

Beethoven may not have read Hamann, but he certainly ascribed to Hamann's idea of an unassailable individual creative genius. Ferdinand Ries recalled that Beethoven rebuffed Haydn's request for him to include "Pupil of Haydn" on the title page of his earliest published works: "This Beethoven refused to do because, as he said, though he had taken a few lessons from Haydn, he never had learned anything from him."[12] For a young composer who had arrived in Vienna to "receive the spirit of Mozart from Haydn's hands," as Count Waldstein famously put it, such a declaration of artistic independence was both an astute response to a shift in the aesthetic winds and a foreshadowing of the stubborn self-regard that would result in many an irascible-Beethoven anecdote.

But as much as he adopted the new Romantic attitudes in public, to judge by the quotations in his 1812–16 journal, Beethoven perhaps remained privately skeptical of post-Kantian metaphysics. Kant charted human existence along dualistic longitudes: reason and faith, thought and sensation; the agenda of the irrationalists that followed Kant was to collapse those dualities into underlying union. Maybe the deaf Beethoven, so confident in his imagination but so cruelly betrayed by his own senses, took stubborn comfort in their continued separation.

SUCH WAS the atmosphere in which E. T. A. Hoffmann decisively appropriated the Fifth and its first four notes for the Romantic cause. Ernst Theodor Amadeus Hoffmann was born

Ernst Theodor Wilhelm in 1776, but adopted "Amadeus" in his thirties as a tribute to Mozart. He was, for much of his life, a refugee, pushed around by the political and military forces of the Napoleonic era. His career as a civil servant and jurist began in his late teens, when his unseemly attentions toward a married woman caused him to be spirited away to clerk for an uncle in Prussian Silesia. Another relocation resulted from Hoffmann's circulating his malicious caricatures of the local military brass. A two-year sojourn in Warsaw, where Hoffmann enjoyed the company of literary society, abruptly ended when Napoléon's liberation of the city put Prussian officials out of work. Hoffmann found himself stuck in Berlin, separated from his wife and family. His young daughter died; a job managing a theater was unraveled by the intrigues of the leading actor. All the while, Hoffmann continued writing—both musical and literary efforts.

The temptation to conflate Hoffmann's biography with his art is omnipresent. A number of his stories feature lost or dying daughters, for example; in *"Das öde Haus,"* an infant daughter is mysteriously kidnapped by gypsies; in *"Rath Krespel,"* the councillor Krespel's daughter Antonia fatally exercises her talent for singing; in *"Der Sandmann,"* the physics professor Spalanzani's daughter, Olimpia, turns out to be a lifeless clockwork automaton. Hoffmann's greatest success as a composer, his 1814 operatic adaptation of Friedrich de la Motte Fouqué's novella *Undine,* tells the story of a fisherman and his wife adopting a water-sprite after their own daughter accidentally drowns.

More interesting is Hoffmann's lifelong fascination with doubles and mirrors. Far from reinforcing the old Kantian dualities, Hoffmann's doubles instead are constantly hinting at hidden, underlying unity. His fiction teems with *doppelgängern*—seeming twins, uncanny resemblances, echoing actions—but the doubles are explained away as either coincidences or parallel, rather than contradictory, phenomena. In Hoffmann's masterpiece,

Lebens-Ansichten des Katers-Murr (*The Life and Opinions of Tom-Cat Murr*), torn-out pages of a printed biography of the musician Johannes Kreisler (one of Hoffmann's more famous characters, and the inspiration for Robert Schumann's *Kreisleriana*) have purportedly been used by Murr to write his own feline memoirs. The book—aptly described by one scholar as "a confluence with constant linkages, with none of the contrasts that we might expect"[13]—is out to undermine its own duality: the narratives of Kreisler and Murr are tangled to the point that separating the threads comes to seem a pedantic waste of time.

Hoffmann's tales remained yet to be written in 1810, when the impoverished writer embarked on some freelance music reviewing. But his choice of Beethoven's Fifth for his first critical exploration foreshadows his later obsessions. The ability to trace the opening through the entire piece, a musical web of seeming doubles, was enticing bait, a glimpse of Hoffmann's own future style—a style not just founded on an ideal of philosophical unity, but narratively revealing the unity beneath a seemingly dualistic surface. The first four notes resemble one of Hoffmann's future protagonists, confronted with a series of mirror images on the path to a realization of wholeness:

> There is no simpler idea than that which the master laid as the foundation of this entire Allegro [here Hoffmann inserts the first four notes as an illustration] and one realizes with wonder how he was able to align all the secondary ideas, all the transitional passages with the rhythmic content of this simple theme in such a way that they served continually to unfold the character of the whole, which that theme could only suggest.

The symphony becomes a very Hoffmann-like tale. The music narrates what is nonetheless completely encapsulated in the brief, startling opening, a glimpse that our finite understanding can't quite circumnavigate, but that pulls us toward the infinite: a frame of reference in which we might finally see that the opening and the entire work, seeming doubles, are in fact one and the same.

Such doubling does not refashion the world so that the world itself makes more sense, but rather so that its contradictions and irrationalities are more stark, and the necessity of some higher, unseen unity is more obvious. Hoffmann's Romantic aesthetic espouses not an art that resolves the world, but one that shows how the world's emotional messiness is a door into a deeper understanding, past logic and reason. The music of the Fifth—unencumbered by plot or text—bumps the listener to the doorstep. "Every passion—love—hate—anger—despair etc., such as we encounter in opera, is clothed by music in the purple shimmer of romanticism, and even that which we experience in life leads us out beyond life into the kingdom of the infinite." Hoffmann shoots the moon with his description, the prose taking on a purple shimmer of its own:

> Glowing beams shoot through this kingdom's deep night, and we become aware of gigantic shadows that surge up and down, enclosing us more and more narrowly and annihilating everything within us, leaving only the pain of that interminable longing, in which every pleasure that had quickly arisen with sounds of rejoicing sinks away and founders, and we live on, rapturously beholding the spirits themselves, only in this pain, which, consuming love, hope, and joy within itself, seeks to burst our breast asunder with a full-voiced consonance of all the passions.

It is fair to say that the readers of the *Allgemeine musikalische Zeitung* had never seen anything quite like this before. Hoffmann was tossing them out into the deepest part of the Romantic wilderness; those who found the surroundings congenial could count themselves among the aesthetic elite. "Romantic taste is rare, Romantic talent even rarer," Hoffmann noted; "this is probably why there are so few who can strike that lyre that opens up the wonderful kingdom of the infinite." The criteria for greatness are being deliberately expanded beyond good and bad. Hoffmann reminds us that "Orpheus's lyre opened the gates of the underworld," and that the door swings both ways. "[T]he soul of every sensitive listener will certainly be deeply and closely gripped by a lingering feeling, which is precisely that unnameable, foreboding longing."

Hoffmann is at pains to demonstrate that the Fifth, as an exemplar of Romantic music ("this should always be understood to refer only to instrumental music"), tells no specific programmatic story, nor acts as an allegory for anything other than itself; nothing even as vague as knocking Fate is mentioned. And yet Hoffmann's review is strongly, almost obsessively narrative. His description of the opening gives a taste of the whole:

> The first Allegro, 2/4 time in C minor, begins with a principal idea that consists of only two measures, and that, in the course of what follows, continually reappears in many different forms. In the second measure a fermata, then a repetition of this idea a tone lower, and again a fermata; both times only string instruments and clarinets. Even the key cannot yet be determined; the listener surmises E-flat major. The second violin begins the principal idea once again, and in the second measure the fundamental note of C, struck by the violoncello and bassoon, delineates the key of C minor, in which viola and violin enter in imitation, until these finally juxtapose two measures with the principal idea, which, thrice repeated (the final time with the entry of the full orchestra), and dying out in a fermata on the dominant, give to the listener's soul a presentiment of the unknown and mysterious . . .

... and so forth. We might chalk up this fanatical play-by-play—which he continues for all four movements—to the fact that most of Hoffmann's readers, like Hoffmann himself, would not have heard the Fifth, nor would have had much prospect to hear it anytime soon. (Hoffmann was reviewing the published score.) Except that Hoffmann then reprints, in full score, the entire excerpt he has just walked us through ("the reviewer inserts it here for his readers to examine").

Orpheus and his lyre should tip us off, though: Hoffmann is, in essence, retelling the Fifth Symphony as a heroic myth. The great classicist John H. Finley Jr. mapped ancient Greek thought into four stages; the first, most basic, was the mythic, what he called the "heroic mind." Finley noted how, in Homer's epics, objects keep their descriptive epithets—he points to Hector's helmet, always "all-shining"—even when the descriptions are irrelevant to the dramatic context. "It is as if in whatever circumstances [the object] keeps its particular being," Finley wrote. The object "does not change because people are sad or happy but remains what it is, one of the innumerable fixed entities that comprise the world." Hoffmann, in laying out the Fifth's fixed entities, exhibits Finley's characterization of a mythic-heroic apprehension, "an outgazing bent of mind that sees things exactly, each for itself, and seems innocent of the idea that thought discerps and colors reality."[14]

On the one hand, Hoffmann's assertion of mythic status fits his Romanticizing agenda nicely. Dennis Ford, citing Finley's mythic category, practically spells out the mechanics of Hoffmann's review. "The sacred realm as articulated by myth is universal, impersonal, timeless, and transcendent. As such, it contrasts with the everyday, profane world that is particular, personal, and time-bound."[15] Hoffmann's repeated longing for the infinite (and/or infinite longing) is reminding the reader what to be listening for as he spins Beethoven's tale, a tale immutable and unchanging in its specific notes and rhythms but, like all epics, a renewable source of metaphysical energy. On the other hand, that space between specificity and universality tips the interpretive prerogative back to the listener—which Romantic aestheticians would have considered a step back.

COMPOSERS' CAREERS are now routinely divided into "early," "middle," and "late" periods; this three-bin laundry sort was first invoked to put a shape on Beethoven's career. At least with Beethoven, critics and musicologists could color within somewhat clear biographical lines: early-period Beethoven starts early; middle-period Beethoven starts with the Heiligenstadt Testament, a reboot of determination in the face of his approaching deafness; late-period Beethoven starts when the deafness finally reaches the point where Beethoven retreats, as the Romantics would eventually portray it, into a world of pure musical imagination.

It is easy to see why the Romantic musical aesthetic, with its championing of art as a deeply personal statement, a missive from the unadulterated Divine to an intellectually qualified reality, would seize on the example of *late-period* Beethoven: the best way to eliminate the messy contamination of the sensed world is to shut it out. For Hoffmann to take the Fifth—one of the high-water marks of Beethoven's middle-period heroic style—as the model for a Romantic symphony is, by comparison, odd: the sheer force of Beethoven's heroic music deflects the personal as much as it amplifies it.

Middle-period Beethoven is not necessarily Heroic Beethoven, but all of Beethoven's heroic works date from the middle period: the *Eroica,* the *Emperor* Concerto, the less sitcom-like portions of *Fidelio,* the *Appassionata* and *Waldstein* Piano Sonatas, and, of course, the Fifth Symphony. From the beginning of his career, Beethoven had a reputation as an innovative rule breaker, and it was the heroic works, especially the Third and Fifth Symphonies, that cemented that image. But to convince an audience that you're breaking the rules, you have to establish a context in which the rules still apply; in Classical terms, Beethoven's heroic music is some of his most conformist, the better to highlight where he goes off script—the "false" horn entrance in the *Eroica*; the distant-key entrance of the second theme in the *Waldstein;* the incursion of the third movement's march into the finale of the Fifth. Even that incursion can be subsumed into an operation that audiences accustomed to Mozart and Haydn would have recognized—just as the end of the third movement dovetails into the finale with a sudden burst of volume, the self-quotation explodes into a repeat of the finale's opening, fulfilling the formal requirement for a recapitulation of the movement's primary theme.

Where the heroic Beethoven breaks from his predecessors is in rhetorical tone. "Heroism is assertive," is how musicologist Michael P. Steinberg puts it. "The heroic style is a style of assertion."[16] Steinberg contrasts that with the Classical pattern of dialogue, themes juxtaposed so that they seem to question and answer each other. Assertion would, at first glance, seem to aid the Romantic program of shifting aesthetic power away from the listener and toward the creator. But Beethoven's assertive style also pushes forward a musical surface so insistent that it becomes something of a firewall—and shifts the power *back* to the listener. The surface energy prevents us from peering behind its curtain, but because we nevertheless want to sense something behind that curtain, we make an educated guess, based on our own emotional experience.

In other words, Beethoven's heroic music is a lot like Steve McQueen's acting. In films such as *The Great Escape, Bullitt,* or *The Getaway,* McQueen offered probably the purest example of a post-1960 Hollywood tough guy; physically dynamic, emotionally inscrutable, stoically cool. Do McQueen's characters have deep reserves of imagination? An internal, intricately interwoven matrix of memory and doubt? Complicated, conflicted inner lives? Who can tell? Novelist and screenwriter William Goldman once described the movie star's preference for an implacable surface over a complex interior: "I don't want to be the man who learns—I want to be the man who *knows.*"[17] (Compare Ralph Waldo Emerson: "Heroism feels and never reasons, and therefore is always right."[18])

The Fifth Symphony knows. Beethoven doesn't so much take the listener on the journey with him as return from the journey and start telling war stories. Both the first movement's struggle and the finale's triumph are very public demonstrations. The energies are directed outward, at the listener, not inward, drawing the listener. This is not to say that Beethoven's *effect*—or McQueen's for that matter—is unemotional, but that, rather than transporting the viewer/listener into a new emotional consciousness, the experience is rather that of a provocative outline for the viewer/listener to fill in. It shifts the determination of musical substance back to the listener.

Besides, Beethoven could eschew action movies when he wanted to. Throughout the middle period, one can almost sense Beethoven alternating between heroic and intimate on a piece-by-piece basis, much like a star following up a blockbuster with that more "personal" project. This, too, would seem to violate the Romantic stricture of organic unity. Intriguingly, variants of the four-note motive turn up in other middle-period works, leaving one to wonder whether it is a coincidence, a stylistic tic, or a deliberate sign of Beethoven's putting asunder a narrative that the Romantic aesthetic would see joined.

Owen Jander[19] has noted how Beethoven's superimposition of stylized quail and cuckoo songs (so labeled in the score) in the "Scene by the Brook" of the *Pastoral* Symphony produces both the three repeated notes and the falling third; taking the Schindler-sourced "Fate" interpretation at face value, he reads the Sixth Symphony, as well as the Fifth, as an autobiographical essay on the composer's advancing deafness. Raymond Knapp goes further,[20] noting numerous similarities of structure between the Fifth and the Sixth (for example, the Sixth's opening phrase, like the Fifth, begins with a three-note pickup and ends with a fermata), and proposing that the Fifth and the Sixth Symphonies be heard as a giant whole. The gentle, caressing classicism of the opening of the Fourth Piano Concerto might be the emotional opposite of the Fifth's haymaker gambit, but a closer look reveals, again, parallel features: three unaccented notes leading into the downbeat, an initial avoidance of the tonic note in the melody, a rhythmically ambiguous held note—we are approaching movie-star catchphrase territory here. And all three of these works had their public premieres in the same concert: first the Sixth, then the concerto, then the Fifth.

Considering the three works as a speculative trilogy at least points up why the Fifth Symphony alone might have made a less awkward soapbox for Romantic proselytizing. The Sixth Symphony's literalism would have put off Romantic proponents (Hoffmann took part of his review of the Fifth to dismiss those of Beethoven's contemporaries who trafficked in such imitative effects); as would, perhaps, the concerto's retro-Mozart tone of Apollonian reticence (when the Romantics finally got around to programmatizing the concerto, they heard in its slow movement, again, the story of Orpheus opening the gates of the underworld). Moreover, taken as a trilogy, one could even read the three-act whole in Kantian terms: raw sense information (the Sixth's naturalism) is processed by the rational mind (the concerto's classicism) by which it is raised beyond the subjective into universal knowledge (the Fifth's singular absoluteness). No wonder the Romantics, their collective eyebrow cocked at Kant's compartmentalization, focused their attention on the Fifth as a self-contained whole.

. . .

BUT EVEN on its own, the Fifth's heroic mettle, its corporeal, visceral presence and apparent narrative of struggle in *this* world, complicates Hoffmann's sense of unnameable longing. (As one critic has put it, the Fifth "would seem to provide one of the least convincing examples of a music that [in Hoffmann's words] 'has nothing in common with the outer sensory world.' "[21]) When Hoffmann describes the ultimate effect of the Andante as calling back "the frightful spirit" of the opening movement "to step forth and threaten every moment from the storm clouds into which it had disappeared," when he ignores the obvious march and martial overtones of the Finale, when he is so intent on demonstrating the symphony's unity that he asserts that the entirety "holds the listener's soul firmly in a *single* mood" (and that the orchestra playing it must be "inspired by a *single* spirit"), it is hard not to surmise that Hoffmann is letting his aesthetic concerns guide his ears, and not the other way around.[22] His review, which did so much to establish Beethoven and Beethoven's Fifth as the benchmark for artistic achievement, also established the Fifth's tabula rasa potential, its ability to be bent to a variety of philosophical and artistic agendas.

Hoffmann's agenda—to promote Romanticism—was not one that had previously made much use of music, Romanticism having been primarily a literary phenomenon. What makes Hoffmann's choice of the Fifth so provocative as an object of Romantic advertising is that it was simultaneously troublesome and ingenious. As easy as it is to point out the rickety parts of Hoffmann's scaffolding, his use of the Fifth to promote music to a Romantic status above and beyond literature was wildly successful. Music was an experience both concrete enough to require explanation and vague enough to admit of a certain latitude in the explaining, a willful running up against the limits of language.

Of course, Hoffmann may have had another agenda; after all,

he wrote in German, not French. In his review of the Fifth, written, as it was, during French occupation, Hoffmann's criticism of French music and the Enlightenment's cultural progeny was circumspect—limited to the disparaging mention of the French vogue for literalistic battle symphonies (ironically, the sort of thing Beethoven would himself produce with *Wellington's Victory*).[23] Nevertheless, Hoffmann's review of the Fifth could easily be tied to the movement for German nationalist renewal in the wake of Napoléon's invasion. And it starts at the beginning; as Stephen Rumph has noted, the use of the first four notes of the Fifth as the basis for the symphony's overall unity paralleled a crucial feature of German nationalistic thought, the unity that "lies at the heart of Romantic political thought": "The Romantics repudiated the mechanistic, atomizing, and utilitarian tendencies of Western liberalism. . . . They upheld instead a vision of the state in which each individual interest was subordinated to the articulated—and hence, hierarchical—structure of the total organism."[24] (Compare Hoffmann, on Beethoven: "Separating what is merely himself from the innermost kingdom of notes, he is thus able to rule over it as an absolute lord.") How much Hoffmann intended his review of the Fifth to be a coded shot across the bow of Napoleonic occupation is unknowable, but he was attuned to the Romantic jargon that would lend itself so well to German nationalistic aspirations.

And the jargon mattered: the wellspring of the patriotism behind that vocabulary, eighteenth-century philosopher Johann Gottfried Herder, was a man fascinated by language. Herder was a scrupulous thinker (he studied with both Kant and Hamann; each held him in high enough regard to later feel betrayed whenever Herder tried to philosophically mediate between their two extremes) whose posthumous reputation was somewhat hijacked by his advocacy of the all-too-easily simplified idea of German nationalism. However, Herder's nationalism was based not around geography or misty conceptions of the medieval Teutonic soul, but around language—German unity was a unification of everyone who spoke German.

While Herder could disparage the French with the best of them—"Spew out the ugly slime of the Seine!" read one poem, "Speak German, O you German!"[25]—his linguistics were strikingly subtle and modern. According to Herder, one's thoughts are imperceptibly channeled in different directions based on what language one thinks in; and languages are hardly universal, each evolving out of its own specific cultural circumstances. Herder thought that the French language was geared too much toward cosmopolitan niceties to get to the philosophical heart of things; as one scholar has summarized it, "The French language suspends the mind above sense experience and therefore refers to nothing but itself; German goes all the way down to brute sense perception and, through it, goes all the way up to higher reason."[26]

Herder's ideas actually undermined straightforward nationalism: any argument for national exceptionalism was actually an argument for linguistic exceptionalism, an argument necessarily expressed within the language one wished to promote, and so on down the philosophical rabbit hole. The German Romantics' introduction of instrumental music into the equation provided an escape hatch: music was an expression beyond speech, and the fact that the most celebrated instrumental composer of the day was German seemed to indicate that there was something exceptional about the German soul that likewise went beyond language.

Hoffmann's exaltation of the Fifth thus lent itself to a self-buttressing argument: only German is adequate to even begin to describe the philosophical striving that he hears the Fifth translating into musical expression, a rhetorical stance that boosts both the prospective nation unified around the German language and the German culture that can uniquely surpass any language, even German. Hoffmann's description of the Fifth charts a treasure map of national renewal. In what is, after all, a wartime review of a wartime piece, Hoffmann rationalizes occupation by making the Fifth a stand-in for German glory, a kingdom of latent power awaiting its realization.

THAT SEEMING PARADOX of the Romantics—the simultaneous extolling of individual expressive prerogative and of collective ethnic identity—hinges around freedom's split personality, the divide between positive and negative liberty most famously analyzed by Isaiah Berlin, the British impresario of political philosophy. It is, basically, the divide between well-intentioned interference and benign neglect.

"Positive" liberty implies a proactive process, springing from the need of individuals to feel as if they are in control of their decisions. The dangerous irony is that the means (for example, the participation in the democratic process) can lead to ends in which individual choice is suppressed by majority rule, even as the individuals are made to *feel* empowered—in Berlin's opinion, making it that much easier to justify tyranny on the grounds that people aren't always aware of what's best for them. ("Recent history has made it only too clear that the issue is not merely academic," he warned.[27]) "Negative" liberty is, by contrast, the absence of meddling in one's individual decisions. "By being free in this sense I mean not being interfered with by others," Berlin put it.[28] The ideal Romantic artist might have embodied a heroic *individual* negative liberty. But outside the realm of aesthetics, while this concept of liberty was prevalent among English thinkers—Hobbes, Bentham, Mill—after the French Revolution, positive liberty held sway on the Continent.

It is easy to consider a performance of Beethoven's Fifth—or any classical repertoire—as a notch in the belt of positive liberty, both in the way we agree to accept the authority of the score (those same first four notes, in the same order, will open every rendition) and the all-too-common atmosphere of improvement, be it moral or aesthetic. It is a short jump from the idea that Beethoven is good for us to the idea that Beethoven was asserting what was good for us, whether we know it or not. Critiques of Western classical music often echo Berlin's critique of positive liberty—it causes us to fool ourselves into thinking we are freer than we are. Bassist and sociologist Ortiz Walton (the first African-American to perform with the Boston Symphony Orchestra, incidentally) was particularly scathing on this point:

> The consumer, or concertgoer, like his counterpart in the world of commerce, has been made into a passive recipient of various sounds. He either accepts the product or rejects it, but never is he allowed to add his own creativity to it. . . . So even though one has heard Beethoven's Symphony Number 5 for the hundredth time, he still keeps listening to it, claiming falsely that he hears something new every time. His participation is limited to applause after the finale or occasional coughing during the section played loud enough to cover the sound.[29]

But, then again, music, by its very incorporeal nature, has a tendency toward negative liberty as well. The connection between music and listener brooks no restriction on interpretation; each of us can hear music as each of us pleases. One is free to pick and choose from two centuries of critical interpretation of Beethoven's Fifth—and, possibly, reject it all—every time fate, as Schindler would have us believe, knocks at the door. Positive liberty helpfully breaks in. Negative liberty peeks through the drapes and decides if it wants to be home.

But Berlin's two concepts of liberty actually admit a third, what Berlin calls "the retreat to the inner citadel": the carving out of some portion of one's thought, persona, soul, that is put out of reach of the external world's stress and strain. Berlin's description of the conditions that give rise to such a retreat might well apply to much of Hoffmann's life: "I am the possessor of reason and will; I conceive ends and I desire to pursue them; but if I am prevented from attaining them I no longer feel master of the situation."[30] And, in fact, in a telling postscript to his review of the Fifth Symphony, Hoffmann would rework his kingdom of the infinite into such a retreat.

As with so many Europeans during the Napoleonic era, war seemed to follow Hoffmann wherever he went. In 1813, he moved to Dresden; within a month, Napoléon was bombarding the city. Hoffmann took refuge in writing, completing a long fictional dialogue called "The Poet and the Composer"; it was published in the *Allgemeine musikalische Zeitung* that December. The dialogue is mostly Hoffmann's take on the venerable operatic contest between music and poetry, as translated into Romantic terms (Hoffmann comes out in favor of a proto-Wagnerian union of both jobs in a single creator). But "The Poet and the Composer" opens with a story set in the midst of urban warfare: "The enemy was at the gates, guns thundered all around, and grenades sizzled through the air amid showers of sparks. The townsfolk, their faces white with fear, ran into their houses; the deserted streets rang with the sound of horses' hooves, as mounted patrols galloped past and with curses drove the remaining soldiers into their redoubts."

This is pure reportage on Hoffmann's part, a glimpse of his own Dresden existence. But then Hoffmann shifts into a fantasy that reflects the escapism of creative activity (around this time, Hoffmann would note that writing "removes me from the pressures of life outside"[31]). And we meet someone who seems more than a little familiar:

Ludwig sat in his little back room, completely absorbed and lost in the wonderful, brightly coloured world of fantasy that unfolded before him at the piano. He had just completed a symphony, in which he had striven to capture in written notation all the resonances of his innermost soul; the work sought, like Beethoven's compositions of that type, to speak in heavenly language of the glorious wonders of that far, romantic realm in which we swoon away in inexpressible yearning.

Not Beethoven, but a name-sharing doppelgänger, one whose symphony, judging by a description nearly self-plagiarized from Hoffmann's 1810 review, is itself a double of the Fifth Symphony. But reality intrudes:

> Then his landlady came into the room, upbraiding him and asking how he could simply play the piano through all that anguish and distress, and whether he wanted to get himself shot dead in his garret. Ludwig did not quite follow the woman's drift, until with a sudden crash a shell carried away part of the roof and shattered the window panes. Screaming and wailing the landlady ran down the stairs, while Ludwig seized the dearest thing he now possessed, the score of his symphony, and hurried after her down to the cellar.
>
> Here the entire household was gathered. In a quite untypical fit of largesse, the wine seller who lived downstairs had made available a few dozen bottles of his best wine, and the women, fretting and fussing but as always anxiously concerned with physical sustenance and comfort, filled their sewing baskets with tasty morsels from the pantry. They ate, they drank, and their agitation and distress were soon transformed into that agreeable state in which we seek and fancy we find security in neighbourly companionship; that state in which all the petty airs and graces which propriety teaches are subsumed, as it were,

into the great round danced to the irresistible beat of fate's iron fist.[32]

The irresistible beat of fate's iron fist. Hoffmann's cellar might be the most tantalizingly plausible source of either Beethoven's post hoc explanation of the Fifth's opening or Schindler's invented poeticization of it. Hoffmann, though, sets up the symphony in opposition to fate, a fate that nevertheless is irresistibly omnipresent, something you can, at best, temporarily ignore. Choose your illusion, he seems to say: either the "sublime siren voices" of art or the fancied security of "neighbourly companionship." If fate is at the door, the purpose of a symphony might just be to drown out the knocking.

In Hoffmann, then, the nineteenth-century philosophical tendencies to depersonalize and externalize both aesthetics and fate found an ideal vessel. The way he found himself buffeted by the winds of chance, politics, and war, perhaps he sensed that the one could vindicate the other, that the terror and awe of the sublime might lend an artistic redemption to the less exalted terror of life during wartime. Surrendering to art gives surrender a good name.

> Here is shewn once more the idiosyncrasy of German nature, that profoundly inward gift which stamps its mark on every form by moulding it afresh from within, and thus is saved from the necessity of outward overthrow. Thus is the German no revolutionary, but a reformer. . . .
>
> —RICHARD WAGNER, "Beethoven"

AND THEN, a strange coda: as German nationalism went from aspirational to imperious, German Romanticism—and, with it, the resonance of the Fifth Symphony—went from mystical to messianic. By the year of the Beethoven centennial, 1870, the anxiety of the Napoleonic Wars and the idealism of the revolutions of the 1840s had been supplanted by imperial brinksmanship, as France (led by once-President, then-Emperor Napoléon III) and Prussia (guided by the conservatively pragmatic hand of Otto von Bismarck) went to war in July after much diplomatic sniping; Prussia scored a decisive upset victory, paving the way for German unification while at the same time scuttling the renascent French monarchy for good. (King Wilhelm I of Prussia was part of a large gathering that observed the Prussian victory at Sedan from a hilly vantage, "a glittering concourse of uniformed notabilities more suitable to an opera-house or a race-course than to a climactic battle which was to decide the destinies of Europe and perhaps of the world."[33]) Bismarck had already secured the allegiance of most of the other German-speaking states after a brief 1866 clash with the Austrian Empire; a story went around that Bismarck, who revered Beethoven, had arranged a command performance of the Fifth Symphony prior to signing the declaration of war. (The concert at which Bismarck heard the Fifth was actually a month earlier.)

Also by 1870, after twelve years in exile, Richard Wagner was once again a German in good standing, albeit living in Switzerland; Wagner acquired a zealous and fortuitous fan in the young King Ludwig II of Bavaria, but jealousy among the Munich court necessitated his leaving. (The composer talked the monarch out of abdicating and following him.) It was still a remarkable change of fortunes.

The 1848 revolutions had taken a full year to reach Dresden, where Wagner was, at the time, kapellmeister of the Royal Saxon Court—patronage that did not keep Wagner from supporting the revolution wholeheartedly. He had been radicalized by August Röckel, a fellow conductor and die-hard activist who lost his own musical position after advocating armed uprising one too many times. Röckel was also connected to Beethoven—his father, Joseph August Röckel, had been Beethoven's Florestan for the second try at *Fidelio;* his aunt was, possibly, the dedicatee of "Für Elise."[34] Röckel introduced Wagner to Mikhail Bakunin, who was going from revolution to revolution, hiding out in Dresden after escaping from Prague—"a really amiable and tender-hearted man," in Wagner's estimation.[35]

In his autobiography, Wagner gave the impression of having been pulled into the uprising by the undertow of the mob ("I suddenly became conscious of the cry raised on all sides: 'To the barricades! to the barricades!' Driven by a mechanical impulse I followed the stream of people"[36]), but he had, in fact, helped plan the rebellion, even ordering a shipment of grenades. The Dresden revolution collapsed in violence, and Wagner was forced to flee, first to Leipzig, then to Paris. He was lucky; Röckel was captured and, after his death sentence was commuted, spent more than a decade in prison.

During his exile, Wagner worked on his massive operatic tetralogy *Der Ring des Nibelungen* and completed the equally expansive *Tristan und Isolde,* but neither of them would be performed until after his exile ended. His marriage collapsed; his affair with Mathilde Wesendonck, the wife of a silk-merchant patron, was in all likelihood unconsummated. He wrote what would prove his most wildly influential essay, *"Das Kunstwerk der Zukunft"* ("The Artwork of the Future"), and his most wildly offensive, *"Das Judenthum in der Musik"* ("Jewishness in Music"), but neither attracted much initial notice. A beloved pet parrot, who had just learned to whistle a scrap of the Fifth Symphony, suddenly died. ("Ah!" he wrote a friend, "if I could say to you what has died for me in this dear creature!!"[37])

Wagner was also introduced to the profoundly pessimistic philosophy of Arthur Schopenhauer. Schopenhauer had published his magnum opus, *The World as Will and Representation,* in 1818. He scorned Hegel and the German Idealists by rewinding back

to Kant; then scorned Kant by rejecting one of Kant's fundamental concepts, the *Ding an sich*, the thing-in-itself, the object
as it exists beyond the context of our senses. Kant thought the
thing-in-itself was, by definition, unknowable; Schopenhauer
thought that our inner experience, our desires, our endeavor to
continue to exist—which he called the "will"—contained knowledge of things-in-themselves. (His specific formulation was that
individual wills were facets of a single, all-knowing Will.) But
the individual will was fundamentally insatiable, forever denying other individual wills, forever unfulfilled by its real-world
translation into "representations," forever making life a vale
of frustration and suffering. Schopenhauer prescribed ascetic
contemplation—the inner citadel could be, if not a refuge from
the will, at least a neutral high ground from which to observe
the hostilities.

It's easy to see why the Wagner of the 1850s, a one-man
band of unfulfilled desire, would be so strongly attracted to
Schopenhauer's bleak analysis. But the attraction persisted
even as Wagner started fulfilling his desires on a regular
basis. For, unlike Kant and Hegel, Schopenhauer had tried to
come to terms with music's power in a way that Wagner found
tellingly sympathetic—and malleable. Wagner's essay upon
the Beethoven centennial, as much about Schopenhauer as
Beethoven, reimagines both figures as stand-ins for Wagner
himself; and Schopenhauer's aesthetics are used to define
Beethoven (and, by extension, Wagner) as the epitome of
German-ness.

For Schopenhauer, music, "since it passes over the Ideas, is
also quite independent of the phenomenal world"—that perpetually miserable domain—"positively ignores it, and, to a certain
extent, could still exist even if there were no world at all, which
cannot be said of the other arts." Music "is by no means like
the other arts, namely a copy of the Ideas, but *a copy of the will*

itself."[38] Wagner takes that ball and runs with it; if music furnishes direct access to the will, then the composer must possess a unique access to "the Essence of things that eludes the forms of outer knowledge."[39] The terms are Schopenhauer's (and, though Schopenhauer would have been loath to admit it, Hegel's), but the empowerment is Wagner's: "the *individual will,* silenced in the plastic artist through pure beholding, awakes in the musician as the *universal Will.*"[40]

Schopenhauer still might have agreed: "It is just this universality that belongs uniquely to music, together with the most precise distinctness," he wrote, "that gives it that high value as the panacea of all our sorrows."[41] But for Wagner, that meant that the creation of music absolved the composer's exercise of will from Schopenhauer's ascetic demands. "[B]reaking-down the floodgates of Appearance," he insists, "must necessarily call forth in the inspired musician a state of ecstasy wherewith no other can compare." Such ecstasy is surpassed only by that of saints, and only because saints do not mediate between their ecstasy and "a perpetually recurrent state of individual consciousness" the way a composer does. That the composer takes on the suffering that results from such alternation, a "penalty for the state of inspiration in which he so unutterably entrances us, might make us hold the musician in higher reverence than other artists, ay, well-nigh give him claim to rank as holy."[42] And none holier than Beethoven, who had one crucial advantage in his access to the universal Will: his deafness.

Like the blind seer Tiresias (who, in one legend, was partially requited for his blindness when Athena opened his ears, giving him the ability to understand birdsong), Beethoven becomes a musical prophet, "the deaf musician who now, untroubled by life's uproar, but listens to his inner harmonies, now from his depths but speaks to that world—for it has nothing more to tell him. So is genius freed from all outside it, at home forever with and in itself."[43] Wagner locates that freed genius within very specific borders, however:

> We know that it was the "German spirit," so terribly dreaded and hated "across the mountains" [i.e., France], that stepped into the field of Art, as everywhere else, to heal this artfully induced corruption of the European race. As in other realms we have hailed our Lessing, Goethe, Schiller and the rest, as our rescuers from that corruption, to-day we have to shew that in this musician Beethoven, who spoke the purest speech of every nation, the German spirit redeemed the spirit of mankind from deep disgrace.[44]

Wagner's overtones of religious trial would become a running motive in Beethoven commentary; as noted by musicologist K. M. Knittel, "writers after Wagner privileged pieces in which [Beethoven's] suffering seemed to manifest itself most clearly."[45] Edward Dannreuther, a German-born pianist who became one of Wagner's great champions in Britain, asserted that "Beethoven is, in the best sense of the word, an ethical, a religious teacher."[46] Sir George Grove, in his *Dictionary of Music and Musicians,* could write how Beethoven's life "formed a Valley of the Shadow of Death such as few men have been called to traverse."[47] When Sir Oliver Lodge, physicist, wireless pioneer, Fabian socialist, and paranormal enthusiast, published a catechism attempting to reconcile science and Christianity, he explained the incarnation of the Divine in man with this analogy: "The spirit of Beethoven is incarnate in his music; and he that hath heard the Fifth Symphony hath heard Beethoven."[48]

> Once more I'm in the ever-juvenile condition of a débutant . . . age, with its fruits, absolutely declines to set in.
>
> —RICHARD WAGNER

WAGNER COMPLETES the full turn of the wheel from the Enlightenment to the Romantic, from controlled logic to subconscious fantasy, from a conviction that reason and rationality can explain the human condition, to the aesthetic ideal represented in the purposefully incomprehensible musical strivings of a deaf composer.

Wagner's deification of deafness came during an outbreak of unusually drama-free circumstances in his life: living in the Swiss countryside, far from urban intrigues, with his longtime mistress (and mother of his children) Cosima von Bülow. In 1870, Wagner would finally marry Cosima, Wagner's first wife having died, Hans von Bülow having granted Cosima a divorce, and Cosima having converted from Catholicism. As Knittel concludes, "[Wagner] was as 'deaf' to the troubles of the world as he could ever have hoped to be."⁴⁹ The isolation, nevertheless, was not entirely placid, as Cosima related to her diary:

> *Friday, February 18 [1870]* Today, children, I committed a grave wrong; I offended our friend, and since this is something I wish never to do again, regarding it as the blackest of sins, I use this instance to identify the pitifulness of our human nature. We were speaking of Beethoven's C Minor Symphony, and I willfully insisted on a tempo which I felt to be right. That astonished and offended R., and now we are both suffering—I for having done it, he for having experienced willfulness at my hands.⁵⁰

Beethoven's metronome strikes again. But the opportunity to instruct the children is in keeping with Wagner's take on Beethoven's music. Cosima again:

> [*January 20, 1873*] . . . R. says he would like to change the time signature of the first movement [of Beethoven's Fifth] into 4/4 because it is so awkward to beat as written, and

the nuances also suffered in this rhythm—it gave rise to too many accents; Beethoven, he thinks, must have felt that people would go wrong in 4/4 and thus wrote it as if for children.[51]

In his centenary essay, Wagner raised Beethoven to Romantic majority by equating Romantic sublimity with a child's innocence: whether in Beethoven's folklike melodic ideas, "in which he recognised that nobility of innocence he dreamt of"; in the Sixth Symphony, in which "the world regains the innocence of its childhood"; or in the "Ode to Joy" from the Ninth Symphony, "the childlike innocence of which . . . breathes upon us as with a saintly breath."

Beethoven's goal, in Wagner's estimation, was "to find the archetype of innocence," an innocence Wagner hears in the Fifth's finale, "where the naïvety of the simple march-tune . . . appeals to us the more as the whole symphony now seems to have been nothing but a straining of our attention for it." Much of that straining, of course, consists of Beethoven's working out of the implications of the opening motive, an intricate operation that might seem more the result of technical plasticity than intuitive inspiration. But Wagner is quick to counter that hearing is not necessarily believing:

> [T]he C-minor Symphony appeals to us as one of those rarer conceptions of the master's in which a stress of bitter passion, the fundamental note of the commencement, mounts rung by rung through consolation, exaltation, till it breaks into the joy of conscious victory. . . . [T]hough it might be doubted whether the purity of Musical Conception would not ultimately suffer by the pursuance of this path, through its leading to the dragging-in of fancies altogether foreign to the spirit of Music, yet it cannot be denied that the master was in nowise prompted by a tru-

ant fit of aesthetic speculation, but simply and solely by an ideal instinct sprung from Music's ownest realm.

That ideal instinct, Wagner goes on, "coincided with the struggle to rescue from every plausible objection raised by his experience of life the conscious belief in human nature's original goodness."[52] The experience of life is an objection to innocence; to rescue it is to rewind life's advance.

In his final nationalistic peroration, Wagner even has the effrontery to mingle such innocence with the then-raging Franco-Prussian War:

And beside [German] valour's victories in this wondrous 1870 no loftier trophy can be set, than the memory of our great *Beethoven*, who was born to the German Folk one hundred years ago. Whither our arms are urging now, to the primal seat of "insolent fashion," there had *his* genius begun already the noblest conquest: what our thinkers, our poets, in toilsome transposition, had only touched as with a half-heard word, the Beethovenian Symphony had stirred to its deepest core: the new religion, the world-redeeming gospel of sublimest innocence, was there already understood as by ourselves.[53]

To double-book German military triumph with German cultural triumph was certainly an inspired move by the German *Geist.* ("The war is Beethoven's jubilee," Cosima remarked to Richard.[54]) But Wagner's insistence on Beethoven's youthful qualities was a glimpse of a juvenile strain that would become more and more prominent as the German Confederation turned into Imperial Germany—from Ludwig II's expensive habit of building fairy-tale castles throughout Bavaria to the destructive childishness of Kaiser Wilhelm II.

Then again, petulance was never far from the surface in

nineteenth-century Europe. In 1845, there was a Beethoven Festival in Bonn, attended by representatives from throughout Europe, featuring the unveiling of a statue of the city's most famous son. Franz Liszt, then at the height of his celebrity, had financially rescued the entire project. The King of Prussia escorted Queen Victoria into the concert hall for the festival's finale, after which followed a huge banquet. If the concert was unsuccessful—long and nearly devoid of Beethoven, apart from the *Egmont* Overture and a bit of the *Archduke* Trio, quoted by Liszt in a specially composed cantata—the dinner was worse. Sir George Smart, Beethoven's English champion, had also made the journey to Bonn; he recorded in his diary that, at the dinner, Liszt made a toast in which he "complimented *all* nations except the French . . . this omission caused dissatisfaction among the French, who, with the Jews, are not popular here." (Liszt's oversight was probably unintentional, a result of giving his speech in German, a language he was less than comfortable with.) The hall was soon consumed by outbursts of recrimination. "This row was noisy," Smart recorded, "and fearing we might get into a scrape we left the Room." Smart saw the Jewish-born Ignaz Moscheles—Beethoven's old colleague, who had translated Schindler's biography into English—leave the banquet, dismayed by anti-Semitic comments. "I am ashamed of my Countrymen!" Moscheles exclaimed.[55]

Liszt wasn't invited back to Bonn for the Beethoven centennial in 1870—the city fathers had been too scandalized when Liszt's ex-mistress, the Irish-born dancer Lola Montez, turned up uninvited at the 1845 banquet, drank too much, and began dancing on a table at the height of the uproar.[56] Thus it was that Liszt ended up composing a second Beethoven cantata for the city of Weimar.

The old text, by Bernhard Wolff, was "a sort of Magnificat of human genius conquered by God," in Liszt's judgment.[57] But the new text, by Adolf Stern, cast Beethoven as a newborn divine, reminding us of "the old legend from distant, pious times of a festival day announced by a star":

> *The star has ascended in this winter's night,*
> *blessed is he for whom the golden ray of splendor lights the way.*
> *Hail Beethoven, Hail!*[58]

And heaven and nature sing.

4

Associations

In every work of genius we recognize our own rejected
thoughts; they come back to us with a certain alienated
majesty.

—RALPH WALDO EMERSON, "Self-Reliance" (1841)

IN 1840, John Sullivan Dwight was ordained as pastor of the Second Congregational Church in Northampton, Massachusetts.
The charge at his ordination was given by William Ellery Channing, the leading theologian of Unitarianism; Channing's 1819
sermon "Unitarian Christianity," a clarion call for tempering
faith in the fire of reason, sparked the emergence of American
Unitarianism as a national movement.

Now, near the end of his life, Channing gave Dwight the sort
of paradoxical advice that elders often give the young as evidence of their hard-won wisdom. "It may be said, that religion
relates to the Infinite; that its great object is the Incomprehensible God; that human life is surrounded with abysses of mystery
and darkness; that the themes on which the minister is to speak,
stretch out beyond the power of imagination . . . that at times
he only catches glimpses of truth, and cannot set it forth in all
its proportions," Channing orated. "All this is true. But it is also
true, that a minister speaks to be understood; and if he cannot
make himself intelligible, he should hold his peace."[1]

Within two years, Dwight had left the ministry and was living at Brook Farm, a Transcendentalist utopian commune just outside Boston. When Lowell Mason's Boston Academy of Music performed Beethoven's Fifth in 1842, Dwight reviewed it, in the process becoming one of the country's first serious critics of classical music.

> The subject is announced with startling directness at the outset, in three short emphatic repetitions of one note falling on the third below, which is held out some time; and then the same phrase echoed, only one degree lower. This grotesque and almost absurd passage, coming in so abruptly, like a mere freak or idle dallying with sounds, fills the mind with a strange uncertainty, as it does the ear.

Where the opening theme embarks on its ping-pong of imitation, Dwight glimpsed an abyss of mystery and darkness. "It is as if a fearful secret, some truth of mightiest moment, startled the stillness where we were securely walking, and the heavens and the earth and hell were sending back the sound thereof from all quarters, 'deep calling to deep,' and yet no word of explanation," Dwight preached. "What is it? What can all this mean?"[2]

Dwight's classmate at Harvard Divinity School, future abolitionist Theodore Parker, wasn't surprised that Dwight didn't make it as a reverend. Dwight, he said, often "mistook the indefinite for the Infinite."[3] Out of such metaphysical optimism would sprout an American cult of Beethoven.

WILLIAM ELLERY CHANNING's nephew, William Henry Channing, was, according to Ralph Waldo Emerson, the catalyst for Transcendentalism. "Dr. Channing took counsel in 1840 [Emerson gets the date wrong; it was actually 1836] with George Ripley, to the point whether it were possible to bring cultivated, thoughtful people together, and make society that deserved the name."[4] Emerson took some pains to paint a casual, accidental air around the founding myth of the intellectual school he would eventually become identified with. The circle, in Emerson's telling, would have been "surprised at this rumor of a school or sect, and certainly at the name of Transcendentalism. . . . From that time meetings were held for conversation, with very little form, from house to house, of people engaged in studies, fond of books, and watchful of all the intellectual light from whatever quarter it flowed. Nothing could be less formal."[5]

And yet, Emerson admitted, members of the group not only produced their own publication, *The Dial* (which "enjoyed its obscurity for four years," Emerson insisted), but also, in 1841, purchased nearly two hundred acres in West Roxbury, Massachusetts, inaugurating the social experiment of Brook Farm. The driving force behind Brook Farm was the above-mentioned George Ripley, like Channing and Dwight, a Unitarian minister. The first meeting of what would be called the Transcendentalist Club (the name "given nobody knows by whom," according to Emerson) was held at Ripley's house.

Transcendentalism always resisted pithy definition; another Transcendental Club member joked that the group referred to themselves as "like-minded; I suppose because no two of us thought alike."[6] But the movement, everyone involved agreed, was heavily influenced by German Romanticism—Germany being to American intellectuals of the time what Paris would be to their 1920s counterparts. The rendition was more enthusiastic than systematic.

Probably because it transmitted much of the aura and reputation of German Romanticism without any specificity, Beethoven's music was a central reference point. Lindsay Swift, an early historian of Brook Farm, insisted that, if "the transplantation of German ideas [is] to be held of much account in the simple story of Boston Transcendentalism, the name of Beethoven must enter any reckoning which includes Goethe and Kant. No external influence has been so potent or lasting in Boston as the genuine love for Beethoven, and for the few other names clustering around the greater genius."[7]

Even Emerson, not much of a music lover, recognized Beethoven's importance. "The music of Beethoven," he wrote, "is said by those who understand it, to labor with vaster conceptions and aspirations than music has attempted before."[8] Beethoven was part of the Transcendentalist ethos from the start, probably introduced by Margaret Fuller, whose awesome erudition and willed self-assurance bewitched and bothered a fair portion of the circle. ("I find no intellect comparable to my own,"[9] she once posited, and she may have been right.) Fuller, drawing on accounts by Goethe and Bettina von Arnim, painted Beethoven in Transcendental colors, shaded with the dialectic: "He traveled inward, downward, till downward was shown to be the same as upward, for the centre was passed."[10]

Fuller, recruited by Emerson to edit *The Dial*, could have been echoing another Transcendentalist—Bronson Alcott, a pioneering educator, a passionate (and sometimes impractical) activist, and, if the encomiums of the rest of the Transcendental Club are to be believed, the true heart of the circle. Alcott's "Orphic Sayings," spread over three issues of *The Dial*, were aphorisms in the German Romantic vein, only more impenetrable; parodies of Alcott's gnomic utterances became a favorite way to mock the New England intellectuals. But Alcott nevertheless came close to both defining the Transcendental ideal and the image of Beethoven they fashioned to match it:

> We need, what Genius is unconsciously seeking, and, by some daring generalization of the universe, shall assuredly discover, a spiritual calculus, a *novum organon*, whereby nature shall be divined in the soul, the soul in God, matter in spirit, polarity resolved into unity; and that power which

pulsates in all life, animates and builds all organizations, shall manifest itself as one universal deific energy, present alike at the outskirts and centre of the universe, whose centre and circumference are one; omniscient, omnipotent, self-subsisting, uncontained, yet containing all things in the unbroken synthesis of its being.[11]

George Ripley himself tried to sum up the Transcendentalists' philosophy in a letter to his Purchase Street Church congregation: "[T]hey maintain that the truth of religion does not depend on tradition, nor historical facts, but has an unerring witness in the soul. There is a light, they believe, which enlighteneth every man that cometh into the world; there is a faculty in all—the most degraded, the most ignorant, the most obscure—to perceive spiritual truth when distinctly presented."[12]

The letter was a last-ditch effort to justify his socially conscious preaching to his increasingly suspicious parishioners, but three months later Ripley tendered his resignation. After giving his farewell sermon in March of 1841, he moved to Brook Farm. Dwight, who was friends with Ripley—Ripley had also preached at Dwight's Northampton ordination—turned up at Brook Farm in November.

RIPLEY ORGANIZED Brook Farm as a joint-stock company, selling shares for $500 each and promising each shareholder 5 percent interest. Emerson declined to join, as did Margaret Fuller, though both would visit often. (One who did sign on was Nathaniel Hawthorne, who initially enjoyed seeing himself as a man of the soil—"Ownest wife, thy husband has milked a cow!!!" he informed his fiancée.[13] But, resistant to Brook Farm's idealism and disappointed in the return on investment, Hawthorne soon left.)

Dwight tolerated being a farmhand; he rather more enjoyed

his work in Brook Farm's school, where he taught Latin and, naturally, music. The curriculum, based around singing and discussion, was heavy on Mozart, Haydn, and Beethoven, and included field trips that took advantage of the burgeoning vogue for the latter. Dwight would lead parties into Boston "to drink in the symphonies, and then walk back the whole way, seven miles at night, and unconscious of fatigue, carrying home with them a new good genius, beautiful and strong, to help them through the next day's labors," according to George William Curtis, who became famous as a writer, public speaker, and government reformer. Curtis was a teenager at Brook Farm, and formed a lifelong friendship with Dwight. In later life Curtis recalled those walks, the radicals descending into moral peril for spiritual sustenance like musical Dantes:

> As the last sounds died away, the group of Brook Farmers, who had ventured from the Arcadia of co-operation into the Gehenna of competition, gathered up their unsoiled garments and departed. Out of the city, along the bare Tremont road, through green Roxbury and bowery Jamaica Plain, into the deeper and lonelier country, they trudged on, chatting and laughing and singing, sharing the enthusiasm of Dwight, and unconsciously taught by him that the evening had been greater than they knew.[14]

If Wagner's brand of nationalist mysticism might be characterized as Hegelianism without socialism, the American energies that produced Brook Farm were socialism without Hegelianism, or at least without the Young Hegelians' ambitious fabric-of-history scope. *The Dial* extolled Brook Farm's back-to-the-land ethos ("The lowing of cattle is the natural bass to the melody of human voices") but reserved the benefits for a certain breed of the intellectually aspirant: "Minds incapable of refinement will not be attracted into this association. It is an Ideal Community, and only to the ideally inclined will it be attractive."[15]

The commune would, indeed, evolve in response to idealized programs rather than practical concerns. The first shift was toward Fourierism, named for Charles Fourier, a French socialist who came up with a scheme for remaking society that was equal parts far-seeing tolerance and numerological eccentricity. He proposed reorganizing human society into communities called phalanxes, each with an ideal population of 1,620—a number Fourier arrived at by categorizing twelve kinds of human passions, which could combine into 810 types of human character, which he then multiplied by two (male and female). Each community would be centered around a phalanstery, a large multipurpose building for which Fourier helpfully provided a detailed architectural layout.

At his most outlandish, Fourier displayed an imagination worthy of science fiction. He assigned personalities to the heavenly bodies: the moon, for example, was a dead mummy that would eventually give way to five living replacements. At its peak, society would reach a stage of Harmony, at which time, Fourier infamously insisted, the oceans would turn to lemonade. Friedrich Engels recommended Fourier, despite his ignorance of Hegelian theory, as a tonic against the tendency of Hegelianism toward arrogant solemnity. "If it has to be," Engels wrote, "I shall prefer to believe with the cheerful Fourier in all these stories rather than in the realm of the absolute spirit, where there is no lemonade at all."[16]

Fourier's ideas were brought to America by his student Alfred Brisbane, who soft-pedaled Fourier's more extravagant fancies; still, enough remained, especially the obsessive streams of impossibly precise numbers, to make even Brisbane's watered-down Fourierism off-the-wall by modern mainstream standards. And yet some of the leading minds of the day—such as New York writer, publisher, and activist Horace Greeley and, in turn, Ripley, Dwight, and others in the Transcendentalist circle—became, for a time, dedicated Fourierists.

Fourier himself had lived through the French Revolution; the meticulous detail of his prospectus can be read as a reaction to that idealistic descent into chaos. In America, though, his prescriptive zeal was something to empower individual freedom. Personal liberty wasn't dependent on status, luck, or power; all one had to do was follow directions. "Life brings to each his task," Emerson wrote, "and, whatever art you select, algebra, planting, architecture, poems, commerce, politics,—all are attainable, even to the miraculous triumphs, on the same terms . . . begin at the beginning, proceed in order, step by step."[17] The appeal of Fourier in America wasn't just his harmonious destination, but that traditional New England holy grail: a turn-by-turn guide for getting there, a path spelled out so that anyone could follow it.

Hand in hand with Fourier's social theories came the religious speculations of Emmanuel Swedenborg. In his fifties, while working on an anatomical study called *The Economy of the Animal Kingdom* (attempting to demonstrate that the soul resided in the blood, since it penetrated the entire body), the well-connected eighteenth-century Swedish gentleman-scientist began having vivid dreams, which soon manifested themselves as revelatory experiences. The Lord himself appeared to him, Swedenborg claimed, anointing him His messenger, letting him travel freely among heaven and hell, conversing with spirits along the way.

The theology that resulted from Swedenborg's fact-finding tours of the next world offered a vision—equal parts Eastern religious traditions and proto-Hegelianism—of mankind graduating from its current materialist existence to a higher, spiritual plane. A connection to Fourier's prospective Harmony was easily made by Transcendental enthusiasts. (Emerson included Swedenborg in his 1850 book *Representative Men,* along with, among others, Shakespeare, Napoléon, and Goethe.) Swedenborg combined the prospect of enlightenment with a prescription of charitable work in a way that appealed to Brook Farmers Ripley and Dwight, both of whom had abandoned the pulpit in search of more concrete action. "Faith without charity is not faith," Swedenborg insisted. "The separation of charity and faith coincides also with the separation of flesh and blood; for the blood separated from the flesh is gore and becomes corruption, and the flesh separated from the blood by degrees grows putrid and produces worms."[18]

What's more, both Fourier and Swedenborg preached tolerance. Fourier was, in essence, an early feminist (one factor behind the proposed phalansteries was to free women from the tyranny of the house), and also thought society should be considerate toward alternative sexualities; Swedenborg believed that the New Jerusalem, the final epoch of Christianity, would most likely take hold in Africa, since Africans were "more interior"[19] and thus more receptive to enlightenment—a stance that, noble-savage overtones aside, fit nicely with the Transcendentalists' abolitionist bent.

Encouraged by Greeley and Brisbane, Brook Farm converted to Fourierism and Swedenborgianism, rebranding themselves from an Association to a Phalanx, and taking over editing and printing of the main Fourierist newspaper in America, now renamed *The Harbinger*. Not all the Brook Farmers went along with change, but Dwight certainly did. He became *The Harbinger*'s music critic, and promptly began pouring his Beethovenian wine into Fourierist bottles, filing composers under Fourier's various human passions: Handel represented Universal Friendship; Haydn, Paternity; and Mozart, Love. Beethoven was Ambition: "the aspiring Promethean spirit, struggling for release from monotony and falseness, sick of the actual, subduing every sincere sadness by heroic triumphs in art, which are like tears brightening into joys of most rapturous, inspired visions of a coming Era, which shall consummate the Unity of all things."[20]

Such prose indicates how radical-by-association, at the time,

Beethoven's reputation could and possibly should be considered. To sum up: Dwight was living on a commune, espousing a far-out political system, delving into a mystical religion. He was, as much as one could be in nineteenth-century America, a hippie. And Beethoven's symphonies were his music of choice. Lest anyone mistake the connection, Dwight spelled it out: "In religion we have Swedenborg; in social economy, Fourier; in music, Beethoven."[21]

The new idols proved false. With a huge part of the farm's income siphoned off to fund the construction of a Fourierist phalanstery, commune-wide economizing took a toll on morale; when the nearly finished phalanstery burned to the ground, in March 1846, Brook Farm was, essentially, financially ruined. "The idealists lingered last, loath to leave a spot endeared by so many associations, hallowed by so many hopes," wrote one chronicler. "One of the last to go, one of the saddest of heart, one of the most self-sacrificing through it all, was John S. Dwight. It may be truly said that Brook Farm dies in music."[22]

At least Brook Farm could measure its span in years; Bronson Alcott, the Orphic idealist, saw his own commune, a ninety-acre tract in Harvard, Massachusetts, dubbed "Fruitlands" ("We rise with early dawn, begin the day with cold bathing, succeeded by a music lesson, and then a chaste repast"[23]) fail after only seven months. His daughter Louisa, after writing her wildly successful novel *Little Women,* revisited the Fruitlands fiasco in a thinly disguised 1873 satire called "Transcendental Wild Oats." Her humor was cutting, but her postmortem, from its Gilded Age vantage, was sympathetic to the fragility of the radical Transcendentalists' idealism in a society increasingly governed by capitalist ambition:

> The world was not ready for Utopia yet, and those who attempted to found it only got laughed at for their pains. . . . To live for one's principles, at all costs, is a dan-

gerous speculation; and the failure of an ideal, no matter
how humane and noble, is harder for the world to forgive
and forget than bank robbery or the grand swindles of cor-
rupt politicians.[24]

Annie Russell Marble, the daughter of one of Emerson's
favorite ministers and herself a literary critic, was sassier, calling
the Transcendentalists "a race who dove into the infinite, soared
into the illimitable, and never paid cash."[25]

Nathaniel Hawthorne also put a sardonic spin on his Brook
Farm memories in his 1852 novel *The Blithedale Romance.* D. H.
Lawrence summarized *The Blithedale Romance* in pithy style:
"[T]he famous idealists and transcendentalists of America met
to till the soil and hew the timber in the sweat of their own brows,
thinking high thoughts the while, and breathing an atmosphere
of communal love, and tingling in tune with the Oversoul, like
so many strings of a super-celestial harp. . . . Of course they fell
out like cats and dogs. Couldn't stand one another. And all the
music they made was the music of their quarrelling."[26]

In Hawthorne's case, the rue is also at least a little
self-directed. He had left Brook Farm after only five months;
even before his final departure, he wrote, "It already looks like
a dream behind me. The real Me was never an associate of the
community: there has been a spectral appearance there, sounding the horn at daybreak, and milking the cows, and hoeing
potatoes, and raking hay, toiling in the sun, and doing me the
honor to assume my name. But this spectre was not myself."[27]
In the form of Miles Coverdale, the narrator of *The Blithedale
Romance,* Hawthorne would be rebuked for that by the novel's
dark feminine presence, Zenobia (modeled, many thought, on
Margaret Fuller):

> "Have you given up Blithedale forever?" I inquired.
> "Why should you think so?" asked she.

"I cannot tell," answered I; "except that it appears all like a dream that we were ever there together."

"It is not so to me," said Zenobia. "I should think it a poor and meagre nature that is capable of but one set of forms, and must convert all the past into a dream merely because the present happens to be unlike it."

Arriving for the interview, Coverdale had "heard a rich, and, as it were, triumphant burst of music from a piano, in which I felt Zenobia's character, although heretofore I had known nothing of her skill upon the instrument."[28] Beethoven's Fifth, maybe? Hawthorne doesn't say.

SEEMING CONTRADICTIONS resulting from the off-the-shelf adoption of Romantic ideas by the Transcendentalists and their progeny might have derailed thinkers less confident of the exceptional nature of the American experience. Dwight's writings on Beethoven manage to evoke both the most progressive strains of Transcendentalism and the American habit of co-opting transcendence in the service of more worldly pursuits. In 1851, Dwight produced a survey of "The Sentiment of Various Musical Composers" for the Philadelphia-based *Sartain's Magazine* (he liked it enough to recycle it for an early issue of *Dwight's Journal of Music* a year later). Beethoven, the best, is saved for last—in terms that make him into an honorary American: "With a many-sidedness like Shakespeare's, there is still one pervading sentiment in all the music of Beethoven. It has more of the prophetic character than any other. The progressive spirit of this age, the expansive social instinct of these new times, accepts it by a strange sympathy. Many a young music-loving American jumps the previous steps of training, through the taste for Haydn, Mozart, Hummel, &c., and with his whole soul loves at once Beethoven."[29]

Dwight's young Americans can be read as model Romantic rule-breakers, but the sentiment could just as well have been invoked in the service of wealth. (Around the same time, the Reverend Darius Mead of New York could rationalize the country's expanding trade as an aid in the conversion of distant heathens: "The love of lucre—the adventurous spirit of Discovery and Commerce—these agencies, supported and strengthened by rapid improvements in the arts and sciences of civilized and christianized society, have already brought the ends of the earth together, and *the valleys* are indeed 'exalted.' "[30] Prophetic character, indeed.)

Dwight goes on:

> It is because Beethoven is, to speak by correspondence, like the seventh note in the musical scale. His music is full of that deep, aspiring passion, which in its false exercise we call ambition, but which at bottom is most generous, most reverent, and yearns for perfect harmony and order. The demands of the human soul are insatiable—infinite.[31]

Dwight recycles his customary cross-breeding of Fourierism and Swedenborgianism with the Hoffmann image of Beethoven. But note the cautious qualification of the Fourierist passion of ambition. And, exported outside the old, specific *Harbinger* contexts, the rhetoric can seem to manifest any number of destinies: "So long as *anything* is not ours, we are poor. So long as *any* sympathy is denied us, we are bereft and solitary. We are to have all and realize all by a true state of harmony *with* all. Is not this the meaning of Beethoven's music?"[32] Ambition is generosity; possession ("to have all") is harmony. (One can imagine a stereotypical plutocrat gravely nodding in agreement.) The heroic Beethoven becomes a transfer point between rarefied Transcendentalism and the American pursuit of wealth.

It took George Ripley some fifteen years to pay off the debt of Brook Farm, but he would die a rich man, having made a fortune in royalties from co-editing *The New American Cyclopedia*. In its entry on the composer, the *Cyclopedia* evoked both the Transcendentalist-Romantic Beethoven and public monuments to civic wherewithal:

> As Gothic architecture is the artistic record of the aspirations of the ages during which it grew to perfection, so the orchestral works of Beethoven are the musical record of the great ideas of his time in the form and likeness which they assumed in his mind. Haydn and Mozart perfected instrumental music in its form—Beethoven touched it, and it became a living soul.[33]

LIKE MANY a hippie after him, Dwight took his youthful enthusiasms for eternal verities. The Fifth Symphony made its impression on him once and indelibly; eschewing any reassessment, Dwight would reprint the salient portion of his review of the Academy of Music's 1842 performance in both *The Harbinger* and *Dwight's Journal of Music*,[34] and subsequently, whenever the subject of the Fifth came up, direct the reader's attention back to the reprints. Dwight was a man eager to make up his mind, and dedicated to keeping it that way.

By standing still as the world shifted around him, Dwight changed from radical to conservative. He admitted as much in the last issue of *Dwight's Journal*, published in 1881. "Lacking the genius to make the old seem new, we candidly confess that what now challenges the world as new in music fails to stir us to the depths of soul and feeling that the old masters did and doubtless always will," he wrote.[35] But Dwight's indefatigable promotion of Beethoven's music as a path to personal and societal progress would bear fruit in the accumulated wealth of post–Civil War America.

To follow Dwight's career is to watch the foundation of the classical-music canon being poured and then gradually hardening. Dwight had only ever heard Beethoven interpreted by either amateur or essentially freelance groups (even the New York Philharmonic, who had performed Beethoven's Fifth on their inaugural concert in 1842, operated as a cooperative until 1909), but toward the end of his career, Dwight evangelized for permanent orchestras. If Beethoven's symphonies offered the prospect of moral uplift, the proselytization required professional institutions, "musicians who play and rehearse together from one end of the season to the other." (Beethoven, who premiered his symphonies with pickup groups, would have been envious.) "The question is: Can our moneyed men, our merchant princes and millionaires, be got to give their money, and give it freely for this object?"[36] They could be got—1881 also saw the debut of the Boston Symphony Orchestra, funded by banker and music lover Henry Lee Higginson; the inaugural season featured no fewer than nineteen Beethoven works, including all nine symphonies.

Dwight's professionalizing crusade had been sparked by the polished performances of German-born conductor Theodore Thomas and his touring orchestra. When Chicago businessman Charles Norman Fay asked Thomas over dinner at Delmonico's if he would move to Chicago to head up a permanent orchestra—for which fifty local barons had contributed $1,000 each—Thomas, the story goes, replied, "I would go to hell if they gave me a permanent orchestra." Thomas pushed for the construction of Chicago's Orchestra Hall; to inaugurate the Hall in 1904, he programmed Beethoven's Fifth Symphony. When Thomas suddenly died a month later, the directors of the Chicago Auditorium Association, another collection of wealthy businessmen, adopted a memorial resolution, calling Thomas "the great missionary—in our country—of the 'music of the brain,'" music which "elevates, refines, ennobles, inspires, stirs, and impassions the mysterious weft of the human mind."[37] The

Transcendentalists' Beethoven had been fully assimilated into the Gilded Age.

The concentration of patronage in large cities paralleled the dilution of the Transcendental focus on nature, which had been so crucial to the original generation. Compare Thoreau— "I wish to speak a word for Nature, for absolute Freedom and Wildness, as contrasted with a Freedom and Culture merely civil"[38]—with the town-*and*-country Transcendentalism of Walt Whitman: "This is the city and I am one of the citizens, / Whatever interests the rest interests me."[39] Whitman's Beethoven likewise seems far from the Concord woods: "Beethoven had the vision of the new need. He interpreted in tones his own environment. What a tone-picture he could have given of our seething, glowing times of great promise! He was the forerunner of the American musician of the modern that will one day appear."[40]

In a similar way, Dr. Henry T. McEwen, a Presbyterian minister in Amsterdam, New York, soft-pedaled nature's obvious effects in telling of how one of his parishioners, a traveling singing teacher and sometime composer named Simeon B. Marsh, was inspired to write his best-known piece. Marsh, in McEwen's telling, was riding through the countryside one autumn morning in 1834 when inspiration struck—but not through the intercession of nature. "The beautiful scenery, because familiar, had nothing new to attract him," McEwen insists; inspiration rather "burned within him." Marsh sat down under an elm—"which then stood," McEwen notes, "where now the four tracks of the New York Central Railway bear a mighty commerce to the sea"—and wrote down his tune on a scrap of paper.[41]

Marsh's tune, which he named "Martyn," would be matched with Charles Wesley's poem "Jesus, Lover of My Soul," after which the song became one of the best-known hymns of the nineteenth century. "Martyn" opens with three repeated notes followed by a descending interval of a third, a contour identical to the opening of Beethoven's Fifth. The resemblance was not lost on an insurance executive, political gadfly, and singular composer—an "American musician of the modern"—Charles Ives.

Man is thus metamorphosed into a thing, into many things.

—RALPH WALDO EMERSON, "The American Scholar"

IN 1837—thirty-seven years before Charles Ives was born—an abolitionist activist and newspaper editor, Elijah Lovejoy, was shot to death by a pro-slavery mob in Alton, Illinois. A month later, at a protest rally in Boston's Faneuil Hall, twenty-six-year-old lawyer Wendell Phillips galvanized the abolitionist movement with a speech that made him famous. Phillips himself would perpetuate the myth that "The Murder of Lovejoy" was a spur-of-the-moment oration, recalling how "I suddenly felt myself inspired, and tearing off my overcoat, started for the platform. My wife seized me by the arm, half terrified, and said, 'Wendell, what are you going to do?' I replied, 'I am going to *speak*, if I can make myself heard.' "[42]

Charles Ives borrowed Beethoven's rhetoric to memorialize Wendell Phillips in a piano study called "The Anti-Abolitionist Riots in the 1830's and 1840's"[43]; in keeping with his penchant for saturating his music with quotations from other tunes, Ives gave over the climax of the piece to clanging iterations of the opening motive from the Fifth Symphony. The use of the Fifth's theme was a common thread in Ives's musical tributes to New England Transcendentalism—Beethoven's first four notes would ring over and over throughout Ives's most encyclopedic realization of his Transcendentalist sympathies, his *Sonata No. 2 for Piano: Concord, Mass., 1840–60*, probably composed between 1916 and 1919, but drawing on a previous decade's worth of works and sketches, and subsequently tinkered with for nearly another thirty years.

Ives was a Transcendentalist born too late and a modernist composer born too soon, and both traits were family legacies. The Transcendentalism grew from location—the Ives family was venerable New England stock—and connection, Emerson having been a family friend. The modernism came directly from his father, George, a free-thinking bandleader who seems to have been regarded as the local eccentric of Danbury, Connecticut. ("George Ives was a kind of original creature," recalled one of Charles's boyhood acquaintances.[44]) Charles Ives would recall his father

> standing without hat or coat in the back garden; the church bell next door was ringing. He would rush into the house to the piano, and then back again. "I've heard a chord I've never heard before—it comes over and over but I can't seem to catch it." He stayed up most of the night trying to find it in the piano.[45]

Both father and son would strive sonically to realize such Romantic images, earnestly blurring the line more-buttoned-down listeners might draw between music and noise. "You won't get a wild, heroic ride to heaven on pretty little sounds," George instructed.[46]

Ives graduated from Yale with a degree in music, and worked for a time as a church organist in New York City, but after the 1902 premiere of his cantata *The Celestial Country,* he decided that the prospective path of a professional composer in turn-of-the-century America was not for him, and turned his career energies to his day job: selling life insurance. Ives and a friend, Julian Myrick, went into business together, and the Ives & Myrick firm was soon selling close to $2,000,000 in policies a year. Ives trained agents during the day and composed at night. He would always insist that his vocations reinforced each other.

If there were unacknowledged conflicts in Ives's double

life, Transcendentalism helped smooth them over, providing a perspective from which the duality might turn out to be
complementary forces. One of his favorite essays was Emerson's "Compensation," an assertion of faith in a self-equalizing,
organic nature. "The world looks like a multiplication-table, or
a mathematical equation, which, turn it how you will, balances
itself," Emerson wrote. "Take what figure you will, its exact value,
nor more nor less, still returns to you."[47] The "exact value" was
Ives's goal in all his varied pursuits, the common thread around
which he organized his clamorous life.

"Truth always finds a natural way of telling her story," Ives
preached, "and a natural way is an effective way, simple or
not." The preaching in this case was not to musicians, but to
insurance agents, in a pamphlet entitled "The Amount to
Carry—Measuring the Prospect," originally written as an article for *The Eastern Underwriter*. Ives's guide went through several
reprints and established him as a pioneer of the modern practice of estate planning. Much of "The Amount to Carry" could
easily be read as a Transcendentalist tract. "[T]he influence of
science will continue to help mankind realize more fully, the
greater moral and spiritual values," Ives wrote. "Life insurance
is doing its part in the progress of the greater life values."[48] Then
again, Emerson's "Compensation" could just as easily be read
as a prophetic description of Ives's music—or, perhaps, his life:

> Each new form repeats not only the main character of the
> type, but part for part all the details, all the aims, further-
> ances, hindrances, energies, and whole system of every
> other. Every occupation, trade, art, transaction, is a com-
> pend of the world, and a correlative of every other. Each
> one is an entire emblem of human life; of its good and ill,
> its trials, its enemies, its course and its end. And each one
> must somehow accommodate the whole man, and recite all
> his destiny.[49]

Historian Robert M. Crunden notes, "The computations of the actuaries, to Ives and to other progressives, were scientific versions of Walt Whitman's lists of democratic events and objects. Once enumerated, they could be of assistance in realizing Transcendental ideals."[50] But it was the enumeration that drove Ives, the adding up, the cumulative force of multiplicity. He spent much of his later life advocating for direct democracy, pushing a constitutional amendment that would enshrine a mechanism for popular referendum at the federal level, promoting—even mandating—that every citizen stand up and be counted. Ives sold his proposed amendment with a testimonial: "Wendell Phillips, a student of history and a close observer of men, as George William Curtis says, rejected the fear of the multitude which springs from the timid feeling that many are ignorant and the few are wise; he believed the saying, too profound for Talleyrand, that EVERYBODY KNOWS MORE THAN ANYBODY."[51]

Everybody gets a say in the *Concord* Sonata—Emerson has his own movement, and so does the skeptical Hawthorne, his "atmosphere charged with the somber errors and romance of eighteenth century New England," as Ives put it.[52] The third movement portrays "The Alcotts"—Bronson Alcott in counterpoint with his house full of daughters. Only Thoreau, in the final movement, seems off by himself, but as the sage of Walden begins to play his flute, Ives writes in an obbligato flute part—the solitary thinker splitting into multiple performers.

Beethoven is a connecting thread—the first four notes of the Fifth turn up in each movement of the *Concord*—but even Beethoven is only part of a chorus of voices. The familiar motive thunders out in the bass on the first page of "Emerson," only to be immediately subsumed into a patchwork of other quotations: Beethoven's op. 106 *Hammerklavier* Piano Sonata, Marsh's "Martyn," as well as another hymn tune, Heinrich Zeuner's 1832 "Missionary Chant."[53] The Fifth will rarely appear in the *Concord* Sonata without being coupled to at least one of its Ivesian doppelgängers. In "Hawthorne," it emerges out of a whirl of demonic ragtime, only to be immediately shunted down the Puritan-guilt alley of "Martyn." Its entrance is delayed in "Thoreau" until the philosopher's flute reverie, at which point it dons the "Missionary Chant" guise (spreading the gospel of *Walden*), before finishing the piece as a distant tolling bell, high on the keyboard.

Ives's use of the motive is most fertile and provocative in "The Alcotts." It opens with the Fifth tidied into a sweet, major-key harmonization redolent of psalm books and parlors. It is Ives's evocation of an idealized childhood, a romanticization of hardship, patterned after the Marches at home in *Little Women* rather than the actual Alcotts freezing at Fruitlands:

> Within the house, on every side, lie remembrances of what imagination can do for the better amusement of fortunate children who have to do for themselves—much-needed lessons in these days of automatic, ready-made, easy entertainment which deaden rather than stimulate the creative faculty. And there sits the little old spinet piano Sophia Thoreau gave to the Alcott children, on which Beth played the old Scotch airs, and played at the *Fifth Symphony*.[54]

But Ives is programmatically setting up family conflict, not family harmony. Beth's playing runs off into improvisatory, chromatic two-part counterpoint, when the Fifth suddenly bursts in again—Bronson Alcott, perhaps, keeping his daughter on task, ensuring her lessons are sufficiently high-minded. As Ives embarks on an extended fantasy on the four-note theme, emphatic and grand, then impressionistic and mysterious, one can hear his description of Bronson, the "kind of hypnotic mellifluous effect to his voice when he sang his oracles—a manner something of a cross between an inside pompous self-assertion and outside serious benevolence."[55] Ives is giving us both the cause and the effect of the Transcendental propaganda on behalf of Beethoven and his music, the sensation of untrammeled power it must have first provided, and its dutiful assimilation into the next generation's domesticity. Bronson is apparently in that perennial parental conundrum, trying to convince his children that he once was cool.

Beth has her revenge, though; in addition to the "old Scotch airs," she appears to know other tunes. One is the "Bridal March" from Wagner's *Lohengrin*, a representative of the new generation Dwight disdained, and which, in the Beethoven-saturated context of "The Alcotts," sounds appropriately like the Fifth Symphony flipped upside-down. The "Bridal March" is followed immediately by another tune, a little curl of melody that then walks upward: the opening phrase of a minstrel song by A. F. Winnemore, "A DUETT," as the 1847 sheet music announces, "Sung by one in imitation of two rival niggers Gumbo & Sambo." That alone would be enough to rile Bronson Alcott, an unflinching abolitionist who was forced to shut down his Temple School in Boston when he admitted—and refused to expel—an African-American child. But the song also undercuts the Romantic image of Beethoven, going all the way back to Schindler's mythologizing. Its title: "Stop Dat Knocking at De Door."[56]

It is, perhaps, Ives's retort to the sentimentalization of Beethoven, the steady stream of sad stories about Beethoven's deafness or loneliness. Ives's sympathies were with Bronson, as it were—Beethoven as an object of Transcendental defiance, not comfortable pity. Ives came no closer to pinning down Transcendentalism than the Transcendentalists themselves, but though one could get there by emulating their effort, by ringing out the "tune the Concord bards are ever playing while they pound away at the immensities with a Beethoven-like sublimity, and with, may we say, a vehemence and perseverance, for that part of greatness is not so difficult to emulate."[57]

As Ives's music began to trickle into musicians' consciousness in the 1930s and '40s, much of the appeal came from Ives's status as a kind of Rip van Winkle, an Emersonian representative man suddenly found living in the modern world. One early Ivesian was the future film composer Bernard Herrmann, who recalled that he "plowed through the movements of the *Concord Sonata*" at Camp Tamiment, a socialist summer camp in the Poconos, in the 1930s.[58] It's possible that the sonata spoiled Beethoven for the opinionated Herrmann; Len Engel, a music editor at Twentieth-Century-Fox, remembered Herrmann holding court at the commissary:

> Benny would sit with us, gravy down his tie, and clobber all his colleagues as well as past composers. The one that knocked me out was Beethoven; he thought Beethoven's Fifth was the worst thing: "Anybody can do da-da-da-dum! What the hell's so unique about that?" The music editors always got a kick out of that, so as we were eating, we'd hum the opening bars of the Fifth; and each time Benny would give us that look.[59]

Herrmann and his jaded ears, however, were preceded by Ives, who came to regard Beethoven's actual notes as, perhaps, a little wan next to the construct of Beethoven in the *Sonata*. Clara Clemens, Mark Twain's daughter (Twain was good friends with Ives's father-in-law), invited the Iveses to a Beethoven recital by her husband, the pianist Ossip Gabrilowitsch (whose name Ives spelled "Ossssssip," a sure sign he didn't consider him manly enough to tackle such repertoire). Ives came away disappointed: "After two and a half hours of the (perhaps) best music in the world (around 1829), there is something in substance (not spirit together) that is gradually missed—that is, it was with me. I remember feeling towards Beethoven [that he's] a great man—but Oh for just one big strong chord not tied to any key."[60]

It was not the only Beethoven performance that frustrated Ives. In a draft letter to Nicolas Slonimsky, Ives blamed the conventionality of American audiences on Toscanini's renditions of the symphonies. The rant offers a glimpse of Ives's usually suppressed penchant for boiling-over tantrums, the composer's unfiltered id:

[A]lmost as bad is the way the lady-birds fall for that $75000 masseur' that old stop-watch, . . . little metronome "Arthur Tascaninny" with his "permanent waves"(in both arms) he hypnotizes the nice boys in purple coats & the silk ladies— & gets their money! He makes Beethoven an Emasculated lily-pad—he plays the notes B. wrote down—plays it nice, even, up-down precise, sweet pretty tone, cissy-sounding way—not the *music* of Beethoven. He makes it easy for bodily part of the box-sitting sap & gets the money! . . . A Nation Mollycoddled by commercialized papp—America losing her manhood—for money—Whatever faults the puritans—they were men—& not effeminate!! Wake up America—kill somebody before breakfast.[61]

The railing against effeminacy is typical for Ives, but, as Ives scholar Thomas Clarke Owens has noted, Ives's silken imagery also symbolizes privilege, a sign of the ambivalence Ives felt toward wealth and success, and a measure of the energy he expended maintaining his life's multiple facets.

The draft was never sent. In its place was a letter from Ives's wife, Harmony: "It wasn't lack of audience & appreciation that made Mr. Ives stop composing. It just happened—the War & the complete breakdown in health. He had worked tremendously hard in his quarry all those years & exhausted the vein I suppose."[62]

.   .   .

My purpose in going to Walden Pond was not to live cheaply nor to live dearly there, but to transact some private business with the fewest obstacles . . .

—HENRY DAVID THOREAU, *Walden*

IVES HAD little use for quasi-Hegelian models of musical progress, thinking they confused personal experience with universal truth. Ives himself admitted to a youthful enthusiasm for Wagner, but by the time of the *Sonata,* Wagner's "music had become cloying, the melodies threadbare." Yet to try to generalize from that, to "try to prove that as this stream of change flows towards the eventual ocean of mankind's perfection . . . the perpetual flow of the life stream is affected by and affects each individual riverbed of the universal watersheds," is to ignore those figures whose true transcendence trumps mere chronology. "Something makes our hypotheses seem purely speculative if not useless," Ives proclaims. "It is men like Bach and Beethoven."[63] Ives's biographer, J. Peter Burkholder, views Ives himself on the same broader, less precise scale: "Ives's career and his music are coherent, once one abandons the expectation that coherence requires consistency, sameness, and a single line of development."[64]

The *Concord* Sonata translates Ives's view of history into musical form: it is cumulative (to use Burkholder's term), not goal-oriented. From the very first page, the quotation of Beethoven's Fifth begins to accrue meanings and mirrors, one among equals in its constellation of similarities, the *Hammerklavier,* the "Missionary Chant," "Martyn." The rhythm is altered, slowed down, smoothed out; Beethoven picks up Ivesian dissonances along the way. The four-note motive is there because of its fame and familiarity, its original power and its power as cliché inseparable. Beethoven's music doesn't come out of the previous generation and lead to the next—it stands outside time, it transcends time, and history coalesces around it.

In the *Essays,* Ives reserves his most personally resonant compliments for Thoreau—who thought that the wind blowing through the trees "wears better than the opera, methinks,"[65] Thoreau who insisted that the "really inspiring melodies are cheap and universal,"[66] Thoreau who called the random counterpoint of a Walden owl and a passing flock of geese "one of the most thrilling discords I ever heard."[67] For Ives, "Thoreau was a great musician, not because he played the flute but because he did not have to go to Boston to hear 'the Symphony.'" Thoreau's symphony was in nature, "he sang of the submission to Nature . . . distinguishing between the complexity of Nature, which teaches freedom, and the complexity of materialism, which teaches slavery." In Ives's portrayal, Thoreau is Beethoven's mirror image: both earned the broadest canvas for their inspiration, but when it came to the accompanying passion, Beethoven "could not but be ever showing it," while Thoreau "could not easily expose it."[68]

Ives accommodates both Thoreau's prickly temperament and his generous ideas by expanding the tapestry into which he weaves Thoreau's musical avatar. What's more, Ives's defense of Thoreau—"The unsympathetic treatment accorded Thoreau on account of the false colors that his personality apparently gave to some of his important ideas and virtues might be lessened if it were more constantly remembered that a command of his today is but a mood of yesterday and a contradiction to-morrow"[69]—could just as easily be read as a defense of Beethoven, or more to the point, as a Thoreau or Beethoven that looks a lot like Charles Ives. Philip Corner, a founding member of the avant-garde Fluxus group, admired Ives's mutability, musical and philosophical: "[H]e puts Beethoven's Fifth into everything he writes. He knows all the good things humanity has left behind—laid up for his, and our, uses. *Not* to be sacrificed to, lest the world be corrupted by a single true idea."[70] The great majority of Ives's lives—radical and conservative, nostalgic and reformer, reclusive artist and evangelizing businessman—were lived at the same time, as it were, but where others might see contradiction, Ives saw simultaneity. He ascribed to Thoreau a habit he shared: "he observed acutely even things that did not particularly interest him"[71]—except that Ives was interested in, seemingly, everything, consumed by a faith that the right aggregation of notes could encompass both the thunder and the bell. (Preparing a revised edition of the sonata, Ives sent emendations and changes to his publisher for seven years, ten proofs in all; at one point, his editor wrote Harmony Ives, begging her to rein in her husband's additions: "The plates absolutely will not stand any more."[72])

Beethoven's Fifth Symphony appears in the music not just as period color, but as its own library of allusions, eager to be cataloged. The *Concord* Sonata, in a way, represents a culmination, a clearinghouse for all the meanings attributed to the opening of Beethoven's Fifth, a comprehensive collection of every varying interpretation and use to which the four notes had ever been put: profound and trivial, sacred and profane, feral and tame, indefinite and infinite. By the time Ives's sonata saw the light of day, Beethoven's image was beginning to fragment, competing exegeses set up in opposition. Ives nonetheless believed he could fully encompass Beethoven's manifold posthumous existence, that every mask ever applied to those four notes deserved to have its vote heard. It was his duty, in more ways than one: the Transcendentalist and the insurance man, tallying up the Beethovenian legacy, making sure the entire estate is covered.

5

Secret Remedies

"One does not always care to feel that fate is knocking at the portal."

"No," she said; "but we have nationalized the sisters. They wear evening gowns nowadays, and we try to propitiate them by asking them to dinner and 'hoping that they are well.'"

—JESSIE VAN ZILE BELDEN, *Fate at the Door* (1895)

FOR A FEW YEARS in the late 1870s, Hans von Bülow and August Manns engaged in a typically Prussian feud, but it is perhaps a small triumph for the spread of German ideas that their feud played out in the British press. Since 1855, Manns, a former army bandmaster, had directed the concerts at London's Crystal Palace, concerts at which Bülow had appeared as a piano soloist on several occasions. The chronically impolitic Bülow, irked at never having been invited to conduct, and dismissive of London's musical life in general, began to disparage Manns in the pages of *The London Figaro*; Manns's slow-burning rage eventually boiled. In November 1878, Bülow took the podium at St. James's Hall, conducting Beethoven's Fifth, and Manns duly reported his impressions to the press.

It was a grand idea of my noble confrere to prefix three silent bars at the beginning of the first movement. I wonder if some New German–principled conductor could add four bars more in order to vex Destiny—who, as we know, is waiting to knock at the door—into a still greater fury than Herr von Bülow did last Tuesday. That Destiny was made impatient through being compelled to wait three bars before it could proceed with its knocking at the door became evident to all who were present; for it did knock with a vengeance after the first beat, and rushed off with such a furious impetuosity that my noble colleague got fairly frightened, and was compelled "to pull up" which had the disastrous effect of destroying, for the rest of the movement, the plastic pose of his left arm, because the left hand had to assist the right one in tightening the reins of infuriated Destiny.[1]

Manns did not, however, mention the reason for Bülow's extra gestural care at the outset: only a small portion of the orchestra was actually watching him, the group being made up of professors and students from the Royal Normal College and Academy of Music for the Blind.

I want to lead the Victorian life, surrounded by exquisite clutter.

—FREDDIE MERCURY

THE INDUSTRIAL REVOLUTION was felt all the more keenly in a Britain that had regarded the political revolutions of the eighteenth century as foreign aberrations, and had managed to keep such wolves at bay. Having resisted change for so long, when the Victorians finally noticed change, it seemed to burst like a thunderbolt. Regarding the era, scholar Walter E. Houghton noted how much more history, it seemed, was being cast aside:

"[T]he past which they had out grown was not the Romantic period and not even the eighteenth century," Houghton wrote. "It was the Middle Ages." It was only in the 1830s, when England could no longer cling to the bulwarks of mythical Albion—the Church of England, the hierarchy of class, the local economies of farms and guilds—that "men suddenly realized they were living in an age of radical change."[2]

For the Victorians, the best psychological defense was a good offense; hence their exuberant mythologizing of commerce and industry, which reached an apotheosis in the Great Exhibition of 1851, housed in the Crystal Palace, a specially built immensity of glass and iron. The Exhibition combined a trade show with an industrial pageant; the Crystal Palace was its cathedral, a sacred space for the worship of stuff.

The organizers of the Great Exhibition saw the effort as utopian and transcendent, marrying the burgeoning theology of Victorian industry to the hazy infinities of the Romantics. Prince Albert, a prime mover behind the Exhibition and the founding president of its Royal Commission, invoked a grand goal: "Nobody who has paid any attention to the particular features of our present era, will doubt for a moment that we are living at a period of most wonderful transition, which tends rapidly to the accomplishment of that great end to which, indeed, all history points—the realisation of the unity of mankind."

A Scottish clergyman, the Rev. John Blakely, approvingly quoted the Prince Consort in an 1856 volume called *The Theology of Inventions*. "True it is," Blakely admitted, "that those nations, which met in the Crystal Palace in mechanical rivalry, have now met in the field of carnage, to decide with the weapons of death the fate of nations. . . . But it furnishes no argument against the truth already announced, regarding the tendency of machinery to promote the brotherhood of nations." The Victorian mind could—indeed, almost had to—rationalize the fallout of misery from the Industrial Revolution as a Divine test; Blakely kept faith with the factories. Mechanical inventions would "unite the separated sons of Adam." The "achievements of the past and the present are but faint types of the future." The machinery heralded a revival: "There is a good time coming."[3]

Beethoven made a cameo appearance at the Great Exhibition, in the form of Gustav Blaeser's "Statue of Louis van Beethoven upon a pedestal, in bronze; with corner figures, representing the Spirits of Chivalry, Religion, Sadness, and Joy"[4]—Blaeser's Beethoven-as-Apollo, a design rejected for the Bonn Beethoven monument, now standing among other examples of Prussian industry, including an "Ælodion, a six-octave keyed instrument, with metal springs, or tongues, caused to vibrate by bellows"; a "large and costly apparatus for the evaporation of syrup, made of beaten copper"; and a "variety of samples of blue and grey military cloths, such as are supplied for the clothing of the Royal Prussian army."[5]

Beethoven would attain a more prominent pedestal after the Crystal Palace was relocated from Hyde Park. The edifice—in essence a giant conservatory, designed by Joseph Paxton, a gardener and greenhouse architect—was rebuilt on Sydenham Hill, a wealthy suburb of London. The enterprise also acquired a new head, officially titled (in the unassuming Victorian manner) Secretary to the Crystal Palace: a railway engineer and music-lover named George Grove.

Victorian convictions were inculcated in Grove by the Rev. Charles Pritchard, Grove's headmaster at the Stockwell and, later, the Clapham Grammar School. Pritchard, according to Grove's biographer, "insisted that the main intention of early education should be the development of the habit of thinking, and he further laid great stress on the necessity of providing resources for the leisure hours of maturer life."[6] Both tenets bore fruit. Though an unruly student—"his circumstantial touches were often trying to the gravity of his instructor"[7]—

Grove would bring to the concert hall the era's faith in educational improvement.

He became a panjandrum of Victorian music, editing his eponymous *Dictionary of Music and Musicians,* and serving as the first director of the Royal College of Music, but his background was that of an enthusiastic amateur. Grove came to music through, Britishly enough, Handel's *Messiah*—while still a teenager, he bought a score for the then-not-inconsiderable amount of a guinea. While an apprentice engineer, Grove spent his off hours copying scores in the British Museum. Working for a specialist in the erection of cast-iron lighthouses, Grove traveled, to Jamaica, to Bermuda. He visited Paris in the revolutionary year of 1848, prior to the election of Louis-Napoléon; a traveling companion remembered him blithely jotting down the notes of "God Save the Queen" for a group of musically minded workers at Notre-Dame.[8]

Grove had switched from building lighthouses to building railway stations and bridges just in time to be caught in the collapse of England's railway bubble; in 1850, influential acquaintances arranged for the increasingly idle Grove to be appointed secretary of the Society of Arts. The president of the Society, Prince Albert, had already convinced the group to mount an industrial showcase; the twenty-nine-year-old Grove found himself in the thick of preparations for the Great Exhibition. After the Exhibition closed, Grove slipped into the secretaryship of the new Crystal Palace without fuss.

With an opportunity to apply the fruits of his all-consuming hobby, Grove took special interest in the presentation of music at the Crystal Palace. At first, the offerings were limited to band concerts under the direction of one Henry Schallehn. But Schallehn's former assistant, Prussian-born former bandmaster August Manns, shrewdly stayed in contact with Grove, sending the secretary programs of his foreign concerts. Impressed by his high-minded repertoire, Grove wrote Manns that he "would give a great deal to have such music done in the Crystal Palace."[9] Schallehn was out; Manns was in.

Manns, who combined military discipline with a certain artist's-privilege aloofness,[10] convinced Grove to let him field a full orchestra. The Palace's first great musical successes were parochial: the chorus-and-orchestra Handel festivals, celebrations of the country's most famous adopted musical son. But with the advent of what became known as the "Analytical Concerts," combining Manns's conducting and Grove's program notes, the Classical-Romantic canon took up residence at the Crystal Palace: Mendelssohn, Schubert, Schumann, and, especially, Beethoven.

The concerts at the Crystal Palace illustrated the increasing permeability of class in Victorian England. Beethoven had been featured as both high and low entertainment before. The Philharmonic Society of London, founded in 1813—the group commissioned Beethoven to write his Ninth Symphony—presented the symphonies as noble endeavors. Prince Albert, himself a musician and composer, occasionally designed concerts for the Philharmonic Society, with Beethoven featured in all but one. (The Fifth was a princely favorite, appearing on four of the fourteen royally programmed concerts, more than any other work.)[11]

On the other end, perhaps, was Louis Antoine Jullien, a Parisian conductor who, having fled his debts to London, became a celebrity in the 1840s and '50s for his flamboyantly showy direction and presentations of huge orchestras, performing grab-bag programs of symphonies, operatic airs, and dance music. When the program came around to Beethoven, Jullien would don clean kid gloves and conduct with a jeweled baton that was brought to him on a silver platter. He augmented the Fifth Symphony with "parts for four ophicleides and a saxophone, besides those of his favourite regiment of side-drums," if a newspaper complaint is to be believed,[12] but all the same he brought the symphonies to a public that would have had little or no access to the Philharmonic Society. When George Grove came to edit his *Dictionary of Music and Musicians,* first published in 1878, he took on Jullien's entry himself. "[W]hat Jullien aimed at was good, and what he aimed at he did thoroughly well," Grove wrote.[13]

Manns and Grove split the difference between the exclusivity of the Philharmonic Society's Hanover Square Rooms and Jullien's shilling-ticket extravaganzas. The result was quintessential Victorian uplift, a musical gospel preached in the era's church of industry, a space blessed with both a royal box and a convenient, cheap railway connection. Like everything else in the Crystal Palace, Beethoven's music became drafted into a campaign of spiritual and commercial betterment.

The Crystal Palace as reconstructed at Sydenham was both larger and more morally didactic than its previous incarnation. Architect Owen Jones, who had designed the Palace's interior layout at Hyde Park, produced a series of ten Fine Arts Courts for Sydenham, each devoted to a historical architectural style: Greek, Byzantine, Medieval, even a court re-creating the decorative ambiance of Jones's architectural benchmark, the Alhambra in Spain. The Egyptian Court featured a commemorative inscription translated into hieroglyphics: "In the 17th year of the reign of her Majesty, the ruler of the waves, the royal daughter, Victoria lady most gracious, the chiefs, architects, sculptors, and painters, erected this palace and gardens."[14] (The artisans who constructed the Fine Arts Courts were largely German, Italian, and French; when Queen Victoria paid a visit to the construction site, the foreigners provided a rendition of "God Save the Queen" "in first-rate style," according to a reporter.[15] Grove would have been pleased.) The Fine Arts Courts were intended to contribute to the improvement of Victorian Londoners, suggesting, in the words of historian Jan Piggott, "a certain politics of empire, a philosophy and even a morality: the fall of proud, wealthy and luxurious civilizations"[16]—a warning to maintain propriety and rectitude, lest an increasingly moneyed British society meet the same fate. (Not for nothing was a Nineveh Court included.) At the same time, the Sydenham Palace—which, unlike the Exhibition, was organized as a commercial, private enterprise—rented shops and stalls, making the building as much a shopping mall as a museum. "[I]t may truly be said, that nowhere can purchases be made with less trouble and fatigue, or with more advantage to the purchasers," the Palace's directors assured patrons.[17] While Prince Albert and the Society of Arts had taken the 1851 Exhibition's profits to build what would become the Victoria and Albert Museum, "the public," as one of the Society's correspondents remarked, "have taken their spare cash to shop down at Sydenham."[18]

Music at the Crystal Palace likewise served both God and Mammon. Victorian cleric and commentator Hugh Reginald Haweis thought that the type of programs that Manns and Grove put on were indicative of the "immense advance of the popular mind"[19] because, though the Palace's shareholders were tempted to "sacrifice everything to attract a paying mob anyhow and anywhen," Grove "stood firm, and he took his stand on music."[20] Grove himself, on the other hand, appreciated the way Beethoven nourished both soul and box office. When he collected his program notes on the Beethoven symphonies into a popular book, Grove introduced the Fifth at the nexus of meaning and fame:

> The C minor Symphony is not only the best known, and therefore the most generally enjoyed, of Beethoven's nine Symphonies, but it is a more universal favourite than any other work of the same class—"the C minor Symphony always fills the room." And this not only among amateurs who have some practical familiarity with music, but among the large mass of persons who go to hear music *pour passer le temps.*[21]

The Fifth most often appeared at the end of Crystal Palace concerts, the better to keep the room filled through any prior novelties. An audience survey during the 1879–80 season put three of Beethoven's symphonies (nos. 3, 5, and 6) in the top five, along with Mendelssohn's *Italian* Symphony and Schubert's *Unfinished*.[22] (And not just at the Crystal Palace: the Fifth was already the preferred symphony of the Royal Philharmonic Society, with thirty-four performances by 1850; from 1858 to 1895, Charles Hallé's orchestra in Manchester played the Fifth eighteen times.[23])

Grove regarded his musical endeavors, and the Victorian promotion of "noble music" in general, as part and parcel with the Industrial Revolution. "It is the division of labour," he wrote, "the spread of machinery" and the concomitant changes in transport and education—"it is these characteristic achievements of the reign of Victoria which have effected so much in literature and music that it is a mere commonplace to us, but which to our fathers and grandfathers was unknown, unexpected, impossible."[24] Something was needed to elevate the newly desirous masses, and something was needed to get them in the door; Beethoven fit the bill on both counts. "[I]n London, in Paris, everywhere else," Grove wrote, "the C minor Symphony has been the harbinger of the Beethoven religion."[25]

Such religions were a growth industry at the time. As industry re-created more and more of the world in its mechanistic image, Victorians began to fear a supplanting of the infinite. As a result, Victorian life was defensively saturated with a hollow exaltation of religion. Reformer and novelist the Rev. Charles Kingsley wrote of his fellow Anglicans "losing most fearfully and rapidly the living spirit of Christianity, and . . . for that very reason, clinging all the more convulsively—and who can blame them?—to the outward letter of it." In the meantime, "the more thoughtful" searched for a substitute, be it Catholicism, commerce, or, most insidiously, art: "an unchristian and unphilo-

sophic spiritualist Epicurism which, in my eyes, is the worst evil
spirit of the three, precisely because it looks at first sight most
like an angel of light."[26] (Kingsley once filled out a literary ques-
tionnaire: "Favourite composer? Beethoven . . . The character
you most dislike? Myself."[27])

In an 1878 issue of *Punch*, "Our Representative Man" reported
hearing Beethoven's Fifth at Covent Garden in the company of
a "Stupendous Musical Amateur," one of Kingsley's spiritualist
epicures *in excelsis*:

> As the *Allegro* finished, my Stupendous Friend rose from
> his seat, and, frowning upon me as though challenging, or
> defying contradiction, addressed me thus. "The *Allegro*," he
> said, firmly and authoritatively, "is the point where Human
> Genius has reached its uttermost limits,"—and with this
> he strode grandly from the box, in so ethereally transcen-
> dental a manner that, had any one met me immediately
> afterwards, and told me "Your friend has gone straight up
> through the roof into the sky above, all among the angels,"
> I should not have been surprised: indeed, I should rather
> have expected it.[28]

The zeal with which George Grove evangelized on Beethoven's
behalf was the result of a relatively late conversion; well into his
thirties, he had remained puzzled by the symphonies. In spite
of his later devotion, researching and writing both his program
notes and the lengthy "Beethoven" entry in the first edition of
his *Dictionary*, Grove again felt a twinge of anxious heresy late in
his life. In poor health, taking the waters at the Swiss resort of
Ragatz, he was suddenly seized with trepidation. "In the dead
of night it came into my mind," he wrote his brother-in-law.
"Had Beethoven written anything sublime?" Grove elaborated
in a letter to his brother. "The sublime, as I take it, must have
a supernatural element in poetry or music. I don't find the

C minor symphony has any of the sublime," he wrote. "*Personal* and *terrible* it is in the first movement, mystical in the Scherzo and connection with the Finale; and triumphantly magnificent in the Finale itself. But I find nothing which . . . makes me silent with awe." To another correspondent, Grove disclosed, "It quite frightens me to admit that there is anything which Beethoven had not, and yet, as I see at present, I must admit he had not *this.*"[29] Even mortal gods fell hard.

BEETHOVEN'S MUSIC at the Crystal Palace, perhaps, was fulfilling the same function in Victorian life as the manufactures that had filled the hall in 1851—talismans of the spiritual validation of earthly goods. The Great Exhibition was not primarily about advancing technology, but about justifying the societal pressure toward consumption that technology created. Scholar Thomas Richards, surveying Victorian "commodity culture," seizes on the Great Exhibition as that culture's inaugural liturgy, a glorification of manufactured goods as self-warranting objects. Richards points out that the Exhibition's most prominent exhibits were not practical machinery, but gadgets, mechanical devices "so specialized as to be practically useless."[30] Just as Beethoven's symphonies had risen to the pinnacle of musical value by exalting pure, unadulterated expression, the gadget could better declare for industry the more it avoided actual function. Absolute music; absolute manufacture.

Richards views the Great Exhibition through the lens of Guy Debord's 1967 Situationist classic, *The Society of the Spectacle.* The radical pranksters of the Situationist International, fomenting revolutionary attitude in 1960s France, might seem far away from nineteenth-century Britain, but their targets were those Victorian novelties, consumption and advertising. "In societies dominated by modern conditions of production, life is presented as an immense accumulation of *spectacles*," Debord wrote. "Everything that was directly lived has receded into a representation."[31] Such spectacles, in Debord's reckoning, are elaborate reinforcements of the ruling order, "its never-ending monologue of self-praise."[32] His analysis drew on Karl Marx (it *is* French theory, after all),[33] but also Hegel—and Hegel by way of Nietzsche. Where Nietzsche posited history itself as an impersonal agent, Debord said that Hegelian "progress" has replaced that historical force with the commodity itself—stuff we manufacture, stuff we consume, turning back on us and controlling our lives. "The spectacle is the stage at which the commodity has succeeded in *totally* colonizing social life," Debord noted. "Commodification is not only visible, we no longer see anything else; the world we see is the world of the commodity."[34]

Many of Debord's aphorisms seem to provocatively glance off both the Victorian predicament and the prominence that Beethoven and the Fifth Symphony accumulated throughout the burgeoning industrial age. The popular programmatic narrative of the symphony's "struggle," for instance, and its status as an exemplar of organic unity: "Although the struggles between different powers for control of the same socio-economic system are officially presented as irreconcilable antagonisms, they actually reflect that system's fundamental unity, both internationally and within each nation."[35] Debord's analysis of movie and television stars might well speak to Beethoven's Victorian celebrity: "As specialists of *apparent life,* stars serve as superficial objects that people can identify with in order to compensate for the fragmented productive specializations that they actually live."[36] And when Debord moves on to culture as a whole, he finds that capitalism has renewed the alienation that first agitated the early Romantics, echoing the young Hegel's line in the sand between Fichte and Schelling; again, as Hegel had put it, "The entire system of relations constituting life has become detached from art, and thus the concept of art's all-embracing coherence has been lost, and transformed into the concept either of superstition or of entertainment."[37] Thus, in Debord's words, culture "detached itself from the unity of myth-based society":

> The history that gave rise to the relative autonomy of culture, and to the ideological illusions regarding that autonomy, is also expressed as the history of culture. And this whole triumphant history of culture can be understood as a progressive revelation of the inadequacy of culture, as a march toward culture's self-abolition. Culture is the terrain of the quest for lost unity. In the course of this quest, culture as a separate sphere is obliged to negate itself.[38]

The alienation and negation Debord saw so clearly in the society of the 1960s was just beginning to be sensed in the 1860s. It would be an oversimplification to regard the Victorian veneration of Beethoven as a deliberate or even unwitting scheme to reinforce the nascent power structure of the Industrial Revolution—even at the remove of a century, the Situationists were still not sure what to make of Beethoven. British playwright Howard Brenton could admire how "the situationists showed how all of them, the dead greats, are corpses on our backs—Goethe, Beethoven—how gigantic the fraud is";[39] but another group of British Situationists could write of how, in the wake of the Industrial Revolution, art "changed from a celebration of society and its ideologies to a project of total subversion. . . . [I]n Beethoven . . . one can see the change from celebrant to subversive within the space of a lifetime."[40] But Raoul Vaneigem, one of the group's leading theoreticians, sensed the Victorians' Beethovenian sea-change in more primal terms in his 1967 book *The Revolution of Everyday Life.* "Nobody seems worried that *joy* has been absent from European music for nearly two centuries; which says everything," he wrote. "Consume, consume: the ashes have consumed the fire."[41]

Indeed, the era confirmed the growing tendency—

subterranean but significant—to underline the Fifth's sense of struggle, rather than triumph. The most striking example is surely the reaction of Fanny Kemble, the celebrated English actress and writer. Kemble temporarily retired from the stage in 1834 to marry the American planter Pierce Butler, but her horror at the treatment of slaves on Butler's plantations, coupled with Butler's infidelities, resulted in their separation. Upon Kemble's discovery of his affairs, Butler had offered a deal: she could retain access to her children on the condition that she forswear the stage and not publish anything in support of abolition; Kemble, trapped, agreed on account of the children.[42] But the arrangement collapsed, Butler took the children, and Kemble returned to Europe. She chronicled a recuperative trip to Italy in *A Year of Consolation*, interspersing the narrative with poems, including this one:

ON A SYMPHONY OF BEETHOVEN.

Terrible music, whose strange utterance
Seem'd like the spell of some dread conscious trance;
Impotent misery, helpless despair,
With far-off visions of things dear and fair;
Restless desire, sharp poignant agonies;
Soft, thrilling, melting, tender memories;
Struggle and tempest, and around it all,
The heavy muffling folds of some black pall
Stifling it slowly; a wild wail for life,
Sinking in darkness—a short passionate strife
With hideous fate, crushing the soul to earth;
Sweet snatches of some melancholy mirth;
A creeping fear, a shuddering dismay,
Like the cold dawning of some fatal day:
Dim faces growing pale in distant lands;
Departing feet, and slowly severing hands;
Voices of love, speaking the words of hate,—

The mockery of a blessing come too late;
Loveless and hopeless life, with memory,—
This curse that music seem'd to speak to me.[43]

Kemble published several volumes of her letters, all scrupulously edited to avoid explicit mention of her marital difficulties. But the fragility and disquiet so vigilantly tamped down
in her epistolary memoirs is palpable in her poetry. If the symphony in question was indeed the Fifth—a likely notion—then
the balance has been decisively shifted away from the Finale ("a
blessing come too late") and toward the first movement's tur-
moil. Cosima Wagner's joke, that the Fifth's climax was a lot of
celebrating over nothing, turns serious, a shout over the abyss
lurking under the shifting ground of Victorian society. Kemble
had fame, success, and influential friends, but also learned that,
in crucial ways, she was performing without a net.

That disquieting opportunity and peril—the newfound ease
with which one could move up the ladder, or down—was delin-
eated as early as 1833 by the politician and indefatigable novelist
Edward Bulwer-Lytton. He blamed the anxiety of social climbing for English reserve and arrogance. "Nobody being really
fixed in society, except the *very* great," Bulwer-Lytton observed,
"in any advance you make to a seeming equal, you may either
lower yourself by an acquaintance utterly devoid of the fictitious
advantages which are considered respectable; or, on the other
hand, you may subject your pride to the mortification of a rebut
from one, who, for reasons impossible for you to discover, considers his station far more unequivocal than your own."[44] The
stiff upper lip was both a shield and a bluff.

In such circumstances, Beethoven's very lack of Englishness
could become a virtue, a chance for a hemmed-in society to
vicariously revel in unfettered foreignness. George Grove once
jotted down these thoughts in a notebook under the heading
"Beethoven": "Such men cannot be judged by the standard of

ordinary men—of Englishmen particularly. They are free from conventions which bind us, they are all nerves, they indulge in strange gestures and utter odd noises and say strange words, and make everyone laugh till we find that the gestures and looks and words are the absolute expression of their inmost feeling."[45]

Beethoven became a proxy, expressing the inmost feelings of Victorians who would never admit that the feelings were their own. Edward Bulwer-Lytton's son, Robert Bulwer-Lytton, followed in his father's literary footsteps, publishing under the pen name of Owen Meredith. ("Genius does what it must," Lytton/Meredith famously wrote, "talent does what it can.") The younger Bulwer-Lytton—"one of the most amateur of all nineteenth-century politicians" in the words of British minister and historian Roy Jenkins[46]—also became a fixture in Victorian diplomacy; as Viceroy of India, Lytton counted on his résumé the Great Indian Famine of the late 1870s as well as the Pyrrhically expensive Second Anglo-Afghan War, the latter decisively contributing to the downfall of Disraeli's final premiership in 1880. Falling upward in the peerage, Lytton was created 1st Earl of Lytton for his efforts. "Never regret, never explain, never apologise," as the Oxford Master Benjamin Jowett was said to have encouraged a generation of Victorian elites;[47] but the veneer could crack, as in Robert Bulwer-Lytton's description of a Beethoven symphony:

> Behold! that anguish—it is thine: that remorse—it is thine own conscience which recognises itself. Recognise this also—it is Faith: and this—it is Hope. What hast thou done with them? That abyss of darkness and chaos—it is thine own soul. Know thyself at last. Ah! didst thou think to lap thee in delightful lies? Up then! confront the universe as it is. Say not, What matters it to me? Thou canst not extricate thyself from the infinite.[48]

The Victorian stereotype of imperturbable pride was well-earned, but the angst it covered up was hidden in plain sight, often under Beethoven's byline.

Beecham's Pills: Aloes, ginger, and soap.

—"PATENT MEDICINES,"
The British Medical Journal, DEC. 26, 1903

BEETHOVEN'S MUSIC became a repository for inchoate Victorian emotions in much the same way that Hoffmann et al., fueled by the anxieties of the Napoleonic era, had traced Romanticism onto the outline of the Fifth Symphony—and in much the same way that the products Victorian factories turned out acquired Romantic mysteries of their own, textiles and patent medicines taking on trappings previously reserved for symphonies. Even Karl Marx—whose exile, it should be remembered, made him a Victorian Londoner—couldn't help but revert to old Romantic ideas when confronted with the era's flood of saleable stuff. Assiduously collecting data, Marx could track how ever-cheaper manufacturing created a growing disparity between use value (what a thing was worth) and money-form (what it cost to produce), but quantifying the larger meaning was more difficult. The imbalance was an opportunity for capitalists—but a philosophical conundrum for Marx.

Romanticism abhors a vacuum, and, much as it colonized the uncharted areas of Enlightenment aesthetics, it filled in the no-man's-land between commodities' use value and their money-form. Marx's sketch of what he called the "Fetishism" of commodities is filled with terminology reminiscent of Hoffmann and Hamann, familiar symbolism papering over a logical void. To make a table out of wood does not change its substance: "the table continues to be that common, every-day thing, wood,"

Marx writes. "But, so soon as it steps forth as a commodity, it is changed into something transcendent." A commodity has "mystical character," it is "enigmatical" and "mysterious," it is, "a very queer thing, abounding in metaphysical subtleties and theological niceties." Commodities become the ether through which people relate, crowding out the reality of the human labor that produced them. Their power is so intangible that Marx tries all sorts of oblique strategies to describe it, finally appealing to a higher power, or at least its worldly illusion: "In order, therefore, to find an analogy, we must have recourse to the mist-enveloped regions of the religious world. In that world the productions of the human brain appear as independent beings endowed with life, and entering into relation both with one another and the human race. So it is in the world of commodities with the products of men's hands."[49]

Perhaps the quintessential Victorian commodity was Beecham's Pills, the near-ubiquitous patent medicine. Formulated by Thomas Beecham, a former livestock keeper who enjoyed experimenting with herbal veterinary treatments, the pills first appeared in the 1840s, part of a brand lineup that included tooth powders and something called "Female's Friend."[50] But it was the pills that became the mainstay of Beecham's company. They worked as laxatives—and not much else—but that didn't stop the company from ascribing to them an almost universal applicability. "Beecham's Pills are admitted by thousands to be worth above a Guinea a Box," read one typical ad,

> for Bilious and Nervous Disorders, such as Wind and Pain in the Stomach, Sick Headache, Giddiness, Fulness and Swelling after Meals, Dizziness and Drowsiness, Cold Chills, Flushings of Heat, Loss of Appetite, Shortness of Breath, Costiveness, Scurvy, Blotches on the Skin, Disturbed Sleep, Frightful Dreams, and all Nervous and Trembling Sensa-

tions, &c. The first dose will give relief in twenty minutes. This is no fiction, for they have done it in thousands of cases. Every sufferer is earnestly invited to try one box of these pills, and they will be acknowledged to be WORTH A GUINEA A BOX. For Females of all ages these Pills are invaluable, as a few doses of them carry off all humours, and bring about all that is required.

That last claim, at least, may have been a deliberately vague accuracy—there is some evidence that the pills, taken in sufficient quantities, could induce abortions.[51] "These are 'facts' admitted by thousands, in all classes of society," the pitch continued, "and one of the best guarantees to the Nervous and Debilitated is that Beecham's Pills have the Largest Sale of any Patent Medicine in the World." In other words, not only did the pills sell because they worked, they worked because they sold. Other advertisements for the pills were even more explicit in their commodity fetishism. "Beecham's Pills have unfailingly carried the message of health and good cheer to the homes of the people"—and the evangelists were so good at proclaiming their gospel that they were self-sufficient. "Personal letters endorsing Beecham's Pills are received by the thousands," the ad goes on, "but it is never necessary to publish them. *The pills recommend themselves.*"

The self-recommending pills were nevertheless the beneficiaries of a startling amount of marketing: appearing before a parliamentary committee in 1913, Sir Joseph Beecham, the founder's son, admitted that the company's spending on advertising had reached £100,000 a year.[52] Among the advertising was a series of *Beecham's Music Portfolios*, cheap songbooks leavened with tunes extolling the benefits of Beecham's Pills. One of the most well known of these set new words to a Mendelssohnian Victorian favorite:

Hark! the herald angels sing!
Beecham's Pills are just the thing,
Two for a woman one for a child . . .
Peace on Earth and mercy mild!

Authorship of the carol was claimed by Sir Joseph's son Thomas. "Look here, my lad," he recalled his father telling him, "I've been spendin' a lot o' brass on your musical education, and now Ah wants you to help me." Even late in life, Sir Thomas Beecham, the greatest British conductor of his time, who went through an estimated hundred-million-pound inheritance founding orchestras and opera companies, remained cheekily proud of his early effort. "These sentiments . . . especially the ellipsis, seemed to me admirably to express the rapture which is occasioned by a good effortless release."[53]

Beecham's father, Sir Joseph, was a music lover himself, and something of an impresario—late in life, he bankrolled a "Grand Season of Russian Opera and Ballet" that included the British premiere of Stravinsky's *Le Sacre du Printemps*. In 1899, for his inauguration as mayor of the town of St. Helens (where he had built the enormous Beecham's factory), Sir Joseph hired the Hallé Orchestra, under director Hans Richter, to play a special gala concert. "Almost at the eleventh hour," Thomas recalled, "the devastating intelligence arrived that Richter could not appear: my father was in despair, his magnificent entertainment seemed threatened with disaster." Sir Joseph asked his son what to do. "I made the suggestion," the son replied, "that I should take the absentee's place." Sir Joseph eventually came around to the idea of a twenty-year-old neophyte taking the podium in front of one of the country's most accomplished professional orchestras, and it was thus that Thomas Beecham made his professional debut, conducting Beethoven's Fifth Symphony. His father, the venerable pill seller, had spied a marketing opportunity—realizing, in his son's words, "being the astutest advertiser of his day, that what had looked like a possible reverse might be worked up to a definite advantage."[54]

The marketing extended to the music. Beecham's branding had so saturated Victorian life that a story went around of an English explorer, deep in uncharted Africa, coming across a tree painted with an advertisement for Beecham's Pills.[55] The Fifth Symphony was similarly established in the Victorian imagination. In Robert Louis Stevenson's 1894 novel *The Ebb-Tide* (written with his stepson, Lloyd Osbourne), the poetically named Robert Herrick, bright and cultured, but "deficient in consistency and intellectual manhood," initially embodies his namesake's *carpe diem* reputation—"While Fates permit us, let's be merry; / Passe all we must the fatall Ferry."[56]

Herrick has abandoned a string of financial failures in England and America, fleeing to Tahiti; as the book opens, he is sick and homeless, sheltering in an abandoned jail. Struck by an acute sense of rootlessness and transition, Herrick decides to add a memorial of his own presence to the building's mass of graffiti:

> From his jarred nerves there came a strong sentiment of coming change; whether good or ill he could not say: change, he knew no more—change, with inscrutable veiled face, approaching noiseless. With the feeling, came the vision of a concert room, the rich hues of instruments, the silent audience, and the loud voice of the symphony. "Destiny knocking at the door," he thought; drew a stave on the plaster, and wrote in the famous phrase from the Fifth Symphony. "So," thought he, "they will know that I loved music and had classical tastes."[57]

The symphony recommends itself.

. . .

THE MOST FAMOUS Victorian advertisement (in the word's original sense) of Beethoven's Fifth actually appeared nearly a decade after Victoria's reign ended. E. M. Forster's novel *Howards End* was published in 1910, the year Victoria's son and successor Edward VII died, taking with him, perhaps, the notion that royal bonhomie, strategic marriage, and noblesse oblige could, on their own, hold civilization together. *Howards End* is Forster's tone poem of the era's fade-out, and the tone is telling: tragedy and farce, jostling for position. Forster—who lived until 1970—would have a chance to observe the twentieth century's harrowing pageant, but his point of view was forever attuned to Victorian shades. Humanist, leftist, and homosexual, Forster made his intellectual home in that English specialty, the curiously central margin—he was a member of the Bloomsbury group, the quintessential band of inside outsiders. "I belong to the fag-end of Victorian liberalism," he noted.[58]

In the fifth chapter of *Howards End*, the middle-class, intellectually inclined, late-Romantic Schlegels—Margaret, Helen, their brother, Tibby—attend a performance of Beethoven's Fifth Symphony in Queen's Hall; even in that "dreariest music-room in London," as Forster judged it, the Fifth, "the most sublime noise that has ever penetrated into the ear of man," is "cheap at two shillings."[59] (The room was, indeed, cheap: while the Crystal Palace offered season tickets for reserved stalls at two guineas, Queen's Hall undercut that price by half—there, at least, Beethoven was worth a guinea a box.)

Forster tells the Fifth through the ears and imagination of Helen, the most volatile of the Schlegels—her precipitate, quickly abandoned engagement to Paul Wilcox, the younger son of his upper-class, business-minded clan, has already set the novel's events in motion. Helen envisions "heroes and shipwrecks" in the opening movement; the relative equanimity of

the Andante doesn't much interest her, even as it engrosses
Frieda, the Schlegels' German cousin, and Frieda's equally German companion.

But with the Scherzo, where the symphony's opening motive
returns in clipped, deliberate translation—the "wonderful
movement," Helen calls it—her poetic impressions combine
Romantic fantasy and Victorian dread. "[T]he music started
with a goblin walking quietly over the universe, from end to
end," she imagines. "Others followed him. They were not aggressive creatures; it was that that made them so terrible to Helen."
The goblins see through the fundamental façade of Victorian
decorum: "They merely observed in passing that there was no
such thing as splendour or heroism in the world." What's left
is, as Helen describes it in her favorite melodramatic phrase,
"panic and emptiness." The return of the Scherzo in the middle
of the triumphant Finale only confirms Helen's enthrallingly
bleak impressions. "The goblins really had been there. They
might return—and they did. It was as if the splendour of life
might boil over—and waste to steam and froth."[60]

Like *Punch*'s Stupendous Amateur, Helen abandons the concert hall after the symphony:

Helen pushed her way out during the applause. She desired
to be alone. The music summed up to her all that had happened or could happen in her career. . . . The notes meant
this and that to her, and they could have no other meaning,
and life could have no other meaning. She pushed right
out of the building, and walked slowly down the outside
staircase, breathing the autumnal air, and then she strolled
home.[61]

Again, Helen's impulsiveness fuels the plot: she has absent-
mindedly walked off with the umbrella of Leonard Bast, an
anxious lower-class dreamer. ("He was not in the abyss, but he

could see it."[62]) The meeting completes the novel's tripartite, low-to-high hierarchy of class: Basts, Schlegels, Wilcoxes, soon to be knotted in dramatic tangles. The Wilcox matriarch tries to leave the family's suburban cottage, Howards End, to Margaret Schlegel, but the Wilcox family suppresses her will. The now-widowed Henry Wilcox marries Margaret, and, through bad business advice, almost offhandedly ruins Leonard Bast. Bast has an affair with Helen, resulting in her pregnancy, before being killed at the hands of Charles, the Wilcox scion. No wonder Helen leaves the concert early; if the Fifth indeed summed up all that could—and does—happen in Helen's career, one could well imagine that any further music would be a bit much.

Forster's pairing of feminine sensation and Beethoven's music drew on a long-standing Victorian commonplace; British and American novels of the nineteenth century teem with young women at the piano, playing their Beethoven. Surveying the throng of fictional female pianists, Mary Burgan summed up the varying rationales for their cultivation of the keyboard: "[P]iano expertise was a commodity in the marriage market, a form of necessary self-discipline, or an innocent entertainment in an otherwise vacuous existence."[63] As part of the essential finishing of a refined girl's education, Beethoven's music became inseparable from Victorian femininity. The progress of one Carrie Crookenden in Lucas Malet's *The Wages of Sin* was typical, if wryly observed: "Carrie had lessons every year when the family went up to London. She was working her way through Beethoven; each year she added, with much conscientious labour a sonata or two to her *répertoire*. She plunged now into the last learned. Her playing was ponderously correct, grandly dull. Meanwhile emotion picked up her trailing skirts and fled."[64] (Lucas Malet was the pen name of Mary St. Leger Kingsley, daughter of Charles Kingsley, who had worried so eloquently over the lack of religion among the smarter, younger, Victorians.)

In John Lane Ford's 1872 novel *Dower and Curse*, wealthy Victor Herbston embarks on a Pygmalion-like scheme to prove his theory of "the immense power of education . . . to modify, even to neutralize, the influence of blood," adopting the poor orphan Annie Scott. Annie is ostracized by the rest of the Herbstons, and takes comfort in familiar music:

> When the family were out she would steal down from her room with some of her favourite pieces in her hand, and sit down and play. She would flood the room with the deep strong Turneresque music of Beethoven. . . .[65]

Annie's education has at least produced a quintessential Victorian woman.

In Mary Braddon's 1882 *Mount Royal*, another orphan provides another reminder of Beethoven's status as an ornament of the upper class. Christabel Tregonell has married into wealth, but when her pianism is put to light-music service at a dinner party, her husband is disconcerted: "Mr. Tregonell had never appreciated Beethoven, being indeed, as unmusical a soul as God ever created; but he thought it a more respectable thing that his wife should sit at her piano playing an order of music which only the privileged few could understand, than that she should delight the common herd by singing which savoured of music-hall and burlesque."[66]

But Beethoven could also gird fictional women against the dual disadvantages of class and gender. In William Makepeace Thackeray's 1860 novella *Lovel the Widower*, Bessy, governess to the title character's children, harbors a secret—she was once a music-hall dancer—that would horrify Lovel's priggish, upper-class mother-in-law. Nevertheless, threatened with exposure, Bessy, a veteran of Victorian femininity's battles with the piano, maintains her equilibrium:

Bessy was perfectly cool and dignified at tea. Danger or doubt did not seem to affect *her*. If she had been ordered for execution at the end of the evening she would have made the tea, played her Beethoven, answered questions in her usual voice, and glided about from one to another with her usual dignified calm, until the hour of decapitation came.[67]

Her past is revealed, but Lovel asks Bessy to marry him, foiling his mother-in-law, resulting in a happy ending. Well, almost—Thackeray's narrator was also among Bessy's suitors; having lost his immortal beloved, he rallies himself to an ersatz-Beethovenian resignation. "I am accustomed to disappointment," he sighs. "Other fellows get the prizes which I try for. I am used to run second in the dreary race of love. Second? Psha! Third, Fourth."[68] (Or even Fifth.)

Once in a while, a novelist would take on Beethoven himself. Elizabeth Sara Sheppard, whose debut novel *Charles Auchester*—peopled with roman à clef versions of Victorian musical celebrities, including Mendelssohn—caught the admiration of both Disraeli and, across the Atlantic, Emerson (she had "the courage of genius," Emerson wrote[69]), went on to create a Beethoven bewitched by femininity in her 1858 novel *Rumour*. The book's Beethoven stand-in, an imperious German composer and organist named Rodomant, vies with Porphyro, a thinly disguised Louis-Napoléon (!), for the hand of one Princess Adelaída (!!). Serving at the court of Adelaída's father, Rodomant, at the novel's climax, defiantly violates the law against pulling all the stops on the organ in the royal chapel.

Down went the pedal which forced the whole first organ out at once, and, as if shouted by hosts of men and by myriad angels echoed, pealed the great Hosanna. The mighty rapture of the princess won her instantly from regret; no peace could be so glorious as that praise . . . her spirit floated on the wide stream with harmonious waves toward the measureless immensity of music at its source.[70]

In pursuit of symphonic perfection, a "fate, of which the chained Prometheus is at once the symbol and the warning," Rodomant finally unleashes the full organ, and, as if in divine retribution, the familiar Beethoven is born: "I have lost my hearing, and it is for ever."[71] Adelaída is crushed when Rodomant leaves the kingdom; but, just as Porphyro is about to propose marriage, the princess's beloved carrier dove—entrusted to Rodomant—returns (and drops dead, having "won its rest, and earned it"[72]), with an entreaty from the composer, mistakenly committed to a Prussian asylum. Adelaída abandons her throne to tend the irascible genius: "He adored her—but frequently tormented her—she loved him all the more."[73]

Ridiculous? No less than Sir George Grove himself speculated that the Fifth had a somewhat related origin. Grove subscribed to Thayer's (erroneous) hypothesis that Beethoven had, for four years, been secretly engaged to Countess Theresa Brunsvik, one of his piano students. Grove noted that the symphony was composed in the middle of what he supposed to be Beethoven's engagement, and related a story of how, some years prior, Beethoven slapped the girl hard on the hand during a lesson and stormed off in anger, and how Theresa, realizing he had left his hat and coat, ran out into the street after him. "Are not the two characters exactly expressed" by the opening two themes—the first four notes being Beethoven, the major-key second section being Theresa? "It surely would be impossible to convey them in music more perfectly," Grove insisted, "the fierce imperious composer, who knew how to 'put his foot down,' if the phrase may be allowed, and the womanly, yielding, devoted girl."[74]

. . .

But the goblins were there. They could return. He had said
so bravely, and that is why one can trust Beethoven when
he says other things.

—E. M. FORSTER, *Howards End*

FORSTER, a discerning music lover and fairly accomplished amateur pianist, could make smart use of such Victorian tropes—for
Lucy Honeychurch, the heroine of *A Room with a View,* to play
Beethoven on the piano might be a contemporary novelistic
commonplace, but for her to choose to play the tempestuous
squall of the op. 111 piano sonata (in C minor, not coinciden-
tally) is an acute characterization on Forster's part.[75] Likewise,
the performance of Beethoven's Fifth within *Howards End* provides an opportunity for deft characterizations of the Schlegel
siblings: Margaret's real-world practicality, Helen's flights of
fancy, Tibby's happy pedantry, following along with the score
on his lap. The set-piece also insinuates the atmosphere of
English-German rivalry: when Elgar's *Pomp and Circumstance*
concludes the concert, Margaret's blustery, über-English aunt
happily taps her foot, while the Schlegels' German visitors discreetly slip out.[76]

And *Howards End* also mirrors the structure of the Fifth Symphony as a whole (an idea suggested by more than one scholar).[77]
One can read, perhaps, the first "movement" as the bringing
together of the Schlegels and the Wilcoxes, and the introduction
of Leonard Bast; the second, beginning with the funeral of the
first Mrs. Wilcox, unfolds, like Beethoven's Andante, as a double
variation: the growing attraction of Henry Wilcox to Margaret
Schlegel, the growing obsession of Helen Schlegel with better-
ing Leonard Bast's lot. For a Scherzo, the goblins observe Helen's
antiheroic efforts to sabotage both Margaret's engagement and
Leonard's marriage. With a double consummation—Margaret

and Henry's marriage, Helen and Leonard's affair—the Finale commences; Leonard's death, like Beethoven's revisit of his Scherzo subject, is an aggressive, desperate interlude encased by a major-key but vaguely hollow triumph.

What would be the unifying motive, the equivalent of the first four notes? Forster himself suggests one possibility at the novel's outset. "One may as well begin with Helen's letters to her sister," he begins, and, of course, Helen's letters begin with their place of origin: "HOWARDS END."[78] As the Victorian Era dovetailed into the Edwardian, prewar twentieth century, Forster looked back and saw how much of England's identity had become bound up in struggles over real estate, both literal and intellectual: properties, colonies, classes, and movements. Howards End becomes a blessed plot fought over along customary fronts: art and business, reform and tradition, propriety and expression, male and female. That it is the middle-class Schlegels who finally take ownership of the place is a trenchant allegory—only a year after the novel's publication, the first Parliament Act was passed, limiting the power of the House of Lords and decisively accelerating the decline of the British landed aristocracy.

Equally apt is the conclusion's ambiguous tone. Forster's ending has, in fact, long bothered critics; after Leonard's death, Charles's imprisonment, Helen's pregnancy, and the near scuttling of Margaret and Henry's marriage, Forster's abrupt string of reconciliations—Margaret reunited with Helen, Margaret preserving her marriage, Margaret joining the families and perpetuating them, in the form of Helen and Leonard's son, whom Margaret and Henry will raise, and who will ultimately inherit Howards End—has seemed, to many readers, unearned and false. Stephen Spender referred to "the curious unreality" of the last scene: "[S]o many social skeletons rattle in the cupboards of *Howards End* that the reader, surely, finds this conclusion almost irrelevant."[79] A. S. Byatt recorded her own disillusionment with the novel: "One used to think: 'This is wonderful, here is a novelist who says we must connect the businessman with the world of the arts,' then you slowly realise that E. M. Forster actually can't do it."[80]

But that is to assume that a connection between business and art is something that Forster himself wants, and not just his characters.[81] To take the ending at face value is to suppose that the reader is not supposed to hear its rattling skeletons. The novel's real truth-teller is Beethoven and the Fifth. Forster's ending is Beethoven's ending: nominally happy, but undermined by the violence and darkness that has preceded it, darkness that even explicitly returns to invade it. "Beethoven chose to make all right in the end," Forster writes, just as the fag-end Victorians chose whatever myth offered the comfort of jubilee, be it England, Progress, Commerce, or even the notion that Beethoven and his music could express the ideals and aspirations of nineteenth-century Britain. Schlegels and Wilcoxes alike settle on the myth of Howards End, but Forster's language gives the game away—Howards End is ending; Helen's concluding announcement of "such a crop of hay as never" casts the whole place and story into the realm of fairy tale with its final word. The "red rust" is creeping across the meadows from London, and both the substance and the color are notable. The goblins are there.

That the characters don't notice is typical of the novel, which makes the overarching presence of Beethoven even more rueful. Beethoven was literally exceptional, in Forster's opinion, in being able to size up a larger conception of Fate in whole. "[T]his musician excited by immensities is unique in the annals of art," Forster once wrote. "No one has ever been so thrilled by things so huge, for the vast masses of doom crush the rest of us before we can hope to measure them. Fate knocks at our door; but before the final tap can sound, the flimsy door flies into pieces, and we never learn the sublime rhythm of destruction."[82] Beethoven is a double-edged sword, his singular glimpse of the infinite so celebrated that, coupled with the era's inclination to blithe confidence, it inspired lesser men to think they, too, could square the immeasurable circle of fate. In *Howards End*, the Schlegels' German-English father—a veteran of Sedan, disillusioned "when he saw the dyed moustaches of Napoleon going grey"—is introduced, in flashback, warning his native and adopted races: "No . . . your Pan-Germanism is no more imaginative than is our Imperialism over here. It is the vice of a vulgar mind to be thrilled by bigness, to think that a thousand square miles are a thousand times more wonderful than one square mile, and that a million square miles are almost the same as heaven."[83]

As if to drive home the inadequacy of mere mortals to comprehend Beethoven's vision, Forster seasons his narrative with dashes of the accrued nineteenth-century imagery surrounding the Fifth—dropped music-appreciation hints that the characters utterly fail to pick up on. Reunited at Howards End, Margaret and Helen fall into reminiscence, but Helen—always the transmitter for Romantic impulses—mixes present and past in the house's garden, via a familiar avian messenger:

"Ah, that greengage tree," cried Helen, as if the garden was also part of their childhood. "Why do I connect it with the dumbbells? And there come the chickens. The grass wants cutting. I love yellow-hammers—"

Margaret interrupted her.[84]

And, at the novel's denouement, when Margaret finally comes into possession of Howards End, it is Paul Wilcox— whose impetuous kiss of Helen Schlegel set the plot in motion, who has disappeared to Nigeria to make his fortune for the bulk of the story, and who appears again now, hostile to Margaret's presence, "manly and cynical" with the habitual intolerance of empire—it is Paul who provides the well-known signal, not with a knock, but a desultory kick: "Clumsy of movement—for he had spent all his life in the saddle—Paul drove his foot against the paint of the front door. Mrs. Wilcox gave a little cry of annoyance. She did not like anything scratched."[85]

Writing on the eve of the Great War, Forster's little detail is prophetic: Fate as the uncoordinated by-product of imperial ambition. Margaret, again, misses its significance. But in her own way, Margaret has fulfilled the symphonic structure, in quintessentially Romantic terms. That Margaret has achieved the novel's final, forced connection within the walls of the novel's titular property is the ultimate mirror of the Fifth Symphony: the opening motive—Howards End itself—becomes the means for realizing organic unity. It just turns out not to be the cure-all everybody thought it would be.

> Thus we assist at a show that would appear comic, if not for the tremendous tragedy it involves.
>
> —HERMANN KEYSERLING,
> "A Philosopher's View of the War"

THE ROMANTICISM that made Beethoven an honorary Victorian would be mercilessly exposed as a placebo by the war. In the introduction to his play *Heartbreak House*, George Bernard Shaw took both the Schlegels and the Wilcoxes of prewar society to task, scolding the latter as incompetent and the former as too polite to point it out. "Thus, like a fertile country flooded with mud," Shaw looked back, "England showed no sign of her greatness in the days when she was putting forth all her strength to save herself from the worst consequences of her littleness."[86] It was a consequence of the unfavorable intellectual economics of politics: "Nature's way of dealing with unhealthy conditions is unfortunately not one that compels us to conduct a solvent hygiene on a cash basis."[87]

Heartbreak House brings all the strains of prewar society together for a country weekend where, under Shaw's richly bleak administration, they show themselves incapable of managing their own fates. The industrial machinery of history has made the characters its servants. Mangan, the pompous business-man, is goaded into admitting that he only runs the factories he has pretended to own; Mazzini, the hapless intellectual, having expected revolution, finds that "nothing happened, except, of course, the usual poverty and crime and drink that we are used to. Nothing ever does happen. It's amazing how well we get along, all things considered." The roaring, doddering Captain Shotover casts his gimlet eye on fate. "Every drunken skipper trusts to Providence," he pronounces. "But one of the ways of Providence with drunken skippers is to run them on the rocks."

When the bombs start falling, the party's female poles, the overbearing Mrs. Hushabye and the dreamy Ellie Dunn, claim the drama as their familiar, feminine birthright:

> MRS. HUSHABYE . . . Did you hear the explosions? And the sound in the sky: it's splendid: it's like an orchestra: it's like Beethoven.
>
> ELLIE By thunder, Hesione: it is Beethoven.[88]

The women's admiration is topically accurate. (And Shavian— a not insignificant part of Shaw's literary output was music criticism.) Beethoven's prewar universality was such that, even in the midst of subsequent wartime anti-German indignation, the indignant could still occasionally forget where Beethoven was from—take Sir Arthur Markham, for instance. In 1915, Markham (a grandson of Joseph Paxton, designer of the Crystal Palace) rose in the House of Commons to denounce Sir Edgar Speyer, Baronet, Privy Councillor, and a patron of music who had personally funded the Promenade Concerts at Queen's Hall for a number of years. Speyer had been born in America to

German-Jewish immigrants, and was made a British subject in 1892; but he remained connected to Germany through his family's banking concern. Anti-German activism targeted Speyer early in the war, and after the Armistice, he would be stricken from the Privy Council—a rare occurrence—and lose his British citizenship. For now, though, Markham seized on Speyer's musical activities:

> I suppose it is because he is of German origin that we in this country are to be treated during the next few weeks by Sir Henry Wood to a series of concerts entirely composed of German music. I have the whole of the programmes here, from which it will be seen that some of the concerts are to be devoted entirely to Wagner's music. . . . I cannot understand how people can go to listen to German music, when every people in the world, except ourselves, would not tolerate during a time of war that they should be entertained by German music. But as the Queen's Hall belongs to him, I suppose we in this country are to be instilled with German virtues.

For Markham, however, there was German and then there was German. Markham's rebuke prompted an exchange:

MR. R. MCNEILL: Is there no Beethoven in the programme?
SIR A. MARKHAM: No, the whole of the programme at some of these concerts contains no music except German.
SIR F. BANBURY: Beethoven was a German.[89]

Edward Goldbeck was less inclined to neutralize Beethoven's Germanic soul. A Berlin native and a German Army veteran, Goldbeck emigrated to the United States, where he wrote theater criticism and cultural commentary. In the shadow of war,

Goldbeck took seriously Beethoven's boast that, had he a military rather than musical mind, he could have defeated Napoléon; the music hovered pointedly between imperious and imperial. The Fifth's opening portrayed a Fate to be overcome through a superior musical offensive: "It is one of his most beautiful and impressive ideas that the 'motive of Fate,' thundering at first, grows more and more muffled, until we hear it only far off and drowned by the trumpets of triumph." No wonder Germany so proudly claimed him as its own. "I doubt very much, however . . . that Beethoven would be a pacifist today. . . . Beethoven had the temperament of a warrior, and music is nothing but architectural and dynamic 'organization' "—the stereotypical wellspring of Prussian military prowess. "The Germany of today is not separated by an abyss from the Germany of the classics," Goldbeck concluded, "the spirit is the same, only the material on which it works is different: it was imagination once, now it is reality."[90]

It was in America that anti-German sentiment would most translate into cultural chauvinism, as German music, operas, and theater—not to mention German names, words, and accents—were cleansed from American life. One of those leading the charge against German repertoire was the New York socialite Mrs. William Jay. (Her husband, a great-grandson of the first Chief Justice of the United States Supreme Court, was a lawyer and the founder of the New York Coaching Club, which, according to his 1915 obituary, "gave a great impetus to the breeding of harness horses in this country, and kept alive a sport which even the automobile has not yet succeeded in killing."[91]) Mrs. Jay, a member of the New York Philharmonic's Board of Directors, headed a wartime group called the Intimate Committee for the Severance of All Social and Professional Relations with Enemy Sympathizers, which advocated the elimination of German repertoire from concert halls and opera houses, "part of a movement directed toward the complete extinction of German influence in this country."[92] The Metropolitan Opera did eliminate German-language repertoire during the war, having decided that productions "might enable Germany, by garbling and patching, to print 'news' dispatches for home consumption which would tend to put heart in the German people."[93]

Even in Boston, the American port of entry for German Romanticism and the birthplace of the American Beethoven cult, German repertoire would nearly vanish during the war. German and Austrian composers accounted for nearly two-thirds of the Boston Symphony Orchestra's programming in the 1916–17 season; in the 1918–19 season, the proportion was less than half that.[94] Along the way, Mrs. Jay and her ilk claimed a particularly valuable scalp: Karl Muck, the orchestra's conductor.

Henry Lee Higginson, still running the orchestra as his personal fiefdom, had first hired Muck, a veteran of Bayreuth and the Royal Opera in Berlin, to lead the group in 1906; Muck opened his tenure with a "brilliant and effective" rendition of Beethoven's Fifth.[95] Higginson convinced him to return for a second tenure in 1912. Muck conducted with an almost stereotypically Prussian demeanor, sober and disinclined to interpretive fantasy, but his authority and discipline raised the Boston Symphony to the pinnacle of American orchestras. Hearing Muck conduct Beethoven's Fifth at Carnegie Hall, critic Frederic Dean pronounced him "the Wendell Phillips of the orchestra—willing to sacrifice sonority to sentiment. . . . He weighs the meaning of a musical phrase as he chooses the exact word for his sentence."[96]

But after the opening concert of the BSO's 1917–18 season— once again featuring the Fifth Symphony—Higginson and the orchestra came under criticism after the American flag was inadvertently left off the Symphony Hall stage. "Until lately my loyalty has never been questioned," Higginson grumbled.[97] The incident may have exacerbated his intransigence when, prior to an October 1917 performance in Providence, Rhode Island, a coterie of local women's and musical clubs sent a telegram to BSO management insisting that the group preface its concert with "The Star-Spangled Banner." Higginson—not about to let anybody tell him how to run his concern—ignored the demand; but the press painted Karl Muck as the villain, a German interloper arrogantly insulting American pride, and the story blossomed into a full-blown scandal. As the orchestra's publicity manager remembered, "The fat was in the fire and blazing high."[98]

In March of 1918, Muck was arrested under the terms of a presidential proclamation regulating enemy aliens. With an unwitting sense of symbolic martyrology, the officials made their move on the eve of Muck's long-awaited performance of Bach's *St. Matthew Passion*; having seized Muck's score of the piece in a raid on his house (apparently without warrant), the police pored over the music, sure that the conductor's markings were coded espionage.[99] (Recall Mrs. Jay's alleged "'news' dispatches.") A series of indiscreet love letters to a twenty-year-old aspiring singer were also found, and, fanned by *Boston Post* reports fulminating against Muck's supposed corruption of American womanhood, resulted in an indictment for violation of postal laws. Faced with prison, Muck opted for internment and eventual deportation.

Muck was transported to a military base in northern Georgia that became as unapologetic an enclave of German culture as ever existed. For the duration of the war, Fort Oglethorpe (built on the Chickamauga battlefield) was home to every German-born businessman, intellectual, artist, or musician in America deemed dangerous enough—that is, German enough—to be interned. A combination of detained cruise ship musicians and military band members provided the camp with performances of Beethoven and the rest of the canon.[100] But the orchestra could only coax a single performance out of Muck; on December 12, 1918, he led the group in works of Brahms and Beethoven. Muck chose not to conduct the Fifth; the accepted narrative of individual struggle and triumph was, perhaps, too much of an irony. Instead, he opted for the anti-Napoléonic *Eroica*—a better outlet for a man whose brief relationship with a powerful republic had turned sour. Muck and his wife were put on a boat in August of 1919; he never again conducted in America. In 1939, a year before he died, Muck appeared in public one last time, accepting the Order of the Golden Eagle from Adolf Hitler.

The same summer Karl Muck sailed back to Europe, Mrs. William Jay announced a cease-fire. "Germany is on her knees before outraged but forgiving humanity," she wrote. There was no need for further protest, "for I know that henceforth materialism will weigh too heavily against a pro-German attitude, and I pray that the former friends of German Kultur will uphold the principles of freedom, honesty, and justice, which they now see triumphant and everlasting."[101] Her ultimately unwarranted optimism was hardly uncommon. (Mrs. Jay, incidentally, was the former Lucy Oelrichs. Her father was a German immigrant, the New York agent for the Norddeutscher Lloyd line of steamships.)

For a time, Henry Lee Higginson had stuck by his Prussian conductor out of pride and stubbornness, but was scandalized by the revelations of possible moral misconduct. In the last year of Higginson's life, the Boston Symphony would decisively pivot away from Germany and toward French and Russian influence. Muck's replacement was Henri Rabaud, a Parisian. When asked whether he would program German composers in Boston, Rabaud was nonplussed. "Such questions are never asked in Paris," he remarked. "Why should we not play beautiful music like Beethoven's C minor Symphony?"[102]

·   ·   ·

BEETHOVEN'S MUSIC would soon enough retake its place at the center of the canon. But the war—an upheaval to bookend the Industrial Revolution—meant that a catholic narrative of the Fifth could no longer be taken for granted; the supposedly universal truths had proven hazardously malleable.

Or maybe a different, unpalatable truth had been there all along. At the height of Victoria's reign, a Manchester journalist, Henry Franks, recalled sitting next to a blind man at a performance of the Fifth. "That blind man, with the fine instincts of culture, listened to Beethoven's symphony in C minor with an upturned face, upon which the emotions played as visibly as the ripples play upon a lake," Franks reported. "I begged him to tell me what he conceived to be the meaning of the theme which recurs so often. After much hesitation, he said that it meant a warning which has come too late."[103] Distracted by the spectacle, most everybody else had only heard what they wanted to hear.

6

Earthquakes

The failing foothold as the shining goal
Appears, and truth so long, so fondly sought
Is blurred and dimmed. Again and yet again
The exulting march resounds. We must win now!
—CHRISTOPHER PEARSE CRANCH,
"Sonnet XXIII: Beethoven's Fifth Symphony" (1878)

IF LUCY HONEYCHURCH'S predilection for Beethoven made for awkward parlor atmosphere in *A Room with a View*, the outbreak of World War I only increased the consternation. In 1958, E. M. Forster revisited the novel's characters in a little sequel called "A View Without a Room"; Lucy and George, we learn, were both conscientious objectors during the war, exacerbating suspicion over Lucy's musical taste: "Hun music! She was overheard and reported, and the police called." But also woven into his fictional reminiscence was an actual experience of Forster's, somewhat closer to the front: an encounter with Beethoven in Egypt, where Forster had spent the bulk of the war working for the Red Cross.

A quiet little party was held on the outskirts of [Alexandria], and someone wanted a little Beethoven. The hostess demurred. Hun music might compromise us. But a young officer spoke up. "No, it's all right," he said, "a chap who knows about those things from the inside told me Beethoven's definitely Belgian."[1]

Forster playfully attributed the propaganda to Cecil Vyse, *A Room with a View*'s self-absorbed, amused aesthete. But tweaking German superiority with Beethoven's Flemish heritage was hardly new: the French had already jumped on that bandwagon, insisting that Beethoven exemplified not German genius, but the *"génie flamand,"* as the poet and critic Raymond Bouyer wrote in his 1905 examination, *Le secret de Beethoven*.[2] Bouyer's selective genealogy was only a particularly flagrant example of French efforts to pry Beethoven's image from the clutches of his German identity. It worked: as Europe stumbled into a second, more destructive reckoning, in the face of the ne plus ultra of German nationalism, Beethoven's Fifth would be brazenly enlisted on the side of the Allies—appropriately, by way of Belgium.

WHEN FRANCE finally got around to revering Beethoven, it did so with zeal, but on French terms. The story was that, at the French premiere of the Fifth Symphony, an old veteran of Napoléon's army was moved to stand up and cry out, "C'est l'Empereur! vive l'Empereur!"[3] Beethoven might have appreciated the sentiment—he had, after all, bragged of his ability to meet Napoléon in battle—but casting Beethoven as a new Napoléon was also a way to bring him into the French fold.

The history of Beethoven in France is that of a hesitant courtship followed by a torrid affair. According to Schindler (and with the requisite accompanying grain of salt), the ice was broken via a blind date with the Fifth. Schindler tells of Louis Sina, a French-born violinist who, as part of Ignaz Schuppanzigh's string quartet, had performed at the Viennese apartments of Beethoven's patron, Prince Lichnowsky. In 1820, Sina returned to Paris, then largely bereft of Beethoven's music (the conductor of the Conservatoire orchestra, François-Antoine Habeneck, had, in Schindler's telling, introduced the *Eroica* at a rehearsal, only to be met with laughter from the players). Sina sent an anonymous letter to Habeneck extolling enough virtues of the C-minor symphony to fire the conductor's curiosity. Schindler: "After considerable hesitation, the symphony was rehearsed. Its reception was favorable! . . . Without losing any time, other symphonies that had likewise remained unknown were tried, and lo! to everyone's surprise they were as well received as the C minor!"[4]

Sina's matchmaking aside, there were institutional reasons for Beethoven's neglect as well. French concertgoers would have had little to no opportunity to hear Beethoven until 1828, the year after Beethoven died: that was when the administration of Charles X (the last of the Bourbon kings of France, whose reign was the high-water mark of post-Revolution French ultraroyalism) subsidized a new concert series at the Paris Conservatoire. Ardor for Beethoven erupted almost overnight. For the second program of the Société des Concerts, Habeneck programmed the *Eroica*; the third program opened with the Fifth.[5] Driven by a "Jeune France" claque of young, passionately zealous artistic types, audiences reportedly reacted with such fervor that overwhelming, transporting enthusiasm became almost a fad. (The Fifth became a perennial favorite at the Société des Concerts, programmed forty times between 1828 and 1848—more than any other symphony.)[6]

Running with the Jeune-France crowd was Hector Berlioz, the composer who dragged his teacher Le Sueur to hear Beethoven's Fifth, and who considered it

the most famous of all his symphonies, [and] also the one in which I think Beethoven first gave free rein to his vast imagination, without recourse to any idea but his own to guide him. . . . It is his intimate thoughts that he means to develop, his secret sorrows, his pent-up anger, his dreams full of dejection, his nocturnal visions, and his outbursts of enthusiasm. Melody, harmony, rhythm, and instrumentation take forms as individual and original as they are noble and powerful.[7]

Berlioz's description is Hoffmannesque,[8] but he is on a different mission. Hoffmann pointed toward a transcendent clarity; Berlioz remains focused on vagueness. Hoffmann was promoting Romanticism; Berlioz is leveraging it.

Some hint at what Berlioz is up to comes in his comparison of the Fifth with the *Eroica*. Beethoven's Third, Berlioz proposes, was inspired by the composer's readings of Homer: "[M]emories of the *Iliad* evidently play a beautiful role." (This was both canny publicity—Leo Schrade, author of the pioneering study *Beethoven in France*, noted that a connection with antiquity "has always been in France the best letter of recommendation"[9]— and, no doubt, a projection of Berlioz's own obsession with the ancient epics.) The Fifth, by contrast, "seems to spring solely and directly from Beethoven's own genius." Except when it doesn't:

> The first movement depicts the chaotic feelings that overwhelm a great soul when prey to despair. It is not the calm, concentrated despair that shows the outward appearance of resignation, nor is it Romeo's dark and mute grief on learning of Juliet's death, but Othello's terrible rage on hearing of Desdemona's guilt from Iago's poisonous lies. . . . Listen to the gasps in the orchestra, to the chords in the dialogue between winds and strings that come and go, sounding ever weaker, like the painful breaths of a dying man.[10]

The German Romantics had revered Beethoven for expressing what was beyond language, but Berlioz, with his explicitly literary programmatic reading of the Fifth (the first four notes as the ominous flutter of Desdemona's handkerchief, maybe?), is expanding the idea of language to encompass Beethoven. Schrade points out how often Berlioz describes the symphonies as "poetic" and the composer as a "poet," epithets Berlioz used "to denote the supreme degree that cannot be surpassed, and in point of language a superlative which cannot be further compared."[11] France was a country where literary elegance and power sat at the summit of cultural achievement. To insist that Beethoven was not just a composer, but a poet, was to make him a little more French.

In *The Arcades Project*, his unfinished analysis of nineteenth-century Paris, critic and philosopher Walter Benjamin devoted an entire section to the flâneur, the perpetually strolling observer so typical of the city—"Paris created the type of the flâneur," Benjamin noted.[12] The rapport the French had established with Beethoven was paralleled in the flâneur's mindset, at least as Benjamin imagined it: "That anamnestic intoxication in which the flâneur goes about the city not only feeds on the sensory data taking shape before his eyes but often possesses itself of abstract knowledge—indeed, of dead facts—as something experienced and lived through."[13] The French experienced the abstract knowledge of Beethoven's symphonies and thus adopted him into the French cultural pantheon. Benjamin jotted down a quote from Pierre Larousse's 1872 *Grand dictionnaire universel*, which, in defining the flâneur, opted for a foreign exemplar:

> In the first years of this century, a man was seen walking each and every day—regardless of the weather, be it sunshine or snow—around the ramparts of the city of Vienna. This man was Beethoven, who, in the midst of his wanderings, would work out his magnificent symphonies in his head before putting them down on paper.[14]

Adolphe Boschot, a critic who also wrote a biography of Berlioz, noted in 1908 how the image of Beethoven had become a standard trope in French art: "In every salon [painters] exhibit for us several canvases showing the author of the nine symphonies. For this has now become the fashion. Once upon a time they manufactured Bonapartes or the 'Temptations of St. Anthony,' now they manufacture Beethovens."[15]

The identification with Beethoven would reach an apotheosis with French sculptor Émile-Antoine Bourdelle, who, as a teenager, perceived a strong resemblance between his own features and an engraving of the composer: "He thought he was seeing himself," Bourdelle's widow surmised, "and it was perhaps this fact, in the first instance, that attracted him."[16] Bourdelle would produce nearly eighty portraits of Beethoven—sketches, finished drawings, sculptures—returning to the subject at periodic intervals between the late 1880s and his death, in 1929. At the very least, Bourdelle's obsession with Beethoven as a subject was indicative of a congruence of artistic intent ("It is my task," Bourdelle wrote, "to construct my own silent orchestra in which the sounds are expressed in terms of planes and of light"[17]); but the progression of his images—Beethoven's head increasingly distorted, craggy, expressionistic—hints at something deeper, what one critic called "a kind of involuntary confession."[18] One of Bourdelle's last essays on the subject, produced shortly before he died, shows Beethoven, his face set in a stoic scowl, leaning against a massive cross.

THE IMAGE of Beethoven as a poet was, nonetheless, also adopted by German writers—and, depending on who was doing the writing, could be read as either sustaining or undermining the crescendo of German nationalism kick-started by the 1870 defeat of France. One notorious poeticization came at the hands of musicologist Arnold Schering. In 1920, on the occasion of Beethoven's 150th birthday, Schering sought to rally post-Armistice Germany, now, in comparison with the glory days of 1870, "a small broken people . . . once again about to celebrate Beethoven." To be great again, Schering advocated a dose of Beethoven's heroism, as inspired by poets:

> The heroic in the highest sense drew him to the heroes of Homer and Plutarch, to Coriolan, to Egmont, to *Fidelio,* where even a woman embodies male heroism. He felt in his own blood something of this heroism. When the *furor teutonicus* came over him, sparks sprayed his imagination and shook the boundaries of what was then possible: in the C-minor Symphony, the *Eroica,* in the first movement of the Ninth Symphony, which in the weak race of 1850 had inspired secret horror.[19]

Homer, Plutarch, Shakespeare, Goethe: Schering would go on to make those literary sparks profoundly literal. Starting with his 1934 book *Beethoven in neuer Deutung* (*Beethoven in a New Interpretation*), Schering set out to demonstrate that Beethoven had actually patterned specific works of music after specific works of literature. The *Eroica* drew on the *Iliad.* The Seventh Symphony followed Goethe's *Wilhelm Meisters Lehrjahre.* The *Appassionata* Sonata was, in reality, scenes from *Macbeth.* The C-sharp minor Piano Sonata, already saddled with the sobriquet *Moonlight,* now became the mirror of act 4 of *King Lear.* In the words of one reviewer, Schering's speculative hermeneutics stood "in the same relation to true musical research as modern astrology stands to physical astronomy."[20]

Berlin critic Paul Bekker also characterized Beethoven as a kind of tone poet, a *"Tondichter,"* in his popular book on Beethoven, first published in 1911. At first glance, Bekker's description of the Fifth seems to be the standard programmatic boilerplate:

> The work deals with the awful powers of Fate and ends with a triumph song of the human will. Underlying the

whole is Beethoven's great idea of the freedom of man. . . . The struggle is to be to the death, involving not the fate of one ideal hero (as in the *Eroica*) but of all humanity. In the first movement of the *Eroica* the hero wrestles with the limitations and crippling emotionalism of his own being in order that his powers may have full scope, but in the fifth symphony humanity wrestles with all these hindrances expressed in the mysterious idea of Fate.[21]

The difference is that Bekker distills that contrast between the *Eroica*'s individual hero and the Fifth's collective protagonist out of the music itself. In the *Eroica,* for instance, Beethoven included extra horns, their more prominent tone symbolic of the hero's presence. In the Fifth's opening, however, "where there is no question of a personal hero, he is content with the traditional complement of instruments." In the Finale, Beethoven reinforces the sound with trombones, "which (in his system) symbolize majestic greatness." Bekker concludes: "It will thus be seen that again in the C-minor symphony the orchestra was recreated in accordance with the underlying 'poetic idea' of the work."[22]

Again, Bekker's analysis might not seem much more than a particularly clever justification of the usual claims of universality made on the Fifth's behalf. But it was the cleverness that so irritated the advocates of German greatness. To reduce Beethoven's works to poetic programs was bad enough, but to analyze such poetry not as something Beethoven musically illustrated, but rather as part and parcel of the musical materials themselves, was to deny music's unique aesthetic status—and, by extension, to deny the supposedly unique German privilege toward all things musical. As conductor and scholar Leon Botstein put it:

Bekker and his allies were concealing the absence of the requisite predisposition—the spontaneous, aesthetic gift and their lack of true talent for music—behind rational arguments. It was a travesty to think that the greatest of all composers, and certainly of all German composers of instrumental music, had been inspired and guided by ordinary thinking and musings easily described in language.[23]

The idea that Beethoven's secrets could be so democratically available, without the intercession of elite, specifically German insight into music's mysteries, bore all the hallmarks of pernicious cosmopolitan (i.e., Jewish) thinking. Thus the question of the extent of poetic inspiration in Beethoven's music became a political wedge. Indeed, at the same time Arnold Schering was working his literary way through Beethoven's catalog, he also characterized "the vague sense of *per aspera ad astra* in the Fifth Symphony" as the "fight for existence waged by a Volk that looks for its Führer and finally finds it."[24]

At the outset of the First World War, the "Culture Pope," German critic Alfred Kerr, had mused on the uneasy place of art during wartime. "The theaters also want to live," he wrote. "The question is what can be played." His solution idealistically combined Germany's greatest cultural hero with a naïve optimism that Germans could avoid discussing him:

> Play, henceforth, the best that we have. Play that which
>   reminds us of our proudest pride [*stolzesten Stolz*].
> And if you know no pieces, then take fifty musicians.
> And speak no word.
> And every evening play Beethoven. Beethoven.
>   Beethoven.[25]

. . .

INDY: Everybody's lost but me.

—*Indiana Jones and the Last Crusade*

IN 1921, Austrian music theorist Heinrich Schenker began to publish a series of pamphlets collectively called *Der Tonwille*, "The Will of Tones," subtitled "Pamphlets in Witness of the Immutable Laws of Music." Schenker, who had trained as a lawyer before casting his lot with music, had already written manuals of harmony and counterpoint. Having thus set down music's statutory law, as it were, *Der Tonwille* continued as an exercise in case law: detailed analyses of musical works, demonstrating their adherence to Schenker's criteria of musical excellence.

The inaugural study of *Der Tonwille* was the first installment of a multipart examination of Beethoven's Fifth. But before that, Schenker had some things to get off his chest, in a prefatory essay called "The Mission of German Genius," such as it stood in "these grave times, in these most grievous of times. . . . Once the artist, in such times, sees how the political parties vying with one another for power sin against art in general, and against his own art in particular, through ignorance and ineptitude, then he must be inflamed."[26]

And Schenker is off on a fevered, incantatory tear, a detailed indictment of the degeneration of German culture. "Shameless betrayal has been perpetrated during the World War on the genius of Germanity": by capitalists ("a spiritually and morally venal fringe group"); by communists ("that trouble-making megalomaniac wage-church of Karl Marx"); by "certain so-called pacifists and professors, their mouths rank with filth"; by commentators who "snored their way loudly" through previous wars "but who, when the Germans had to defend themselves against an invasion long premeditated by nations whose virulent envy of it exceeded their incompetence, suddenly woke up to discover, oh-so-smugly, the spiritual and moral truth that peace was more humane than war";[27] and, most of all, by the siren song of democracy:

[I]f democracy is really what was exemplified by those Western nations before, during, and after Versailles, then let
the German democrat simply take a good look at democracy and do exactly what he sees Americans, Frenchmen,
Englishmen, Italians, Poles, Czechs, etc. doing. Let him
break promises, violate treaties, infringe international law,
steal private property, falsify maps, deface monuments, des-
ecrate war-graves, lie, and commit murder as they do, and
use words most pleasing unto man and God in the process,
just as they do.[28]

And so on, page after page—until Schenker circles back around
to his underlying point: "The task of these pamphlets will thus
be to show what constitutes German genius in music."[29]

Few people embodied the tensions running through early-
twentieth-century *Mitteleuropa* as thoroughly as Schenker. From
his Viennese vantage, Schenker saw the rise of fin-de-siècle
modernism, cosmopolitan sophistication, and democratic
ferment—and hated it all. He created a style of music theory
specifically designed to prove the superiority of the classic
Austro-Germanic repertoire: Bach, Beethoven, Brahms. And yet
the theory's mechanism—analytical, legalistic, pointedly devoid
of poetic imagery—seemed to breathe a coolly scientific air in
curious counterpoint to its creator's Kantian notions of genius
and his extremely Right-Hegelian conservatism. One senses he
realized the rift, hoping to compensate with a fiercely argumen-
tative style gleaned from his legal studies: a two-pronged attack,
evidential logic buttressed by emotional appeals to the jury.

No biblical prophet was more convinced of his righteous-
ness. In a codicil to his will, Schenker provided his own epitaph:
"Here lies the body of one who perceived the soul of music and
communicated its laws, as the great musicians understood them,
and as no one before him had done."[30] He once wrote to a student
about the fate of his "monotheistic music-teaching": "[A]fter

2,000 years the successors to the Germanic people may disavow Schenker as they disavow Rabbi Jesus, but all along the teaching has made its effect and achieved propagation in the world."[31]

Schenkerian analysis did propagate—particularly in America, where his techniques became a standard part of academic music training—but it did so in the absence of his heated rhetoric: belligerent sections of his treatises were left untranslated, and missionaries of his ideas focused on the analysis, not the oratory. (Allen Forte's article on Schenker for the 1980 edition of *Grove's Dictionary,* for example, avoids any hint of Schenker's combative prose, and doesn't even mention his legal background.[32]) Smoothing over Schenker's sharp edges makes him more palatably modern and universal, taking him out of the tumult of his own era. But it was the era that drove him, the chaos he sensed descending on civilization prompting both the escalating rationality of his theory and the emotional fury with which he shouted it into the whirlwind.

IN HIS CLASSIC TEXT of analytic aesthetics, *Languages of Art,* American philosopher Nelson Goodman considered "the rather curious fact that in music, unlike painting, there is no such thing as a forgery of a known work."[33] This is because in music (unlike painting) there is a score. We consider a performance authentic if it follows the score, and it has to follow the score to be authentic: "If we allow the least deviation, all assurance of work-preservation and score-preservation is lost; for by a series of one-note errors of omission, addition, and modification, we can go all the way from Beethoven's *Fifth Symphony* to *Three Blind Mice.*"[34]

For Schenker, though, being able to get from Beethoven's Fifth to "Three Blind Mice," step by analytical step, was the sign of true musical understanding. Having commenced *Der Tonwille* with livid indignation, Schenker abruptly shifted into theoretical discourse: a short essay to introduce the *Urlinie,* the "fundamental line." This was the concept that increasingly occupied Schenker's thought for the rest of his life: a simple descending scale, sometimes eight notes, sometimes five, but in its most basic form, only three notes (i.e., the opening phrase of "Three Blind Mice"), ending on the tonic, the pole star and goal of any piece of tonal music. When a three-note *Urlinie* is combined with a do-sol-do bass line, the result is an *Ursatz,* a fundamental structure, the simple architecture at the core of all Schenker-approved great music.

"The Urlinie bears in itself the seeds of all the forces that shape tonal life"; the *Urlinie* supersedes all other musical creation stories. Schenker's goal is to demonstrate a work's Austro-Germanic fitness by reverse-engineering its presented musical surface all the way back to the *Urlinie.* "With the cooperation of the harmonic degrees," Schenker goes on, "the *Urlinie* indicates the paths to all elaboration and so also to the composition of the outer voices, in whose intervals the marriage of strict and free composition is so wonderfully and mysteriously consummated."[35] Beginning with the fundamental line and structure, great composers elaborate that structure, layer by layer, into musical monuments, every transition from simpler to more complex governed by the strict rules of counterpoint and voice-leading that Schenker, thorough as he was, had already codified in his harmony and counterpoint guides. Background pattern to middle-ground expansion to foreground surface: the evolution of true music, that is, Austro-German music, as helpfully defined by Heinrich Schenker.

It is only after the rant and the reason that Schenker is ready to pull back the curtain on Beethoven's Fifth. The different channels actually are working in tandem, yoking together the emotion and logic of Schenker's thinking—and hinting at that thinking's legal origins. For Schenker's framework paralleled a particular conservative-Hegelian, pro-German theory of law and civilization. It was a theory Schenker would have heard expounded by one of his law professors at the University of Vienna, Georg Jellinek, who happened also to be a rabbi's son. And in the background of the theory was a goal that Schenker and Jellinek, both proud, highly educated German Jews, never lost sight of: assimilation.

Georg Jellinek's father, Adolf, head of the Leopoldstädter Tempel, Vienna's largest synagogue, advocated Jewish assimilation, the better to be "true, loyal, and selfless sons of the fatherland."[36] His sons epitomized it: Georg held law professorships in Vienna, Basel, and Heidelberg; Max, also a professor, specialized in German linguistics, and became a member of the Austrian Academy of Sciences; Emil moved to France and became, among other business-related things, a pioneering car dealer. (Emil's daughter Mercédès lent her name to the cars being sold.) Georg fashioned himself into the very model of a Prussian academic.[37] Yet assimilation only went so far: Georg Jellinek, despite having converted to Christianity, was never made a full professor in Vienna on account of his Jewish ancestry.

Jellinek's view of the law was shaped by the French Revolution—specifically, everything that he saw as being wrong with it—which put him in the nineteenth-century conservative mainstream. His thinking was in line with the historical school of jurisprudence, which predicted doom for any society that tried to impose theoretical "rights" and "laws" that weren't rooted in that society's own history and traditions. In other words: don't do what the French did. The most widely read of Jellinek's writings during his lifetime was a scholarly takedown of the French Revolutionary *Déclaration des droits de l'homme et du citoyen*, showing what the declaration had borrowed from primarily English and colonial American constitutional sources; to give the French "rights of man" a specific genealogy was to undermine any claim of their universality. Jellinek instead advocated that laws and legal institutions evolved, country by country, out of specific national traits: societal structures, economic relationships, language.

In his effort to refashion laws and institutions as if the Bastille had never been stormed, Jellinek even achieved the rare feat of making a Hegelian synthesis run in historical reverse—the real being rational only up to a certain historical point. The Scylla and Charybdis of Jellinek's ideal state were the extremes of ancient Roman law—too much authoritarian order—and modern democratic law—too much unruly individual freedom and equality. The golden mean was, for Jellinek, the Teutonic law of medieval feudal German states: an aristocratic class structure, with limited individual freedoms not imposed on the state as a given right but cultivated within the boundaries provided by the weak nature of any central authority.[38]

> [L]iberty accordingly was not created but recognized, and recognized in the self-limitation of the state and in thus defining the intervening spaces which must necessarily remain between those rules with which the state surrounds the individual. What thus remains is not so much a right as it is a condition.[39]

Liberty survives in the "intervening spaces"—the *Zwischenräume*—beyond the state's purview. Freedom is not a right but rather a DMZ between the state and the individual.

For Jellinek, the study of law was the study of the rules by which a society gradually evolved, step by complicating step, from basic values to fully functional institutions—a pattern recapitulated in Schenker's music theory. And Schenker's acknowledgment was often explicit, as in this passage from his posthumously published composition manual *Der freie Satz* (*Free Composition*):

> The origin of every life, whether of nation, clan, or individual, becomes its destiny. . . .

The inner law of origin accompanies all development
and is ultimately part of the present.

Origin, development, and present I call background,
middleground, and foreground; their union expresses the
oneness of an individual, self-contained life.[40]

Schenker even borrowed some of Jellinek's terminology:
Zwischenraum, for example, becomes the melodic mediation
between the end of a trill and the subsequent note.[41] Schenker
also picked up Jellinek's disdain for revolutionary arbitrariness;
as the latter criticized imposed rights and freedoms, Schenker dismissed the autarky of Wagner and his followers, their
self-consciously novel harmonic experiments, to say nothing of
the conjectures of atonality. The parallels between Schenkerian
theory and Jellinek's historical jurisprudence go on and on, and
in both directions; for, ultimately, Schenker's aim is not just to
explain musical greatness but to reinforce the politics he shared
with his professor. To properly understand the music is to properly understand the world.[42]

The pose of objectivity Schenker and Jellinek adopted was
in large part just that, a pose. In his magnum opus, the multi-
volume *Allgemeine Staatslehre* (*General Theory of the State*), Jellinek
insisted that historicism was a truly objective approach. "The
doctrine of public laws," he wrote, "is *a science of standards*. These
standards sharply diverge from propositions about the state as
a social phenomenon."[43] When the first part of Jellinek's theory
was published in France, however, the translator, Georges Fardis
("with the authorization of the author," according to the title
page), added an explanation to this section that flipped the scientific claim on its head. Fardis compared the disputed "natural" origin of laws and rights to the way a natural scientist would
explain a symphony: as "a series of vibrations in the objective
world," or "the acousto-psychological processes that arise" during a performance. The historicist perspective was more, well,

Romantic (and the symphony in question thus appropriately chosen):

> But if we are placed in the field of aesthetics? The view is completely different. . . . There is, in the world of artistic sensations, a truth that has nothing in common with that of the natural world of knowledge. Beethoven's Symphony in C minor is, from the point of view of feeling and musical perception, the deepest reality, the most indubitable truth, the most powerful: all of natural science can do nothing against the consciousness of this reality.

"Things are similar within the law," Fardis continues. "The legal world is a world of ideas, it behaves vis-à-vis the tangible world as the world of art vis-à-vis the world of natural science."[44] Schenker's style of analysis, despite its graphs and jargon and chains of evidence, was likewise more art than science.

The intellectual manner of both Jellinek and Schenker could plausibly be called Talmudic—their close readings of sources, their marshaling of extensive evidence, their mistrust of surface truths, always drilling down, looking for deeper, holistic structure. (Nicholas Cook connects Schenker to another Jewish thinker, Sigmund Freud, given that both their styles of analysis were "predicated on suspicion of the obvious."[45]) So—getting back to the Fifth, now—when Schenker insists that the fundamental motive of the first movement of Beethoven's Fifth is the first *eight* notes, not the first four, it goes well past mere contrarian provocation. It is, in fact, the fundamental text of his theory of the *Urlinie*. The first four notes form but a generic first impression, while the first eight notes hint at the password to the inner sanctum of the true Austro-Germanic musical tradition. In Schenker's analysis, the Fifth spells out the entrance requirements to German civilization.

In looking at the first eight notes of the Fifth, one can see how it might have been this symphony that inspired Schenker to imagine the *Urlinie*. The fourth and eighth notes, the ones emphasized by the two fermatas—E-flat and D—give two-thirds of the *Urlinie* right at the outset, setting up a tension that will eventually require the line to descend one more step, down to C, the tonic. Much of Schenkerian analysis requires teasing the outlines of such structures out of the busy tapestry of the musical surface, but in the Fifth's opening, Beethoven seems to be doing Schenker's analytical job for him, placing the *Urlinie* in ready-made, obvious relief.

Musicologist Scott Burnham has elegantly summed up the ties that bind the Fifth and the *Urlinie*:

> Either this piece was made to order for Schenker's way of thinking, or Schenker's way of thinking was made to order for this piece. Yet either/or misses the mark here, for this is clearly both: Beethoven's compelling surface influences Schenker, while Schenker appropriates that selfsame quality for his *Urlinie*. Think what Schenker gains from this. His *Urlinie* is here made palpable, for it becomes identified with the inexorable thrust of Beethoven's line. Thus Schenker attempts to validate his theoretical concepts by appropriating one of the most engaging openings in all of music as a direct demonstration and sounding confirmation of his ideas.[46]

Schenker allowed that less-percipient listeners might be misled into a shallow hearing of the opening, grouping the first four notes into a theme rather than the first eight: how "the fermatas and the sequential formation in the adjoining bars" might fool "the untrained ear" into "the impression of a motive as early as the first fermata."[47] Untrained ears, it turns out, belonged to a fairly distinguished crowd—Schenker calls out a lengthy list of Romantics who were led down the road to a two-bar perdition. With their "dissemination of legends," Czerny and Schindler obviously fell into this trap; himself ensconced in legend, Richard Wagner, "a total stranger to absolute music, succumbed to the mysterious eloquence of note repetition in the same way."[48] It is the repetition that makes fools of so many: "[M]erely by taking pleasure in recognizing the motive as it recurs so many times, one imagines that one is actually hearing and feeling."[49] Schenker painstakingly indicts every previous celebrated interpreter of the Fifth. Hoffmann? "One can see that Hoffmann's ear is not ready for higher musical connections, which makes his presentation merely a hollow duplication in words of the musical events."[50] Schindler's story of fate knocking at the door? "Pious nonsense!"[51] Adolph Bernhard Marx is set up and knocked down. Sir George Grove "is nothing more than a windbag, and sounds so simple-minded."[52] Paul Bekker's dramatic narratives are saved for last, epitomizing (to Schenker) the worst sort of hermeneutics, having the effrontery to look God in the face, as it were. "To be sure, the work of a Beethoven, being the work of man, addresses mankind. Should that itself be sufficient grounds to justify, conversely, mankind addressing the work?"[53] (This from a man who, remember, once compared himself to Jesus.)

There are times where Schenker seems so convinced of even the musicians' lack of understanding that performance itself is still too great a distortion of musical truth: "For most people, a symphony by Beethoven has to be performed by an orchestra and a conductor or in the form of a piano reduction for two or four hands. But what the *performers* play—is it really the symphony by Beethoven? . . . [W]hat if one had to say that *none* of the known renditions even approximates what is to be expressed? That, indeed, is the truth of the matter!"[54] That was Schenker in the preface to the first volume of his

counterpoint manual, published in 1910. The second volume
didn't appear until 1922, and the intervening war sharpened
his pen:

> The World War resulted in a Germany which, although
> unvanquished in battle [!], has been betrayed by the dem-
> ocratic parties. . . . This Germany has taken over from the
> hostile nations of the West their lie of "liberty." Thus the last
> stronghold of aristocracy has fallen, and culture is sold out
> to democracy, which, fundamentally and organically, is hos-
> tile to it—for culture is selection, the most profound syn-
> thesis based on miraculous achievements of the genius.[55]

Against such democratic debasement of genius, Schenker
imagines Germany, the *true* Germany, giving the dissolute
Entente Powers a magnificently Teutonic kiss-off: "[T]he German bourgeois and worker should band together, become musicians, and, under the baton of a chosen one, thunder the last
movement of Beethoven's Fifth Symphony to the West with the
force thirty million strong until the people there, deeply moved
by the German genius, would gladly kiss any German hand
in gratitude that a German man had opened his chamber to
them."[56]

Though initially sympathetic to the Nazis' nationalism,
Schenker was too critically attuned to overlook their excesses,
and his enthusiasm turned to skepticism within months of Hitler's 1933 assumption of the chancellorship.[57] But even as the
Nazis consolidated their power, Schenker was still couching his
theories in nationalist terms, as in this section from *Der freie Satz*
(a section discreetly omitted from English translations):

> [T]he question of Beethoven's nationality is incontrovert-
> ibly decided: he is not "only half a German," as some have
> wished—and still wish—to have it. No, the creator of such

linear progressions must be a German even if foreign blood perhaps flowed in his veins! In this regard, the bringing to fulfillment of extended tension-spans is better proof than any evidence from racial science.

Strip away the historical context and the loaded vocabulary ("foreign blood," "racial science") and the statement expresses an assimilatory ideal: being German isn't a matter of religion or bloodlines, but of a mastery of German culture, of the linear progressions and tension-plans that Schenker posited into his definition of German greatness. But, in this case, the context is inescapable. National Socialists had, early on, tackled the question of Beethoven's racial makeup in order to bring the composer into the fold of a pure Germany, burnishing, rationalizing, and even outright ignoring the historical record along the way. (One article went so far as to deny that Beethoven's father was alcoholic, instead giving him "a heroic fighting nature of Nordic essence."[58])

The campaign culminated in an article in *Volk und Rasse* (the "Journal of the Reich Committee for the Volk's Health Service and the German Society for Racial Hygiene") giving Beethoven a clean bill of Aryan health—and doing so with logic not far off from Schenker's: "Nordic are, above all, the heroic aspects of his works which often rise to titanic greatness. It is significant that today, in a time of national renovation, Beethoven's works are played more often than any others, that one hears his works at almost all events of heroic tenor"[59]—therefore, Beethoven was an unalloyed German. Schenker's argument is laced with a fierce irony: the Nazi powers would hardly apply the benchmark to Schenker himself.[60] (Schenker would be posthumously derided in the Nazi-produced *Lexikon der Juden in der Musik*, his theories willfully caricatured as abstract "mathematical games"; his widow, Jeanette, would perish in the Theresienstadt concentration camp.) So sure of his musical perception, Schenker

remained profoundly tone-deaf to the way Hitler and his followers cynically elaborated the basic *Urlinie* of German pride into a
pervasive, racist virulence.

Schenker died before Nazi anti-Semitism made it to his door.
The assimilation he believed in (and built into his theoretical edifice), already severely eroded, was finally shattered in November
of 1938, in a massive, Nazi-orchestrated outburst of anti-Jewish
violence throughout Germany and Austria: *Kristallnacht*. Along
with most of the rest of Vienna's synagogues, the Leopoldstädter
Tempel, where Adolf Jellinek had encouraged his fellow Jews to
be selfless sons of the Fatherland, was destroyed.

IN 1941, Victor de Laveleye was looking for a way for the Belgian
resistance to be more efficient in their graffiti. "[T]he people of
Belgium were chalking up the letters R.A.F. on walls, sidewalks,
and even on Nazi vehicles," he later remembered. De Laveleye, a
former Belgian justice minister, now in charge of underground
BBC broadcasts into his Nazi-occupied homeland, thought a
one-letter tag more amenable to avoiding the Gestapo. "The
problem was to find the one letter that would mean the same
thing to those who spoke Flemish and French."[61] The solution:
the letter *V*, symbolizing victory (*victoire*) in French and freedom
(*vrijheid*) in Flemish.

The BBC broadcast word of the new symbol on January 14, 1941, and the V sign soon spread throughout Belgium to
France. De Laveleye's British colleagues brainstormed how else
to exploit the letter, out of which emerged the notion of using
the Morse Code symbol for V—dot-dot-dot-dash—as an on-air
signal. One story attributes the idea to C. E. Stevens, an archaeologist and Oxford don—according to one remembrance, "a
grimy figure from a Hardy novel"[62]—then moonlighting as an
assistant to John Lawrence (who had helped set up the BBC's
Foreign Service).[63] Apart from his war work, Stevens had made

time in 1941 to publish a lengthy critique of the sixth-century cleric Gildas and his historical sermon *De Excidio et Conquestu Britanniae* (*On the Ruin and Conquest of Britain*), an important source for British history of the era following the Roman occupation; one suspects that, for all the scrupulously detached scholarship, the subject matter had taken on new resonance. In particular, Stevens was concerned with parsing Gildas's use of oral histories and traditions: "They are the matter of history dramatized on the lips of men for whom changes of political relations came no longer from the invisible and almost mechanical activities of councils and cabinets but from the dramatic encounters of personalities."[64]

Another story divides the glory, telling of a meeting among Lawrence, Stevens, and Jonathan Griffin, the BBC's European Intelligence Officer (later a distinguished poet and translator): Stevens, it is said, came up with the Morse Code symbol as an audible tag; Griffin noted its congruence with Beethoven's motive.[65]

The signal was initially thumped out on a drum in a BBC studio by the eminent percussionist James Blades. "The experiments tried with woodwind, brass and stringed instruments proved unsatisfactory," he recalled. "Among the numerous instruments assembled none equalled the arresting note obtained from an African drum." Blades poetically likened the sound to that of Drake's Drum, an instrument carried by Sir Francis Drake on his voyages and subsequently bequeathed to the nation; legend holds that its ghostly beat could be heard during times of British crisis or triumph.[66] The Beethovenian drumbeat—and, later, the theme itself—was soon crisscrossing Europe by radio.

(The namesake of Morse Code was, ironically, an isolationist. No one has ever been able to determine whether Samuel F. B. Morse—or Alfred Vail, Morse's more technically adept assistant, who did the bulk of the work in developing what came to be called Morse Code[67]—had Beethoven in mind when the encoding of the alphabet reached V, the Roman numeral of the symphony it seems to echo. But, in becoming such successful propaganda for a cross-Atlantic alliance, the code became a posthumous riposte to Morse's own politics.

"Who among us," Morse wrote, "is not aware that a mighty struggle of *opinion* is in our days agitating all the nations of Europe; that there is a war going on between *despotism* on one side, and *liberty* on the other."[68] Except that in Morse's eyes, the threat was a conspiracy between Metternich and the Roman Catholic Church to undermine the American experiment through a combination of popery and dilution of the national stock. After the telegraph became a success, Morse divided his time between lawsuits—trying to establish himself as the sole inventor of the telegraph—and nativist, Know-Nothing activism and propaganda: running for mayor of New York, "editing" a purported tell-all called *Confessions of a French Catholic Priest.* Morse probably would have been horrified had he lived to see the advent of the Second World War: electronic communication shrinking the distance between Europe and America, his favored isolationism now most insistently preached—over the radio, no less—by the Catholic Father Coughlin.)

The "V" signal became one of the most effective propaganda memes of all time. The Nazis tried to counter it—for a time, Joseph Goebbels pushed a *V-für-Viktoria* campaign of his own—but to no avail. The seeming irony of the Allied appropriation of a monument of German culture was actually a crucial ingredient in the success of the symbol. Thomas Mann's daughter Erika touted the Fifth as a devilishly effective double agent, a mole in the midst of the Third Reich. "This British 'V' Blitz will drive the enemy mad by weapons he is unable to match or even account for," she wrote. "Nazi concentration camps will hammer 'V' rhythm into minds of their slave drivers, and the first notes of Beethoven's Fifth will be sung by children on their way to Nazi schools, whistled in Nazi-dominated factories, played by orchestras tuning their instruments for the Nazi hymn."[69] (The BBC eventually began preceding the four notes with a warning to lower the volume—"This transmission contains music"—a sign of how effectively the propaganda had rebounded against German cultural pride: the sound of Beethoven's Fifth coming over a radio in Germany was now cause to suspect treason.)[70] In her memoir of the Girls' Orchestra of Auschwitz, French singer Fania Fénelon recalled performing the Fifth, gleefully noting that the players and the guards were, in essence, hearing two different pieces; what was "a monument of German music" to the SS was a message from the Resistance to the inmates.[71]

In Europe, the code became a rallying cry; in America, it became something closer to a brand name. A "Bundles for Britain" poster encouraged spreading the propaganda "V" in all its iterations, with helpful illustrations: "use it as a greeting" (the two-finger salute); "wear it on your coat" (a V-pin); and, of course, "whistle the tune of it" (the first four notes of the Fifth). The "V-Club of America" printed the opening of the Fifth on mail-in cards where one could list other prospective members.[72] Mail for the overseas troops became V-Mail (converted to microfilm, V-Mail saved space when shipped—and also streamlined censorship); specially recorded music performances, pressed onto vinyl for GI consumption, were labeled V-Discs.

For Armistice Day, 1943, the New York Philharmonic and conductor Bruno Walter added a musical observation to their scheduled concert: "The 'Victory' theme of the Beethoven Fifth Symphony" (the first nine measures) was followed by a minute of silence, then "The Star-Spangled Banner."[73] Beethoven had been fully conscripted into the Allied cause.

After the war, at least one Ally continued to use the brand. Winston Churchill was not very musical; his onetime son-in-law, comedian and pianist Vic Oliver, recorded a pall being cast over an impromptu wartime musicale at Chequers when Oliver began to play the *Appassionata* Sonata, only to have Churchill confuse it with Handel: "Nobody plays the *Dead March* in my house," the bulldog growled.[74] Nevertheless, he made Beethoven's four-note victory tattoo his personal calling card. When, in 1954, the Houses of Parliament celebrated Churchill's eightieth birthday, the honoree's climactic entrance into Westminster Hall was preceded by "an eerily expectant silence broken only by a Guardsman thumping out a repetitive refrain on his big drum: 'da-da-da-DUM.' "[75] A good theme is a good theme. Even decades later, the V-for-Victory association was still attached to the Fifth. An advertisement from the early 1970s for the "Beethoven Bicentennial Edition," a mail-order series of LPs from Time-Life Records, used it to tout the music's power:

> The theme of one work alone—his immortal Fifth Symphony—was an inspiration to millions in World War II who risked their lives in the name of freedom.[76]

The performance of the Fifth in the "Beethoven Bicentennial Edition" was conducted by Herbert von Karajan, a onetime member of the Nazi Party.

WHILE A SNIPPET of Beethoven fueled the Resistance, performances of the full symphony continued throughout the war. In 1939, Adolf Hitler requested a performance of Beethoven's Fifth for a "Party Conference on Peace," a conference canceled because the Nazis invaded Poland the day it was scheduled to take place.[77] Wilhelm Furtwängler, the German conductor, who had been specified by Hitler to lead the concert, was probably relieved.

Furtwängler had stayed in Germany after the Nazis took over, his loyalty to the timeless, Romantic Germany superseding his distaste for the new regime. Arnold Schoenberg once called Furtwängler "one of those old-fashioned Deutschnationale" from the nineteenth century, "when you were national because of those Western states who went with Napoleon."[78] The conductor saw his role as preserving German culture from the vagaries of politics, writing in 1944: "I am one of the most convincing proofs that the real Germany is alive and will remain alive. The will to live and work in me is, however critically I view myself, that of a completely unbroken nation."[79] Furtwängler used his status to do what he could for musicians whose careers and lives were targeted by the Third Reich, calling in favors from the Nazi bureaucracy, sending money to exiles. That status, though, was maintained by his being—and staying—Hitler's favorite conductor; Furtwängler's own political sense, which tended toward the magisterially blunt, left him unable to notice how effectively his image and music-making were drafted into Nazi propaganda, how, from the Reich's standpoint, his modest gestures of independence were a small price to pay for the prestige his presence lent the regime. ("He is worth the trouble," Goebbels once said.[80]) Still, the conductor's idiosyncratic loftiness galled some of Hitler's associates, Himmler in particular; near the end of the war, Furtwängler slipped into Switzerland, fearing possible retribution.[81] The Nazis' actual revenge on Furtwängler would end up being all the more effective for being so subtle—they did nothing. Despite being cleared at his denazification trial, Furtwängler was never able to shake the impression that he had cut some deal with the Nazi regime.

Beethoven was at the center of Furtwängler's musical universe. His wartime conception of the Fifth, with the Berlin Philharmonic, was recorded in concert in June of 1943; Furtwängler never conducted a Fifth more fiercely grand. The repetitions of the motive almost step on one another's heels, goading the music forward; the fermatas sear. The tempo is on the slow side—the first movement hovers around 88 beats per minute—but delivered with energetic weight, Furtwängler enunciating every phrase, the orchestra annealing every note.

The flexibility is astounding; after the recapitulation's oboe solo, the music takes off, 100 half notes per minute, like a dark flock suddenly turning with the wind. Was it a rebuke to the Nazis, underlining and emphasizing Beethoven's powerful freedom, a forceful reminder of the true Germany Furtwängler was trying to preserve? The Nazis probably just heard it as another expression of their martial ethos.

Despite their very different temperaments, Arturo Toscanini had nonetheless recommended Furtwängler to replace him as director of the New York Philharmonic in 1936. (It was probably at least partially a ploy to pry him loose from the Nazis; Furtwängler declined, afraid that if he took work outside of Germany, he would not be allowed back in.)[82] Ardently anti-Fascist, Toscanini left Italy in 1938 after a skirmish with the Italian government over his passport.

In 1943, conducting the NBC Orchestra—created for him— Toscanini marked the fall of Mussolini with a concert called "Victory Symphony, Act I"; on it he programmed the first movement of Beethoven's Fifth, promising the rest when Germany was defeated. Good as his word, Toscanini conducted a complete Fifth on VE-Day, May 8, 1945. It was his fastest performance: the opening movement actually exceeded Beethoven's 108-beats-per-minute marking, the orchestra hurtling across the surface of the score. It was as if Toscanini was annexing Beethoven back from the Nazis with a blitzkrieg of his own.

A MORE EQUIVOCAL settling of accounts with the Fifth would come at the hands of the iconoclastic composer Arnold Schoenberg. Back in 1914, Schoenberg had published a short article called "Why New Melodies Are Difficult to Understand." It was a defense of the early atonal rhetoric that Schoenberg was busy developing—but also an implicit rebuke to the kind of motivic construction Beethoven's Fifth exemplified. "The more primitive, the more artless the melody is, then the more modest the variation and the more numerous the repetitions," Schoenberg wrote. "The lower the demands which may be put upon the capacity for comprehension, the quicker the tempo of repetitions, then the more inferior must be its inner organization." The newer, more concentrated melodies would require a new kind of listener. "Such 'brevity' is disagreeable to him who wants to enjoy his comfort," he allowed. "But why should the privileges of those who think too slowly be preserved?"[83]

Heinrich Schenker, despite having once taken no less than Wagner to task for succumbing to the comfort of repetition, took what (for Schenker) might rank as mild offense at Schoenberg's article, calling Schoenberg "this Don Quixote of compositionally undeveloped chords," comparing him to Paul Bekker—poor company indeed, in Schenker's eyes. "Never once in his unspeakably miserable incompetence does he recognize the repetitions in the works of our masters; there he flails at all those who cannot or will not sink as rapidly with him into the depths of ignorance," Schenker wrote.[84]

In 1939, Schoenberg stumbled across a copy of Schenker's riposte, and jotted down his thoughts. He was no longer so down on short, digestible motives as he once was. And, with Schenker dead, Schoenberg could afford a bit of magnanimity—but only a bit. "Enough," he sighed. "He is defenseless today. Indeed, I am, too, for who still reads this sort of thing?"[85]

By that time, Schoenberg was living in the Brentwood neighborhood of Los Angeles, California; he had wasted no time in emigrating once Hitler took power, arriving in America in the fall of 1933. The twelve-tone music that Schoenberg pioneered had not exactly taken America by storm—"a new chaos, without form, and void," commented the New York *Sun*[86]—but the presence of Schoenberg himself was an ideological victory. "Germany's loss will be this country's musical gain," commented George Gershwin.[87]

When, in 1942, Schoenberg received a commission from the League of Composers for a chamber work, he decided that the times justified what was, for him, a novelty: an explicitly political piece. At first, he considered writing something about bees. "I could not see," Schoenberg considered, "why a whole generation of bees or of Germans should live only in order to produce another generation of the same sort, which on their part should also fulfill only the same task: to keep the race alive." Schoenberg rather thought that bees and Germans were in the thrall of a more ominous fate, surmising that bees "instinctively believed their destiny was to be successors of mankind, when this had destroyed itself"; only "a goal of world domination" could sufficiently explain why Germans had willingly let their society be transformed into a hive of discrimination, subordination, and killing.[88]

For a text, Schoenberg first considered the Dutch writer Maurice Maeterlinck, a playwright whose conception of Fate was so capitalized that he once said he preferred marionettes to actors. In his 1901 book-length essay, *The Life of the Bee*, Maeterlinck, an amateur beekeeper, arranged his observations of his hobby into elegant philosophical allegory. At times, the dramatization rises to a sort of expressionist pitch that Schoenberg might have found appropriate:

Where the path once lay open to the kindly, abundant reservoirs, that so invitingly offered their waxen and sugary mouths, there stands now a burning-bush all alive with poisonous, bristling stings. The atmosphere of the city is changed; in lieu of the friendly perfume of honey, the acrid odour of poison prevails; thousands of tiny drops glisten at the end of the stings, and diffuse rancour and hatred. Before the bewildered parasites are able to realise that the happy laws of the city have crumbled, dragging down in most inconceivable fashion their own plentiful destiny, each one is assailed by three or four envoys of justice; and these vigorously proceed to cut off his wings, saw through the petiole that connects the abdomen with the thorax, amputate the feverish antennae, and seek an opening between the rings of his cuirass through which to pass their sword.[89]

But ultimately, Maeterlinck's description of apian society, however apposite, just wasn't edgy enough: "Maeterlinck's poetic philosophy gilds everything."[90] Instead, Schoenberg had his UCLA student Leonard Stein drive him to Campbell's Bookstore in Westwood Village, where he bought a volume of poetry by Lord Byron.[91] In it was Byron's fevered 1814 "Ode to Napoleon Buonaparte."

At the outset, Byron had been as enamored of Napoléon as Beethoven had been, but Byron's crush proved more ironclad. Where Beethoven judged Napoléon in absolute terms—taking an emperor's crown was an irrevocable break with democratic ideals—Byron's point of view was more pragmatic: crown or no crown, as long as Napoléon continued to frighten and disturb the rest of conservative Europe, he retained his heroic stature. What finally disillusioned Byron was not Napoléon's imperial ambitions or his cult of personality, but his abdication and exile to Elba; better that he had died, a martyr in battle, than to have capitulated.

The aristocratic Byron cultivated a revolutionary enthusiasm that bore more than a whiff of radical chic, but he held the pose impressively well, rarely missing a chance to rhetorically and poetically castigate what he saw as reactionary power (the Tory government's foreign minister, Lord Castlereagh, was a favorite target), and inventing that enduring personification of brooding antiauthoritarianism, the Byronic hero. Byron's own persona was both model for and modeled after his template; given how much he identified with Napoléon as well, for the former First Consul to quit the field of battle anticlimactically, to reveal his "fronts of brass, and feet of clay," as Byron put it, felt like unusually personal treachery.

At the climax of the "Ode to Napoleon Buonaparte," Byron imagines Napoléon stewing in exile:

> Thou Timour! in his captive's cage
> What thoughts will there be thine,
> While brooding in thy prisoned rage?

Byron compares the fate to that of Prometheus, that favorite figure of the Romantics, what with his Beethoven-like combination of daring, divine access, and subsequent suffering:

> Or like the thief of fire from heaven,
> Wilt thou withstand the shock?
> And share with him, the unforgiven,
> His vulture and his rock!

But such approbation as afforded Prometheus (and Beethoven) is denied the compromised Napoléon:

> Foredoomed by God—by man accurst,
> And that last act, though not thy worst,
> The very Fiend's arch mock

To drive home the extent of the betrayal, the reference— "O, 'tis the spite of hell, the fiend's arch-mock, / To lip a wanton in a secure couch, / And to suppose her chaste!"—is from Shakespeare: Iago in *Othello*.

Such was the poem's original ending. But as the editions piled up—the anonymously published "Ode" was a literary hit—Byron's publisher requested a few more stanzas to fill out the pages. Byron obliged him with a Gallant to Napoléon's Goofus:

> The Cincinnatus of the West,
>   Whom envy dared not hate,
> Bequeath'd the name of Washington.

The poem's reference to both Schoenberg's original home ("And she, proud Austria's mournful flower, / Thy still imperial bride; / How bears her breast the torturing hour?") and his adopted one completed the allegorical circle.[92] But if the poetic content of Schoenberg's *Ode* was a rather obvious appropriation of Byron into the fight against perverted German nationalism, the musical content would make subtle but pointed use of another mascot: Beethoven.[93]

Schoenberg set Byron's poem not in melody but in *Sprechstimme,* a rhythmically specified and melodically contoured declamation, somewhere between singing and oratory. The speaker was accompanied by string quartet and piano. Schoenberg thoroughly plotted the piece: he typed out the poem and then annotated it in extensive precompositional detail, mapping out motives, planning musical connections between distant stanzas.[94] The music is dense, chromatic, mercurial.

But then, about a quarter of the way in, as the speaker ruefully recalls Napoléon's former martial glory—"The triumph, and the vanity, / The rapture of the strife— / The earthquake voice of Victory"—the violins and piano offer an eminent bit of commentary: the first four notes of Beethoven's Fifth. The speaker echoes it:

of Victo- | **ry**

Schoenberg makes the connection between the Napoleonic era and World War II in a single stroke.

Schoenberg attached great import to the quotation, which provocatively yoked so much history into one charged gesture. He showed Leonard Stein "with barely concealed pride and excitement" the "serendipitous discovery." "Now it was rather unusual for Schoenberg to show anybody his works in progress," Stein remembered, "so he must have been struck by the remarkable inspiration which produced in combination the 'Marseillaise' and the motive of the Beethoven Fifth Symphony."[95] The revolutionary echoes could be remastered in service of another century's struggle. But Beethoven's appearance in Schoenberg's *Ode* is by no means a moment of unclouded triumph. The entire piece, in fact, is arguing with history, undermining the privileges of a civilization that, in Schoenberg's opinion, thought too slowly to be preserved. The friction can be heard in the way Schoenberg applies the technique he was most identified with: the twelve-tone method.

The twelve-tone method was originally conceived, in part, as a systematic way to remove any hint of nineteenth-century tonality from a work's musical vocabulary. By basing a piece around a row—the twelve tones of the chromatic scale, rearranged and permutated, but threaded through a piece consistently, such that no one pitch took precedence over the other eleven—a composer could escape the fetters of a tonal center, a tonal point of departure and return (C, for instance, in the case of Beethoven's Fifth). Triads—the familiar harmonies of tonal music—were to be avoided, lest they set up aural expectations of resolution and arrival. The idea was to make sounds, structures, and rhetoric more fluid, their expressivity more instantaneous and powerful.

The application of twelve-tone principles in the *Ode*, though, is unusually loose. The row is hardly consistent: Schoenberg partitions the row into three-, four-, six-note sections, which he then freely reorders. Once Schoenberg preached avoiding octaves, on the ground that they would give too much weight to the pitches being doubled; but the *Ode* doubles pitches at the octave all over the place. And Schoenberg deliberately flies in the face of the music's nominal atonality by constantly engineering his row so it throws off old-fashioned triads. The *Ode* is a twelve-tone piece that is bending over backward to sound tonal. The piece ends on a grand, fat E-flat major chord.

But the *Ode* is not really tonal: rather, it is taking the vocabulary of tonality and turning it into disorienting, churning rhetoric; the music runs away from tonal grammar, shifting through harmonies too quickly to allow any sort of anchor. And that may be part of the work's satiric intent—the *Ode* does to familiar musical sounds what the Nazis did to language.

Victor Klemperer was a professor and philologist in Dresden up until 1935, when he was dismissed on account of his Jewish heritage. Since his wife was not Jewish, Klemperer avoided the camps, but spent the rest of the war shuffled between factory jobs. All the while, he kept notes on the Nazis' gradual appropriation of the German language; after the war, he compiled a book on what he called *LTI*—"Lingua Tertii Imperii," the language of the Third Reich. It was a language of distortion, not invention. "The Third Reich coined only a very small number of the words in its language, perhaps—indeed probably—none at all," Klemperer wrote. "But it changes the value of words and the frequency of their occurrence, it makes common property out of what was previously the preserve of an individual or a tiny group, it commandeers for the party that which was previously common property and in the process steeps words and groups of words and sentence structures with its poison."[96]

If Klemperer analyzed a twisted language, Schoenberg's *Ode to Napoleon* critiques a twisted cultural heritage. Since coming to America, Schoenberg had written a handful of works in a traditionally tonal style (a neo-Baroque Suite in G for strings, a modernistic but tonally anchored "Kol Nidre" setting), and many of his dodecaphonic works of the 1930s and '40s hinted at tonal centers. But the *Ode to Napoleon* is different, a funhouse mirror of tonality, a familiar language after a breakdown. It is at the original peroration of Byron's poem, when Napoléon's once-proud image is rendered most brittle—when Byron most mercilessly dismantles "That spirit pour'd so widely forth— / So long obey'd—so little worth!"—that Schoenberg suddenly wrings a stream of triads from his row: G major, E-flat minor, C-sharp minor, F major, G-flat major, D minor, and so on, the sequence divesting the familiar chords of their familiar meaning. The great inheritance of musical tradition, bequeathed from the Fifth Symphony through the Romantics, through Wagner, through Schenker, had, in the end, done nothing to forestall the conflagration of war. When it came to improving human nature, the edicts of music, so long obeyed, showed, ultimately, little worth.

The allusions to Beethoven in the *Ode* are similarly double-edged. The opening of the Fifth is clearly echoing V-themed Allied propaganda—but the poetic "voice of Victory" it underlines is Napoléon's. The E-flat major ending makes reference to the *Eroica* Symphony, but the piece it completes is a thorough dismantling of a heroic image. After the war, a generation of European composers would take Schoenberg's twelve-tone method to extremes, eager to flush from their music any vestige of the nineteenth-century tradition that, in their estimation, had paved the way for war. A piece like the *Ode to Napoleon* would have been regarded as old-fashioned, but, in a way, the *Ode* was designed to engineer its own obsolescence. In the *Ode*, Schoenberg came not to praise the nineteenth century, but to bury it.[97]

WHEN SCHOENBERG died, in 1951, Pierre Boulez published a famous left-handed eulogy titled "*Schoenberg est mort*" ("Schoenberg Is Dead"). Boulez sought polemically to rescue Schoenberg's fundamental innovation—the twelve-tone method—from Schoenberg's late-Romantic habits and allusions. Schoenberg's American period, in Boulez's opinion, was marked by "utter disarray and the most wretched disorientation";[98] the technique needed to be claimed by a superseding, progressive aesthetic (one, naturally, corresponding to Boulez's own). Schoenberg would have recognized the gambit; it's what he himself was trying to do to an earlier master in the *Ode*. From his expatriate vantage point, Schoenberg was proclaiming that Beethoven—or, at the very least, the truculent nationalism that deified him—was dead.

Sometimes, when Germans had bristled at using the Italian term *Eroica*, the equivalent word, *Heldenhafte*, was instead applied to Beethoven's Third Symphony. In the 1880s, the composer and historian Wilhelm Langhans had used the term to rate the Fifth Symphony higher than the Third: the Fifth described "the heroic [*heldenhafte*] struggle of man with an overpowering destiny, and victory over it, in even more poignant way than the *Eroica*."[99]

Victor Klemperer later recorded the Nazi destiny of *heldenhaft*:

> In December 1941 Paul K. returned from work one day beaming. *En route* he had read the military despatch. "They are having a terrible time in Africa," he said. I asked whether they were really admitting it—usually they only report victories. "They write: 'Our troops who are fighting *heldenhaft*.' *Heldenhaft* sounds like an obituary, you can be sure of that."

> Subsequently *heldenhaft* sounded like an obituary in many, many more bulletins and was never misleading.[100]

The German army's defeat at Stalingrad, in February of 1943, was too great even to euphemize. German radio announced that "all theatres, cinemas, and variety halls in the Reich were to close for three days." The announcement was followed by a broadcast of Beethoven's Fifth Symphony.[101]

7

Samples

IT TOOK the Second World War to find a steady movie role for
the Fifth Symphony. It had not been used very often, possibly
being already too much of a cliché even for Hollywood. But the
success of the "V-for-Victory" meme gave the Fifth its big break:
war movies. The four-note motive, along with the Marseillaise
and "Rule Britannia," became an essential tool for cinematic
pro-Allied sentiment. (It even worked its way into the plot on
occasion: in Universal's 1942 *Sherlock Holmes and the Voice of Ter-*

ror, which brought the Victorian detective forward thirty years to battle the Nazis, Holmes [Basil Rathbone] analyzes radio broadcasts of the Fifth with an oscilloscope in order to unmask a Lord Haw-Haw–like propagandist.) [2]

Animated cartoons, already a playground for free-floating semiotic bits of music, seized on the association. *Fifth Column Mouse* (1943) brings in the theme to punctuate the war effort success of a group of mice, shaving a Hitleresque cat's fur into a dot-dot-dot-dash pattern. [3] In *Scrap Happy Daffy* (1943), newspaper reports of Daffy Duck's Brobdingnagian pile of Allied-bound scrap metal inspire a burst of the Fifth on the soundtrack, the combination driving a cartoon Hitler into an unintelligible fury. [4] Carl Stalling, the longtime music director for the Warner Bros. animation department, had the particularly apt idea of matching the Fifth's incessant motivic rhythm to modern, mechanized war production; both 1942's *Ding Dog Daddy* (in which a none-too-bright dog falls for a bronze-sculpture counterpart, only to see her carted off in a scrap drive) and 1943's *The Home Front* (one of a series of cartoons produced for the U.S. Army starring the irrepressibly irresponsible Private Snafu) featured factories that hummed to Beethoven's beat. [5]

Dramatic films about the war made *during* the war had a tendency to use the Fifth to send the audience out with a dose of Allied resolve—as in Jules Dassin's 1942 *Reunion in France,* which ends with Michele de la Becque (Joan Crawford) and her double-agent fiancé (Philip Dorn) gazing up as a defiant skywriter offers occupied France *COURAGE,* to the accompaniment of familiar, pealing Fate. [6] Postwar, Beethoven could be drafted for more casual purposes: Max Steiner's score for William Wellman's 1958 *Darby's Rangers* reorchestrates the Fifth's theme for flutes and muted trumpets, a comic sting for an American lothario (Corey Allen) knocked out by a British soldier after trying to steal his girl. [7] (Allen collapses under a poster reading "Be Kind to Our Allies.")

Samuel Fuller's 1959 *Verboten!* uses the Fifth Symphony for dread rather than uplift, ominously setting the film's opening scene: a burned-out German town, an American platoon trying to flush out a Nazi sniper.[8] (The sequence of the first few minutes is positively surreal: the Fifth's opening bars over the RKO logo, a fade-in to gunfire, then Paul Anka's syrupy title song, then back to the story and the Fifth.) Fuller builds the entire sequence around the symphony's first movement, and any intended sense of victory is undermined, as two American soldiers are killed and a third wounded before the threat—and the music—is over. (Fuller, a veteran of the U.S. Army, 16th Infantry, once told of billeting on the floor of Beethoven's house in Bonn; to Fuller, who idolized the composer, it was like "finding an oasis in the desert."[9])

Producer Darryl F. Zanuck's 1962 D-Day epic *The Longest Day* managed to be sparing yet unsubtle in its use of the Fifth, opening with a stark, BBC-style drumbeat of the motive over a close-up shot of an army helmet upturned on a Normandy beach.[10] Like one of the film's roll call of big stars in small roles, Beethoven's Fifth appears fleetingly, and reduced to its most familiar essence, never getting any further than the first eight notes.

And, like *Verboten!*, *The Longest Day* almost seems to give Beethoven's Fifth back to the Germans, associating it more with Nazi foreboding than Allied triumph. The motive only appears in full orchestral guise twice: near the beginning, just after *Generalfeldmarschall* Erwin Rommel (played by Werner Hinz) promises the Allies, should they invade, the titular ordeal; and then just before the German Major Werner Pluskat (Hans Christian Blech) memorably spots the invading force itself (*"Auf mich zu direkt!"*).

Alan Sillitoe's 1960 novel *The General*, about a traveling orchestra captured by an enemy during war, specified neither the war nor the orchestra's repertoire; but, as the enemy general, "dwelling on one of the mass surprise attacks for which he had become famous," listens to the concert he forces the orchestra to play, the images are familiar: "The music illuminated his vision, and its final symphonic beats synchronized his resignation to the slow steps of advancing fate."[11]

When *The General* was made into a movie, it became very specific indeed: *Counterpoint* (1967, directed by Ralph Nelson) takes place during World War II; the orchestra is an American group on a USO tour; their captor is the German General Schiller (played by Maximilian Schell), who engages in a battle of wills with his egotistical equal, conductor Lionel Evans (Charlton Heston).[12] Evans's conducting bona fides are established at the outset with a performance of the Fifth; at movie's end, with Evans left behind at the now-abandoned German headquarters, Allied artillery coming ever closer, the four-note motive again emerges from Bronislau Kaper's score, eventually swelling into full, grim Beethovenian force.

Inevitably, though, memories of the war faded, and the Fifth would accompany situations that could simultaneously utilize and satirize its distracting familiarity. Woody Allen's 1998 *Celebrity* opened with a funhouse version of *Reunion in France:* the Fifth comes crashing in as a skywriter over New York spells out *HELP.*[13] (It turns out to be part of a movie shoot.) Playing a neurotic Californian in 1991's *L.A. Story,* Steve Martin, showing an English journalist played by Victoria Tennant around the city, takes her to the "Museum of Musicology," which proudly displays Verdi's baton, Mozart's quill, and (*da-da-da-dum*) "Beethoven's balls," a donation from "The Austrian School of Castration"— a common allegorical Hollywood fate, one surmises.[14]

The other place the Fifth Symphony turned up in movies was, of course, in movies about Beethoven himself. Abel Gance's *Un Grand Amour de Beethoven* (1936) plays it over the opening credits, almost as if to get it out of the way.[15] The 1994 biopic *Immortal Beloved,* directed by Bernard Rose, also opens with it, but under much more appropriately fateful circumstances:

Beethoven (Gary Oldman), on his deathbed, expiring to an impeccably timed clap of thunder—and the first five bars of the Fifth Symphony."[16]

Immortal Beloved's MORTAL BEGINNING echoes a variant of Schindler's story of Fate knocking at the door, one that replaces Fate with Death. *The Musical Times* used it in 1911, for instance, mocking the new fad of adapting classical themes into popular songs with a most inappropriate hypothetical: "We would not, for instance, like to hear the low comedian chanting his quips, say, to the 'death-knocking-at-the-door' theme in Beethoven's C minor."[17]

It's possible the knock of Death was appropriated from a work that Romantic opinion often heard as a direct precursor to Beethoven: Mozart's *Don Giovanni*, in which death (in the form of the Commendatore's statue) really does knock at the door. But the notion is an old one, going back to the Roman poet Horace:

Pallida Mors aequo pulsat pede pauperum tabernas regumque turris (*Odes* 1.4)

As translated by Christopher Smart in 1767:

Pale death alike knocks at the poor man's door . . . and the royal dome.[18]

The image made its way into the repertoire of English allusion, and thereafter nudged its way into the lore surrounding the Fifth Symphony. There are even translations that hint at the crossover, such as that by Philip Francis, first published in 1742: "With equal pace, impartial Fate / Knocks at the palace as the cottage gate."[19]

With the *Fate/gate* rhyme foreshadowing Schindler and/or

Beethoven's *Schicksal* and *Pforte,* one can almost imagine some product of an English education, somewhere along the line, making the unconscious transfer from Horace to the Fifth. (It's tempting to make the connection between Horace and Beethoven himself—the poet was one of Beethoven's favorites from among antiquity—but the German translations Beethoven would have read are nowhere near as close to the Schindler/ Beethoven formulation.[20])

The Death-at-the-door interpretation gained traction around the turn of the twentieth century, a reflection of the heightened emotional stakes of art and music in the wake of the Romantic era. The Danish composer Carl Nielsen salted his Sixth Symphony, premiered in 1925, with versions of Beethoven's motive; in the final movement, a theme-and-variations, a near-quotation is thwacked out by a large drum. Nielsen told a friend that this particular variation was, indeed, meant to symbolize "Death knocking at the gate."[21] (Nielsen had suffered a series of heart attacks after completing his own Fifth Symphony; the Sixth would be his last. In a bit of defiance, Nielsen followed his Death-knocking Variation IX with a brash, concluding Fanfare.)

Replacing Fate with Death also brought Beethoven's Fifth into the fold of old-time, fire-and-brimstone religion. The image had long been a favorite of preachers (such as seventeenth-century Presbyterian William Jenkyn: "Death may knock next and remember he will easily break into thy body, though thy Minister could not get into thy soul"[22]); as Schindler's tale became commonly known, enterprising proselytizers seized on the resemblance. Edmund S. Lorenz, composer of such favorite revivalist hymns as "There's Power in Jesus' Blood" and "Tell It to Jesus," provided this exhortation in 1909, illustrating "Why a Minister Should Study Music":

Who can hear the Fifth Symphony of Beethoven with its *motif* of Death knocking at the door without being deeply impressed, and stimulated to an intense degree? Now with one instrument, now with another, the hand of Death is heard knocking, knocking, persistently knocking. The phrase is mysterious, haunting, ever recurring, sometimes sweet and plaintive, sometimes with the roar of the ocean sounding through its measures, sometimes crashing and pounding with brass and cymbal as though siege guns were being trained upon the heart.[23]

A good example of the Death-at-the-door variant is found in Pat Conroy's *The Water Is Wide*, his memoir of a year spent teaching on an isolated island off the coast of South Carolina. One day, Conroy decides to play for his poor, undereducated Gullah students—descendants of freed slaves—a record of Beethoven, whom the students promptly dub "Bay-Cloven."

"Now one of Beethoven's most famous songs was written about death. Death knocking at the door. Death, that grim, grim reaper coming to the house and rapping at the door. Does death come to everybody's door sometime?"

"Yeah, death come knocking at Dooney's door last year," Big C said.

"Well, Beethoven thought a little bit about death, then decided that if death were really knocking at the door, he would sound something like this: da-da-da-*da*. Now I am going to place this little needle on this valuable record and we are going to hear death knocking at Bay Cloven's door."

The first notes ripped out. Ol' death, that son of a bitch.

"Do you hear that rotten death?" I yelled.

"Don't hear nuttin'," said Prophet.

"Sound like music," said Lincoln.

"Shut up and listen for that bloodsucker death," I yelled again.

"Yeah, I hear 'im," Mary said.

"Me, too," a couple of the others agreed.

Finally, everyone was hearing old death rapping at the door. Once we labeled death and identified him for all time, I switched to the Triumphal March from *Aida*.[24]

The scene touches on every aspect of the Death story that made it particularly resonant in America. There are the religious overtones, the revivalist style that Lorenz promoted, and also the call-and-response traditions of the African-American church. The repertoire of Negro spirituals often opts for similar imagery; Thomas Wentworth Higginson (a cousin of the founder of the Boston Symphony Orchestra) recorded one such spiritual during his Civil War days as the colonel of a black regiment:

> For Death is a simple ting,
> And he go from door to door,
> And he knock down some, and he cripple up some,
> And he leave some here to pray.[25]

There's also the point that Horace was trying to make: death's universality. That, too, would have taken on special meaning in the United States, a country where the ideal of democracy was perpetually celebrated, if only intermittently realized. If the fate knocking at the door was to be specified, Americans might well imagine it as death, the most democratic fate of all.

ON NEW YEAR'S DAY, 1863, a jubilant crowd of Boston abolitionists celebrated the arrival of Lincoln's Emancipation Proclamation with a concert featuring Beethoven's Fifth Symphony.[26] Ralph Waldo Emerson read a new poem, called "Boston Hymn":

To-day unbind the captive,
So only are ye unbound;
Lift up a people from the dust,
Trump of their rescue, sound![27]

The novelist Ralph Ellison was named for Emerson. In a 1955 article for *High Fidelity* magazine, Ellison recalled his days as an aspiring writer living in a noisy apartment. The Basie fan next door and the singing barflies who would stumble into the backyard court were profound annoyances, but there was another musical intrusion that provoked "feelings of guilt and responsibility": an opera singer, practicing hour after hour. This "more intimate source of noise . . . got beneath the skin and worked into the very structure of one's consciousness—like the 'fate' motif in Beethoven's Fifth or the knocking-at-the-gates scene in *Macbeth*."[28]

The feelings were rooted in the past. Before turning to writing, Ellison had aspired to music. A budding trumpeter, he hung around Oklahoma City's vital jazz scene, yearning for entry. At the same time, he nurtured a desire to be a great Negro composer, bringing black American vernacular sounds into the temples of European high art. "[H]ere I was with a dream of myself writing the symphony at twenty-six which would equal anything Wagner had done at twenty-six," he recalled. "This is where my ambitions were."[29] Ellison took lessons in trumpet, analysis, and composition from Ludwig Hebestreit, a German immigrant, music educator, and conductor, who founded the Oklahoma City Junior Symphony Orchestra. (Since Hebestreit taught at a segregated high school, Ellison's lessons were, by necessity, private; he got a break on the fees by mowing Hebestreit's lawn.)[30] He enrolled at the Tuskegee Institute as a music major, to study with the conductor and composer William L. Dawson, whom Ellison ranked as "the greatest classical musician in that part of the country."[31]

Ellison may have imagined that he would satisfy mind and soul by pursuing both jazz and classical music; instead, all he felt was tension. Hence the unease that his opera-singer neighbor brought flooding back, along with Ellison's recollection of his own obsessive practicing (and of the discomfort it caused his own neighbors) in pursuit of a troublesome goal: "For while our singer was concerned basically with a single tradition and style, I had been caught actively between two: that of Negro folk music, both sacred and profane, slave song and jazz, and that of Western classical music. It was most confusing."[32]

It is at a point of acute confusion that Beethoven and his Fifth Symphony enter Ellison's most famous piece of writing, his 1954 novel *Invisible Man*. The protagonist, once a favored standout at a black college, is working at a paint factory after a series of disillusioning setbacks; after causing a boiler explosion, he wakes up in a hospital, in the middle of shock treatment.

Somewhere a machine began to hum and I distrusted the man and woman above me.

They were holding me firm and it was fiery and above it all I kept hearing the opening motif of Beethoven's *Fifth*—three short and one long buzz, repeated again and again in varying volume, and I was struggling and breaking through, rising up, to find myself lying on my back with two pink-faced men laughing down.

"Be quiet now," one of them said firmly. "You'll be all right." I raised my eyes, seeing two indefinite young women in white, looking down at me. A third, a desert of heat waves away, sat at a panel arrayed with coils and dials. Where was I? From far below me a barber-chair thumping began and I felt myself rise on the tip of the sound from the floor. A face was now level with mine, looking closely and saying something without meaning. A whirring began that snapped and cracked with static, and suddenly I seemed to be crushed between the floor and ceiling. Two forces tore savagely at my stomach and back. A flash of cold-edged heat enclosed me. I was pounded between crushing electrical pressures; pumped between live electrodes like an accordion between a player's hands. My lungs were compressed like a bellows and each time my breath returned I yelled, punctuating the rhythmical action of the nodes.

"Hush, goddamit," one of the faces ordered. "We're trying to get you started again. Now shut up!"[33]

The Beethoven reference is not just a throwaway; as in the symphony, Ellison builds his gambit into a whole movement, the entire experience itself echoing the opening of the Fifth. The opening rest (*"Be quiet now," one of them said firmly*); the initial attack (*I felt myself rise on the tip of the sound*); the repetitive anacrusis (*A face was now level with mine, looking closely and saying something without meaning*); and then the held note, the fermata, delivered with the drawn-out excess recommended by Wagner: *I seemed to be crushed between the floor and ceiling. . . . My lungs were compressed like a bellows* (Wagner: "Then shall life be drained to the last blood-drop"). Eventually, though, the fermata yields (*We're trying to get you started again*).

The symbolism, too, becomes more nuanced on closer inspection. At first, it seems a wedge, a bit of white, European culture meant to torture a black man into docility, for his own good. But in bringing in the Fifth, Ellison also brings in all of the symphony's encrusted narratives: fate, struggle, defiance.

Ellison's idea of art was decidedly Beethovenian. In one famous description of another musical touchstone, the blues, Ellison's language might have come directly from a description of the Fifth Symphony: "Their attraction lies in this, that they at once express both the agony of life and the possibility of conquering it through sheer toughness of spirit."[34] As the civil rights movement picked up steam, Ellison stood outside it, defending his Beethoven-like retreat into his art; the social impact of *Invisible Man* was "the result of hard work undertaken in the belief that the work of art is important in itself, that it is a social action in itself."[35] Critic Jerry Gafio Watts writes of Ellison in a way that recalls Beethoven's complicated pas de deux with Napoléon: "Heroic individualists, like most ambitious fine artists, are not fundamentally democratically minded. They may espouse democratic ideology, but they tend to view themselves as a select group, select by virtue of talent but more importantly by virtue of their sheer artistic willpower and bravery."[36]

Ellison once wrote that "being a Negro American involves a *willed* (who wills to be a Negro? *I* do!) affirmation of self as against all outside pressures."[37] (*Muss es sein? Es muss sein!*) In that sense, Beethoven's cameo in *Invisible Man* echoes Ellison's individualism, echoes his protagonist's need to find an identity that transcends the preexisting roles in which both blacks and whites would cast him.

Nevertheless, Ellison is also picking a fight with Beethoven, and Ellison's Sunday punch is the way he rewrites the recognized instance of the Fifth Symphony's opening as an expansive, intricate description, neutralizing the music's temporality by lingering over each moment. Early in the book, the protagonist muses on what he's learned from listening to Louis Armstrong, likening it to a boxing match between a skilled pro and an amateur. Like the first movement of the Fifth, the prizefighter's body "was one violent flow of rhythmic action. He hit the yokel a hundred times while the yokel held up his arms in stunned surprise." But the yokel, coming from outside the world of tradition and conventional tactics, lands his blow. "The smart money hit the canvas. The long shot got the nod. The yokel had simply stepped inside of his opponent's sense of time."[38] Retelling his protagonist's experience as a stretched-out version of the Fifth's opening, Ellison could get inside Beethoven's sense of time.

.   .   .

The past is valid only in relation to whether the present recognises it.

—NADINE GORDIMER,
Beethoven Was One-Sixteenth Black and Other Stories

IN THE STORY "Beethoven Was One-Sixteenth Black," by South African writer Nadine Gordimer, that particular assertion of Beethoven's heritage, heard by a white former antiapartheid activist and slightly alienated academic, prompts a reflection on the unknowable distance between him and his own ancestors, and how the needs of the present shape the perception of the past. "Once there were blacks, poor devils, wanting to claim white," he notes. "Now there's a white, poor devil, wanting to claim black. It's the same secret."[39]

The idea of Beethoven having African ancestry inched into the mainstream along with the civil rights movement of the 1950s and '60s. Malcolm X often claimed that Beethoven was black, as in a 1963 *Playboy* interview: "Well, Hannibal, the most successful general that ever lived, was a black man. So was Beethoven; Beethoven's father was one of the blackamoors that hired themselves out in Europe as professional soldiers. Haydn, Beethoven's teacher, was of African descent."[40]

Haydn's alleged blackness didn't make much of a ripple, but Beethoven's did, even reaching the ears of Schroeder, the Beethoven-idolizing pianist of Charles Schulz's comic *Peanuts:* "Do you mean to tell me," he asked, "that all these years I've been playing 'soul' music?"[41]

The classification of Beethoven as some fraction black—one-sixteenth, or one-sixty-fourth, or even one-fourth, depending on where one reads—is often traced back to J. A. Rogers. A journalist, historian, and quintessential "race man" of the first half of the twentieth century, Rogers made the assertion that Beethoven was of African ancestry in the 1940s, in a three-volume study titled *Sex and Race: Negro-Caucasian Mixing in All Ages and All Lands,* citing numerous descriptions of Beethoven's swarthy complexion and curly hair, hinting at Moorish ancestors, going so far as to assert that "there is not a single shred of evidence to support the belief that he was a white man."[42]

That sort of burden-of-proof fallacy might give rational pause, though perhaps it helped make Rogers the go-to source on Beethoven's blackness: for those inclined to believe, a published reference; for those inclined to doubt, an argument that never ventured beyond the circumstantial. And Rogers's contention was not new. In the first decade of the twentieth century, the mixed-race English composer Samuel Coleridge-Taylor had asserted a black Beethoven, sardonically noting that "if the greatest of all musicians were alive today, he would find it somewhat difficult, if not absolutely impossible, to obtain hotel accommodation in certain American cities."[43]

There is no positive evidence to support African ancestry for Beethoven. There is always the possibility that Beethoven's Flemish ancestors deliberately obscured the documentation; perhaps the Eighty Years' War, which dominated the Dutch Renaissance, occasioned a dalliance between one of Beethoven's forebears and an occupying Spanish sailor, one with Moorish or African blood, a connection whitewashed for the sake of propriety. But, given its fundamental reliance on speculation, the idea of a black Beethoven ends up as something like the Fifth Symphony: a convenient screen onto which anyone can project their own concerns.

Those concerns came into conflict in 1988, at Stanford University. During a freshman orientation at Ujamaa House, an African and African-American-focused dormitory, two white students got into an argument with a black student over Beethoven's alleged blackness; later, the white students drunkenly defaced a Stanford Symphony poster featuring a picture of Beethoven, coloring it brown, giving it frizzy hair, big lips, red eyes—Beethoven in blackface—and then hung it up outside the black student's room. Tensions rose and feelings frayed amid charges of overt and covert racism.

The Ujamaa Incident, as it came to be known, engendered passionate if somewhat predictable reaction from all shades of the political spectrum—from grim denunciations of political correctness run amok to reinterpretations of legal case theory that attempted to square regulation of hate speech with the First Amendment. Nobody, though, mentioned the curiosity of finding Beethoven, a long-dead product of long-dead German city-states, at the center of a late twentieth-century American clash over race and prejudice.[44]

On the one hand, the incident was a warped tribute to Beethoven's iconic status; how many other figures would inspire such a heated reaction? (One commentator asked if the reaction would have been the same if one insisted that Beethoven was Danish; the better comparison would be a claim of blackness for someone as obscure as, say, Jean-François Le Sueur.)[45] But the incident also hinted at how the direction of Beethoven's fame had shifted from the music to the man. It was the figure of Beethoven, not the music, that was still potent enough to occasion both the black student's debate trump card and the white students' ill-considered response.

Critics of the hand-wringing the incident produced suggested that black students overreacted; but one might also wonder what it was about the possibility of Beethoven being black that so unnerved the white students. How much difference would an African ancestor make in the way we hear the Fifth Symphony? The notes would still be the same. Schroeder wondered if he had been playing soul music; but the whole idea that music has soul only gained traction with Beethoven in the first place. (Hoffmann, writing of the Fifth's innovatory nature:

"Beethoven bears musical romanticism deep within his soul and expresses it in his works with great genius and presence of mind."[46]) Ralph Ellison once cautioned blacks that they didn't have a monopoly on soul: "Anyone who listens to a Beethoven quartet or symphony and can't hear *soul* is in trouble."[47] In light of the Ujamaa Incident, Ellison's warning might be extended to all races.

The Stanford Symphony poster the students defaced was, in fact, a recruitment poster—an ironic footnote to the whole saga of Beethoven's blackness, since at the heart of the matter was the question of who got to claim Beethoven. Even as Malcolm X extolled Beethoven's blackness, other radical black activists saw Beethoven as recruiting for the other side, seeing the music-appreciation idolization of Beethoven as a kind of propaganda designed to assimilate blacks into white modes of living. The Howard University sociologist Nathan Hare regarded Beethoven as an affectation of "black Anglo-Saxons," as he put it; Hare told of a party where "the guests sighed with boredom amid strains of Beethoven's Fifth Symphony," until Hare surreptitiously put on a record by Little Richard.[48] The poet and playwright LeRoi Jones was, not surprisingly, even more harsh; in his 1966 black-power "Morality Play" *Madheart,* an archetypically posited Black Man speaks of "the nightmare in all of our hearts. Our mothers and sisters groveling to white women, wanting to be white women." Later, one of those mothers prays to the idols of the (white-controlled) media: "Tony Bennett, help us please. Beethoven, Peter Gunn . . . deliver us in our sterling silver headdress . . . oh please deliver us."

"This is enough of this stuff," the Black Man scolds.[49]

Dominique-René de Lerma, one of the great scholars of black music, was scholastically compelled to dismantle the Beethoven-is-black theory as unsupported conjecture, but found one equally compelling benefit in engaging with Rogers and the idea of Beethoven's African-tinged features. "No matter how circumstantial or speculative Rogers's arguments might be," he wrote, they "are most provocative for those who still think of a black/white dichotomy."[50] (Go back far enough, and we are all African.)

The most prominent leader of the civil rights movement, the Rev. Dr. Martin Luther King Jr., had a musical taste that ran more to opera, and was more likely to cite spirituals than symphonic composers, though King would occasionally mention Beethoven as part of a sequence directed at seemingly more humble toilers: "If it falls your lot to be a street sweeper, sweep streets like Raphael painted pictures; sweep streets like Michelangelo carved marble; sweep streets like Beethoven composed music."[51] But Beethoven made it into King's movement, wittingly or not; it was at the 1963 March on Washington—a century after the Boston abolitionists had celebrated Emancipation with the Fifth—that King honed to perfection a piece of rhetoric he had been trying out for some weeks, a peroration built on the power of a short, repeated theme, perhaps the most famous *quartus paeon* in oratorical history:

I have a | **dream**

As Ellison said, the motive does get beneath the skin.

A 1987 PROMOTIONAL AD for ABC network programming found Beethoven hammering out the Fifth at a piano: "If Beethoven were alive today, could he make it in the music business?" Beethoven dons sunglasses, electric guitars wail. "Find out what it takes . . . this week on *Good Morning America!*"

The first attempt at cross-fertilizing Beethoven's Fifth and rock-and-roll didn't make that much of a splash. "Rock and Roll Symphony," in two movements (the A and B sides of a 45), was released in 1961, credited to "The Back Beat Philharmonic."

The Fifth's opening is duly invoked before the piece slides into a string-laden, light-rock instrumental—only to come back around to quote a version of the Fifth's ending. The Philharmonic was a one-off, the product of accordionist Frank Metis and guitarist Randy Starr (the pseudonym of a Manhattan dentist, Dr. Warren Nadel). As The Islanders, Metis and Starr had previously scored a hit with their instrumental "The Enchanted Sea." *Billboard* highlighted the record as one of its "Spotlight Winners of the Week"—"Both sides come across well and should make strong instrumentals"—but "Rock and Roll Symphony" failed to chart.[52]

In Japan, the Fifth Symphony's pop infiltration received an assist from California surf culture, namely, the instrumental rock group The Ventures, whose wildly successful 1965 Japanese tour inspired the genre known as *eleki* (after the electric guitars that defined the sound). One of the leading *eleki* artists, guitarist Takeshi Terauchi, filled his tenth LP, *Let's Go Classics,* with surf-guitar versions of classical themes. The opening track reworked the opening of Beethoven's Fifth; "Let's Go *Unmei*" ("Let's Go Fate") won the 1967 Japan Record Prize for Best Arrangement.

The trend reached Europe the following year. In 1968, the Dutch jazz-rock group Ekseption won an award at the Loosdrecht Jazz Festival, the prize being a record contract with the conglomerate Philips; Ekseption recorded two songs by the early jazz trumpeter Bix Beiderbecke, which the record company pronounced too old-fashioned and refused to release. Having been impressed by an English group, The Nice, whose organ player, Keith Emerson, liked to combine classical and rock (a combination he would epitomize with his next group, Emerson, Lake & Palmer), Ekseption's keyboard player, Rick van der Linden, was inspired to work up his own rock-flavored, organ-and-bass-heavy arrangement of the opening movement of Beethoven's Fifth. For fun, he also worked in the theme from the *Moonlight* Sonata, as well as a 5/4 version of the opening of Beethoven's op. 2, no. 1 Piano Sonata. The band regarded the arrangement as little more than a novelty, but went along and recorded it.[53] "The Fifth"—backed by an arrangement of Khachaturian's *Sabre Dance*—spent seven weeks in the top ten in Holland, and was a hit throughout Europe.

The British group Electric Light Orchestra, another rock out-fit that flaunted classical overtones, redeemed an obvious joke by the skill with which they worked the Fifth into their 1973 cover of Chuck Berry's "Roll Over Beethoven," using the entire opening paragraph as a lead-in, and then contrapuntally thread-ing the four-note motive throughout the arrangement. Yngwie Malmsteen, the Swedish heavy metal guitar hero, signaled the ambition behind his neoclassical style by playing a highly electri-fied solo arrangement of the Fifth on his 1980s concert tours.

It was, however, the advent of disco that would allow Beethoven to leave his most indelible mark on the pop music landscape. Disco started off as danceable defiance for a con-fluence of demographics—black, Latino, gay—shut out from the overwhelmingly white-straight-male world of mainstream rock. Originally limited to underground parties and clubs, disco began to enter the mainstream (and the mainstream pop charts) around 1973. In retrospect, it seems amazing that it took even as long as it did for the disco style—lush, string-laden, with a basic, readily adaptable four-on-the-floor beat—to be applied to the classical repertoire. But it was only in 1976 that a matchmaker emerged in jingle writer and former *Tonight Show* arranger Walter Murphy.

Accidentally recapitulating a Hegelian model of progres-sive German music history, Murphy was inspired to arrange Beethoven by an arrangement of J. S. Bach. In 1972, a fleeting British studio group called Apollo 100 had scored an American hit with a pop-flavored version of Bach's "Jesu, Joy of Man's Desir-ing."[54] Murphy worked up a demo of a disco Beethoven's Fifth that convinced a short-lived label called Private Stock Records to sign on to the project. (Private Stock's biggest successes had been Frankie Valli solo albums, but the label also cornered the market on unlikely dance records: another 1976 release was *Bicentennial Gold*, an album of disco versions of American patriotic songs like "The Marines' Hymn" and "You're a Grand Old Flag.")[55]

"A Fifth of Beethoven," credited to "Walter Murphy and the Big Apple Band," reached the top of the *Billboard* singles chart in October 1976.[56] (The "Band" was a label-imposed fiction that irked Murphy, who noted, "I wrote the song, arranged it, played most of the parts; it was basically my own doing"[57]—apparently taking the Fifth's motive as, essentially, common property.) The acerbic rock critic Robert Christgau admitted that the track was "great schlock, transcendent schlock even,"[58] but none of Murphy's subsequent classical-disco experiments ever approached its success. (As if to amplify its novelty aspects, it was knocked out of the number one spot by radio DJ Rick Dees's "Disco Duck.") That didn't stop producer Robert Stigwood from licensing the track for the soundtrack to his movie project, *Saturday Night Fever*. "A Fifth of Beethoven" was accorded prime placement in the film, accompanying Tony Manero (John Travolta) and his coterie as we see them enter the 2001 Odyssey club like a prince and his retinue. Again, the song functions as an entrée into the world of disco by way of the most common entrée into classical music. For all its opportunistic sheen, "A Fifth of Beethoven" transcended mere novelty by deftly averaging a host of cultural vectors: inside and outside, black and white, gay and straight, art and commerce, eternal and ephemeral.[59]

Musically, "A Fifth of Beethoven" domesticates the Fifth Symphony while subverting its accumulated history. Murphy changes the meter from 2/4 to 4/4; the three eighth notes become three sixteenth notes, the entire anacrusis falling within a single beat, rather than across the center of the original's ambiguously fast two-beat bar. This makes the fourth note of the motive proportionally longer, almost like a fermata every time, but the continuing steady changes of harmony leave no doubt as to the underlying grid of time. After a somewhat faithful rendition of the original's first paragraph, Beethoven's contribution is boiled down to merely the four-note riff, punctuating sections that venture ever further from the symphony's material.

The only real vestige of Beethoven's ambiguity is in the opening, a fairly literal quote of the first five bars, but the context mitigates that original disorientation; "A Fifth of Beethoven" both plays upon and depends on the Fifth Symphony's celebrity. With the same passage with which Beethoven sought to jolt and confuse listeners, Murphy draws them into comfortable familiarity. Those inclined to dance will wait through the opening because it's Beethoven; those inclined toward Beethoven will, maybe, stay through the dance because it's Beethoven.

Much of the effectiveness of "A Fifth of Beethoven" vis-à-vis Beethoven's original derives from how much the disco sound, with its swooping strings and hypnotically incessant beat, already matches the Romantic descriptions of the Fifth Symphony that would become music-appreciation boilerplate: transcendence, otherworldliness. (English critic Richard Dyer once wrote of how disco creates a Hoffmann-like "'escape' from the confines of popular song into ecstasy."[60]) The seeming juxtaposition of high and low is an illusion, even a ruse; disco and Beethoven are revealed as long-lost cousins. One of the cousins just happens to be gay.

In much the same vein as avowals of an African ancestor for Beethoven, there have been periodic speculations that Beethoven was a deeply closeted homosexual. The most famous claim was made by psychoanalysts Editha and Richard Sterba in their 1954 analysis *Beethoven and His Nephew*, citing Beethoven's repeated self-sabotage of his relationships with women, his unhealthily intense obsession with his nephew, even the cross-dressing at the center of the plot of *Fidelio*.[61] The claim is most assuredly questionable. "A Fifth of Beethoven" is much more shrewd in its appropriation: rather than Beethoven himself, it is Beethoven's music that is conscripted into gay culture, polishing another facet of the Fifth's universality. In the words of Philip Brett and Elizabeth Wood, it was in "A Fifth of Beethoven" that "the opening of Beethoven's Fifth Symphony, that quintessential model of heroic masculinity, met its gay destiny."[62]

The Fifth also fulfilled its black destiny by gaining a place, via "A Fifth of Beethoven," in hip-hop and R&B. The VHB—the Vintertainment House Band, the production team for Vincent Davis's Brooklyn-based Vintertainment Records, which featured the influential DJ Chuck Chillout—produced a 1984 hip-hop adaptation, "Beethoven's Fifth (Street) Symphony," that relied heavily on Murphy's framework. (And if "A Fifth of Beethoven" counted on the listener to remember the actual Fifth, "Beethoven's Fifth (Street) Symphony" alters the source material in a way that sounds like the musicians themselves were trying to remember how the piece goes.)

The Fifth has been sampled, looped, and layered into other songs' backing tracks. The music could lend weight, either ironic (the British rap group Gunshot used the opening to kick off their debut single, "Battle Creek Brawl," in suitably imposing style) or earnest (producer Antoine Clamaran, under the name Omega, had a French club hit with "Dreaming of a Better World," making a transition in the middle of the song with a swath of the Fifth, much as another DJ might use a sampled drum break). "A Fifth of Beethoven" specifically could signify both sophistication and retro connoisseurship, as when the rapper A+ (Andre Levins) used Murphy's version as the foundation of his 1999 single "Enjoy Yourself," a night-out boast that updates Tony Manero's entrance into the 2001 Odyssey for a hip-hop generation.

But as remixed culture evolved into something more fluid, the disco Fifth found a niche in which the symphony's more deep-rooted celebrity could also be acknowledged: an ironic counterpoint of history and parallel musical tradition. A pair of related dance tracks from the vibrant mash-up community that sprung up in San Francisco in the 2000s made especially trenchant commentary: first the DJs Adrian & Mysterious D mixed the Fifth and Kanye West's 2005 single "Gold Digger"; in tribute to that track's popularity, fellow DJ Party Ben worked the Fifth into a more elaborate collage built around Kanye's "Love Lockdown." Beethoven's monumentality made fluent combination with Kanye, a rapper and producer whose musical ambition and self-regard (he once appeared on the cover of *Rolling Stone* as Jesus in a crown of thorns)[63] might well be called Beethovenian. The grandeur suits him.

Hip-hop artist Bonita "D'Mite" Armah used the Fifth's theme as a backing for his 2007 single "Read a Book," which recast basic self-improvement advice—brush your teeth, take care of your kids, invest in real estate—as a full-on, thumping crunk anthem, redolent with profanity ("read a muh'fuckin' book"). Satire with an edge that fine was bound to offend, especially after Black Entertainment Television turned the song into an animated short that showcased seemingly every negative hip-hop stereotype extant; a crowd five hundred strong protested outside the home of BET's chairperson.[64] But Beethoven's presence was one key to Armah's intent, to parody a style that had grown so focused on style that any content would fit. "People tell me all the time, 'You know, I'm thrown off by how ridiculous the song is,'" Armah said. "I was like, yes, it's ridiculous, isn't it? It shows kind of where we've gone as a culture, and as an art."[65]

It was the brilliantly edgy Irish band A House that had, perhaps, the best take on pop Beethoven, with their 1992 single "Endless Art." The verses—lists of deceased artists, writers, and musicians, often cited with their birth and death dates—lead into the chorus, built on a sample of the first movement of the Fifth: "All dead, yet still alive."[66]

"HOW DIFFERENT life must have been before the tape-recorder. Fine things evaporated like rain drops. Nowadays, even rubbish has a chance of immortality. That is progress indeed."

The words of Stephen, a music critic, "dictating into the latest Japanese device" in Peter Ustinov's play *Beethoven's Tenth*. Later, Beethoven himself shows up at Stephen's house (knocking on the door in predictable rhythm) and, after being outfitted with a hearing aid, spends three days listening to his own works—many for the first time—via Stephen's record collection. Beethoven notes the productive virtue of his shelved expanse of vinyl: "From there to there," he boasts.[67]

Beethoven's Fifth had been a soundtrack for the recording industry's technological milestones—the 1910 Fifth by Friedrich Kark and the Odeon-Orchester had been the first complete symphony put on record, while RCA Victor had introduced the long-playing record with the Philadelphia Orchestra playing the Fifth, conducted by Leopold Stokowski—but, with the advent of the LP era, Beethoven's Fifth itself could make the pitch, and cheaply. In 1940, for example, the Southern California Gas Company began sponsoring nightly programs of classical music on radio station KFAC; a report in *Public Utilities Fortnightly* explained the rationale: "The theory: That people who like classical music are mostly nice people, who like nice things, have nice homes, constitute a sort of upper crust to the community pie—and therefore should be the folks to talk about the latest appliances."[68]

The programs actually exceeded that demographic, drawing a cross-section that would be any marketer's dream. "The listening audience is large, includes all population and economic groups, commands attention longer than any other form of advertising, and gets close to its audience, as a very personal thing," the report noted. "As a friend-maker, it is in its own class."[69]

But, with the advent of rock-and-roll, Beethoven-as-pitchman could go back to courting that theoretical, upper-crust (or upper-crust-aspiring) audience. Thus, for instance, Orson Welles—from 1978 until 1981, the television spokesperson for the California winemaker Paul Masson—was, in one ad, discovered by the camera listening to Beethoven's Fifth Symphony on the stereo:

> It took Beethoven four years to write that symphony. Some things can't be rushed. Good music . . . and good wine: Paul Masson's Emerald Dry—a delicious white wine. Paul Masson's wines taste so good because they're made with such care. What Paul Masson himself said nearly a century ago is still true today: We will sell no wine before its time.[70]

In theory, that was the place of Beethoven's Fifth in advertising—as a kind of underhanded appeal to snobbery, a shorthand for good taste. In practice, though, it was the Fifth's sheer recognizability that won out.

The strength of wartime V-for-Victory associations initially put a damper on the Fifth's mass-media advertising presence. In the early 1950s, the fledgling jingle-writing team of Bobby Cassotto (who would later adopt the stage name Bobby Darin) and Don Kirshner (who would later produce the Monkees) had used the opening of the Fifth Symphony as the basis of a radio ad for a German airline; not surprisingly, the pitch was rejected.[71] By the 1970s, though, an ad for the pain reliever Vanquish could successfully commercialize the war, with the Fifth ringing out as a construction worker flashed the V sign to indicate the defeat of his headache. (Churchill might have demurred, but Sir Thomas Beecham would have been proud.)

A 1990 television spot for Nike shoes, starring NBA center David Robinson, used a nifty remix of the Fifth to set up Robinson's dig at fellow Nike spokesman Bo Jackson: "Bo may know Diddley, but Mr. Robinson knows *Beethoven*." It was a widespread intelligence, and one that became the Fifth's main selling point—what better way to drill a name or a product or a slogan into the customer's head than to leash it to a tune that seemingly everybody already knew?

The association could be positive—as in an Italian television commercial for the cleaner Vim ("vi-vi-vi-Vim")—or negative, as in a Swedish radio commercial for Nicorette gum, starring a choir coughing out the Fifth. Then there was Hyundai's 2007 "Big Duh" campaign, in which the glossy poetry-in-motion images of automobiles standard to such commercials were backed by famous songs, "remixed" into a cappella renditions consisting solely of the word "duh"—"based on the idea that it's a no-brainer to pick a Hyundai," according to Jeff Goodby, chairman and chief creative officer of Goodby, Silverstein & Partners, who came up with the ads. Among the songs was, perhaps inevitably, the Fifth Symphony. "Beethoven would be rolling over in his grave," reported *Advertising Age* magazine.[72] Nevertheless, the campaign "earned the highest ranking for consumer recall," according to the advertising analysts IAG Research.[73] The *quartus paeon* still works.

The Fifth Symphony also became a calling card for the composer, especially in Japan, where Beethoven himself (or a reasonable facsimile thereof) was often pressed into advertising service. In a 2006 commercial for Tokyo Gas, a Japanese Beethoven bursts out of an armoire, announcing himself by singing the first four notes of the Fifth. (After cajoling the armoire's owner into letting him use the shower, and learning he can simultaneously wash his clothes without losing hot water—thanks to Tokyo Gas and its new "Eco-Jozu" water heater—Beethoven runs to the piano, clad in a towel, shampoo in his hair, and pounds out the motive in triumph.)

A commercial for NewTouch Sugomen, a line of frozen noodle bowls manufactured by the Yamadai corporation, showed Beethoven enjoying the product in question in rhythm—slurp, slurp, slurp, sluuurrrrp. Beethoven expressing his satisfaction by shouting "*Unmei*" (Fate), the popular Japanese name for the Fifth, but also aurally close to "*umai*"—"excellent."[74]

In South America, the advertising agency W/Brasil ingeniously used the motive to hint at Beethoven's presence as part of a television commercial for the French-based media/electronics retailer Fnac: an overhead shot showed a customer flipping through a rack of compact discs, the plastic cases clacking in the Fifth's opening rhythm, until the desired Beethoven album is located and retrieved. (The campaign won a 2003 Gold CLIO award.)

The Fifth could even stand in for the customer rather than Beethoven, at least over the phone. In 1986, composers and recording engineers Mitch and Ira Yuspeh produced and marketed "Crazy Calls," songs in various styles with lyrics designed to work as outgoing messages on tape-based telephone answering machines. Promoting the collection through television commercials, the brothers sold over a million cassettes. The message utilizing the Fifth Symphony's opening theme was probably the best-known of the set. "Nobody home," it sang, "nobody home."

IN THE EARLY 1980s, chipmaker General Instrument released the AY-3-1350, an integrated circuit capable of providing synthesized tunes for "toys, musical boxes, and doorchimes" (the latter especially)—among the twenty-five preprogrammed "popular and classical tunes chosen for their international acceptance" were Beethoven's Fifth and Ninth Symphonies.

(Also included were the Marseillaise, the "William Tell" Overture, and the theme from *Star Wars*.)[75] Hobbyists soon figured out how to wire an AY-3–1350 to an existing phone, creating the first Beethoven's Fifth ringtone.[76]

Beginning in 1996, when the Japanese telecom company NTT DoCoMo released the Digital Mova N103 Hyper, the first cell phone preprogrammed with multiple melodic ringtones, the notion of a phone call announced by Beethoven's Fifth really began to seep into cultural consciousness. In reality, both "Für Elise" and the "Ode to Joy" (the latter was programmed into phones supplied by the organizers of the 1998 Nagano Olympic games) seemed to be more common. But Beethoven's Fifth became a common reference for writing about the possibility of a classical ringtone. (After all, the original already *sounds* like a ringtone.)

As early as 2000, the prevalence of Beethoven's Fifth as a ringtone, or, more to the point, the prevalence of the *idea* of Beethoven's Fifth as a ringtone, was enough for *InfoWorld* editor-at-large Dan Briody to include it in the second of a list of ersatz-Mosaic cell-phone commandments. "Thou shalt not set thy ringer to play *La Cucaracha* every time thy phone rings," he preached. "Or Beethoven's *Fifth*, or the Bee Gees, or any other annoying melody."[77] (Was it the mere translation into ringtone that made the melody annoying? Briody's placement corresponded to either the prohibition against worshipping graven images or the misuse of the Lord's name, depending on whether one adopts a Talmudic or Augustinian numeration.)

But as the technology advanced to the point of sampled, not synthesized, ringtones, popular music began to dominate the market. Where Beethoven's Fifth *did* become enormously popular as a ringtone is in the universe of mass-market fiction. Instantly familiar and unsusceptible to cultural obsolescence, the Fifth fairly rings off the hook in such writing. Pick up a thriller, mystery, or romance novel at your local airport, and chances are, if a cell phone rings during the story, it will ring Beethoven's Fifth.

To trace the symbolism of these fictional ringtones is to revisit familiar contexts for Beethoven's Fifth, and Beethoven's reputation in general. Sometimes it hints at a more privileged path through life; in Christopher Reich's 2002 thriller *The First Billion*, Hans-Uli Brunner, the Swiss Minister of Justice, receives an untimely interruption on the links, the melodic content an indication of his class:

> As he stroked the putter toward the ball, an ominous tune chimed from within his golf bag. The first bars of "Beethoven's Fifth." The blade met the ball askew and it sailed three feet past the cup.
> "Damn it!"[78]

With the advent of technology that allows multiple ringtones, tailored to particular incoming callers, Schindler's fate-knocking-at-the-door story again surfaces. For example, disillusioned political wife Helene Zaharis in Beth Harbison's 2007 *Shoe Addicts Anonymous* programs political calls to ring "with the ominous opening of Beethoven's Fifth Symphony."[79] Parents are often the symbolized authority, as in Caroline Cooney's *Hit the Road*, in which the sixteen-year-old Brit embarks on an illegal road trip: "For her mother's ring, Brit had chosen the Beethoven's Fifth theme, that ominous one: dum dum dum daaaaah."[80] (In the 2007 *Rear-Window*-for-teens movie thriller *Disturbia*, the girl-next-door Ashley similarly has the Fifth to warn her of a maternal call.) One can even find the American death-knocking variant, as in E. R. Webb's Christian-inspirational serial-killer novel *Gemini's Cross*, as part of the usual cat-and-mouse game:

> Immediately a phone rang somewhere in the shop. The ring tone was Beethoven's Fifth Symphony. Da-da-da-dum.

Death, knocking at the door. Da-da-da-dum. Following the sound, Baxter looked under the table. Nothing. He turned over the chairs, one by one. . . .

There it was, a cell phone taped under the chair. He ripped it off and put it to his ear.

"Okay, Darrell. I'm here."

"Good. Remember what I said about law enforcement."

"I'm alone."[81]

Jonathan Kellerman, in his 2005 detective novel *Rage*, uses the Fifth to hint at a character's Beethovenian outsider gruffness:

He downed two Bengal premiums, called for the check, and was slapping cash on the table when his cell chirped Beethoven's Fifth. . . .

Rising to his feet, he motioned me toward the exit. Some of the twenty-somethings stopped laughing and looked at him as he loped out of the restaurant. Big, scary-looking man. All that merriment; he didn't fit in.[82]

Then there is the Fifth as an affectation to be mocked. In Linda Ladd's *Die Smiling*, detective Clare Morgan considers the Fifth to reflect poorly on her partner, Bud Davis ("he's pretentious sometimes that way").[83] On the other hand, in Christine McGuire's serial-killer mystery *Until Judgment Day*, DA investigator Donna Escalante's ringtone impresses sheriff's chief of detectives James Miller, echoing the turn-of-the-century use of the symphony as a signal of feminine refinement—or perhaps passion:

"Is that your phone chirping or mine?" Miller asked Escalante. . . .

"Yours," she said. "When mine rings, it plays music."

"What music?"

"The first four notes of Beethoven's Fifth Symphony."
"Pretty classy."[84]

And sometimes, fictional phones ring out the Fifth simply as a play on the convenience of recognizability, as with Moxy Maxwell, the stubborn ten-year-old heroine of Peggy Gifford's series of children's books.

Moxy was so quick on the draw when she picked up her cell phone that Ajax often remarked that she would have made a first-rate gunslinger in the Old West. And this time was no exception.

After the second but before the third note of Beethoven's Fifth Symphony, Moxy was saying "Yes" into the phone. "Yes" was what Moxy said instead of "Hello," unless it was someone she didn't know.[85]

If Beethoven's Fifth stops after the first two notes, is it still Beethoven's Fifth? Moxy does not have time for your trumped-up pop koans. But the joke only works if the tune is something everybody knows, once again both reinforcing and perpetuating the ubiquity of the Fifth Symphony's iconic opening. The fictional progress of the Beethoven ringtone, then, encapsulates the progress of the symphony itself in Western culture: from an exotic novelty, to a prepackaged interpretive meme, to a neutered, omnipresent cultural artifact.

THE OPENING of Beethoven's Fifth had become a non-Kantian thing-in-itself, a self-sufficient cultural push-button. Its very familiarity could work against it. In Anthony Burgess's 1962 novel *A Clockwork Orange,* the Pavlovian aversion treatment by which the delinquent Alex is "cured" of his violent tendencies, the Ludovico Treatment, included the Fifth Symphony at its center, accompanying a film of Nazi brutality. A decade later, for the film adaptation, director Stanley Kubrick cast the Fifth aside in favor of the Ninth; only the Fifth's opening motive remained, in the form of the doorbell to the home of the writer Mr. Alexander, attacked by Alex and his gang—a grim fate rendered as a grim pun.[86]

Kubrick's version of *A Clockwork Orange* was stylistically indebted to Toshio Matsumoto's 1969 film *Bara no Sōretsu* (*Funeral Parade of Roses*), a hallucinatory, nonlinear modernization of *Oedipus Rex* set in Tokyo's gay underground.[87] The movie also featured a cameo by the Fifth, a joke at both the Fifth's and the film's own avant-garde expense. A conversation turns to a movie that Eddie, the transvestite main character, has been acting in, a movie that may very well be *Bara no Sōretsu* itself. Someone asks if the movie is interesting. "I'm not sure," Eddie replies. "It's unique, though"—and Beethoven's opening phrases sound, as a title card informs the audience: *Awaiting your esteemed applause!*

Even that was more pointed than the Fifth's appearance in the opening scenes of Clara Law's 2000 film *The Goddess of 1967*; we see glimpses of the life of a young Japanese man as he carries on an Internet negotiation for the purchase of a Citroën DS automobile—the "Goddess" (*déesse*) of the title.[88] Each shot produces a jump cut on the soundtrack, each a different genre and mood—the Fifth's opening turns up in the middle, neither portentous nor ironic, just one of a host of fragments and objects out of which a modern identity is constructed.

The tendency of such digital interconnectedness, while at the same time making the entire corpus of culture more and more immediately accessible, was to encourage consumption of information in more and more concentrated packets. Matt Wand, a cofounder of the British avant-garde sound collage group Stock, Hausen & Walkman, summarized the aesthetic: "MP3 is a codec designed to remove 'redundant' audio information, to make a sound file 5 to 10 times smaller, in effect to create 'MUSIC-lite'—a kind of diet music in which all the sound information our ears supposedly don't need to hear is removed. . . . [H]ow much better would it be if the software truly stripped out all the redundant material, Beethoven's 5th reduced down to its first 4 notes, a repetitive dance hit cut right down to the one repeating loop that is its main constituent?"[89]

In a 2005 episode of *The Simpsons*, Marge Simpson spearheads the construction of a new Frank Gehry–designed concert hall in Springfield—but at the opening concert, the entire audience gets up to leave after the first five bars of the Fifth. "We've already heard the duh-duh-duh-dum," Chief Wiggum explains. "The rest is just filler."[90]

THEODOR W. ADORNO saw it all coming. In 1945, he wrote: "There exists today a tendency to listen to Beethoven's Fifth as if it were a set of quotations from Beethoven's Fifth."[91]

At the time, Adorno was living in exile in Los Angeles, California. A native of Frankfurt, he had fled the Nazis in 1934, first to England, then to America, having been invited by his colleague Max Horkheimer to rejoin the Institute for Social Research, the think tank that had employed both of them back in Germany; the Institute had followed Horkheimer to New York.

Adorno's insight into the Fifth's fragmentation was a by-product of another American invitation. Shortly after his arrival, Adorno was recruited into a Rockefeller-sponsored study of mass media, centered at Princeton, and known as the Radio Project. He was already interested in radio and recordings, in the way it affected how people listened to and understood music, the way it promoted what he called "regressive listening": "Not only do the listening subjects lose, along with freedom of choice and responsibility, the capacity for conscious perception of music, which was from time immemorial confined to a narrow group, but they stubbornly reject the possibility of such perception." And, foreshadowing his diagnosis about the Fifth: "They fluctuate between comprehensive forgetting and sudden dives into recognition."[92] Music over the radio, to Adorno, was all sensuality and no structure. (He once wondered whether "Beethoven actually *wanted* to go deaf—because he had already had a taste of the sensuous side of music as it is blared from loudspeakers today."[93])

Adorno left the project in 1941, critical of the project's methodology. Paul Lazarsfeld, the sociologist who headed the project, and Frank Stanton, later to become president of CBS, had come up with a gadget they nicknamed "Little Annie," which could instantaneously and continuously record audience likes and dislikes.[94] (It was an early version of that staple of instant polls and focus groups, the dials that a viewer can turn from positive to negative to mirror their reaction.)

The flow of data that "Little Annie" and other such methodologies provided was, to Adorno, misleadingly, dangerously context-free. One of the main underpinnings of the critical theory that he and Horkheimer and the Institute for Social Research had developed was that reactions *always* have a social context—in fact, it is the very context of society itself that most reveals its own critique. To regard any data, any reaction, any cultural artifact as somehow separable from the society that produced it was liable to blind one to the ways in which society shapes artifacts and reactions in order to reinforce its own status quo.

No status quo was excepted. The Institute and its researchers were Marxists, but Marxists who were dismayed at the way Marxism had been hijacked and bureaucratized in order to lend unqualified support to this or that Communist movement. Adorno's resistance toward such sloganeering would resurface in the late 1960s, after he had returned to Germany, after he had resumed his teaching career, his classrooms full of young radicals. But when those radicals became *soixante-huit* would-be revolutionaries, Adorno drew back, censuring their reliance on revolutionary formula rather than critical engagement. His lectures were disrupted by demonstrations; he died during a Swiss retreat, taken after canceling the year's remaining classes. His last letter was to his Institute colleague, Herbert Marcuse, who had supported the student uprisings. "I am the last person to underestimate the merits of the student movement," Adorno wrote. "But it contains a grain of insanity in which a future totalitarianism is implicit."[95]

HE WAS BORN Theodor Wiesengrund, but, around the time of his emigration to America, settled instead on Adorno, his mother's maiden name. (For a time, he also wrote reviews under the name "Hektor Rottweiler.")[96] His father was a well-to-do assimilated Jew, carrying on the family wine trade; his mother was an opera singer of Corsican ancestry and Catholic faith. Theodor enjoyed a fairy-tale childhood, if the fairy tale had been written by a German intellectual. The philosopher Siegfried Kracauer was a family friend; every week they would read Kant, Theodor becoming attuned to "the play of forces at work under the surface of every closed doctrine."[97] He learned the canon of classical music by playing piano duets with his aunt. He was precocious, sheltered, and spoiled. A friend remembered Adorno enjoying "an existence you just had to love—if you were not dying with jealousy of this beautiful, protected life."[98]

Adorno was probably the most accomplished musician to ever become a professional philosopher. He was welcomed into the circle of the Second Viennese School, studying piano with Eduard Steuermann, and composition with Alban Berg; the latter relationship was particularly close, with Berg extolling Adorno's music to Schoenberg while Adorno helped facilitate Berg's love affair with Hanna Fuchs-Robettin.[99] Adorno's music, in the pre-dodecaphonic, freely atonal expressionist style, shows a talent and technique far beyond mere dilettantism. In the early 1930s, he began his most ambitious work, an opera based on Mark Twain's *Tom Sawyer* called *Das Schatz der Indianer-Joe* (*The Treasure of Indian Joe*). The subject might seem a strange fit, but Adorno's libretto brought out themes of fear and conformity lurking within Twain's tale:

[*Huck and Tom*]	A man has died
	Two saw it happen
	All are guilty.
With emphasis	As long as they don't talk.[100]

But the increasing uncertainty of his status in Germany, not to mention the unenthusiastic response of his friend and fellow cultural critic Walter Benjamin, led Adorno to abandon the project after only two numbers.

Adorno focused on his other vocation, philosophy. As might be expected from his childhood weekends, Adorno's philosophy was strongly shaped by the German Idealists, by Kant and, especially, Hegel. But Adorno was wary of the implications of Hegel's dialectic, the way it seemed to be led by the nose toward the Absolute by subjective thought—for Adorno, a subjective point of view didn't exist outside of the objective society that shaped it. This was not simply metaphysical hair-splitting; it was, for Adorno, at the core of why the Enlightenment-born Western world had not only not prevented suffering, but had produced suffering on an unprecedented level. The Idealistic focus on subjectivity had missed the objective suffering happening all around it.

Adorno instead would call for a "negative dialectic," one that would put asunder the illusory unities that subjective thought imposes on the objective world—"to break the compulsion to achieve identity, and to break it by means of the energy

stored up in that compulsion and congealed in its objectifica-
tions."[101] In the words of one of Adorno's best interpreters, Robert Hullot-Kentor: "What Adorno wanted to comprehend was
the capacity of thought—of identity itself—to cause reality to
break in on the mind that masters it."[102] Adorno's thought used
contradiction—often self-contradiction—to jostle reason out of
its subjective biases. The result is his difficult, reflexive, fragmentary writing style—there is, as Hullot-Kentor puts it, "the
sense, on entering any one of Adorno's essays, that even in their
very first words one has already arrived too late to find out for
sure what any of the concepts mean."[103] But better that than the
false assimilation of the concepts into a point of view unaware
of its own distortions.

ODDLY ENOUGH, a good place to start to understand Adorno's
perception of Beethoven is in his analysis of another type of
music, an analysis that Adorno, in many ways, got remarkably
wrong. Adorno's writings on jazz are infamous. In his 1936 essay
"Über Jazz" (originally published under the "Hektor Rottweiler"
byline), he rehearsed a critique that he never abandoned: jazz
was mechanical, rigid music, repackaging an illusion of freedom in such a way that only inculcated the conformity necessary
for a capitalist, industrial society to maintain the status quo. Any
sensation of freedom in jazz is just a veneer, detached from the
underlying structure, a structure that encourages obedience,
not rebellion.

Beethoven's syncopation had been "the expression of an accumulated subjective force which directed itself against authority until it had produced a new law out of itself."[104] But in jazz,
"the objective sound" (the harmonic and rhythmic repetition)
"is embellished by a subjective expression" (the misdirections
of solos, syncopation, &c.) "which is unable to dominate it and
therefore exerts a fundamentally ridiculous and heart-rending

effect." The improvisatory elements of jazz are, thus, just sentimental window dressing, a halfhearted revolt "against a collective power which it itself is; for this reason its revolt seems ridiculous and is beaten down by the drum just as syncopation is by the beat."[105]

The standard backlash against Adorno's jazz writing was that he was simply an insufferable elitist, misreading jazz in order to preserve "high" culture. (As one critic puts it: "The aesthetic net must not be cast too wide lest it drag up trash."[106]) But to classify Adorno's criticism as mere snobbery is a misreading as well: Adorno had some regard for the low end of the high-low cultural continuum. In his book on film music, written with fellow émigré Hanns Eisler, Adorno allowed that movies "such as 'westerns' or gangster and horror pictures often are in a certain way superior to pretentious grade-A films."[107] In *Dialectic of Enlightenment*, Adorno and Horkheimer scolded the "culture industry" for its antipathy to difference, no matter the provenance: "The eccentricity of the circus, peepshow, and brothel is as embarrassing to it as that of Schönberg."[108] Even cartoons are made to converge on respectability—browbeaten into insisting on "the very ideology which enslaves them," audiences end up favoring the properly punished troublemaking of Donald Duck over the consequence-free hedonism of Betty Boop.[109]

In other words, Adorno's problem with jazz is not that it isn't high culture—it's that it is neither high-culture *nor low-culture* enough to elude the culture industry. Only art at the extremes of the high-low continuum could avoid being appropriated: high art because it was transcendent, low art because it was anarchic. Middlebrow culture was Adorno's real target—all the aura of art, but none of its threat to order. Both critics and apologists have noted that Adorno's jazz analyses would better correspond to light jazz, "sweet" jazz, the Paul-Whiteman-like arrangements that would have been prevalent on the radio, if not in those clubs where "hot" jazz reigned. Conflating the styles made hash of Adorno's musicology. But maybe that was part of his point: jazz had been fairly easily defanged for mass consumption. (Ralph Ellison had *Invisible Man*'s narrator imagine re-creating jazz's potency in a way reminiscent of Stefan Wolpe's Dada experiments with the Fifth: "I'd like to hear five recordings of Louis Armstrong playing 'What Did I Do to Be So Black and Blue'—all at the same time."[110])

It is no wonder that it was in America, where the appropriation of culture was conspicuous, even celebrated, that Adorno was most primed to dialectically expose it, and not just in jazz and popular music. Adorno's *Philosophy of New Music,* which warns of the fetishizing nature of serialism, dates from his exile, as does his and Horkheimer's *Dialectic of Enlightenment,* which took Western rationality to similar task.

But it was also in America that Adorno's fascination with Beethoven crystallized into a book—one he never finished.[111] The surviving fragments of the project are a particularly diffuse constellation; one nevertheless can perceive Adorno trying to carve out space for the exceptional nature of Beethoven's music.

THE FRAGMENTATION of the Fifth was, for Adorno, the mechanism by which mass media and mass culture dragged Beethoven toward middlebrow status. "Radio symphonies," as Adorno called them—an on-air mediation of the canon so thoroughgoing that it created a new genre—promoted a kind of music-as-trivia-answer, substituting recognition for comprehension, encouraged hearing a part to listening to the whole. It was the difference between musical understanding and music appreciation.

In 1954, the Book-of-the-Month Club introduced "Music-Appreciation Records," in which recordings of the standard repertoire were backed with spoken analysis and musical examples, "to help you understand music better and enjoy it more."[112] The free, no-obligation tryout record was Beethoven's Fifth: "You have heard this great work countless times—what have you heard in it? And what may you have failed to hear?" Notice the aim of the two-pronged sales pitch—inducing anxiety that one's individual experience both requires re-categorization (*what have you heard?*), and is still somehow lacking in comparison with majority opinion (*what may you have failed to hear?*).

Such pressure to conform was at the heart of Adorno's quarrel with mass media over music, no matter how altruistic mass media's intent. Adorno once wrote a scathing analysis of NBC's long-running *Music Appreciation Hour,* a show aimed at schoolchildren, hosted and conducted by Walter Damrosch. The show's procedure was familiar—break a symphony down into its constituent themes, and point out structural signposts. But such "atomistic listening," in Adorno's reckoning, was a deliberate alienation from music's power. "While apparently urging recognition in order to help people to 'enjoy' music, the Music Appreciation Hour actually encourages enjoyment, not of the music itself, but *of the awareness that one knows music.*"[113] Understanding, as Adorno posits it—what he calls a "life-relationship" with music—is open-ended and individual, and thus far too inefficient for mass media, which relies on the mere illusion of an individual relationship. Recognition, though, is instant gratification; not everyone can experience the Fifth as transcendent, but everyone can recognize when the main theme comes back. It is in such recognition that the media advances its own interests over that of Beethoven's:

Here lies the connection between the categories of consumer goods, particularly commercial entertainment, and the sort of practical aesthetics advocated by the Hour. Something must be pleasing and worth its money to be admitted to the market. On the contrary, the work of art really raises postulates of its own, and it is more essential

for the listener to please the Beethoven symphony than for
the Beethoven symphony to please the listener.[114]

Reducing the Fifth to a parade of themes subordinates
it by substituting a kind of musical score-keeping for a true
engagement with the musical whole. It was the same sort of
bait-and-switch that Adorno sensed in one of Walter Benjamin's
critical experiments: Benjamin had attempted an analysis of
Baudelaire consisting solely of juxtaposed quotations of Baudelaire's own writings, a mosaic list that would, in theory, produce
a self-evident argument. Adorno chided him: "You supersti-
tiously attribute to material enumeration a power of illumina-
tion that is never kept."[115]

So what? The full Fifth would still remain, available to those
who, instinctively or consciously, rejected its division into easily
digestible parts. The problem, for Adorno, is that by the time
we would know enough to reject such hearing, the damage is
already done—and it has flipped Beethoven's philosophical content upside-down, reversed the music's dialectic. And it is in that
dialectic that Beethoven's true importance lies. The material
enumeration of Beethoven's symphonies, privileging themes
over the whole, irresponsibly makes something out of what
Adorno perceives as the core of Beethoven's music: nothing.

"IN BEETHOVEN everything can become anything, because it 'is'
nothing," Adorno wrote.[116] And the "nothing" Adorno is referring to is not just the silence Beethoven's music arises out of, but
the themes themselves, their brevity, their circumscribed sim-
plicity. Adorno talks of "the nothing of the first bars"[117] of the
Fifth, of how such themes are "formulas of tonality, reduced to
nothingness as things of their own."[118]

The idea connects Beethoven directly to the German idealists.
"Being is indeed nothing at all," Hegel said, but "within becom-

ing, being is no longer simply being; and nothing, through its oneness with being, is no longer simply nothing."[119] Beethoven's music acts out this genesis: the "nothing" of his themes is transformed into being by the way Beethoven uses the themes to build his musical forms. The theme of the Fifth is nothing by itself; the whole symphony—"not so much the production of forms, as their reproduction out of freedom"[120]—brings the theme into union with its being through the process of its becoming.

Freedom is, for Adorno, the key to Beethoven's music, a freedom both philosophically deep and elemental. Hegel, remember, treated such aspects of music as an analogy to the mechanism of the intellect. For Adorno, it was something more. Musicologist Daniel P. K. Chua puts it this way:

> [I]t is precisely what Adorno calls the "nullity of the particular" that allows the symphonic will to determine the material in any way it chooses; the will is poised at the point of adequation, totally indifferent to the empty plenitude of the material; the elements merely form a vacuum for the frictionless activity of freedom.[121]

In the "empty plenitude" is endless possibility. Everything can become anything: absolute freedom.

Thus, in Beethoven's music, German idealism is taken back from Hegel's circumspect complexities to its revolutionary origins. Adorno's Beethoven, in fact, echoes one of Hegel's earliest writings, a fragmentary note, sometimes attributed to Friedrich Hölderlin, the so-called "Oldest Programme for a System of German Idealism"—probably a memorandum of student conversations with Hölderlin and Schiller: "The first idea is, of course, the representation *of myself as* an absolutely free being. With this free, self-conscious being a whole *world* comes into existence—out of nothing—the only true and conceivable *creation from nothing*." The "Programme" goes on to advocate enlightened anarchy. "We must thus also progress beyond the state" to "absolute freedom of all spirits, who carry the intelligible world in themselves and may seek neither god nor immortality *outside of themselves.*"[122]

This foreshadows the words of a fictional Adorno, the Devil in Thomas Mann's novel *Doctor Faustus,* just before he transforms into a very Adorno-like manifestation: "Take Beethoven's notebooks. There is no thematic conception there as God gave it. He remoulds it and adds 'Meilleur' "[123]—("better"). (Adorno and Mann, fellow temporary Californians, had discussed music as the book was being written.) Where the fictional Adorno had Beethoven improving on God, the real Adorno had him improve on society—again, in terms that echo the "Oldest Programme":

> Let us reflect on Beethoven. If he is the musical prototype of the revolutionary bourgeoisie, he is at the same time the prototype of a music that has escaped from its social tutelage and is esthetically fully autonomous, a servant no longer. . . . The central categories of artistic construction can be translated into social ones. . . . It is in fitting together under their own law, as becoming, negating, confirming themselves and the whole without looking outward, that [Beethoven's] movements come to resemble the world whose forces move them; they do not do it by imitating that world. [124]

Beethoven's music has progressed beyond the state—"its social tutelage"—and carries the intelligible world in itself.

But Beethoven's music is, nevertheless, in the world, the historical world, and that is where the freedom at its core becomes troublesome. "[T]he works themselves are not self-sufficient, are not indifferent toward the time," Adorno warned. "Only because they transform themselves historically, unfold and wither in time; because their own truth-content is historical and not a pure essence, are they so susceptible to that which is allegedly inflicted on them from outside."[125] This is why Adorno so insistently harangued against their fragmentation. Hearing the Fifth as quotations from the Fifth was not just a trivializing annoyance but struck directly at the heart of Beethoven's power to resist appropriation. It asserted something-ness for Beethoven's themes while denying them their Hegelian becoming. It turned the music's absolute freedom into a liability.

"The primal cells in Beethoven are nothing *in themselves*, mere concentrates of the tonal idiom to which *only the symphony* lends voice," Adorno warned. "Torn from their context, their artful irrelevance becomes the commonplace which, as the initial motif of the Fifth, was to be exploited up to the hilt by international patriotism."[126] The war conveniently acted out a negative dialectic on this point: in his notes for his Beethoven book, Adorno saved a newspaper cutting, an Associated Press report, dateline Bonn, March 10, 1945:

> The birthplace of the composer Ludwig van Beethoven, the opening notes of whose Fifth Symphony have been used by the Allies as a symbol for victory, was virtually destroyed in the fight for this old university city.[127]

SINCE HIS DEATH, in 1969, Adorno's reputation has waxed and waned—mostly the latter. The complexity of his writing was a persistent barrier. His analysis of the way societies leveraged enjoyment to maintain control was all too easily read as an indictment of enjoyment itself. His German Idealist lineage did not endear him to the rising post-modernist school. His Marxism, however idiosyncratic, eroded his prestige as international Communism collapsed under the weight of its own corruption.

Nevertheless, there is at least one aspect of Adorno that deserves a continuing place in human thought: his optimism.

It is odd to think of Adorno, the virtuoso of the negative dialectic, the scold who insisted on the objectivity of suffering, as an optimist, but he was. There is a transcript of a conversation between Adorno and Horkheimer in which Adorno defends himself from a criticism that his ideas are naïve:

> ADORNO: . . . Is not this criticism already an admission that one no longer believes in happiness? Is not [my] naïveté a higher form of knowledge than the unnaïve knowledge of analysis?
> HORKHEIMER: I have not given up the claim to happiness, but I do not believe in happiness. Whoever really believes in happiness is in the worst sense naïve.
> ADORNO: We must be at once more naïve and much less naïve.[128]

It was this optimism that led Adorno back to Beethoven again and again: he heard in the music a way past the modern world—his modern world—of war and exile and totalitarianism. Beethoven achieved in music what the world forever tries and fails to achieve: the better society. "[T]his is imprinted in Beethoven's music, the sublime music, as a trait of esthetic untruth: by its power, his successful work of art posits the real success of what was in reality a failure."[129] And: "That Beethoven never goes out of date is connected, perhaps, to the fact that reality has not yet caught up with his music."[130]

That is itself an optimistic statement—one might just as plausibly say that reality has caught up with the Fifth all too well, forever smudging it with two centuries of interpretive fingerprints. The list of those who have tried to claim it—revolutionaries and reactionaries, Hegelians both Right and Left, radical Transcendentalists and proper Victorians, the Nazis and the Allies—is forbiddingly long and frequently contradictory. But, if we believe

Adorno, it is in contradiction that reality can again break into the mind. Adorno's dialectic puts the lie to any single reading of the Fifth by allowing the measure of all of them—the sheer number of attempted appropriations is a testament to the persistent power of Beethoven's reality.

Can that reality break through again? "The first bars of the Fifth Symphony, properly performed," Adorno insisted, "must be rendered with the character of a thesis, as if they were a free act over which no material has precedence."[131] Even after all the intrusions of poetics, programs, sentiment, and technology, he thought it could still be done. To know what the Fifth has been burdened with is to know what to clear away. You have to start somewhere.

Epilogue

THE PREMIERE, incidentally, was something of a disaster. The most famous account of the concert comes from Johann Friedrich Reichardt, a composer and writer who lived a virtual summation of eighteenth- to nineteenth-century European history. As a teenager, he was encouraged to study philosophy by Immanuel Kant; as a composer, he set texts and libretti by Goethe, and was also friends with Herder and Schiller. Achim von Arnim and Clemens Brentano (Bettina von Arnim's husband and brother, respectively) dedicated their famous collection of German folk poems, *Des Knaben Wunderhorn*, to Reichardt (although Brentano later soured on Reichardt, on account of his incessant social climbing and gossiping).[1] He supported the French Revolution (for which he was fired) before turning against Napoleon (for which he was exiled).

Toward the end of his life, Reichardt was trying to make a career in Vienna; on December 22, 1808, he found himself sitting in the box of Prince Lobkowitz, Beethoven's patron, at the Theater-an-der-Wien. "There we continued, in the bitterest cold, too, from half past six to half past ten," he recalled, "and experienced the truth that one can easily have too much of a good thing—and still more of a loud."[2] The concert included:

the Sixth Symphony;

the concert aria "Ah! Perfido";

273

the "Gloria" from the Mass in C Major, op. 86;

the Fourth Piano Concerto, with composer at the
    keyboard;

the Fifth Symphony;

the "Sanctus" from the Mass in C Major;

a piano improvisation;

and, finally, the Choral Fantasy for piano, orchestra, and
    chorus, op. 80.

At one point, Beethoven had considered ending the concert
with the Fifth, but, in the words of Alexander Thayer, "to defer
that work until the close was to incur the risk of endangering
its effect by presenting it to an audience too weary for the close
attention needful on first hearing to its fair comprehension and
appreciation."[3] Beethoven's response to that dilemma was to
make the concert longer: the Choral Fantasy was a last-minute
addition, written for the concert.

Reichardt enjoyed the Fourth Piano Concerto, especially the
slow movement; Beethoven "sang on his instrument with deep
melancholy feeling." But as for the Fifth:

A large, very elaborate, too long symphony. A gentleman
next to us assured us that, at the rehearsal, he had seen
that the violoncello part, which was very busy, alone covered thirty or forty pages.[4]

Reichardt nevertheless allowed that music copyists were
doubtless as skilled as their legal counterparts in stretching out
their work and boosting their per-page fees. And even after four
hours of difficult music in a freezing hall, Reichardt was sym-

pathetic: "Poor Beethoven, who from this, his own concert, was having the first and only scant profit that he could find in a whole year, had found in the rehearsals and performance a lot of opposition and almost no support."[5]

The concert, advertised as a "musical *Akademie*," was organized by Beethoven himself. The evening had been at least two years in the making: in order to reserve the space, Beethoven needed the permission of Joseph Hartl, the Viennese Court Councillor in charge of the city's theaters. Hartl also was in charge of Vienna's public charities, and used access to the theaters as bait in order to lure performers for benefit concerts. Beethoven hated him. In one letter, he complained of having to repeatedly wait on Hartl in order to press his request for an *Akademie*: "I am so annoyed that all I desire is to be a bear so that as often as I were to lift my paw I could knock down some so-called great ———ass."[6]

Beethoven nonetheless lent his talents and compositions to three charity concerts between 1807 and 1808, the last coming on November 15 of that year. (November 15 is the feast-day of Leopold, the patron saint of Vienna.) During rehearsals for this concert, Beethoven somehow enraged the players; according to Joseph Röckel (father of August, who plotted revolution in Dresden with Richard Wagner), the breaking point was a rehearsal where Beethoven pounded with such ferocity that he knocked the candles from the piano. Whatever the cause, the players refused to continue unless Beethoven was banished from the hall; notes were relayed back and forth from rehearsals to composer via the concertmasters.

Such was the atmosphere in which November's concert proceeded, and it hardly bode well for Beethoven's own concert a month later, which would necessitate drawing on the same pool of musicians. To make matters worse, another benefit concert, this one benefiting the Widows and Orphans Fund, was also scheduled for December 22. In a letter to the publishers Breitkopf and Härtel, Beethoven sensed a conspiracy, led by his onetime teacher:

> The promoters of the concert for the widows, out of hatred for me, Herr Salieri being my most active opponent, played me a horrible trick. They threatened to expel any musician belonging to their company who would play for my benefit—[7]

If the accusation was not mere paranoia, it would give Salieri the distinction of having intrigued against both Mozart and Beethoven.

Beethoven was writing to Breitkopf and Härtel because he had sold them the Fifth Symphony. It was the second time he had sold it. The symphony had originally been commissioned by Franz von Oppersdorff, a Silesian count wealthy enough to maintain his own private orchestra. For 500 florins, Count Oppersdorff had received the Fourth Symphony—the score along with exclusive rights to it for six months—and liked it so much that he commissioned another, for another 500 florins. However, after collecting 350 of those florins, Beethoven wrote to the Count, "You will look at me in a false light, but necessity compelled me to sell to someone else the symphony which was written for you and another as well"—the Fifth and the Sixth, for which Beethoven had already been negotiating with Breitkopf and Härtel for some months.[8]

It was a good thing Beethoven had gotten 350 florins out of the Count, as he came out on the short end of the negotiations with Breitkopf and Härtel. After initially proposing a price of 900 florins for "two symphonies, a Mass [in C major], and a sonata for pianoforte and violoncello [op. 69]," Beethoven eventually settled for 600 florins, in return for "two symphonies, a sonata with violoncello obbligato, two trios for pianoforte, violin and violoncello (since such trios are now rather scarce), or, instead of these last two trios, a symphony"—plus the Mass for free. ("I pay attention not only to what is profitable but also to what brings honour and glory," Beethoven explained, though he may also have felt the need to repair his ego over the Mass, which its dedicatee, Prince Nikolaus Esterházy II, had criticized.)[9]

So Beethoven went into his *Akademie* with too much music, surly musicians, and the pressure to turn a profit. The result was about as one would expect. The audience grew restless. The singers were noticeably shivering in the winter cold. The Choral Fantasy ran off the rails in performance, and Beethoven was forced to stop the orchestra and start over.

Still, Beethoven convinced himself that the concert had gone over well—"the public nevertheless applauded the whole performance with enthusiasm"—though he expected the worst from the critics. "[S]cribblers in Vienna will certainly not fail to send again to the Musikalische Zeitung some wretched stuff directed against me," he predicted.[10]

The *Allgemeine musikalische Zeitung*, however, perhaps having caught some glimpse of the Fifth Symphony's future all-purpose ubiquity, opted for discretion.

[This] new, grand symphony by Beethoven . . . in its fashion, in accordance both with the ideas and with their treatment, once again stands so much apart from all others that even the trained listener must hear it several times before he can make it his own and arrive at a definite opinion.[11]

APPENDIX: Eight Interesting Recordings

BERLIN PHILHARMONIC
Arthur Nikisch, conductor
(HMV 040784/91, recorded 1913)

Originally released on eight single-side 78 rpm discs (and now available on multiple CD transfers), Nikisch's complete Fifth is a remarkable glimpse of Romantic extravagance, alternating between intemperate languor and impetuosity. Phrases ebb and flow; Nikisch repeatedly draws out the tempo to an organ-like sustain and then slams on the gas. More indulgence than modern ears might be accustomed to, but more flair, too.

BERLIN PHILHARMONIC
Wilhelm Furtwängler, conductor
(recorded June 30, 1943)

Furtwängler's live, wartime recording of the Fifth (available on at least six different labels) is heightened on so many levels that even Furtwängler's other recordings of the symphony don't quite match its overwhelming impact. The fervency of the interpretation, the brilliance of the playing, and the ominous shadow of the Third Reich troubling every note: the struggle between Beethoven's music and the darkest impulses of humanity is palpable. (Arturo Toscanini's VE-day performance with the NBC Philharmonic is also available, on Music & Arts 753: disciplined and astonishingly, relentlessly fast—the Toscanini style at its most zealous.)

GLENN GOULD
piano
(Columbia MS 7095, 1968)

Gould revived Franz Liszt's piano solo transcription of the Fifth as, maybe, a wry play on of his reputation as a hermit, but the result is thrilling and surprising. The first movement has hammered force, Gould reveling in the heavy crush of the piano's bass, while his eccentric exaltation comes to the fore in the Andante: he takes a tempo far slower than any orchestra could ever hope to sustain, and both he and we get wondrously lost in it. Worth seeking out on LP for Gould's hilarious parody-review liner notes.

THE NEW PHILHARMONIA ORCHESTRA
Pierre Boulez, conductor
(Columbia M 30085, 1970)

To hear Boulez's infamous reading of the Fifth requires a bit of searching; it was left out of Sony Classical's "Pierre Boulez Edition" of reissues (although a CD reissue was released in Japan). Often criticized as temperamentally slow and dryly unidiomatic, Boulez's long march through the Fifth nonetheless uncovers new shadings, a modern reading full of modern bleakness, a giant machine both inexorable and imprisoning.

VIENNA PHILHARMONIC
Carlos Kleiber, conductor
(Deutsche Grammophon 2530-518, 1975)

For many years, this was considered the gold standard of the Fifth on record, and it's not hard to hear why: the playing is gorgeously plush, the reading is full of charging momentum. If Beethoven's Fifth were the golden age of luxury jet travel, this is what it would sound like, hurtling forth in grand style.

ORCHESTRE RÉVOLUTIONNAIRE ET ROMANTIQUE
John Eliot Gardiner, conductor
(Archiv 447062, 1995)

Gardiner founded this group to explore the musical echoes of the French Revolution on period instruments; their Fifth is one of the best of the historically informed performances, being dedicated to speed, élan, and the pursuit of unabashed rabble-rousing. As a description of the Fifth, "revolutionary" has become a bland commonplace, but Gardiner and his cadres make you want to go out and guillotine an aristocrat.

ENSEMBLE MODERN
Peter Eötvös, conductor
(BMC Records CD 063, 2001)

A recording that ropes the microphone into its conspiracy; Eötvös and the chamber-sized Ensemble Modern, new-music specialists, amplify every instrument in close-up, then remix and balance the sound into a coordinated assault. The rock-style sonic punch is matched by the interpretation, lean and solidly muscular.

THE PORTSMOUTH SINFONIA
on The Portsmouth Sinfonia Plays the Popular Classics
(Columbia KC 33049, 1973)

Formed by students at England's Portsmouth School of Art in 1970, spearheaded by the experimental composer Gavin Bryars, the Sinfonia eschewed technical skill: members were either non-musicians or musicians playing unfamiliar instruments. Their recording of the Fifth—a medley of all four movements, in 1-4-2-3 order—is a glorious mess of wrong notes, fudged rhythms, and untrammeled enthusiasm. That it is still recognizably the Fifth is part of the cheeky point.

Acknowledgments

The book was Marty Asher's idea, and he shepherded it through with enthusiasm and editorial focus. Andrew Carlson and Jeff Alexander conscientiously and thoughtfully brought the manuscript through the final stages of publication. Alex Ross vouched for the author, and vouchsafed the author by generously reviewing drafts of the book, as did Jeremy Eichler, Marti Epstein, Katie Hamill, Phyllis Hoffman, Robert Hoffman, Rebecca Hunt, Ethan Iverson, Mark Meyer, and Jack Miller; any remaining errors—factual, interpretive, or stylistic—are mine alone. Moe distracted the author into crucial, enforced, procrastinatory reflection.

Lucy Kim made the entire book possible, just as she has made possible every other even remotely worthwhile thing I have ever done. To journey with someone of such beauty, discernment, and resilience is a joy that the word "love" can only begin to encompass.

Framingham, Massachusetts
March 4, 2012

Notes

PREFACE

1. Jeph Jacques, "Number 1336: Canathesia," *Questionable Content*, http://
questionablecontent.net/view.php?comic=1336.
2. Robert Haven Schauffler, *Beethoven: The Man Who Freed Music* (New York:
Tudor Publishing Co., 1944), p. 217.
3. According to the poet Christoph Kuffner. See Alexander Wheelock
Thayer, *Thayer's Life of Beethoven*, Elliot Forbes, ed. (Princeton University
Press, 1967), p. 674. (Hereafter "Thayer-Forbes.")
4. James F. Green, "Beethoven's Fifth Symphony: A Forgotten Anecdote Discovered," *The Beethoven Journal*, 25, no. 1 (Summer 2010): 36–37. Upon
the death of Albert, King of Saxony, in 1902, a correspondent to *The Spectator* recalled the ruler telling a similar story: "Beethoven, said the King,
was once asked by a profound thinker the 'meaning' of the mysterious
opening notes of the C Minor Symphony. The composer replied in a dras-
tic German phrase (which has its equivalent in other languages) whose
four monosyllables fitted the four quavers, and, at the same time, were a
suitable reply to an asinine question." ("X.Y.Z.," "The King of Saxony. [To
the editor of the 'Spectator.']" *The Spectator* [London], no. 3861 [June 28,
1902]: 1005–6.)

CHAPTER 1. Revolutions

1. David Cairns, *Berlioz: Volume One: The Making of an Artist 1803–1832* (University of California Press, 2000), p. 268.
2. Carl Woideck, *Charlie Parker: His Music and Life* (University of Michigan
Press, 1998), p. 205.
3. Austin Clarkson, "Lecture on Dada by Stefan Wolpe," *The Musical Quarterly*
72, no. 2 (1986): 213–14.
4. See, most notably, Edward T. Cone, *Musical Form and Musical Performance*
(New York: W. W. Norton & Co., 1968), pp. 11–31.
5. See, for example, Nicky Lossoff, "Silent Music and the Eternal Silence," in
Silence, Music, Silent Music, Nicky Lossoff and Jenny Doctor, eds. (Aldershot:
Ashgate, 2007), pp. 205–22.
6. Jacques Derrida, *The Truth in Painting*, Geoffrey Bennington and Ian
Macleod, trans. (University of Chicago Press, 1987), p. 61. See also

Robin Marriner, "Derrida and the *Parergon*," in Paul Smith and Carolyn Wilde, eds., *A Companion to Art Theory* (Oxford: Blackwell, 2002), 349–59. For another musical view, see Richard C. Littlefield, "The Silence of the Frames," *Music Theory Online* 2.1 (1996), http://mto.societymusic theory.org/issues/mto.96.2.1/mto.96.2.1.littlefield.html. Critic Winthrop Sargeant told this story: "A friend of mine took a Buddhist monk to hear the Boston Symphony perform Beethoven's Fifth Symphony. His comment was 'Not enough silence!'" Sargeant, "Musical Events," *The New Yorker* 47, no. 52 [February 12, 1972]: 73.

7. Wesley Wehr, *The Eighth Lively Art: Conversations with Painters, Poets, Musicians, & the Wicked Witch of the West* (University of Washington Press, 2000), p. 236.

8. See Eric Johnson, "A Composer's Vision: Photographs by Ernest Bloch," *Aperture* 16, no. 3 (Nov. 1972).

9. Richard Wagner, *On Conducting (Ueber das Dirigiren)*, Edward Dannreuther, trans. (London: William Reeves, 1887), p. 30.

10. Felix Weingartner, *On the Performance of Beethoven's Symphonies*, Jessie Crosland, trans. (London: Breitkopf und Härtel, 1907), p. 61.

11. Norman Del Mar, *Conducting Beethoven. Volume I: The Symphonies* (Oxford: Clarendon Press, 1992), p. 71.

12. Gunther Schuller, *The Compleat Conductor* (Oxford University Press, 1998), p. 119.

13. Del Mar, *Conducting Beethoven*, p. 74.

14. Emily Anderson, ed. *The Letters of Beethoven, Collected, Translated and Edited with an Introduction, Appendixes, Notes and Indexes* (New York: St. Martin's Press, 1961), vol. 1, p. 217.

15. Ibid., p. 60.

16. Ibid., p. 217.

17. Quoted in Thayer-Forbes, p. 373.

18. Ibid., p. 358.

19. Maynard Solomon, *Beethoven Essays* (Harvard University Press, 1990), p. 93.

20. A. McCombe et al., "Guidelines for the Grading of Tinnitus Severity, the Results of a Working Group Commissioned by the British Association of Otolaryngologists, Head and Neck Surgeons, 1999," *Clinical Otolaryngology & Applied Sciences* 26, no. 5 (Oct. 2001): 388–93.

21. [Alexander Wheelock Thayer], "From My Diary. No. XVI," *Dwight's Journal of Music*, 2, no. 19 (Feb. 12, 1853): 149.

22. Annette Maria DiMedeo, *Frances McCollin: Her Life and Music* (Lanham, MD: Rowman & Littlefield, 1990), p. 5.

23. Alessandra Comini, *The Changing Image of Beethoven, A Study in Mythmaking* (Santa Fe, NM: Sunstone Press, 2008), p. 160.

24. William McGuffey, *McGuffey's Fifth Eclectic Reader* (American Book Co., 1879), p. 303. *The Crofton Boys* was first published in 1842, only fifteen years after Beethoven's death, making Hugh's mother pretty culturally hip for a London druggist's wife. Martineau was a pioneering journalist and

sociologist who advocated for feminism, abolitionism, and the positivist theories of August Comte, whose popular historical "law of three stages" (theocratic, metaphysical, scientific) was another manifestation of the nineteenth-century fetish for three-part intellectual structures that also gave us the early-middle-late division of Beethoven's career.

25. For example, on page 27 of Jack Mingo and Erin Barrett's *Just Curious About History, Jeeves* (New York: Simon & Schuster, 2002), a collection of historical trivia: "[B]y the time [Beethoven] reached his early thirties his hearing was gone, and he could no longer play the piano properly." In a teaching guide called *Breaking Away from the Textbook: The Enlightenment through the 20th Century* (by Ron H. Pahl [Lanham, MD: R&L Education, 2002], p. 90), one reads that "[Beethoven] called himself a 'tone poet' and he was deaf by the time he was thirty, but that did not stop him from reinventing music." Another educational workbook, *Editing Skills: Practical Activities Using Text Types, Ages 11+* (Balcatta, Australia: R.I.C. Publications, 2005, p. 83), designed to train students to spot errors of spelling and grammar, reiterates the trope in a convincingly imitated semiliterate style: "By the age of 30, Beethoven was profowndly deaf yet he still managed to compose brilliant music examples of these works are the symphones, 'Eroica' and 'Pastoral.'"

26. *Ludwig van Beethovens Konversationshefte*, Band 9, Grita Herre, ed. (VEB Deutscher Verlag für Musik Leipzig, 1988), pp. 290–91.

27. Owen Jander, "'Let Your Deafness No Longer Be a Secret—Even In Art': Self-Portraiture and the Third Movement of the C-Minor Symphony," *The Beethoven Journal* 8 (2000): 25.

28. Quoted in Rita Steblin, *A History of Key Characteristics in the Eighteenth and Early Nineteenth Centuries* (University of Rochester Press, 2002), p. 111.

29. Ibid., p. 231.

30. Ibid.

31. Thayer-Forbes, p. 209.

32. E. T. A. Hoffmann, "Review," in Wayne M. Senner, translator, and Robin Wallace and William Meredith, editors. *The Critical Reception of Beethoven's Compositions by His German Contemporaries*, 2 vols. (University of Nebraska Press, 1999 [vol. 1], 2001 [vol. 2]), vol. 2, p. 98.

33. See Michael C. Tusa, "Beethoven's 'C-minor Mood,' Some Thoughts on the Structural Implications of Key Choice," *Beethoven Forum* 2 (1993): 6–10.

34. Leonard Bernstein, *The Joy of Music* (New York: Simon and Schuster, 1959), p. 89.

35. Steblin, *A History of Key Characteristics*, pp. 232–33.

36. See Konrad Ulrich, "Mozart's Sketches," *Early Music* 20, no. 1 (Feb., 1992), for a useful overview.

37. The best survey of Landsberg 6 is Rachel W. Wade, "Beethoven's *Eroica* Sketchbook," *Fontes artis musicae* XXIV, no. 4 (Oct.-Dec. 1977): 254–90. Dating the sketches can be a tricky business, but the presence of early sketches for *Fidelio*—which Beethoven first turned his attention to at the end of

1803—makes early 1804 a plausible date for the sketches of the Fifth. See also the detailed discussion of the sketchbook in Douglas Johnson, et al., *The Beethoven Sketchbooks* (University of California Press, 1985), pp. 137–45.

38. The catalog of Landsberg's Beethoven collection is reproduced in Johnson et al., *The Beethoven Sketchbooks*, p. 32.

39. See Gustav Nottebohm, *Ein Skizzenbuch von Beethoven aus dem Jahre 1803* (Leipzig: Breitkopf und Härtel, 1880), pp. 70–71.

40. Robert Haven Schauffler, *The Unknown Brahms* (New York: Dodd, Mead and Company, 1933), pp. 139–40. Schauffler's musical biographies can sometimes rival Schindler for engendering skepticism, but here he is quoting Brahms's friend and biographer Max Kalbeck.

41. Homer, *The Iliad of Homer*, Samuel Butler, trans. (London: Longmans, Green & Co., 1898), p. 76.

42. Aristotle, *The "Art" of Rhetoric*, J. H. Freese, trans. (Harvard University Press, 1926), pp. 385–86. (The translator uses the spelling *paean*.)

43. Quintilian, *Quintilian's Institutes of Oratory*, John Selby Watson, trans. (London: George Bell and Sons, 1876), vol. 2, p. 237.

44. Edwin E. Gordon, *Tonal and Rhythm Patterns: An Objective Analysis* (State University of New York Press, 1976), pp. 66, 71.

45. Ibid., p. 123.

46. Friedrich Kerst, *Der Erinnerungen an Beethoven* (Stuttgart: Julius Hoffmann, 1913), Band 1, p. 54. (*"Viele Motive Beethovens entstanden durch zufällige äußere Eindrücke und Ereignisse. Der Gesang eines Waldvogels (der Ammerling) gab ihm das Thema zur C-Moll-Sinfonie, und wer ihn fantasieren gehört hat, weiß, was er aus den unbedeutendsten paar Tönen zu entwickeln wußte."*) Czerny had contributed his reminiscences of Beethoven to Otto Jahn, an archaeologist and historian whose 1856 biography of Mozart still remains one of the great monuments of musical scholarship. Jahn never got around to writing his Beethoven biography, but Czerny's notes survived to be published.

47. Christoph Christian Sturm, *Reflections on the Works of God in Providence and Nature, for Every Day in the Year*, Adam Clarke, trans. (New York: McElrath, Bangs & Herbert, 1833), p. 183.

48. The conversation books mention an intellectual dispute between Oken and Ignaz Troxler that was enough to pass for news of the day; see Alexander Wheelock Thayer, *Ludwig van Beethovens Leben*, Vierter Band (Leipzig: Breitkopf und Härtel, 1907), p. 154. Troxler, a doctor and philosopher, was an acquaintance of Beethoven's in Vienna.

49. See Stephen Jay Gould, *The Flamingo's Smile: Reflections in Natural History* (New York: W. W. Norton & Co., 1985), pp. 199–211.

50. Wilhelm Christian Müller, "Something on Ludwig van Beethoven," in Senner et al., *The Critical Reception of Beethoven's Compositions by His German Contemporaries*, vol. 1, p. 106. Müller knew Beethoven largely through his daughter Elise, a pianist and composer who corresponded with Beethoven, and, scholarly temptation aside, most likely was *not* the dedicatee of "Für Elise."

51. Olivier Messiaen, the most famous of ornithologically inspired composers, always placed the yellowhammer's final note a whole step *higher* than the

repeated notes, but dialects vary; see, for instance, Gundula Wonke and Dieter Wallschläger, "Song dialects in the yellowhammer *Emberiza citrinella*: bioacoustic variation between and within dialects," *Journal of Ornithology* 150, no. 1 (Jan. 2009): 117–26.

52. See Owen Jander, "The Prophetic Conversation in Beethoven's 'Scene by the Brook,'" *The Musical Quarterly* 77, no. 3 (Autumn 1993): 520.

53. Harvey Grace, "Interludes," *The Musical Times*, Sept. 1, 1920: p. 595.

54. As in Haydn's 104th Symphony, for instance:

55. As quoted in Sandra P. Rosenbaum, *Performance Practices in Classic Piano Music* (Indiana University Press, 1991), p. 368.

56. Richard Wagner, *On Conducting*, William Ashton Ellis, trans., in *Richard Wagner's Prose Works*, vol. 4 (London: Kegan Paul, Trench, Trübner & Co., Ltd., 1912), p. 311.

57. For a fascinating look at such technology, see George Thomas Ealy, "Of Ear Trumpets and a Resonance Plate: Early Hearing Aids and Beethoven's Hearing Perception," *19th Century Music* 17, no. 3 (Spring 1994): 262–73.

58. Gustav Nottebohm, *Beethoveniana. Aufsätze und Mittheilungen* (Leipzig: Verlag von C. F. Peters, 1872), p. 135.

59. Felix Weingartner, *On Conducting*, pp. 35–36.

60. Weingartner, *On the Performance of Beethoven's Symphonies*, Ernest Newman, trans. (London: Breitkopf und Härtel, 1906), p. 61.

61. Gunther Schuller, *The Compleat Conductor*, pp. 148–49. (This table seems to be more precise than the one on page 123.)

62. Quoted in Joseph Horowitz, *Understanding Toscanini* (University of California Press, 1994), p. 339.

63. Jean Vermeil, *Conversations with Boulez*, Camille Naish, trans. (Portland, OR: Amadeus Press, 1996), p. 71.

64. See Schumann's letter to Friedrich Hiller, April 25, 1853, in Gustav F. Jansen, ed., *Robert Schumanns Briefe: Neue Folge* (Leipzig: Breitkopf und Härtel, 1904), pp. 370–71.

65. See William Malloch, "Carl Czerny's Metronome Marks for Haydn and Mozart Symphonies," *Early Music* 16, no. 1 (Feb. 1988): 72–82, which also includes a reproduction of Beethoven's own metronome-marking table from the December 1817 *Allgemeine musikalische Zeitung*.

66. Peter Stadlen makes this point in "Beethoven and the Metronome," *Soundings* 9 (1982): 38–73.

67. Kielan Yarrow et al., "Illusory Perceptions of Space and Time Preserve Cross-Saccadic Perceptual Continuity," *Nature* 414 (Nov. 15, 2001): 302–5.

68. For effects of musical training, see, for example, Bruno H. Repp, "Sensorimotor Synchronization and Perception of Timing," *Human Movement Science* 29 (2010): 200–213. For a study of the deafness aspect, see Joanna Kowalska and Elzbieta Szelag, "The Effect of Congenital Deafness on Duration Judgment," *Journal of Child Psychology and Psychiatry* 47, no. 9 (Sept. 2006): 946–53.

69. See Helga Lejeune and J. H. Wearden, "Vierordt's *The Experimental Study of the Time Sense* (1868) and Its Legacy," *European Journal of Cognitive Psychology* 21 (2009): 941–60. Vierordt's book has never been translated into English.

70. Simon Grondin, "Timing and Time Perception: A Review of Recent Behavioral and Neuroscience Findings and Theoretical Directions," *Attention, Perception, & Psychophysics* 72 (2010): 581, n. 4.

71. Ibid., p. 564.

72. One can compare three notable recordings from the 1980s that took up the historically informed Beethovenian challenge. The Hanover Band, led by Roy Goodman, takes the first movement of the Fifth at around 104 on their 1984 recording (Nimbus NIM 5007); Christopher Hogwood and the Academy of Ancient Music hover just under the 108 threshold on their 1987 version (Decca L'Oiseau-Lyre 417–615 2); Roger Norrington and the London Classical Players (EMI 7-49656-2) deliver their 1989 reading at a solid 108.

73. Richard Taruskin, "On Letting the Music Speak for Itself: Some Reflections on Musicology and Performance," *The Journal of Musicology* 1, no. 3 (July 1982): 338–49.

74. Jean-Paul Sartre, *War Diaries: Notebooks from a Phoney War 1939–40*, Quentin Hoare, trans. (London: Verso, 1999), p. 221.

75. Jean-Paul Sartre, *Situations*, vol. 4, Benita Eisler, trans. (New York: G. Braziller, 1965), p. 222.

76. Jules Michelet, *Historical View of the French Revolution*, Charles Cocks, trans. (London: George Bell and Sons, 1888), p. 439.

77. Maynard Solomon, "Beethoven's '*Magazin der Kunst*,'" *19th-Century Music* 7, no. 3 (April 1984): 207.

78. The news was duly transmitted by a professor in Beethoven's hometown of Bonn, B. L. Fischenich, to Schiller's wife:

> I am enclosing a musical setting of the Feuerfarbe [a poem by Sophie Mereau, a friend of Schiller's] and I would like to know your opinion of it. It is by a young man from here, whose musical talents are praised everywhere and whom the Elector has sent to Haydn in Vienna. He is also going to set Schiller's *Joy* with all the verses to music.

Quoted in Tia DeNora, *Beethoven and the Construction of Genius: Musical Politics in Vienna, 1792—1803* (University of California Press, 1995), p. 85. Settings of the "Ode" were hardly rare, but Beethoven knew that Fischenich was on letter-writing terms with the Schillers, and that his own setting might stand a better-than-average chance of standing out from the crowd. Beethoven's "Feuerfarbe" was published as op. 52, no. 2.

79. Friedrich Schiller, *On the Aesthetic Education of Man,* Elizabeth M. Wilkinson and L. A. Willoughby, trans. (Oxford University Press, 1983).

80. Ibid., p. 191.

81. Schiller to Goethe, March 2, 1798 (*"die Reiche der Vernunft"*). In Friedrich Schiller, *Schillers Werke. Nationalausgabe. Neunundzwanzigster Band: Schillers Briefe 1796–1798,* Norbert Oellers and Frithjof Stock, eds. (Weimar: Hermann Böhlaus Nachfolger, 1977).

82. Solomon, "Beethoven and Schiller," in *Beethoven Essays,* p. 208.

83. Franz Wegeler and Ferdinand Ries, *Beethoven Remembered: The Biographical Notes of Franz Wegeler and Ferdinand Ries,* Frederick Noonan, trans. (Arlington, VA: Great Ocean Publishers, 1987), p. 68.

84. Solomon, *Beethoven,* p. 182.

85. See Nicholas Mathew, "History Under Erasure: *Wellingtons Sieg,* the Congress of Vienna, and the Ruination of Beethoven's Heroic Style," *The Musical Quarterly* 89, no. 1 (Spring 2006): 17–61.

86. Leo Braudy, *The Frenzy of Renown* (New York: Vintage Books, 1997), p. 409.

87. Henri Brunschwig, *Enlightenment and Romanticism in Eighteenth-Century Prussia,* Frank Jellinek, trans. (University of Chicago Press, 1974), p. 139.

88. As suggested by Solomon in *Beethoven,* pp. 219–26.

89. Thayer-Forbes, p. 536.

90. *Beethoven's Letters (1790–1826) from the Collection of Dr. Ludwig Nohl,* Lady Wallace, trans. (London: Longmans, Green and Co., 1866), vol. 1, pp. 114–15.

91. Quoted in Thayer-Forbes, *Thayer's Life of Beethoven,* p. 538.

92. Quoted in ibid., p. 403, n. 10.

93. Rodeina Kenaan. "Staff Try to Save Battered Hotel That Was Journalist's Haven," Associated Press, Feb. 25, 1987.

94. All examples from Paul-Édouard Levayer, ed., *Chansonnier révolutionnaire* (Paris: Éditions Gallimard, 1989).

95. Michael Broyles, *Beethoven: The Emergence and Evolution of Beethoven's Heroic Style* (New York: Excelsior Music Publishing Co., 1987), p. 125.

96. Arnold Schmitz, *Das romantische Beethovenbild* (Berlin und Bonn: Ferd. Dümmlers Verlag, 1927), pp. 166–67. Also see Broyles, Ibid., pp. 120–23.

97. Jean-François Le Sueur, "Chant du 1er Vendémiaire An IX," in Constant Pierre, *Musique des fêtes et cérémonies de la révolution française,* p. 167:

For comparison, Cherubini's *"L'Hymne du Panthéon"* can be found on p. 367 of the same volume.

98. Julien Tiersot, *Les Fêtes et Les Chants de la Révolution Française* (Paris: Librairie Hachette et Cie., 1908), pp. 313–15.
99. See David Charlton's preface to his edition: Étienne Nicolas Méhul, *Symphony no. 1 in G minor* (Madison: A-R Editions, Inc., 1985), p. ix.
100. Robert Schumann, *Music and Musicians: Essays and Criticisms*, Fanny Raymond Ritter, trans. (London: William Reeves, 1891), p. 385.
101. Jean Mongrédien, *French Music from the Enlightenment to Romanticism 1789–1830*, Sylvain Frémaux, trans. (Portland, OR: Amadeus Press, 1996), pp. 319–20.
102. Étienne Nicolas Méhul, *Euphrosine, ou Le Tyran Corrigé*, libretto by François Hoffmann (New York and London: Garland Publishing, Inc., 1980) (facsimile of the first printed edition), p. 2 (mm. 23–27); see also p. 5 (mm. 87–89), a particularly Beethovenian instance.
103. Étienne Nicolas Méhul, *Ariodant*, libretto by François Hoffmann (New York and London: Garland Publishing, Inc., 1980) (facsimile of the first printed edition), pp. 70–73.
104. Étienne Nicolas Méhul, *Uthal*, libretto by Jacques Benjamin Saint-Victor (New York and London: Garland Publishing, Inc., 1980) (facsimile of the first printed edition), p. 48.
105. Although the printed score of Méhul's G-minor symphony is for a small, Mozart-size orchestra, some manuscript fragments indicate that Méhul either arranged or made an arrangement from a version including trumpet and trombone; see appendices to Charlton's edition.
106. Quoted by David Charlton in the preface to his edition of Méhul's *Symphony no. 1*, p. ix.
107. Quoted by David Charlton in the preface to his edition of Étienne Nicolas Méhul, *Three Symphonies* (New York and London: Garland Publishing, 1982), p. xiii.
108. Henri Radiguier, "La Musique Française de 1789 à 1815," in Albert Lavignac and Lionel de la Laurencie, eds., *Encyclopédie de la musique et dictionnaire du conservatoire*, p. 1638. Lavignac famously assigned characteristics to all the keys; his C minor was "gloomy, dramatic, violent."
109. Alexander L. Ringer, "A French Symphonist at the Time of Beethoven: Etienne Nicolas Méhul," *The Musical Quarterly* 37, no. 4 (Oct. 1951): 551.
110. Paul Virilio, *Speed and Politics*, Mark Polizzotti, trans. (Los Angeles: Semiotext[e], 2006), p. 43.
111. Ibid., p. 44.
112. "The Great Lower Rhine Music Festival at Düsseldorf, Whitsuntide 1830," in Senner et al., *The Critical Reception of Beethoven's Compositions by His German Contemporaries*, vol. 2, p. 132.
113. Igor Stravinsky, *An Autobiography* (New York: W. W. Norton & Co., 1962), pp. 116–17.
114. Priscilla Robertson, *Revolutions of 1848: A Social History* (Princeton University Press, 1959), p. 26.

115. From "The Eighteenth Brumaire of Louis Bonaparte," in Karl Marx, *The Essential Marx: The Non-Economic Writings—a Selection*, Saul K. Padover, ed. (New York: New American Library, 1978), p. 234.

116. "La Marseillaise" was performed in Gossec's standard orchestration, originally written for his 1792 opera *L'Offrande à la liberté*. The concert closed with the final "Hallelujah, Amen" from Handel's *Judas Maccabeus*. See Prod'homme, *"La musique et les musiciens en 1848,"* *Sammelbände der Internationalen Musikgesellschaft* 14, no. 1 (Oct.-Dec. 1912): 158.

117. Quoted in Beate Angelika Kraus, "Beethoven and the Revolution: The View of the French Musical Press," in *Music and the French Revolution*, Malcolm Boyd, ed. (Cambridge University Press, 1992), p. 307.

CHAPTER 2. Fates

1. Kurt Münzer, *Mademoiselle*, in *Die flammende Venus: Erotische Novellen*, Reinhold Eichacker, ed. (Munich: Universal-Verlag, 1919), pp. 122, 121. (*"Mademoiselle langte nach dem Beethovenband. Sie schlug die Symphonie auf, legte das Heft auf das Notenpult und setzte sich neben Eduard zurecht. 'Erste, zweite, drit–te –,' begann sie und schlug an. Aber Eduard ließ plötzlich die Hände sinken und sagte, ohne das Fräulein anzusehen. 'Heut,' sagte er leise, 'heut sprach der Brunner aus der Obersekunda mit mir, der einmal Klavierkünstler werden will. Ich erzählte ihm, daß wir diese Symphonie spielten, und da nannte er sie die Schicksals-Symphonie. Diese ersten Noten, sagte er, bedeuten: so klopft das Schicksal an die Pforte.' Und er schlug die Töne an und summte leise dazu: 'So klopft das Schick- / sal an die Pfor–te.' 'Natürlich', sagte Mademoiselle gedankenlos. Gott weiß, wo ihre Gedanken waren."*)

2. Anton Schindler, *The Life of Beethoven*, Ignace Moscheles, trans. and ed. (London: Henry Colburn, 1841), vol. 2, p. 150.

3. Anton Schindler, *Biographie von Ludwig van Beethoven*, vol. 1, p. 158. As translated by Donald W. MacArdle in Anton Schindler, *Beethoven as I Knew Him* (New York: Dover Publications, 1996), p. 147.

4. Felix Weingartner, *On Conducting*, Ernest Newman, trans. (London: Breitkopf und Härtel, 1906), p. 35.

5. Margaret Fuller, *Papers on Literature and Art* (New York: John Wiley, 1848), Part I, pp. 86–87.

6. William Mason, *Memories of a Musical Life* (New York: The Century Co., 1902), p. 80.

7. Ibid., pp. 81–82.

8. William S. Newman, "Yet Another Major Beethoven Forgery by Schindler?" *The Journal of Musicology* 3, no. 4 (Autumn 1984): 397–422.

9. Standley Howell, "Beethoven's Maelzel Canon: Another Schindler Forgery?" *The Musical Times* (December 1979): 987–90.

10. See Peter Stadlen, "Schindler's Beethoven Forgeries," *The Musical Times* (July 1977): 549–52, and Dagmar Beck et al., *"Einige Zweifel an der Überlieferung der Konversationshefte,"* in *Bericht über den Internationalen Beethoven-Kongreß 20. bis 23. März 1977 in Berlin*, Harry Goldschmidt et al., eds. (VEB Deutscher Verlag für Musik Leipzig, 1978), pp. 257–74.

11. Philip Hale, *Philip Hale's Boston Symphony Programme Notes*, John N. Burk, ed. (Garden City, NY: Doubleday, Doran, & Co., 1935), p. 23.

12. Emily Anderson, ed., *The Letters of Beethoven, Collected, Translated and Edited with an Introduction, Appendixes, Notes and Indexes* (New York: St. Martin's Press, 1961), pp. 66–68.

13. Maynard Solomon, "Beethoven's Tagebuch of 1812–1818," In *Beethoven Studies 3*, Alan Tyson, ed. (Cambridge University Press, 1982), p. 212.

14. Ibid., p. 249. Beethoven's original (*"Zeige deine Gewalt Schicksal! Wir sind nicht Herrn über uns selbst; was beschlossen ist, muß seyn, und so sey es dann!"*) is a slight misquotation of Christoph Martin Wieland's translation (*"Schiksal, zeige deine Macht: Wir sind nicht Herren über uns selbst; was beschlossen ist, muß seyn, und so sey es dann!"*). Shakespeare, *Shakespear Theatrikalische Werke*, Christoph Martin Wieland, trans. (Zürich: Orell, Geßner und Comp., 1766), VIItr. Band, p. 437.

15. Solomon, "Beethoven's Tagebuch of 1812–1818," p. 232.

16. Editha and Richard Sterba, *Beethoven and His Nephew: A Psychoanalytical Study of Their Relationship* (New York: Schocken Books, 1971), p. 10.

17. Johann Kasper Lavater, *Hundert Christliche Lieder* (Zurich: Orell, Gessner, Füßli und Comp., 1776), p. 46. Lavater, who once tried to convert Moses Mendelssohn, was, incidentally, indirectly responsible for the existence of Beethoven's death mask; his 1778 *Physiognomische Fragmente* spurred the vogue for such casts.

18. James Macpherson, *Die Gedichte Ossians eines alten Celtischen Dichter*, Michael Denis, trans. (Vienna: Johann Thomas Edlen v. Trattern, 1769), Dritter Band, p. 157.

19. German: *Der Koran: oder Das gesetz der Moslemen durch Muhammed den sohn Abdallahs*, translated by Friedrich Eberhard Boysen (Halle: *"in der Gebauerschen Buchhandlung,"* 1828), p. 343; English: *The Koran*, translated by J. M. Rodwell (London: Williams and Norgate, 1861), p. 204.

20. A. W. Schlegel, *Kritische Schriften und Briefe* (Stuttgart: W. Kohlhammer Verlag, 1962), vol. 4, p. 37. See also Nicholas A. Germana, *The Orient of Europe: The Mythical Image of India and Competing Images of German National Identity* (Cambridge Scholars Press, 2009).

21. Friedrich Schiller, "The Mission of Moses," in *Schiller's Complete Works*, C. J. Hempel, ed. and trans. (Philadelphia: I. Kohler, 1861), vol. 2, p. 359.

22. Thayer-Forbes, p. 240.

23. See Maynard Solomon, "Beethoven, Freemasonry, and the *Tagebuch* of 1812–1818," *Beethoven Forum* 8 (2000): 101–46.

24. Malcolm C. Duncan, *Duncan's Masonic Ritual and Monitor* (New York: Dick & Fitzgerald, 1866), pp. 59–60.

25. August von Kotzebue, *Theater von August v. Kotzebue* (Verlag von Ignaz Klang in Wien und Eduard Kummer in Leipzig, 1841), vol. 35, p. 17.

26. Lewis Lockwood, *Beethoven: The Music and the Life* (New York: W. W. Norton & Co., 2005), p. 230.

27. See Frithjof Haas, *Hans von Bülow: Leben und Wirken* (Wilhelmshaven: Florian Noetzel Verlag, 2002), pp. 332–33.

28. George Gordon Byron, *Lord Byron's Cain: Twelve Essays and a Text with Variants and Annotations*, Truman Guy Steffan, ed. (University of Texas Press, 1968), p. 163.

29. Ibid., p. 254.

30. Richard Wagner to Hans von Bülow, October 10, 1854, in Wagner, *Sämtliche Briefe*, Band VI, Hans-Josef Bauer et al., eds. (VEB Deutscher Verlag für Musik Leipzig, 1986), Band VI, pp. 257–61.

31. C. A. Barry, "Hans von Bülow's 'Nirvána,'" *Zeitschrift der Internationalen Musikgesellschaft* 2, no. 9 (June, 1901): 298.

32. G. W. F. Hegel, *Hegel's Philosophy of Right*, S. W. Dyde, trans. (London: George Bell and Sons, 1896), p. xxvii.

33. G. W. F. Hegel, *Hegel's Lectures on the History of Philosophy*, E. S. Haldane, trans. (London: Routledge & Kegan Paul Ltd., 1955), vol. 1, p. 279.

34. As translated in Philip Wheelwright, *Heraclitus* (Princeton University Press, 1959), pp. 29, 90.

35. See Hegel, *The Difference Between Fichte's and Schelling's System of Philosophy*, Walter Cerf and H. S. Harris, trans. (Albany: SUNY Press, 1977). In time, Hegel's reputation would eclipse both subjects of his initial foray into philosophy. Schelling, who outlived his onetime friend, would bitterly claim to have taught Hegel everything he knew. Fichte's revenge was more subtle—the simple thesis-antithesis-synthesis dialectic so often and somewhat inaccurately associated with Hegel's thought was originally popularized by Fichte.

36. Ibid., p. 172.

37. Hegel, *Lectures on the Philosophy of History*, p. 466.

38. Ibid., p. 212.

39. Ibid., p. 257.

40. Hegel, *The Difference Between Fichte's and Schelling's System of Philosophy*, p. 92.

41. For a discussion that analyzes Hegel's ambivalence as an attempt to dialectically mediate between formalism and anti-formalism, see Richard Eldridge, "Hegel on Music," in *Hegel and the Arts*, Stephen Houlgate, ed. (Northwestern University Press, 2007), pp. 119–45.

42. Hegel, *Aesthetics: Lectures on Fine Art*, T. M. Knox, trans. (Oxford: Clarendon Press, 1975), vol. 2, p. 895.

43. Ibid., p. 902.

44. Ibid., p. 896.

45. Ibid., p. 895.

46. Hegel, *Hegel's Philosophy of Mind*, pp. 172–74.

47. Sidney Lanier, "To Beethoven," in *Poems of Sidney Lanier* (New York: Charles Scribner's Sons, 1888), p. 98.

48. Ludwig Nohl, *Life of Beethoven*, John J. Lalor, trans. (Chicago: Jansen, McClurg & Co., 1881), p. 97. (Emphasis added.) (Originally published in Germany by Ernst Julius Günther, Leipzig, in 1867.)

49. Scott Burnham, "Introduction" to A. B. Marx, *Musical Form in the Age of Beethoven*, Scott Burnham, ed. and trans. (Cambridge University Press, 1997), p. 4.

50. A. B. Marx, *Musical Form in the Age of Beethoven*, p. 66.

51. Ibid., p. 63.

52. Ibid., p. 92.

53. Charles Rosen, *Sonata Forms* (New York: W. W. Norton & Co., 1980), p. 292.

54. A. B. Marx, "A Few Words on the Symphony and Beethoven's Achievements in This Field," in Senner et al., *The Critical Reception of Beethoven's Compositions by His German Contemporaries* (University of Nebraska Press, 1999), vol. 1, pp. 59–77, 66.

55. Maynard Solomon, "Beethoven's Tagebuch of 1812–1818," in *Beethoven Studies 3*, Alan Tyson, ed. (Cambridge University Press, 1982), p. 239.

56. Friedrich Engels to Marie Engels, late 1838, in Marx and Engels, *Karl Marx/Friedrich Engels: Collected Works*, vol. 2 (London: Lawrence & Wishart, 1975), p. 403.

57. Friedrich Engels to Marie Engels, March 11, 1841, in ibid., p. 430.

58. Tristram Hunt, *Marx's General: The Revolutionary Life of Friedrich Engels* (New York: Metropolitan Books, 2009), pp. 28–29.

59. Friedrich Engels to Schlüter, May 15, 1885, in Karl Marx and Frederick Engels, *Karl Marx and Frederick Engels: Letters to Americans, 1848–1895*, Alexander Trachtenberg, ed. (New York: International Publishers, 1953), p. 145.

60. Hunt, *Marx's General*, p. 45.

61. Wilhelm Liebknecht, *Karl Marx: Biographical Memoirs*, Ernest Untermann, trans. (Chicago: Charles H. Kerr & Co., 1906), pp. 146, 149.

62. Karl Marx, *A Contribution to the Critique of Political Economy*, Salo Ryazanskaya, trans. (New York: International Publishers, 1979), p. 20.

63. Marx never finished his critical survey of Hegel's philosophy; the project's endpoint receded from Marx the more he worked on it. He did publish, in 1844, an Introduction to "A Contribution to the Critique of Hegel's Philosophy of Right," which, its tentative title notwithstanding, finds Marx in his best pugilistic, aphoristic style. It is here that, combating Hegel's focus on the Absolute, Marx tosses his most famous antireligious grenade, calling religion "the opium of the people." But the next sentence makes it clear that what Marx is really against is the false comfort he senses in Hegel's history, how it seems to let the present off the hook in favor of an Ideal in the future. "The abolition of religion as the illusory happiness of the people," Marx writes, "is a demand for their true happiness" (Marx, *Critique of Hegel's "Philosophy of Right,"* Joseph O'Malley, trans. and ed. [Cambridge University Press, 1977], p. 131.) Feuerbach's subject-predicate stratagem fits hand in glove with Marx's disdain for religion: Hegel's insistence on the agency of the Absolute is inverted into man's invention of the divine.

64. Friedrich Engels, *Dialectics of Nature*, C. P. Dutt, trans. (New York: International Publishers, 1960), p. 27.

65. Karl Kautsky, *Terrorism and Communism*, W. H. Kerridge, trans. (http://www.marxists.org/archive/kautsky/1919/terrcomm/index.htm), chapter 8.

66. Leon Trotsky, *Dictatorship vs. Democracy (Terrorism and Communism): A Reply to Karl Kautsky* (New York: Workers Party of America, 1922), p. 45.

67. T. S. Eliot, "Tradition and the Individual Talent" (1922), as quoted in Slavoj Žižek, *In Defense of Lost Causes* (London and New York: Verso, 2008), p. 313.

68. A. B. Marx, "A Few Words on the Symphony and Beethoven's Achievements in This Field," in Senner et al., *The Critical Reception of Beethoven's Compositions*, vol. 1, p. 75.

69. Anatoly Lunacharsky, *On Literature and Art*, Avril Pyman and Fainna Glagoleva, trans. (Moscow: Progress Publishers, 1965), p. 112.

70. Amy Nelson, *Music for the Revolution: Musicians and Power in Early Soviet Russia* (Pennsylvania State University Press, 2004), p. 187.

71. Richard Taruskin, "Public Lies and Unspeakable Truth: Interpreting Shostakovich's Fifth Symphony," in *Shostakovich Studies*, David Fanning, ed. (Cambridge University Press, 1995), p. 29.

72. Quoted in Alan N. Nothnagle, *Building the East German Myth: Historical Mythology and Youth Propaganda in the German Democratic Republic, 1945–1989* (University of Michigan Press, 1999), p. 77.

73. "Back Into the Darkness," *Time*, September 6, 1968, http://www.time .com/time/magazine/article/0,9171,900324,00.html.

74. See Sheila Melvin and Jindong Cai, *Rhapsody in Red: How Western Classical Music Became Chinese* (New York: Algora Publishing, 2004), pp. 231–34.

75. Ibid., p. 266.

76. This particular power struggle was Jiang Qing's yearlong "Criticize Lin, Criticize Confucius" movement, the "Lin" being Lin Biao, the former army chief who had died in a 1971 plane crash, apparently fleeing a failed anti-Mao coup, and the ancient Chinese sage Confucius being recast as a reactionary who supported landowners against the centralized control of Shang Yang during the Qin dynasty.

77. Xiyun Yang, "U.S. Orchestra Performs in China, in Echoes of 1973," *The New York Times*, May 7, 2010.

78. Melvin and Cai, *Rhapsody in Red*, p. 286.

79. "Beethoven's 5th—Courtesy of the Police." *Hong Kong Human Rights Monitor Newsletter* (July 1997). At http://www.hkhrm.org.hk/english/reports/enw/enw0797a.htm.

80. Leon Trotsky, "In 'Socialist' Norway" (1936), http://www.marxists.org/archive/trotsky/1936/12/nor.htm.

81. Leon Trotsky, *My Life: An Attempt at an Autobiography* (New York: Charles Scribner's Sons, 1930), p. 581.

82. Friedrich Nietzsche, *On the Genealogy of Morals and Ecce Homo*, Walter Kaufmann and R. J. Hollingdale, trans. (New York: Vintage Books, 1989), p. 258.

83. Nietzsche, *The Gay Science*, Walter Kaufmann, trans. (New York: Vintage Books, 1974), pp. 273–74.

84. Nietzsche, *Thus Spoke Zarathustra*, R. J. Hollingdale, trans. (London: Penguin Books, 2003), pp. 178–79.

85. Peter Hallward, *Out of This World: Deleuze and the Philosophy of Creation* (London: Verso, 2006), p. 54.
86. Nietzsche, *Twilight of the Idols and The Anti-Christ*, R. J. Hollingdale, trans. (London: Penguin Books, 1990), p. 65.
87. Nietzsche, *Human, All Too Human*, R. J. Hollingdale, trans. (Cambridge University Press, 1986), p. 281.
88. Joachim Köhler, *Richard Wagner: Last of the Titans*, Stewart Spencer, trans. (Yale University Press, 2004), p. 508.
89. As translated by Malcolm Brown in his online *Nietzsche Chronicle* (http://www.dartmouth.edu/~fnchron/1872.html).
90. Nietzsche, *On the Genealogy of Morals and Ecce Homo*, Walter Kaufmann and R. J. Hollingdale, trans. (New York: Vintage Books, 1989), p. 247.
91. Nietzsche, *Human, All Too Human*, pp. 97–98.
92. Ibid., pp. 99, 100.
93. Nietzsche, *Untimely Meditations*, R. J. Hollingdale, trans.; Daniel Breazeale, ed. (Cambridge University Press, 1997), p. 91.
94. As translated in Fritz Stern, *The Varieties of History* (New York: Meridian Books, 1956), p. 57.
95. Nietzsche, *Untimely Meditations*, p. 91.
96. Ibid., p. 92.
97. The quotation comes from Leopold von Ranke, *Fürsten und völker von Süd-Europa*, vol. 2 (Berlin: Duncker und Humblot, 1834), p. 34.
98. Nietzsche, *Untimely Meditations*, p. 105.
99. Ibid., p. 97.
100. Ibid., p. 93.
101. Nietzsche, *Human, All Too Human*, p. 243.
102. Münzer, *Mademoiselle*, pp. 129–30. (*"Von neuem klang das geheimnisvolle, strenge, drohende Motiv auf. Unvorgeschriebene Dissonanzen erhöhten seine Schauerlichkeit. . . . 'Ich weiß nicht,' sagte aber da ihr harmloser Gatte. 'Mir klingt es mehr falsch als sozusagen pikant.' 'Adolf,' rief die Justizrätin entrüstet, 'das ist eben das Unglück deiner einseitigen juristischen Ausbildung. Du hast nie etwas für deine musikalische Erziehung getan. Jetzt rächt es sich und du vermagst nicht, der künstlerischen Einsicht deiner Familie zu folgen.' Der Schluß des ersten Satzes übertraf den vom Mittag noch um ein beträchtliches an ungelöster Dissonanz, denn diesmal spielte das Fräulein richtig, und nur Eduard geriet plötzlich in Fis-dur hinein. Der Justizrat zuckte empfindlich zusammen und stöhnte hörbar, aber die Justizrätin wand sich sozusagen vor Wonne und sagte im Tone tiefster Verachtung: 'Richard Strauß!!'"*)
103. Ibid., p. 132. Ellipsis in the original. (*"Da lächelte sie und öffnete leise, gütig und liebevoll die unverschlossene Tür des Knabenzimmers. . . ."*)

CHAPTER 3. Infinities
1. Karl Marx, "Neumodische Romantik," in Karl Marx and Frederick Engels, *Marx-Engels-Gesamtausgabe*, I. Abteilung, Band 1 (Berlin: Dietz Verlag, 1975), p. 675. (*"Das Kind, das, wie ihr wißt, an Göthe schreib, / Und ihm weis machen wollt', er hab' sie lieb, / Das Kind war einst im Theater zugegen, / 'ne*

Uniform thut sich bewegen. / Es blickt zu ihr gar freundlich lächelnd hin: / 'Bettina wünscht, mein Herr, in ihrem Sinn, / Das Lockenhaupt an sie zu lehnen, / Gefaßt von wundersamem Sehnen.' / Die Uniform erwiedert gar trocken drauf: / 'Bettina laß dem Willen seinen Lauf!' / 'Recht, spricht sie, weißt du wohl, mein Mäuschen, / Auf meinem Kopf giebts keine Läuschen!'")

2. As translated in Maynard Solomon, "Beethoven's Tagebuch of 1812–1818," in *Beethoven Studies 3,* Alan Tyson, ed. (Cambridge University Press, 1982), p. 261.

3. Immanuel Kant, *The Critique of Judgement,* James Creed Meredith, trans. (Oxford: Clarendon Press, 1952), p. 60.

4. Ibid., p. 89.

5. Ibid., p. 82.

6. For a particularly good analysis of this idea, see James Kirwan, *The Aesthetic in Kant: A Critique* (London: Continuum, 2004).

7. Frederick C. Beiser, *The Fate of Reason: German Philosophy from Kant to Fichte* (Harvard University Press, 1987), pp. 19–20.

8. Quoted in Isaiah Berlin, *The Magus of the North: J. G. Hamann and the Origins of Modern Irrationalism* (London: John Murray, 1993), p. 20.

9. J. G. Hamann, "Aesthetica in nuce: A Rhapsody in Cabbalistic Prose," Joyce P. Crick, trans., in *Classic and Romantic German Aesthetics,* J. M. Bernstein, ed. (Cambridge University Press, 2003), p. 13.

10. Ibid., p. 4.

11. Quoted in Berlin, *The Magus of the North,* p. 99.

12. Quoted in Oscar Sonneck, *Beethoven: Impressions by His Contemporaries* (New York: Dover Publications, 1967), p. 49.

13. Eric A. Blackall, *The Novels of the German Romantics* (Cornell University Press, 1983), p. 236.

14. John H. Finley, *Four Stages of Greek Thought* (Stanford University Press, 1966), pp. 3–4.

15. Dennis Ford, *The Search for Meaning: A Short History* (University of California Press, 2008), p. 30.

16. Michael P. Steinberg, *Listening to Reason: Culture, Subjectivity, and Nineteenth-Century Music* (Princeton University Press, 2004), p. 71.

17. William Goldman, *Adventures in the Screen Trade* (New York: Warner Books, 1983), p. 134.

18. Ralph Waldo Emerson, "Heroism," in *The Complete Works of Ralph Waldo Emerson,* vol. 2 (Boston: Houghton, Mifflin and Company, 1903–04), p. 250.

19. See Owen Jander, "The Prophetic Conversation in Beethoven's 'Scene by the Brook,'" *The Musical Quarterly* 77, no. 3 (Autumn 1993): 508–59.

20. See Raymond Knapp, "A Tale of Two Symphonies: Converging Narrative of Divine Reconciliation in Beethoven's Fifth and Sixth," *Journal of the American Musicological Society* 53, no. 2 (Summer 2000): 291–343.

21. Hoffmann's habit of cherry-picking to suit his Romanticism is the most common criticism of his review of the Fifth. Robin Wallace refers to the "almost irrational consistency" of Hoffmann's focus on the kingdom of the

infinite, saying that Hoffmann's "foremost aim was always to explain how the music worked upon his emotions, and he chose to do so as directly as possible, even when that meant overlooking important passages in favor of those which suited him best." And Abigail Chantler notes how Hoffmann isolated and rhetorically amplified certain features of the symphony—the somewhat unusual key relationships in the Andante, the use of the timpani in bridging the last two movements—in order to shoehorn everything into his organically unified whole, how he "attributed to unrelated musical features an extra-musical kinship in order to justify their inclusion in the work." (See Wallace, *Beethoven's Critics* [Cambridge University Press, 1986], pp. 24, 26; Chantler, *E.T.A. Hoffmann's Musical Aesthetics* [Ashgate Publishing, 2006], p. 75.)

22. Stephen Rumph, "A Kingdom Not of This World: The Political Context of E.T.A. Hoffmann's Beethoven Criticism," *19th-Century Music* 19, no. 1 (Summer 1995): 51. Steven Cassedy has speculated that Hoffmann's formulation may be echoing a rather casual reading of Kant; see his "Beethoven the Romantic: How E. T. A. Hoffmann Got It Right," *Journal of the History of Ideas* 71, no. 1 (Jan. 2010): especially pp. 2–4.

23. After Napoléon's exile, Hoffmann's criticism of the French would be more explicit. In 1814, he would chastise the "unutterable sacrilege of that nation [France]" that "led finally to a violent revolution that rushed across the earth like a devastating storm"; by 1821, he could disdain the operas of the great French composer Jean-Baptiste Lully, wondering "how it was that this empty, monotonous sing-song . . . could be regarded as music for almost a hundred years, at least by the French." (Hoffmann, *"Alte und neue Kirchenmusik,"* as translated in Rumph, "A Kingdom Not of This World," p. 56; Hoffmann, "Further Observations on Spontini's Opera *Olimpia*," in *E. T. A. Hoffmann's Musical Writings*, David Charlton, ed. Martyn Clarke, trans. [Cambridge University Press, 2004], p. 435.)

24. Rumph, "A Kingdom Not of This World," p. 61.

25. Johann Gottfried Herder, *"An die Deutschen,"* as translated in Elie Kedourie, *Nationalism*, 4th ed. (Oxford, UK: Blackwell Publishers, 1994), p. 53.

26. Harold Mah, *Enlightenment Phantasies: Cultural Identity in France and Germany 1750–1914* (Cornell University Press, 2003), pp. 60–61.

27. Berlin, *Four Essays on Liberty* (Oxford University Press, 1969), p. 134.

28. Ibid., p. 123.

29. Ortiz M. Walton, "A Comparative Analysis of the African and Western Aesthetics," in *The Black Aesthetic*, Addison Gayle Jr., ed. (Garden City, NY: Doubleday & Company, Inc., 1971), p. 165.

30. Berlin, *Four Essays on Liberty*, p. 135.

31. Hoffmann to Carl Friedrich Kunz, August 19, 1813, in *E. T. A. Hoffmanns Briefwechsel*, Erster Band, Friedrich Schnapp, ed. (München: Winkler-Verlag, 1967), p. 409 (*"so wird es Ihnen nicht sehr darauf ankomme[n]"*).

32. Hoffmann, "The Poet and the Composer," Martyn Clarke, trans., in *E. T. A. Hoffmann's Musical Writings*, pp. 189–90.

33. Michael Howard, *The Franco-Prussian War: The German Invasion of France, 1870–1871* (London: Routledge, 2001), p. 212.

34. As proposed by Klaus Martin Kopitz. See his *Beethoven, Elisabeth Röckel und das Albumblatt "Für Elise"* (Köln: Verlag Dohr, 2010).

35. Richard Wagner, *My Life*, vol. 1 (New York: Dodd, Mead & Co., 1911), p. 469.

36. Ibid., p. 476.

37. Wagner to Theodor Uhlig, February 1851, in Wagner, *Richard Wagner's Letters to His Dresden Friends*, J. S. Shedlock, trans. (New York: Scribner and Welford, 1890), p. 94.

38. Arthur Schopenhauer, *The World as Will and Representation*, E. F. Payne, trans., vol. 1 (New York: Dover Publications, 1969), p. 257.

39. Ibid., p. 69.

40. Ibid., p. 72.

41. Ibid., pp. 261–62.

42. Richard Wagner, "Beethoven," William Ashton Ellis, trans., in *Richard Wagner's Prose Works*, vol. 5 (London: William Reeves, 1896), pp. 72–73.

43. Ibid., p. 92.

44. Ibid., p. 84.

45. K. M. Knittel, "Wagner, Deafness, and the Reception of Beethoven's Late Style," *Journal of the American Musicological Society* 51, no. 1 (Spring 1998): 73.

46. Edward Dannreuther, "Beethoven and His Works: A Study," *Macmillan's Magazine* 34 (July 1876): 194.

47. George Grove, "Beethoven," in J. A. Fuller Maitland, ed., *Grove's Dictionary of Music and Musicians* (New York: Macmillan, 1911), p. 262.

48. Oliver Lodge, *The Substance of Faith Allied with Science: A Catechism for Parents and Teachers* (London: Methuen & Co., 1907), p. 87.

49. Knittel, "Wagner, Deafness, and the Reception of Beethoven's Late Style," p. 82.

50. *Cosima Wagner's Diaries: Volume I, 1869–1877*, Martin Gregor-Dellin and Dietrich Mack, eds., Geoffrey Skelton, trans. (New York and London: Harcourt Brace Jovanovich, 1978), p. 191.

51. Ibid., p. 586.

52. Richard Wagner, "Beethoven," pp. 99–100.

53. Ibid., p. 126. Ellis renders Wagner's *frecher Mode* as "shameless Mode"; "insolent fashion" is Edward Dannreuther's translation.

54. *Cosima Wagner's Diaries: Volume I*, p. 246.

55. Percy M. Young, *Beethoven: A Victorian Tribute; based on the papers of Sir George Smart* (London: Dennis Dobson, 1976), pp. 82–85.

56. Alan Walker, *Franz Liszt: The Virtuoso Years, 1811–1947* (Ithaca: Cornell University Press, 1987), p. 424.

57. Ryan Minor, "Prophet and Populace in Liszt's 'Beethoven' Cantatas," in *Liszt and His World*, edited by Christopher H. Gibbs and Dana Cooley (Princeton University Press, 2006), p. 118.

58. Ibid., p. 150.

CHAPTER 4. Associations

1. William E. Channing, *The Works of William E. Channing, D.D. Eleventh Complete Edition, with an Introduction* (Boston: George G. Channing, 1849), vol. 5, p. 308.

2. John Sullivan Dwight, "Academy of Music—Beethoven's Symphonies," *The Pioneer* 1, no. 2 (Jan.–Feb. 1843): 57.

3. Lindsay Swift, *Brook Farm: Its Members, Scholars, and Visitors* (New York: Macmillan Company, 1900), p. 154.

4. Ralph Waldo Emerson, "Life and Letters in New England," in *The Complete Works of Ralph Waldo Emerson*, vol. 10 (Boston: Houghton, Mifflin and Company, 1903–04), p. 340.

5. Ibid., p. 343.

6. James Clarke Freeman, quoted in James Elliot Cabot, *A Memoir of Ralph Waldo Emerson* (Cambridge, MA: Riverside Press, 1888), p. 249.

7. Swift, *Brook Farm*, p. 156.

8. Ralph Waldo Emerson, "Thoughts on Modern Literature," *The Dial* 1, no. 2 (October 1840): 149.

9. As related by Emerson in *Memoirs of Margaret Fuller Ossoli*, vol. 1 (Boston: Phillips, Sampson and Company, 1852), p. 234.

10. Margaret Fuller, "Lives of the Great Composers, Haydn, Mozart, Handel, Bach, Beethoven," *The Dial* 2, no. 2 (Oct. 1841): 202.

11. A. Bronson Alcott, "Orphic Sayings," *The Dial* 1, no. 1 (July, 1840): 93.

12. Octavius Brooks Frothingham, *George Ripley* (Boston: Houghton, Mifflin and Company, 1886), pp. 84–85.

13. Ibid., p. 9.

14. George Willis Cooke, *Early Letters of George Wm. Curtis to John S. Dwight* (New York and London: Harper and Brothers Publishers, 1898), pp. 58–59.

15. Quoted in Frothingham, *George Ripley*, p. 124.

16. Ibid., p. 613.

17. Emerson, "The Conduct of Life," in *The Complete Works of Ralph Waldo Emerson*, vol. 6, pp. 276–77.

18. Emmanuel Swedenborg, *The True Christian Religion; Containing the Universal Theology of the New Church* (New York: American Swedenborg Printing and Publishing Society, 1855), pp. 376, 388.

19. Ibid., p. 804.

20. John Sullivan Dwight, "Musical Review: Music in Boston During the Last Winter," *The Harbinger* 1, no. 8 (Aug. 2, 1845): 124.

21. John Sullivan Dwight, "Review: *Festus, a Poem*," *The Harbinger* 2, no. 2 (Dec. 20, 1845): 27. "Festus" was a long philosophical poem by the English poet Philip James Bailey which had some currency in nineteenth-century America (Tennyson, for example, admired it). Dwight concluded his Swedenborg-Fourier-Beethoven thought by asking, "and shall we not say, in poetry, 'Festus?'" He had at least enough critical perspicacity to include the qualifying question mark.

22. Frothingham, *George Ripley*, p. 192.

23. A. Bronson Alcott and Charles Lane to A. Brooke, August 1843, in Clara

Endicott Sears, *Bronson Alcott's Fruitlands* (Boston: Houghton Mifflin Company, 1915), p. 50.

24. Louisa M. Alcott, "Transcendental Wild Oats," in Sears, *Bronson Alcott's Fruitlands*, p. 169.

25. Quoted in Thomas Wentworth Higginson, *Part of a Man's Life* (Boston: Houghton, Mifflin and Company, 1905), p. 12.

26. D. H. Lawrence, *Studies in Classic American Literature* (Penguin Classics, 1991), p. 112.

27. Nathaniel Hawthorne to Sophia Peabody, September 3, 1841, in Hawthorne, *The Letters, 1813–1843*, Thomas Woodson et al., eds. (Ohio State University Press, 1984), p. 566.

28. Nathaniel Hawthorne, *The Blithedale Romance and Fanshawe* (Ohio State University Press, 1964), pp. 165, 162.

29. John Sullivan Dwight, "The Sentiment of Various Musical Composers," *Sartain's Union Magazine of Literature and Art* VIII, no. 2 (Feb., 1851): 133.

30. Rev. Darius Mead, "Part of a Speech on 'Divine Electricity,'" in Mead, ed., *The American Literary Emporium or Friendship's Gift* (New York: C. H. Camp, 1848), p. 15.

31. John Sullivan Dwight, "The Sentiment of Various Musical Composers," p. 133.

32. Ibid.

33. George Ripley and Charles A. Dana, eds., *The New American Cyclopaedia: A Popular Dictionary of General Knowledge* (New York: D. Appleton and Company, 1861), vol. 3, p. 71.

34. See John Sullivan Dwight, "Musical Review: Music in Boston During the Last Winter.—No. III," *The Harbinger* 1, no. 10 (Aug. 16, 1845): 154–57, and his "Beethoven's Symphony in C Minor," *Dwight's Journal of Music* IV (Oct. 8, 1853): 1–3.

35. Dwight, "Valedictory," *Dwight's Journal of Music* XLI (Sept. 3, 1881): 123.

36. Dwight, "What Lack We Yet?" *Dwight's Journal of Music* XL (Sept. 11, 1880): 150.

37. George P. Upton, ed., *Theodore Thomas: A Musical Autobiography*, vol. 1 (Chicago: A. C. McClurg & Co., 1905), p. 310.

38. Henry David Thoreau, "Walking," in *Civil Disobedience and Other Essays* (New York: Dover Publications, 1993), p. 49.

39. Walt Whitman, "Song of Myself," in *Leaves of Grass* (New York: Modern Library, 1921), p. 67.

40. Quoted in Herbert Bergman, "Whitman on Beethoven and Music," *Modern Language Notes* 66, no. 8 (Dec. 1951): 557.

41. Allan Sutherland, *Famous Hymns of the World: Their Origin and Their Romance* (New York: Frederick A. Stokes Company, 1906), p. 22.

42. Stearns, *Sketches from Concord and Appledore* (New York: G. P. Putnam's Sons, 1895), p. 187. See also Louis Ruchames, "Wendell Phillips' Lovejoy Address," *The New England Quarterly* 47, no. 1 (March 1974): 108–17.

43. In a memo, Ives considered including the study in a set of pieces, with the

reminder "Wendell Philips [*sic*]—Faneuil Hall." See James B. Sinclair, *A Descriptive Catalogue of the Music of Charles Ives* (Yale University Press, 1999), p. 613. Ives also apparently began to orchestrate the study for his *Three Places in New England*: "There was another movement started but never completed, about the Wendell Phillips row and the mob in Faneuil Hall." Ives, *Charles E. Ives: Memos*, John Kirkpatrick, ed. (New York: W. W. Norton & Company, 1991), p. 87.

44. Vivian Perlis, *Charles Ives Remembered: An Oral History* (Yale University Press, 1974), p. 16.

45. Charles Ives, "Some 'Quarter-Tone' Impressions," in *Essays Before a Sonata, The Majority, and Other Writings*, Howard Boatwright, ed. (New York: W. W. Norton & Co., 1970), p. 111.

46. Ives, *Charles E. Ives: Memos*, p. 132.

47. Ralph Waldo Emerson, "Compensation," in *The Complete Works of Ralph Waldo Emerson*, vol. 2, p. 102.

48. Ives, "The Amount to Carry—Measuring the Prospect," in *Essays Before a Sonata*, pp. 240, 236.

49. Emerson, "Compensation," in *The Complete Works of Ralph Waldo Emerson*, vol. 2, p. 101.

50. Robert M. Crunden, *Ministers of Reform: The Progressives' Achievement in American Civilization, 1889–1920* (University of Illinois Press, 1984), p. 124.

51. Charles Ives, "Concerning a Twentieth Amendment," in *Essays Before a Sonata*, pp. 206–07. ("Williams Curtis" in original.)

52. Ives, *Essays Before a Sonata*, p. 40.

53. Compare the left hand in measure 3—

Beethoven's Fifth

—with the left hand in measures 6–7:

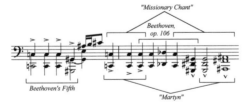

54. Ives, *Essays Before a Sonata*, p. 47. (Beth Alcott, who, like her *Little Women* counterpart, died young, was also the only Alcott daughter to share a name with her fictional characterization.)

55. Ibid., p. 45.
56. A. F. Winnemore, "Stop Dat Knocking at De Door" (Boston: Geo. F. Reed, 1847). As Ives quotes it:

57. Ives, *Essays Before a Sonata,* pp. 47–48.
58. Perlis, *Charles Ives Remembered,* p. 161.
59. Steven C. Smith, *A Heart at Fire's Center: The Life and Music of Bernard Herrmann* (University of California Press, 1991), p. 180.
60. *Charles E. Ives: Memos,* p. 44.
61. Thomas Clarke Owens, *Selected Correspondence of Charles Ives* (University of California Press, 2007), p. 126.
62. Harmony Ives to Nicolas Slonimsky, July 6, 1936, in Owens, *Selected Correspondence of Charles Ives,* p. 128.
63. Ives, *Essays Before a Sonata,* p. 73.
64. J. Peter Burkholder, "Ives and the Four Musical Traditions," in *Charles Ives and His World* (Princeton University Press, 1996), p. 5.
65. Thoreau, *The Journal of Henry D. Thoreau* (Boston: Houghton, Mifflin and Company, 1906), vol. 2, p. 492 (Nov. 9, 1853).
66. Ibid., p. 379 (Aug. 6, 1851).
67. Thoreau, *Walden,* vol. 2, p. 421.
68. Ives, *Essays Before a Sonata,* p. 51.
69. Ibid., p. 58.
70. Philip Corner, "Thoreau, Charles Ives, and Contemporary Music," in Walter Harding et al., eds., *Henry David Thoreau: Studies and Commentaries* (Fairleigh Dickinson University Press, 1972), p. 68.
71. Ibid., p. 54.
72. James B. Sinclair, *A Descriptive Catalogue of the Music of Charles Ives* (Yale University Press, 1999), p. 197.

CHAPTER 5. Secret Remedies

1. Alan Walker, *Hans von Bülow: A Life and Times* (Oxford University Press, 2009), p. 267.
2. Walter E. Houghton, *The Victorian Frame of Mind, 1830–1870* (Yale University Press, 1957), pp. 1–2.
3. Rev. John Blakely, *The Theology of Inventions, or, Manifestations of Deity in the Works of Art* (New York: Robert Carter & Brothers, 1856), pp. 138–39, 141.
4. *Great Exhibition of the Works of Industry of All Nations, 1851. Official Descriptive and Illustrated Catalogue,* vol. 4 (London: Spicer Brothers, Wholesale Stationers; W. Clowes and Sons, Printers, 1851), p. 1067.

5. Ibid., pp. 1053, 1047, 1054.
6. Charles L. Graves, *The Life & Letters of George Grove, C.B.* (London: Macmillan and Co., 1903), p. 9.
7. Ibid., p. 10.
8. Ibid., p. 28.
9. See Henry Saxe Wyndham, *August Manns and the Saturday Concerts: A Memoir and a Retrospect* (London: Walter Scott Publishing Co., Ltd., 1909), pp. 21–32.
10. Manns had been singled out as a bandmaster by Albrecht von Roon, later the Prussian Minister of War during Bismarck's tenure, but soured on army life after a junior officer opined that the buttons on his band's uniforms were insufficiently polished. See Saxe Wyndham, *August Manns and the Saturday Concerts*, pp. 14–15.
11. Complete lists of Prince Albert's programs for both the Antient Concerts and the Philharmonic Society are in Theodore Martin, *The Life of His Royal Highness the Prince Consort* (London: Smith, Elder & Co., 1875), pp. 494–501.
12. Adam Carse, *The Life of Jullien* (Cambridge: Heffer, 1951), p. 65.
13. See "Jullien, Louis Antoine," in George Grove, ed., *A Dictionary of Music and Musicians,* vol. 2 (London: Macmillan & Co., 1880), p. 45.
14. Jan Piggott, *Palace of the People: The Crystal Palace at Sydenham, 1854–1936* (University of Wisconsin Press, 2004), p. 74.
15. Ibid., p. 47.
16. Ibid., p. 75.
17. *The Crystal Palace Penny Guide* (Sydenham: Crystal Palace Printing Office, 1863), p. 17.
18. "Delta," "Home Correspondence: The Royal Commission and the Surplus," *The Journal of the Society of Arts,* vol. 2 (London: George Bell, 1854), p. 343.
19. Hugh Reginald Haweis, *Music and Morals* (New York: Harper and Brothers, 1872), p. 419.
20. Hugh Reginald Haweis, *Travel and Talk: 1885–93–95,* vol. 2 (London: Chatto & Windus, 1897), p. 244.
21. George Grove, *Beethoven and His Nine Symphonies* (London and New York: Novello, Ewer and Co., 1896), p. 137.
22. Michael Musgrave, *The Musical Life of the Crystal Palace* (Cambridge University Press, 1995), pp. 84, 120.
23. Cyril Erlich, *First Philharmonic: A History of the Royal Philharmonic Society* (Oxford University Press, 1995), p. 44; Peter Gay, *Pleasure Wars: The Bourgeois Experience: Victoria to Freud* (New York: W. W. Norton & Co., 1998), p. 81.
24. *A Short History of Cheap Music as Exemplified in the Record of the House of Novello, Ewer & Co., with Especial Reference to the First Fifty Years of the Reign of Her Most Gracious Majesty Queen Victoria with Three Portraits and a Preface by Sir George Grove, D.C.L., &c.* (London and New York: Novello, Ewer and Co., 1887), pp. vi–vii.

25. Grove, *Beethoven and His Nine Symphonies*, p. 139.
26. Charles Kingsley, *Yeast: A Problem* (New York: Harper and Brothers, 1851), pp. iii–iv.
27. [Frances] Kingsley, *Charles Kingsley: His Letters and Memories of His Life*, vol. 2 (London: Henry S. King & Co., 1877), pp. 399–400.
28. "Our Representative Man," *Punch*, Sept. 14, 1878, p. 117.
29. Graves, *The Life & Letters of George Grove*, pp. 399–401.
30. Thomas Richards, *The Commodity Culture of Victorian England* (Stanford University Press, 1990), p. 33.
31. Guy Debord, *The Society of the Spectacle*, Ken Knabb, trans., http://www.bopsecrets.org/SI/debord/, p. 1.
32. Ibid., p. 5.
33. Explaining the Situationist concept of *détournement*, a kind of cultural hijacking, Debord and Gil Wolman offered as an example that "it wouldn't be a bad idea to make a final correction to the title of the 'Eroica Symphony' by changing it, for example, to 'Lenin Symphony.'" See Debord and Wolman, "A User's Guide to Détournement," Ken Knabb, trans., http://www.bopsecrets.org/SI/detourn.htm. (Originally in *Les Lèvres Nues*, May 1956.)
34. Debord, *The Society of the Spectacle*, p. 10.
35. Ibid., p. 15.
36. Ibid., p. 16.
37. G. W. F. Hegel, *The Difference Between Fichte's and Schelling's System of Philosophy*, Walter Cerf and H. S. Harris, trans. (Albany: SUNY Press, 1977), p. 92.
38. Debord, *The Society of the Spectacle*, p. 57.
39. Howard Brenton, "Petrol Bombs Through the Proscenium Arch," interview by Catherine Itzen and Simon Trussler, *Theatre Quarterly* 5, no. 17 (March–May 1975): 20.
40. Tim Clark, Christopher Gray, Charles Radcliffe, and Donald Nicholson-Smith, "The Revolution of Modern Art and the Modern Art of Revolution," unpublished pamphlet, 1967, http://www.notbored.org/english.html. Authors Clark, Gray, and Nicholson-Smith were formally excluded from the Situationist International in 1969 (Charles Radcliffe had earlier resigned), exclusion having become a main activity of the SI post-1968. See "The Latest Exclusions," *Internationale Situationniste* #12 (Paris: Sept. 1969), Ken Knabb, trans., http://www.bopsecrets.org/SI/12.exclusions.htm.
41. Raoul Vaneigem, *The Revolution of Everyday Life*, Donald Nicholson-Smith, trans. (Welcombe: Rebel Press, 2001), p. 44.
42. See Dierdre David, *Fanny Kemble: A Performed Life* (University of Pennsylvania Press, 2007), pp. 202–7. Kemble's *Journal of a Residence on a Georgian Plantation in 1838–1839* became an abolitionist best-seller upon its publication in 1863.
43. Fanny Kemble, *A Year of Consolation*, vol. 2 (New York: Wiley & Putnam, 1847), pp. 87–88.
44. Edward Bulwer-Lytton, *England and the English* (Paris: Baudry's European Library, 1836), p. 14.

45. Graves, *The Life & Letters of George Grove*, p. 337.
46. Roy Jenkins, *Gladstone* (New York: Random House, 1997), p. 191.
47. The exhortation has been widely attributed; Jowett's claim comes courtesy of a eulogy in the *Oxford Chronicle*, October 7, 1893, quoted in Cecil Day Lewis and Charles Fenby, *Anatomy of Oxford* (London: Jonathan Cape, 1938), p. 139.
48. Robert Bulwer-Lytton, "Beethoven," *The Fortnightly Review* XII, no. LXVII (July 1, 1872): 32.
49. Karl Marx, *Capital*, Samuel Moore and Edward Aveling, trans.; Frederick Engels, ed., vol. 1 (Chicago: Charles H. Kerr & Co., 1909), pp. 81–83.
50. See Stuart Anderson and Peter Homan, "'Best for me, best for you'— a history of Beecham's Pills 1842–1998," *The Pharmaceutical Journal* 269 (Dec. 21/28, 2002).
51. Etienne Van de Walle and Elisha P. Renne, *Regulating Menstruation: Beliefs, Practices, Interpretations* (University of Chicago Press, 2001), p. 99.
52. "The Parliamentary Committee on Proprietary Remedies. Evidence Regarding Beecham's Pills," *The British Medical Journal* 1, no. 2718 (Feb. 1, 1913): 234. At the same hearing, Sir Joseph was asked whether his father had known of any medical value in Beecham's Pills before he started selling them:

> [T]he witness said he did not know whether his father was the discoverer of the therapeutic value of the drugs used in Beecham's pills; it was a case of the discovery of an excellent combination.
>
> Mr. Lawson: He discovered the money value. (Laughter.)

53. Neville Cardus, *Sir Thomas Beecham: A Memoir* (London: Collins, 1961), p. 12.
54. Sir Thomas Beecham, *A Mingled Chime* (New York: G. P. Putnam's Sons, 1943), pp. 51–52.
55. James C. Whorton, *Inner Hygiene: Constipation and the Pursuit of Health in Modern Society* (Oxford University Press, 2000), p. 51.
56. Robert Herrick, "To Enjoy the Time," in *The Poetical Works of Robert Herrick*, F. W. Moorman, ed. (Oxford: Clarendon Press, 1915), p. 172.
57. Robert Louis Stevenson and Lloyd Osbourne, *The Ebb-Tide: A Trio and Quartette* (New York: Charles Scribner's Sons, 1913), pp. 7, 46. Herrick punctuates his Beethoven with a quotation from Virgil: *terque quaterque beati Queis ante ora patrum*—"three and four times blessed were those fated to die before their parents' eyes." British homesickness could easily colonize Germany and Rome.
58. E. M. Forster, "The Challenge of Our Time," in *Two Cheers for Democracy* (New York: Harcourt, Brace & World, Inc., 1951), p. 56.
59. E. M. Forster, *Howards End* (Mineola, NY: Dover Publications, 2002), p. 21. The sentiment may be echoing Goldsworthy Lowes Dickinson's remedy for easing the tension of reconciling "the Western flight down Time with the Eastern rest in eternity": "When you feel dead you should go to church;

but not in a 'sacred edifice.' Beethoven, even in the Queen's Hall, is better." Dickinson, a Cambridge historian and philosopher, was a longtime friend of Forster, and his companion on his first trip to India (eventually yielding Forster's final novel, *A Passage to India*); Dickinson's family was reportedly the inspiration for the Schlegel sisters and their London house in *Howards End*. Forster speculated that Dickinson, a lifelong pacifist, may have been the one to coin the term "League of Nations." But toward the end of his life, Dickinson would admit that the prospects for the League were dim, writing to an Indian correspondent in 1931: "When one enters into politics one enters the region of passion, interest, prejudice, and at last, fighting, which, however it begins, always ends in the destruction of all that was best and most generous in those who perhaps inaugurated it." (For the Beethoven quote, see Goldsworthy Lowes Dickinson, *Appearances* [New York: Doubleday, Page & Company, 1915], pp. 134, 135; for the connection with *Howards End*, see Paul Cadmus's letter to *The New York Times*, April 12, 1992; for the League of Nations and Dickinson's disillusion, see E. M. Forster, *Goldsworthy Lowes Dickinson* [New York: Harcourt Brace Jovanovich, 1962], pp. 163 and 229–30.)

60. Forster, *Howards End*, pp. 22–23.

61. Ibid., p. 23.

62. Ibid., p. 31. Forster's fellow Bloomsburyan Leonard Woolf had a friend, B. F. Dutton, who reminded him of Leonard Bast: "He spent his evenings writing poetry about elves and fairies, and playing, endlessly, an arrangement of Beethoven's Fifth Symphony, the C Minor, on his out-of-tune piano. . . . The fascination of Dutton for Leonard was that Dutton was a terrifyingly degraded version of himself." See Victoria Glendinning, *Leonard Woolf: A Biography* (New York: Free Press, 2006), p. 77.

63. Mary Burgan, "Heroines at the Piano: Women and Music in Nineteenth-Century Fiction," *Victorian Studies* 30, no, 1 (1986): 61.

64. Lucas Malet, *The Wages of Sin*, vol. 3 (London: Swan Sonnenschein and Co., 1891), pp. 31–32.

65. John Lane Ford, *Dower and Curse*, vol. 1 (London: Tinsley Brothers, 1872), pp. 6, 167.

66. Mary Elizabeth Braddon, *Mount Royal* (London: John and Robert Maxwell, 1883), p. 282.

67. William Makepeace Thackeray, *Denis Duval: Lovel the Widower: and Other Stories* (London: Smith, Elder & Co., 1869), p. 237.

68. Ibid., p. 256.

69. Linda Allardt et al., eds., *The Journals and Miscellaneous Notebooks of Ralph Waldo Emerson* (Harvard University Press, 1982), p. 255.

70. Elizabeth Sara Sheppard, *Rumour*, vol. 3 (London: Hurst and Blackett, 1858), p. 219. "Adelaída" combines aspects of Louis-Napoléon's empress, the Spanish-born Eugénie de Montijo, with a name borrowed from both the Beethoven song and Queen Victoria's niece, Princess Adelheid of Hohenlohe-Langenburg, to whom Louis-Napoléon had unsuccessfully proposed marriage.

71. Ibid., p. 227.
72. Ibid., p. 312.
73. Ibid., p. 347.
74. Grove, *Beethoven and His Nine Symphonies*, pp. 155–56.
75. See Michelle Fillion, "Edwardian Perspectives on Nineteenth-Century Music in E. M. Forster's *A Room with a View*," *19th-Century Music* 25, no. 2/3 (Autumn 2001–Spring, 2002): 266–95.
76. See the "Introduction: Biographical and Historical Contexts," in Alistair M. Duckworth, *Howards End: Case Studies in Contemporary Criticism* (Basingstoke: Palgrave Macmillan, 1996), p. 16.
77. See, for instance, Anna Foata, "The Knocking at the Door. A Fantasy on Fate, Forster, and Beethoven's Fifth," *Cahiers victoriens et édouardiens* 44 (1996): 135–45, or Andrea K. Weatherhead, "*Howards End*: Beethoven's *Fifth*," *Twentieth Century Literature* 31, no. 2/3 (E. M. Forster Issue) (Summer-Autumn 1985): 247–264. Weatherhead's use of musical terminology is highly dubious; a tangle such as "Beethoven's first themes in A flat and C major are 'relative minors.' They have completely different scales but may be combined to produce a series of chords in minor thirds" (p. 256)—is, at the very least, misunderstanding both relative key relationships and mistaking a major third for a minor. But her overall thesis, that the novel roughly tracks the symphony's structure, is plausible. (My own mapping of symphony to novel varies from both Foata and Weatherhead; for instance, Foata matches the Andante to the relationship between Margaret Schlegel and Ruth Wilcox, and Weatherhead proposes Helen's repeated cries of "panic and emptiness" as a unifying motive.)
78. Forster, *Howards End*, p. 1.
79. Stephen Spender, *The Creative Element* (London: Hamish Hamilton, 1953), p. 90.
80. Quoted in "Bah, humbug! The classics we secretly loathe," *The Times* (London), December 23, 2009, http://entertainment.timesonline.co.uk/tol/arts_and_entertainment/specials/article6964184.ece.
81. One should not even trust the seeming voice of the author. It is one of Forster's more elegant confidence games that one should end up assuming that the intrusive, judgmental, and frequently deflating narrator of *Howards End* is both omniscient and a stand-in for Forster himself. Like the tantalizingly palpable but elusive composer-stand-in protagonist of the Fifth Symphony, Forster's narrator only seems straightforward. Francis Gillen has suggested that the narrator is a kind of devil's-advocate Socratic teacher ("I'll fool you sometimes, suggest, as a good teacher, a false or oversimplified conclusion, then show you your mistakes in accepting it," as he characterizes him); Paul Armstrong makes him a deliberately subversive figure, asserting conventional authority in order to reveal conventional authority's fragile arbitrariness (a notion often linked to Forster's homosexuality); Elizabeth Langland questions whether the narrator is even a he at all. See Gillen, "*Howards End* and the Neglected Narrator," *NOVEL: A Forum on Fiction* 3, no. 2 (Winter 1970): 140; Armstrong, *Play and the*

Politics of Reading: The Social Uses of Modernist Form (Cornell University Press, 2005), pp. 111–26; Langland, "Gesturing Toward an Open Space: Gender, Form and Language in E. M. Forster's *Howards End*," in Laura Claridge and Elizabeth Langland, eds., *Out of Bounds: Male Writers and Gender(ed) Criticism* (University of Massachusetts Press, 1990), pp. 252–67.

82. E. M. Forster, "The C Minor of That Life," in *Two Cheers for Democracy*, p. 125.

83. Forster, *Howards End*, p. 20.

84. Ibid., pp. 213–14.

85. Ibid., p. 244.

86. Shaw, "Heartbreak House and Horseback Hall," in *Complete Plays with Prefaces*, vol. 1, p. 471.

87. Ibid., p. 453.

88. George Bernard Shaw, *Heartbreak House*, in *Complete Plays with Prefaces*, vol. 1 (New York: Dodd, Mead & Co., 1962), p. 595.

89. *Hansard Parliamentary Debates*, Commons, 5th series, vol. 73 (1915), column 2326 (debate of July 28, 1915).

90. Edward Goldbeck, "Beethoven," *Chicago Daily Tribune*, Jan. 2, 1916, p. 5. Goldbeck's wife was the actress, singer, and later theatrical producer Lina Abarbanell; his son-in-law was the composer Marc Blitzstein.

91. "Col. William Jay Expires Suddenly," *The New York Times*, March 29, 1915, p. 9.

92. "No Power to Bar Papers: Court Enjoins Mount Vernon from Banning Hearst by Law," *The New York Times*, June 5, 1918, p. 22. This article is a brief roundup of anti-German sentiment. Other items: The city of Mount Vernon, New York, tried to ban German-language newspapers; a school commissioner in Summit, New Jersey, unsuccessfully sought to end German-language instruction in the town. Another resolution by the same commissioner, "to have all books entitled 'Im Vaterland' collected and reserved until July 4, when they will be turned over to the Fourth of July celebration committee, with instructions to use them for a bonfire and to use other German propaganda papers to kindle the blaze, took the same course."

93. "German Opera Cut from List at Metropolitan," *New York Tribune*, Nov. 2, 1917, p.1.

94. Barbara L. Tischler, "One Hundred Percent Americanism and Music in Boston during World War I," *American Music* 4, no. 2 (Summer 1986): 172.

95. "The Boston Orchestra Under Dr. Karl Muck," *The New York Times*, Oct. 13, 1906, p. 9.

96. Frederic Dean, "Some Conductors and Their Batons," *The Bookman* 46, no. 5 (Jan. 1918): 589–90.

97. Janet Baker-Carr, *Evening at Symphony: A Portrait of the Boston Symphony Orchestra* (Boston: Houghton Mifflin Company, 1977), p. 56.

98. William E. Walter, "Culled From the Mail Pouch: Miss Farrar Remembers Karl Muck's War Problem," *The New York Times*, March 10, 1940, p. 159.

99. Edmund A. Bowles, "Karl Muck and His Compatriots: German Conductors in America During World War I (And How They Coped)," *American Music* 25, no. 4 (Winter, 2007): n. 41: 433–34.

100. The nucleus of the ensemble was a naval band formerly posted to the German protectorate of Tsing-Tao, China; after the capture of Tsing-Tao by Japanese and British troops in 1914, the band—noncombatants under the terms of the Geneva Convention—had made its way to the United States, where its members were detained once America entered the war. Previously, the Tsing-Tao Band had performed at a 1916 Carnegie Hall memorial for German war dead. Among the speakers at the concert was the Rev. Dr. G. C. Berkemeier, one of the leading Lutheran ministers in America. "Dr. Berkemeier said that the war had united Germany, and that the spirit which prompted her in the war would win. He was applauded loudly when he said that England was prompted by love of Mammon, France, by love of Vengeance, and Russia—'well, Russia, there are all the devils of hell.' " (See "Germans Honor War Dead: Hear Opera Singers and Orators at Carnegie Hall Meeting," *The New York Times*, May 30, 1916, p. 7.) The band gave the Camp Oglethorpe group its name: the *Tsingtauer Orchester*. See Bowles, "Karl Muck and His Compatriots."

101. "Mrs. Jay Quits: Announces She Will Lead No More Uprisings Against German Art," *The New York Times*, July 3, 1919, p. 11.

102. "German Music? Maybe; Muck's Successor Undecided on Symphony Policy," *New York Tribune*, Oct. 30, 1918, p. 9.

103. Henry Franks, "Geist," in *Papers of the Manchester Literary Club* (London: Abel Heywood and Sons, 1878), vol. 4, pp. 95–106.

CHAPTER 6. Earthquakes

1. E. M. Forster, "A View Without a Room: Old Friends Fifty Years Later," *The New York Times Book Review*, July 27, 1958, p. 4.

2. Quoted in Leo Schrade, *Beethoven in France* (Yale University Press, 1942), p. 187.

3. As reported in Alexandre Oublicheff, *Beethoven, ses critiques et ses glossateurs* (Paris: Jules Gavelot, 1857), in such a way that hinted at the story's already-wide currency.

4. Schindler, *Beethoven as I Knew Him*, Donald W. MacArdle, trans. (New York: Dover Publications, 1996; orig. 1860), p. 502.

5. James H. Johnson, *Listening in Paris: A Cultural History* (University of California Press, 1995), p. 258.

6. Beate Angelika Kraus, *Beethoven-Rezeption in Frankreich* (Bonn: Verlag Beethoven-Haus, 2001), p. 111.

7. Hector Berlioz, *The Art of Music and Other Essays*, Elizabeth Csicery-Rónay, trans. (Indiana University Press, 1994), p. 19.

8. Berlioz even adopts Hoffmann's epic style of alternating emotional impressions with unusually specific musical descriptions: "There is a striking example in [the first] movement of the effect produced in some contexts by the excessive doubling of parts, and also of the untamed quality of the

six-four chord above the supertonic, otherwise known as the second inversion of the dominant chord," and so forth. Ibid., p. 20.

9. Schrade, *Beethoven in France* p. 29.

10. Berlioz, *The Art of Music and Other Essays*, p. 19.

11. Schrade, *Beethoven in France*, p. 52.

12. Walter Benjamin, *The Arcades Project*, Howard Eiland and Kevin McLaughlin, trans. (Harvard University Press, 2002), p. 417.

13. Ibid., p. 417.

14. Quoted in ibid., p. 454.

15. Quoted in Schrade, *Beethoven in France*, p. 177.

16. Quoted in Angelica Zander Rudenstine, *Modern Painting, Drawing & Sculpture Collected by Emily and Joseph Pulitzer, Jr.*, vol. 4 (Harvard University Art Museums, 1988), p. 587.

17. Ibid., p. 588.

18. Emile-François Julia, *Antoine Bourdelle: Maitre d'Œuvre* (Paris: Librairie de France, 1930), p. 110 (*"une sorte de confession involontaire"*).

19. Arnold Schering, *Beethoven und der deutsche Idealismus: rede gehalten beim Festakt zur feier der 150* (Leipzig: Verlag von C. F. Kahnt, 1921), pp. 3–4, 20. (*"[E]in niedergebrochenes Volk, stehen wir abermals im Begriff, Beethoven zu feiern"; "Das Heroische in diesem höchsten Sinne zog ihn du den Helden Homers und Plutarchs, zu Coriolan, zu Egmont, zu 'Fidelio', wo gar ein Weib männliches Heldentum verkörpert. Er selbst spürte im eigenen Blute etwas von Heroentum. Wenn der furor teutonicus über ihn kam, so sprühte seine Phantasie Funken und rüttelte an den Schranken des damals praktisch Möglichen: in der C-Moll-Symphonie, der Eroica, im ersten Satze der neunten Symphonie, die einem so schwachen Geschlecht wie dem um 1850 geheimes Grauen einflöste."*)

20. "A.E.," "*Beethoven und die Dichtung*" (review), *Music & Letters* 18, no. 2 (April 1937): 208.

21. Paul Bekker, *Beethoven*, M. M. Bozman, trans. (London and Toronto: J. M. Dent & Sons, Ltd., 1932), p. 170.

22. Ibid., p. 171.

23. Leon Botstein, "The Search for Meaning in Beethoven: Popularity, Intimacy, and Politics in Historical Perspective," in Scott Burnham and Michael P. Steinberg, eds., *Beethoven and His World* (Princeton University Press, 2000), p. 355.

24. Quoted in David B. Dennis, *Beethoven in German Politics, 1870–1989* (Yale University Press, 1996), p. 151.

25. Alfred Kerr, *Eintagsfliegen, oder Die Macht der Kritik, Die Welt im Drama IV* (Berlin: S. Fischer Verlag, 1917), pp. 163, 165 (*"Die Theater wollen auch leben. Fragt sich, was gespielt werden kann . . . . Spielt künftig das Beste, das wir haben. Spielt, was an unsren stolzesten Stolz erinnert. Und wenn ihr keine Stücke wißt, so nehmt euch fünfzig Musiker. Und sprecht kein Wort. Und spielt an jedem Abend Beethoven. Beethoven. Beethoven."*).

26. Heinrich Schenker, *Der Tonwille: Pamphlets in Witness of the Immutable Laws of Music*, William Drabkin, trans., vol. 1 (Oxford University Press, 2004), p. 3.

27. Ibid., pp. 4–5.

28. Ibid., p. 12.

29. Ibid., p. 20.

30. Hellmut Federhofer, *Heinrich Schenker: Nach Tagebüchern und Briefen in der Oswald Jonas Memorial Collection, University of California, Riverside* (Hildesheim: Georg Olms Verlag, 1985), p. 37n. (Emphasis added.)

31. Quoted in Nicholas Cook, *The Schenker Project: Culture, Race, and Music Theory in Fin-de-Siècle Vienna* (Oxford University Press, 2007), p. 208.

32. Allen Forte, "Heinrich Schenker," in *The New Grove Dictionary of Music and Musicians*, Stanley Sadie, ed., vol. 16 (London: Macmillan, 1980): 627–28.

33. Nelson Goodman, *Languages of Art: An Approach to a Theory of Symbols* (New York: Bobbs-Merrill, 1968), p. 112.

34. Ibid., p. 187. For a fascinating exploration of the implications and interpretations of this passage, see Lydia Goehr, "Three Blind Mice: Goodman, McLuhan, and Adorno on the Art of Music and Listening in the Age of Global Transmission," *New German Critique* 104, vol. 35, no. 2 (Summer 2008): 1–31.

35. Schenker, *Der Tonwille*, vol. 1, p. 21.

36. Cook, *The Schenker Project*, p. 203.

37. Even stories of Georg Jellinek's lighter side are Teutonically heavy: "Some of [Jellinek's] students will recall the perplexed *Dienstmann* who once appeared at the door of his classroom and stood there as though nailed to the spot. Upon hearing the stern command 'Heraus mit dir' (out with you) of the apparently enraged professor, the bewilderment of the man-servant changed to sudden fright, followed by a hasty retreat. For a moment the class believed the professor's anger genuine, but it soon dawned upon us that it was a mere outburst of German humor, and all joined in a hearty laugh over the poor fellow's discomfiture." ("George Jellinek," *The American Journal of International Law* 5, no. 3 [July 1911]: 717–18.)

38. See Wayne Alpern, "Music Theory as a Mode of Law: The Case of Heinrich Schenker, Esq.," *Cardozo Law Review* 20 (1998–1999): 1468–74.

39. Georg Jellinek, *The Declaration of the Rights of Man and of Citizens*, Max Farrand, trans. (New York: Henry Holt and Company, 1901), p. 97.

40. Heinrich Schenker, *Free Composition (Der freie Satz): Volume III of New Musical Theories and Fantasies*, Ernst Oster, trans. (New York: Longman, 1979), p. 3.

41. Alpern, "Music Theory as a Mode of Law," pp. 1474–75.

42. See, for instance, this passage from Schenker's *Harmony*: "The relationships of the tone are established in its systems. . . . A tone dominates the others if it subjects them to its superior vital force, within the relationship fixed in the various systems. In this sense, a system resembles, in anthropomorphic terms, a constitution, regulation, statute, or whatever other name we use to grasp conceptually the manifold relationships we enter." (Heinrich Schenker, *Harmony*, Oswald Jonas, ed.; Elisabeth Mann Borgese, trans. [University of Chicago Press, 1954], p. 84.)

43. Georg Jellinek, *Allgemeine Staatslehre* (Berlin: Verlag von O. Häring, 1905), p. 49. (Emphasis added.) (*"Die Staatsrechtslehre ist . . . eine Normwissenschaft.*

Ihre Normen sind von den Aussagen über das Sein des Staates als sozialer Erscheinung scharf zu trennen.")

44. Georg Jellinek, *Introduction à la Doctrine de L'État*, Georges Fardis, ed., trans. (Paris: Albert Fontemoing, 1904), pp. 84–85. (*"Veut-on se placer dans le domaine de l'esthétique? Le point de vue devient tout autre. . . . Il existe ainsi, dans le monde des sensations d'art, une vérité qui n'a rien de commun avec celle du monde des connaissances naturelles. La symphonie en ut mineur de Beethoven est, au point de vue du sentiment et de la perception musicale, la réalité la plus profonde, la plus indiscutablement vraie, la plus puissante: toute la science naturelle ne peut rien contre la conscience de cette réalité. . . . Les choses se comportent d'une manière analogue eu matière de droit. . . . Le monde juridique est un monde d'idées, il se comporte vis-à-vis du monde tangible comme le monde de l'art vis-à-vis du monde des sciences naturelles."*)

45. Cook, *The Schenker Project*, p. 212.

46. Scott Burnham, *Beethoven Hero* (Princeton University Press, 2000), pp. 99–100.

47. Heinrich Schenker, *Der Tonwille*, vol. 1, p. 27.

48. Ibid., pp. 27–29.

49. Ibid., p. 29.

50. Ibid., p. 187.

51. Ibid., p. 187.

52. Ibid., p. 196.

53. Ibid., p. 30.

54. Henrich Schenker, *Counterpoint*, John Rothgeb and Jürgen Thym, trans., Book 1 (New York: Schirmer Books, 1987), p. xviii.

55. Ibid., Book 2, pp. xiii.

56. Ibid., Book 2, p. xvi.

57. Cook, *The Schenker Project*, p. 150.

58. Quoted in Dennis, *Beethoven in German Politics*, p. 147.

59. Ibid., p. 149.

60. Schenker's argument might also be read as an example of a Teutonically heavy sense of humor; see Cook, *The Schenker Project*, p. 148.

61. "Reunion in San Francisco," *Billboard*, May 5, 1945, p. 9.

62. Paul Johnson, "When Daring Dons Sported Through the Unguarded Groves of Academe," *The Spectator* 282, no. 8914 (June 12, 1999): 29.

63. As related in "Tam-tam-tam-ta," *Der Spiegel* (Sept. 3, 1970). See also Jeremy Bennett, *British Broadcasting and the Danish Resistance Movement, 1940–1945* (Cambridge University Press, 1966), p. 40.

64. C. E. Stevens, "Gildas Sapiens," *The English Historical Review* 56, no. 223 (July 1941): 358.

65. See, for example, Sir John Lawrence's version of the story in Anthony Rudolf, *Sage Eye: The Aesthetic Passion of Jonathan Griffin* (Berkeley, CA: Menard Press, 1992), p. 61. Lawrence attributes to Stevens the notion of an audible signal, but credits the Morse Code idea to "a large cigar smoking man from the Ministry of Warfare, whose name I forget."

66. James Blades, *Percussion Instruments and Their History* (New York: Frederick A. Praeger, 1970), p. 68.

67. See Franklin Leonard Pope, "The American Inventors of the Telegraph," *The Century* 35, no. 6 (April 1888).

68. Samuel F. B. Morse, *Foreign Conspiracy Against the Liberties of the United States: The Numbers Under the Signature of Brutus, Originally Published in the New York Observer* ("Seventh Edition") (New York: American and Foreign Christian Union, 1855), pp. 33–34.

69. Quoted in Nicolas Slonimsky, *A Thing or Two About Music* (New York: Allen, Towne, & Heath, 1948), p. 81.

70. Dennis, *Beethoven in German Politics*, p. 170.

71. Ibid., p. 173. A 1953 episode of the television program *This Is Your Life*, telling the story of Hanna Bloch Kohner, a Holocaust survivor, would use the Fifth to underscore the liberation of Hanna and the other inmates from the Mauthausen concentration camp. See Jeffrey Shandler, *While America Watches: Televising the Holocaust* (Oxford University Press, 1999), pp. 30–32.

72. Both the poster and the card are reproduced in Diane DeBlois and Robert Dalton Harris. "Morse Code V for Victory: Morale through the Mail in WWII," Smithsonian National Postal Museum, September 27, 2008, http://www.postalmuseum.si.edu/symposium2008/DeBlois-Harris-V_for_Victory-paper.pdf.

73. The Philharmonic-Symphony Society of New York, program for November 11–12, 1943. (Thanks to Will Robin for finding this program in the New York Philharmonic's digital archives: http://archives.nyphil.org/index.php/artifact/2e25ab01-fdca-416e-9d2a-dfae3ddf78b8.)

74. Martin Gilbert, *The Churchill War Papers: The Ever-Widening War, 1941*, vol. 3 (New York: W. W. Norton & Co., 2001), p. 705.

75. Jonathan Aitken, *Heroes and Contemporaries* (London: Continuum, 2006), p. 22.

76. As in *Life* magazine, vol. 73, no. 1 (July 7, 1972), p. 21.

77. Dennis, *Beethoven in German Politics*, p. 166.

78. Schoenberg to Kurt List, January 24, 1946, in Schoenberg, *Arnold Schoenberg: Letters*, Erwin Stein, ed. (University of California Press, 1987), p. 238.

79. Sam H. Shirakawa, *The Devil's Music Master: The Controversial Life and Career of Wilhelm Furtwängler* (Oxford University Press, 1992), p. 280.

80. Richard J. Evans, *Rereading German History 1800–1996: From Unification to Reunification* (London: Routledge, 1997), p. 192. Furtwängler was on Goebbels' *Gottbegnadeten* ("God-gifted") list, a register of those artists the Reich Minister of Propaganda deemed irreplaceable to the regime and, thus, exempt from military service.

81. How much danger from the Nazi regime Furtwängler was ever in is not clear. Both Shirakawa and German musicologist Fred K. Prieberg have proposed that Himmler actively sought Furtwängler's arrest, suspecting him of being sympathetic to the 20 July plot to assassinate Hitler; but Michael H. Kater, in particular, has strongly doubted this theory: see Michael H. Kater,

The Twisted Muse: Musicians and Their Music in the Third Reich (Oxford University Press, 1999), p. 202.

82. Harvey Sachs, *Toscanini* (New York: Harper & Row, 1988), p. 244.

83. As translated in Bryan R. Simms, "New Documents in the Schoenberg-Schenker Polemic," *Perspectives of New Music* 16, no. 1 (Autumn-Winter 1977): 115–16.

84. Ibid., p. 113.

85. Ibid., p. 124.

86. Quoted in Nicolas Slonimsky, *Lexicon of Musical Invective* (New York: W. W. Norton & Co., 2000), p. 162.

87. "Funds for Study with Schoenberg," *The New York Times*, Sept. 26, 1933.

88. Arnold Schoenberg, "How I Came to Compose the Ode to Napoleon," in Joseph Auner, *A Schoenberg Reader: Documents of a Life* (Yale University Press, 2003), pp. 290–91.

89. Maurice Maeterlinck, *The Life of the Bee*, Alfred Sutro, trans. (New York: Dodd, Mead, and Company, 1903), pp. 351–52.

90. Auner, *A Schoenberg Reader*, p. 291.

91. Leonard Stein, "A Note on the Genesis of the *Ode to Napoleon*," *Journal of the Arnold Schoenberg Institute* II, no. 1 (Oct. 1977), p. 52.

92. According to one report, Schoenberg at first worked with a German translation of the poem, which lacked the final verses, and was "thrilled immeasurably" when he saw the complete version's reference to Washington; see Walter H. Rubsamen, "Schoenberg in America," *The Musical Quarterly* 37, no. 4 (Oct., 1951): 478. However, Schoenberg's typed copy of the poem in English, with extensive precompositional notes, indicates that Schoenberg was in possession of the full version before starting work on the piece. See Martha M. Hyde, "The Format and Function of Schoenberg's Twelve-Tone Sketches," *Journal of the American Musicological Society* 36, no. 3 (Autumn 1983): 468–70.

93. After Napoléon's return from exile—the adventure of the Hundred Days—Byron renewed his affection, hoping that a victory might produce a radical shift in European society. Napoléon's final defeat forestalled that possibility. The Boston-based scholar George Ticknor was visiting the poet when the news arrived:

> After an instant's pause, Lord Byron replied, "I am d——d sorry for it"; and then, after another slight pause, he added, "I didn't know but I might live to see Lord Castlereagh's head on a pole. But I suppose I sha'n't, now." And this was the first impression produced on his impetuous nature by the news of the battle of Waterloo.

Napoléon himself might have long since ceased to be anything but a symbol to Byron, but the collapse of what he symbolized—the prospect of a fit retribution for a conservative Europe—crushed the Emperor's onetime castigator. See Ticknor, *Life, Letters, and Journals of George Tick-*

nor (Boston and New York: Houghton Mifflin Company, 1909), vol. 1, p. 60.

94. Hyde, "The Format and Function of Schoenberg's Twelve-Tone Sketches," pp. 468–70.

95. Stein, "A Note on the Genesis of the *Ode to Napoleon,*" p. 53.

96. Victor Klemperer, *The Language of the Third Reich: LTI—Lingua Tertii Imperii: A Philologist's Notebook,* Martin Brady, trans. (London: Athlone Press, 2000), p. 16.

97. Schoenberg's unease was, perhaps, anticipated by that of the Russian novelist Leo Tolstoy. In 1900, composer Sergei Rachmaninoff was invited to visit the great man (it was the composer's second meeting with Tolstoy). Asked to play something, Rachmaninoff and Feodor Chaliapin performed Rachmaninoff's song "Fate" (op. 21, no. 1), the music of which liberally quotes the opening of Beethoven's Fifth. As Rachmaninoff later recalled:

> When we finished, we felt that all were delighted. Suddenly the enthusiastic applause was hushed and everyone was silent. Tolstoy sat in an armchair a little apart from the others, looking gloomy and cross. For the next hour I evaded him, but suddenly he came up to me and declared excitedly: "I must speak to you. I must tell you how I dislike it all!" And he went on and on: "Beethoven is nonsense, Pushkin and Lermontov also." It was awful. (Sergei Bertensson and Jay Leyda, *Sergei Rachmaninoff: A Lifetime in Music* [New York University Press, 1956], p. 89.)

The following year, Tolstoy would be excommunicated from the Russian Orthodox Church for his espousal of anarcho-pacifist principles.

98. Pierre Boulez, "Schoenberg Is Dead," *Stocktakings from an Apprenticeship,* Paule Thévenin, ed.; Stephen Walsh, trans. (Oxford: Clarendon Press, 1991), p. 213.

99. Wilhelm Langhans, *Die Geschichte der Musik des 17. 18. und 19. Jahrhunderts* (Leipzig: Verlag von F. E. C. Leuckart, 1887), Zweiter Band, p. 232.

100. Klemperer, *The Language of the Third Reich,* p. 8.

101. Ernst Kris and Hans Speier, *German Radio Propaganda: Report on Home Broadcasts During the War* (Oxford University Press, 1944), pp. 431–32.

CHAPTER 7. Samples

1. W. P. Lehmann, "Decoding of the Martian Language," *The Graduate Journal* (University of Texas at Austin) 7, no. 1 (Dec. 1965): 269. The December 1965 issue of *The Graduate Journal* of the University of Texas at Austin was dedicated to "Planets and People"; Lehmann's contribution was this speculative article disguised as a science-fiction story, detailing the efforts of future humans to decipher the musically based missives of Martians.

2. *Sherlock Holmes and the Voice of Terror.* Dir. John Rawlins. Universal Pictures, 1942.

3. *Fifth Column Mouse.* Dir. I. Freleng. Warner Bros. Pictures, 1943.

4. *Scrap Happy Daffy.* Dir. Frank Tashlin. Warner Bros. Pictures, 1943.

5. *Ding Dog Daddy*. Dir. I. Freleng. Warner Bros. Pictures, 1942; *The Home Front*. Dir. Frank Tashlin. Warner Bros./U.S. Army Signal Corps, 1943.

6. *Reunion in France*. Dir. Jules Dassin. Metro-Goldwyn-Mayer, 1942.

7. *Darby's Rangers*. Dir. William Wellman. Warner Bros. Pictures, 1958.

8. *Verboten!* Dir. Samuel Fuller. RKO Pictures, 1959.

9. Samuel Fuller, *A Third Face: My Tale of Writing, Fighting, and Filmmaking* (New York: Alfred A. Knopf, 2002), pp. 208–9. Fuller returned to the scene in his 1974 black-comedy thriller *Dead Pigeon on Beethoven Street*.

10. *The Longest Day*. Dir. Ken Annakin, Andrew Marton, and Bernhard Wicki. 20th-Century-Fox, 1962.

11. Alan Sillitoe, *The General* (New York: Alfred A. Knopf, 1961), pp. 126–27.

12. *Counterpoint*. Dir. Ralph Nelson. Universal Pictures, 1967.

13. *Celebrity*. Dir. Woody Allen. Miramax Films, 1998.

14. *L.A. Story*. Dir. Mick Jackson. TriStar Pictures, 1991.

15. *Un Grand Amour de Beethoven*. Dir. Abel Gance. Général Productions, 1936.

16. *Immortal Beloved*. Dir. Bernard Rose. Columbia Pictures, 1994.

17. "Occasional Notes," *The Musical Times* (Feb. 1, 1911), p. 88.

18. Horace, *The Works of Horace*, Christopher Smart, trans., vol. 1 (London: W. Flexney; Mess. Johnson and Co.; T. Caslon, 1767), p. 23.

19. Horace, *A Poetical Translation of the Works of Horace*, Philip Francis, trans. (Edinburgh: Alexander Donaldson, 1779), p. 11.

20. For instance, compare Karl Wilhelm Ramler's version, dating from 1769: "*Früh und spat pochet der Tod mit mächtigem Fuss an Fürstenschlosser / Und Schäferhütten*." Horace, *Horazens Oden*, Karl Wilhelm Ramler, trans. (Berlin: Sandersche Buchhandlung, 1818), p. 11.

21. Quoted in Colin Roth, "Carl Nielsen and the Danish Tradition of Storytelling," *Carl Nielsen Studies*, vol. 4 (2009): 178.

22. In Samuel Annesley, ed., *A Supplement to the Morning-Exercise at Cripple-Gate* (London: Thomas Cockerill, 1674), p. 93. Jenkyn was nearly executed for his part in Christopher Love's plot to restore Charles II to the throne. Samuel Annesley was the grandfather of John and Charles Wesley.

23. Edmund S. Lorenz, *Practical Church Music: A Discussion of Purposes Methods and Plans* (New York: Fleming H. Revell Company, 1909), p. 65.

24. Pat Conroy, *The Water Is Wide* (Boston: Houghton Mifflin Company, 1972), pp. 53–54.

25. Thomas Wentworth Higginson, *Army Life in a Black Regiment* (Boston: Houghton, Mifflin, and Company, 1900), p. 286.

26. John Sullivan Dwight, "Music in Boston," in Justin Winsor, ed., *The Memorial History of Boston, Including Suffolk County, Massachusetts, 1630–1880*, vol. 4 (Boston: James R. Osgood and Company, 1883), p. 436.

27. Ralph Waldo Emerson, *Poems* (Boston and New York: Houghton, Mifflin and Company, 1884), p. 177.

28. Ralph Ellison, "Living with Music," in *Shadow and Act* (New York: Random House, 1964), p. 189.

29. James Alan McPherson, "Indivisible Man" (1969), in Maryemma Graham

and Amritjit Singh, eds., *Conversations with Ralph Ellison* (University Press of Mississippi, 1995), p. 181.

30. Arnold Rampersad, *Ralph Ellison: A Biography* (New York: Alfred A. Knopf, 1997), pp. 41–42.

31. Ralph Ellison, "The World and the Jug," in *Shadow and Act*, p. 135.

32. Ellison, "Living with Music," in ibid., p. 190.

33. Ellison, *Invisible Man* (New York: Vintage Books, 1995), p. 232.

34. Ellison, "Richard Wright's Blues," in *Shadow and Act*, p. 94.

35. Ellison, "The World and the Jug," in ibid., p. 137.

36. Jerry Gafio Watts, *Heroism and the Black Intellectual: Ralph Ellison, Politics, and Afro-American Intellectual Life* (University of North Carolina Press, 1994), p. 110.

37. Ralph Ellison, "The World and the Jug," in *Shadow and Act*, p. 132.

38. Ellison, *Invisible Man*, p. 8.

39. Nadine Gordimer, "Beethoven Was One-Sixteenth Black," in *Beethoven Was One-Sixteenth Black and Other Stories* (New York: Farrar, Straus and Giroux, 2007), p. 7.

40. Alex Haley, "Playboy Interview: Malcolm X," *Playboy* (May 1963), p. 53.

41. Charles Schulz, *Peanuts*, July 7, 1969.

42. J. A. Rogers, *Sex and Race: Volume III: Why White and Black Mix in Spite of Opposition* (New York: J. A. Rogers, 1944), p. 306.

43. Quoted in Dominique-René de Lerma, "Beethoven as a Black Composer," *Black Music Research Journal* 10, no. 1 (Spring 1990): 120.

44. And, perhaps, a *specifically* American clash; a 2004 advertisement for the Belgian radio station Klara similarly put Beethoven in blackface (with the tagline "New, Jazz on Your Classical Radio"), with apparently little or no outcry. See Corey Keating, "WEBeethoven: Advertimento," *The Beethoven Journal* 25, no. 1 (Summer 2010): 44.

45. Adrian Piper, "Passing for White, Passing for Black," *Transition* 58 (1992): 20.

46. Hoffmann, E. T. A., "Review," in Senner et al., *The Critical Reception of Beethoven's Compositions by His German Contemporaries*, vol. 2, p. 98.

47. Steve Cannon et al., "A Very Stern Discipline: An Interview with Ralph Ellison," in Graham and Singh, *Conversations with Ralph Ellison*, p. 132.

48. Nathan Hare, "The Black Anglo-Saxons." *Negro Digest* 11, no. 7 (May 1962): 55.

49. LeRoi Jones, *Four Black Revolutionary Plays* (Indianapolis and New York: Bobbs-Merrill Company, 1969), pp. 76, 83.

50. de Lerma, "Beethoven as a Black Composer," p. 120.

51. Martin Luther King Jr., "Some Things We Must Do," in *The Papers of Martin Luther King, Jr.: Volume IV: Symbol of the Movement, January 1957–December 1958*, Clayborne Carson et al., eds. (University of California Press, 2000), p. 338. King also used the trope in his sermon "The Three Dimensions of a Complete Life." He credited it to one of his mentors, Dr. Benjamin Mays.

52. "Spotlight Winners of the Week," *Billboard*, May 1, 1961, p. 21.

53. For the history of Ekseption, see Alex Gitlin's *Nederpop* page on Trace (Rick van der Linden's follow-up band): http://www.alexgitlin.com/trace.htm.

See also Ralf Hoffmann, *"Der Grenzgänger"* (interview with Rick van der Linden), *Okey!*, July-August 2001, http://www.okey-online.com/artikel /041_report/index.html.

54. Apollo 100's version of "Jesu, Joy of Man's Desiring" was, in fact, nearly identical to one recorded by the group Jigsaw two years earlier.

55. Patrice Eyries et al, "Private Stock Album Discography," http://bsnpubs.com /nyc/privatestock/privatestock.html.

56. Fred Bronson, *The Billboard Book of Number 1 Hits* (New York: Billboard Books, 2003), p. 444.

57. Quoted in Ken McLeod, "'A Fifth of Beethoven': Disco, Classical Music, and the Politics of Inclusion," *American Music* 24, no. 3 (Autumn 2006): 352.

58. Robert Christgau, *Rock Albums of the '70s: A Critical Guide* (New York: Da Capo Press, 1990), p. 271.

59. For a further take on this idea, see McLeod, "'A Fifth of Beethoven.'"

60. Richard Dyer, *Only Entertainment* (London: Routledge, 2002), p. 156.

61. See Editha and Richard Sterba, *Beethoven and His Nephew: A Psychoanalytical Study of Their Relationship* (New York: Schocken Books, 1971), particularly pp. 97–111.

62. Philip Brett and Elizabeth Wood, "Lesbian and Gay Music," in Brett et al., *Queering the Pitch: The New Gay and Lesbian Musicology* (New York and Abingdon: Routledge, 2006), p. 371.

63. See the cover of *Rolling Stone*, Feb. 9, 2006.

64. Maria Aspan, "BET Says Cartoon Was Just a Satire," *The New York Times*, August 27, 2007, http://www.nytimes.com/2007/08/27/business /media/27bet.html.

65. "Man Behind BET's 'Read a Book' Responds to Critics," *Tell Me More*, National Public Radio, Sept. 17, 2007, http://www.npr.org/templates /story/story.php?storyId=14466377.

66. A House, "Endless Art," *I Am the Greatest* (recording), songs by A House, produced by Edwyn Collins. Setanta Records SETLP3 (1992).

67. Peter Ustinov, *Beethoven's Tenth: A Comedy in Two Acts* (New York: Samuel French, Inc., 1985), pp. 7, 49.

68. James H. Collins, "Beethoven Gets a Public Relations Job," *Public Utilities Fortnightly* 41, no. 9 (April 22, 1948): 546.

69. Ibid., p. 548.

70. A similar ad made reference to Stradivarius violins. During the recording session, Welles balked: "Come on, gentlemen, now really! You have a nice, pleasant little cheap wine here. You haven't got the presumption to compare it to a Stradivarius violin. It's odious." See Barbara Leaming, *Orson Welles* (New York: Penguin Books, 1985), p. 490.

71. Al DiOrio, *Bobby Darin: The Incredible Story of an Amazing Life* (Philadelphia: Running Press, 2004), p. 42.

72. Jean Halliday, "Hyundai Push Not for Classical-Music Purists," *Advertising Age,* July 19, 2007. http://adage.com/article?article_id=119412.

73. "Hyundai's 'Big Duh' Campaign Snares Top Spots in Consumer Recall Study,"

press release, March 31, 2008. http://www.hyundainews.com/Corporate
_News/Corporate/03_31_2008_2774.asp.

74. As noted by Jeffrey Rowe, who portrayed Beethoven in the com-
    mercial: "Yamadai Sugomen TVCM," *Jetset*, June 20, 2008, http://
    jeff.jetsets.jp/?p=75.
75. General Instrument, *Microelectronics Data Catalog* (1982): 5–26.
76. See, for example, Steve Ciarcia, "Ciarcia's Circuit Cellar: A Musical Tele-
    phone Bell," *Byte* 9, no. 7 (July 1984), pp. 125–33.
77. Dan Briody, "Thou shalt learn and abide by the Ten Commandments of
    cell-phone etiquette," *InfoWorld* (June 12, 2000): 59B.
78. Christopher Reich, *The First Billion* (New York: Random House, 2003),
    p. 385.
79. Beth Harbison, *Shoe Addicts Anonymous* (New York: Macmillan, 2008),
    p. 151.
80. Caroline B. Cooney, *Hit the Road* (New York: Random House, 2005),
    p. 16.
81. E. R. Webb, *Gemini's Cross* (Tate Publishing, 2007), p. 276.
82. Jonathan Kellerman, *Rage* (New York: Ballantine Books, 2005), p. 127.
83. Linda Ladd, *Die Smiling* (Pinnacle Books, 2008), p. 13.
84. Christine McGuire, *Until Judgment Day* (New York: Simon and Schuster,
    2003), pp. 255–56.
85. Peggy Gifford, *Moxy Maxwell Does Not Love Writing Thank-You Notes* (New
    York: Random House, 2008), p. 51.
86. *A Clockwork Orange*. Dir. Stanley Kubrick. Warner Bros. Pictures, 1971.
87. *Bara no Sōretsu*. Dir. Toshio Matsumoto. Art Theatre Guild, 1969.
88. *The Goddess of 1967*. Dir. Clara Law. New South Wales Film & Television
    Office, 2000.
89. Jon Nelson, "Stock, Hausen & Walkman," *Some Assembly Required*, Oct.
    31, 2009, http://www.blog.some-assembly-required.net/2009/10/stock
    -hausen-walkman.html.
90. Bill Odenkirk, writer; Matthew Nastuk, director, "The Seven-Beer Snitch,"
    The Simpsons, season 16, episode no. 349 (first aired April 3, 2005).
91. Theodor W. Adorno, "A Social Critique of Radio Music," *Kenyon Review* 7,
    no. 2 (Spring 1945): 214.
92. Adorno, "On the Fetish-Character in Music and the Regression of Listen-
    ing," Maurice Goldbloom, trans., in Theodor W. Adorno, *Essays on Music*,
    Richard D. Leppert, ed.(University of California Press, 2002), p. 303.
93. Adorno, *Beethoven: The Philosophy of Music*, Rolf Tiedemann, ed.; Edmund
    Jephcott, trans. (Cambridge: Polity Press, 2002), .p. 31.
94. For the history of "Little Annie," see Susan J. Douglas, *Listening In: Radio
    and the American Imagination* (University of Minnesota Press, 2004),
    pp. 137–39.
95. Quoted in Detlev Clausen, *Theodor W. Adorno: One Last Genius*, Rodney Liv-
    ingstone, trans., vol. 2 (Harvard University Press, 2008), p. 10.
96. Max Paddison, *Adorno's Aesthetics of Music* (Cambridge University Press,
    1997), p. 8.

97. Theodor W. Adorno, "The Curious Realist: On Siegfried Kracauer," in Theodor W. Adorno, *Notes to Literature*, vol. 2, Shierry Weber Nicholson, trans., vol. 2, (Columbia University Press, 1992), p. 59.

98. Leo Löwenthal, as quoted in Stefan Müller-Doohm, *Adorno: A Biography* (Cambridge: Polity Press, 2005), p. 30.

99. Ibid., pp. 97, 91.

100. Quoted in ibid., p. 163.

101. Theodor W. Adorno, *Negative Dialectics*, E. B. Ashton, trans. (New York: The Seabury Press, 1973), p. 157.

102. Robert Hullot-Kentor, *Things Beyond Resemblance: Collected Essays on Theodor W. Adorno* (Columbia University Press, 2006), p. 15.

103. Ibid.

104. Adorno, "On Jazz," translated by J. Owen Daniel, *Discourse* 12, no. 1 (Fall-Winter 1989–90): 66.

105. Ibid., pp. 67–68.

106. Harry Cooper, "On *Über Jazz*: Replaying Adorno with the Grain," *October* 75 (Winter 1996): 133.

107. Theodor W. Adorno and Hanns Eisler, *Composing for the Films* (Oxford University Press, 1947), p. 16.

108. Theodor W. Adorno and Max Horkheimer. *Dialectic of Enlightenment*, John Cumming, trans. (New York: Herder and Herder, 1972), p. 136.

109. Ibid., p. 134. See also Esther Leslie, *Hollywood Flatlands: Animation, Critical Theory, and the Avant-Garde* (London and New York: Verso, 2004), pp. 158–99.

110. Ralph Ellison, *Invisible Man*, p. 8. For possible correspondences between Ellison's and Adorno's critiques of jazz, see James M. Harding, "Adorno, Ellison, and the Critique of Jazz," *Cultural Critique* 31 (Autumn 1995): 129–58.

111. As late as 1969, Adorno still included the Beethoven book on a list of works-in-progress that he intended to complete. See Theodor W. Adorno, *Beethoven: The Philosophy of Music*, p. viii.

112. June Bundy, "Book-of-Mo. Starts Classic Disk Club." *Billboard* (Sept. 4, 1954), p. 11. For a typical advertisement, see *Life* (Nov. 15, 1954), p. 9.

113. Theodor W. Adorno, "Analytical Study of the NBC 'Music Appreciation Hour.'" *The Musical Quarterly* 78, no. 2 (Summer 1994): 358.

114. Ibid., p. 355.

115. Quoted in Robert Hullot-Kentor, *Things Beyond Resemblance*, p. 175.

116. Theodor W. Adorno, *Beethoven: The Philosophy of Music*, p. 26.

117. Ibid., p. 121.

118. Ibid., p. 46.

119. G. W. F. Hegel, *Lectures on Logic*, Clark Butler, trans. (Indiana University Press, 2008), pp. 92, 95.

120. Theodor W. Adorno, *Beethoven: The Philosophy of Music*, p. 34.

121. Daniel P. K. Chua, "The Promise of Nothing: The Dialectic of Freedom in Adorno's Beethoven," *Beethoven Forum* 12, no. 1 (Spring 2006): 20. Much of my discussion is indebted to Chua's argument.

122. Friedrich Hölderlin, "Oldest Programme for a System of German Idealism" (1796). Stefan Bird-Pollan, trans., in *Classic and Romantic German Aesthetics*, edited by J. M. Bernstein (Cambridge University Press, 2003), pp. 185–86.
123. Thomas Mann, *Doctor Faustus*, H. T. Lowe-Porter, trans. (New York: Alfred A. Knopf, 1948), p. 237.
124. Theodor W. Adorno, *Beethoven: The Philosophy of Music*, p. 46.
125. Ibid., p. 122.
126. Ibid., p. 121. (Emphasis added.)
127. Reproduced in Adorno, *Beethoven: The Philosophy of Music*, p. 48.
128. Quoted in Robert Hullot-Kantor, *Things Beyond Resemblance*, p. 30.
129. Theodor W. Adorno, *Beethoven: The Philosophy of Music*, p. 47.
130. Ibid., p. 32. Adorno added a note: "real humanism"—the term is from Marx and Engels, referring not to the intellectualized humanism of the German Idealists, but the practical humanism of socialist reformers.
131. Ibid., p. 121.

EPILOGUE

1. See John F. Fetzer, *Romantic Orpheus: Profiles of Clemens Brentano* (University of California Press, 1974), pp. 22–23.
2. Quoted in Thayer-Forbes, *Thayer's Life of Beethoven*, p. 448.
3. Ibid.
4. Quoted in Alexander Wheelock Thayer, *Ludwig van Beethoven's Leben*, Dritter Band (Berlin: W. Weber, 1879), p. 58.
5. Thayer-Forbes, p. 448.
6. Beethoven to Heinrich Joseph von Collin, Feb. (?) 1808, in Emily Anderson, ed., *The Letters of Beethoven, Collected, Translated and Edited with an Introduction, Appendixes, Notes and Indexes* (New York: St. Martin's Press, 1961), p. 186.
7. Beethoven to Breitkopf und Härtel, January 7, 1809, in Anderson, *Letters*, vol. 1, p. 212.
8. Thayer-Forbes, pp. 433–34.
9. Beethoven to Breitkopf und Härtel, June 8, 1808; July 8, 1808; and July 16, 1808, in Anderson, *Letters*, vol. 2, pp. 188–93.
10. Beethoven to Breitkopf und Härtel, Jan. 7, 1809, in Anderson, *Letters*, vol. 1, p. 212.
11. "News. Leipzig," in Wayne M. Senner et al., *The Critical Reception of Beethoven's Compositions by His German Contemporaries*, vol. 2 (originally published in *Allgemeine musikalische Zeitung* 11, Feb. 1, 1809), p. 92.

Bibliography

A House. *I Am the Greatest* (recording), songs by A House, produced by Edwyn Collins. Setanta Records SETLP3 (1992).

"A.E." "*Beethoven und die Dichtung*" (review). *Music & Letters* 18, no. 2 (April 1937): 206–11.

Adams, Douglas. *The Original Hitchhiker Radio Scripts.* Edited by Geoffrey Perkins. New York: Harmony Books, 1985.

Adorno, Theodor W. "Analytical Study of the NBC 'Music Appreciation Hour.'" *The Musical Quarterly* 78, no. 2 (Summer 1994): 325–77.

Adorno, Theodor W. *Beethoven: The Philosophy of Music.* Edited by Rolf Tiedemann; translated by Edmund Jephcott. Cambridge: Polity Press, 2002.

Adorno, Theodor W. "The Curious Realist: On Siegfried Kracauer." In Theodor W. Adorno, *Notes to Literature,* volume 2, translated by Sherry Weber Nicholson, pp. 58–75. Columbia University Press, 1992.

Adorno, Theodor W. *Negative Dialectics.* Translated by E. B. Ashton. New York: Seabury Press, 1973.

Adorno, Theodor W. "On Jazz." Translated by J. Owen Daniel. *Discourse* 12, no. 1 (Fall-Winter 1989–90): 39–69.

Adorno, Theodor W. "On the Fetish-Character in Music and the Regression of Listening." Translated by Maurice Goldbloom. In Theodor W. Adorno, *Essays on Music,* edited Richard D. Leppert, pp. 288–317. University of California Press, 2002.

Adorno, Theodor W. "A Social Critique of Radio Music." *Kenyon Review* 7, no. 2 (Spring 1945): 208–17.

Adorno, Theodor W., and Hanns Eisler. *Composing for the Films.* Oxford University Press, 1947.

Adorno, Theodor W., and Max Horkheimer. *Dialectic of Enlightenment.* Translated by John Cumming. New York: Herder and Herder, 1972.

Aitken, Jonathan. *Heroes and Contemporaries.* London: Continuum, 2006.

Alcott, A. Bronson. "Orphic Sayings." *The Dial* 1, no. 1 (July 1840): 85–98.

Allardt, Linda, David W. Hill, and Ruth H. Bennett, editors. *The Journals and Miscellaneous Notebooks of Ralph Waldo Emerson,* vol. 15. Harvard University Press, 1982.

Alpern, Wayne. "Music Theory as a Mode of Law: The Case of Heinrich Schenker, Esq." *Cardozo Law Review* 20 (1998–1999): 1459–1511.

Anderson, Emily, ed. *The Letters of Beethoven, Collected, Translated and Edited with an Introduction, Appendixes, Notes and Indexes.* New York: St. Martin's Press, 1961.

Anderson, Stuart, and Peter Homan. "'Best for me, best for you'—a history of Beecham's Pills 1842–1998." *The Pharmaceutical Journal* 269 (December 21/28, 2002): 921–24.

Annesley, Samuel, editor. *A Supplement to the Morning-Exercise at Cripple-Gate.* London: Thomas Cockerill, 1674.

Aristotle. *The "Art" of Rhetoric.* Translated by J. H. Freese. Harvard University Press, 1926.

Armstrong, Paul B. *Play and the Politics of Reading: The Social Uses of Modernist Form.* Cornell University Press, 2005.

Aspan, Maria. "BET Says Cartoon Was Just a Satire." *The New York Times*, August 27, 2007, http://www.nytimes.com/2007/08/27/business/media/27bet.html.

Auner, Joseph, editor. *A Schoenberg Reader: Documents of a Life.* Yale University Press, 2003.

"Back Into the Darkness." *Time*, September 6, 1968, http://www.time.com/time/magazine/article/0,9171,900324,00.html.

"Bah, humbug! The classics we secretly loathe." *The Times* (London), December 23, 2009, http://entertainment.timesonline.co.uk/tol/arts_and_entertainment/specials/article6964184.ece.

Baker-Carr, Janet. *Evening at Symphony: A Portrait of the Boston Symphony Orchestra.* Boston: Houghton Mifflin Company, 1977.

Barry, C. A. "Hans von Bülow's 'Nirvána.'" *Zeitschrift der Internationalen Musikgesellschaft* 2, no. 9 (June 1901): 295–99.

Beck, Dagmar, and Grita Herre. "Einige Zweifel an der Überlieferung der Konversationshefte." In *Bericht über den Internationalen Beethoven-Kongreß 20. bis 23. März 1977 in Berlin*, edited by Harry Goldschmidt, Karl-Heinz Köhler, and Konrad Niemann, pp. 257–24. VEB Deutscher Verlag für Musik Leipzig, 1978.

Beecham, Thomas, Sir Bart. *A Mingled Chime.* New York: G. P. Putnam's Sons, 1943.

"Beethoven's 5th—Courtesy of the Police." *Hong Kong Human Rights Monitor Newsletter* (July 1997). At http://www.hkhrm.org.hk/english/reports/enw/enw0797a.htm.

Beethoven's Letters (1790–1826) from the Collection of Dr. Ludwig Nohl. Translated by Lady Wallace. London: Longmans, Green and Co., 1866.

Beiser, Frederick C. *The Fate of Reason: German Philosophy from Kant to Fichte.* Harvard University Press, 1987.

Bekker, Paul. *Beethoven.* Translated by M. M. Bozman. London and Toronto: J. M. Dent & Sons, Ltd., 1932.

Benjamin, Walter. *The Arcades Project.* Translated by Howard Eiland and Kevin McLaughlin. Harvard University Press, 2002.

Bennett, Jeremy. *British Broadcasting and the Danish Resistance Movement, 1940–1945.* Cambridge University Press, 1966.

Bergman, Herbert. "Whitman on Beethoven and Music." *Modern Language Notes* 66, no. 8 (December 1951): 556–58.

Berlin, Isaiah. *Four Essays on Liberty.* Oxford University Press, 1969.

Berlin, Isaiah. *The Magus of the North: J. G. Hamann and the Origins of Modern Irrationalism.* London: John Murray, 1993.

Berlioz, Hector. *The Art of Music and Other Essays.* Translated by Elizabeth Csicery-Rónay. Indiana University Press, 1994.

Bernstein, Leonard. *The Joy of Music.* New York: Simon and Schuster, 1959.

Bertensson, Sergei, and Jay Leyda. *Sergei Rachmaninoff: A Lifetime in Music.* New York University Press, 1956.

Blackall, Eric A. *The Novels of the German Romantics.* Cornell University Press, 1983.

Blades, James. *Percussion Instruments and Their History.* New York: Frederick A. Praeger, 1970.

Blakely, the Rev. John. *The Theology of Inventions, or, Manifestations of Deity in the Works of Art.* New York: Robert Carter & Brothers, 1856.

"The Boston Orchestra Under Dr. Karl Muck." *The New York Times,* October 13, 1906: 9.

Botstein, Leon. "The Search for Meaning in Beethoven: Popularity, Intimacy, and Politics in Historical Perspective." In *Beethoven and His World,* Scott Burnham and Michael P. Steinberg, editors, pp. 332–66. Princeton University Press, 2000.

Boulez, Pierre. *Stocktakings from an Apprenticeship.* Collected and presented by Paule Thévenin; translated by Stephen Walsh. Oxford: Clarendon Press, 1991.

Bowles, Edmund A. "Karl Muck and His Compatriots: German Conductors in America during World War I (And How They Coped)." *American Music* 25, no. 4 (Winter 2007): 405–40.

[Braddon, Mary Elizabeth.] *Mount Royal.* London: John and Robert Maxwell, 1883.

Braudy, Leo. *The Frenzy of Renown.* New York: Vintage Books, 1997.

Brenton, Howard. "Petrol Bombs Through the Proscenium Arch." Interview by Catherine Itzen and Simon Trussler. *Theatre Quarterly* 5, no. 17 (March–May 1975): 4–20.

Brett, Philip, Elizabeth Wood, and Gary C. Thomas, editors. *Queering the Pitch: The New Gay and Lesbian Musicology,* 2nd ed. New York and Abingdon: Routledge, 2006.

Brewster, Anne M. H. *St. Martin's Summer.* Boston: Ticknor and Fields, 1866.

Briody, Dan. "Thou shalt learn and abide by the Ten Commandments of cell-phone etiquette." *InfoWorld,* June 12, 2000: 59B.

Bronson, Fred. *The Billboard Book of Number 1 Hits.* New York: Billboard Books, 2003.

Broyles, Michael. *Beethoven: The Emergence and Evolution of Beethoven's Heroic Style.* New York: Excelsior Music Publishing Co., 1987.

Brunschwig, Henri. *Enlightenment and Romanticism in Eighteenth-Century Prussia.* Translated by Frank Jellinek. University of Chicago Press, 1974.

Bulwer-Lytton, Edward. *England and the English.* Paris: Baudry's European Library ("from the London Fifth Edition"), 1836.

Bulwer-Lytton, Robert. "Beethoven." *The Fortnightly Review* XII, no. LXVII (July 1, 1872): 19–38.

Bundy, June. "Book-of-Mo. Starts Classic Disk Club." *Billboard,* September 4, 1954.

Burgan, Mary. "Heroines at the Piano: Women and Music in Nineteenth-Century Fiction." *Victorian Studies* 30, no. 1 (1986): 51–76.

Burkholder, J. Peter, editor. *Charles Ives and His World.* Princeton University Press, 1996.

Burnham, Scott. *Beethoven Hero.* Princeton University Press, 2000.

Byron, George Gordon. *Lord Byron's Cain: Twelve Essays and a Text with Variants and Annotations.* Edited by Truman Guy Steffan. University of Texas Press, 1968.

Cabot, James Elliot. *A Memoir of Ralph Waldo Emerson.* Cambridge, MA: The Riverside Press, 1888.

Cairns, David. *Berlioz: Volume One: The Making of an Artist 1803–1832.* University of California Press, 2000.

Cardus, Neville. *Sir Thomas Beecham: A Memoir.* London: Collins, 1961.

Carse, Adam. *The Life of Jullien.* Cambridge: Heffer, 1951.

Cassedy, Steven. "Beethoven the Romantic: How E. T. A. Hoffmann Got It Right." *Journal of the History of Ideas* 71, no. 1 (January 2010): 1–37.

Channing, William E. *The Works of William E. Channing, D.D. Eleventh Complete Edition, with an Introduction.* Boston: George G. Channing, 1849.

Chantler, Abigail. *E.T.A. Hoffmann's Musical Aesthetics.* Ashgate Publishing, 2006.

Christgau, Robert. *Rock Albums of the '70s: A Critical Guide.* New York: Da Capo Press, 1990.

Chua, Daniel P. K. "The Promise of Nothing: The Dialectic of Freedom in Adorno's Beethoven." *Beethoven Forum* 12, no. 1 (Spring 2006): 13–35.

Ciarcia, Steve. "Ciarcia's Circuit Cellar: A Musical Telephone Bell." *Byte* 9, no. 7 (July 1984): 125–33.

Clark, Tim, Christopher Gray, Charles Radcliffe, and Donald Nicholson-Smith. "The Revolution of Modern Art and the Modern Art of Revolution." Unpublished pamphlet, 1967, http://www.notbored.org/english.html.

Clarkson, Austin. "Lecture on Dada by Stefan Wolpe." *The Musical Quarterly* 72, no. 2 (1986): 202–15.

Clausen, Detlev. *Theodor W. Adorno: One Last Genius.* Translated by Rodney Livingstone. Harvard University Press, 2008.

"Col. William Jay Expires Suddenly." *The New York Times,* March 29, 1915: 9.

Collins, James H. "Beethoven Gets a Public Relations Job." *Public Utilities Fortnightly* XLI, no. 9 (April 22, 1948): 545–51.

Comini, Alessandra. *The Changing Image of Beethoven: A Study in Mythmaking.* Santa Fe, NM: Sunstone Press, 2008.

Cone, Edward T. *Musical Form and Musical Performance.* New York: W. W. Norton & Co., 1968.

Conroy, Pat. *The Water Is Wide*. Boston: Houghton Mifflin Company, 1972.
Cook, Nicholas. *The Schenker Project: Culture, Race, and Music Theory in Fin-de-Siècle Vienna*. Oxford University Press, 2007.
Cooke, George Willis, editor. *Early Letters of George Wm. Curtis to John S. Dwight: Brook Farm and Concord*. New York and London: Harper and Brothers Publishers, 1898.
Cooney, Caroline B. *Hit the Road*. New York: Random House, 2005.
Cooper, Harry. "On *Über Jazz*: Replaying Adorno with the Grain." *October* 75 (Winter 1996): 99–133.
Cranch, Christopher Pearse. *Ariel and Caliban; with Other Poems*. Boston and New York: Houghton, Mifflin and Company, 1887.
Crunden, Robert M. *Ministers of Reform: The Progressives' Achievement in American Civilization, 1889–1920*. University of Illinois Press, 1984.
The Crystal Palace Penny Guide ("by authority of the directors"). Sydenham: Crystal Palace Printing Office, 1863.
Dannreuther, Edward. "Beethoven and His Works: A Study." *Macmillan's Magazine* 34 (July 1876): 193–209.
David, Dierdre. *Fanny Kemble: A Performed Life*. University of Pennsylvania Press, 2007.
Day Lewis, Cecil, and Charles Fenby. *Anatomy of Oxford*. London: Jonathan Cape, 1938.
de Lerma, Dominique-René. "Beethoven as a Black Composer." *Black Music Research Journal* 10, no. 1 (Spring 1990): 118–22. (Originally published in *Black Music Research Newsletter* 8, no. 1 [Fall 1985].)
Dean, Frederic. "Some Conductors and Their Batons." *The Bookman* 46, no. 5 (January 1918): 586–91.
DeBlois, Diane, and Robert Dalton Harris. "Morse Code V for Victory: Morale through the Mail in WWII." Smithsonian National Postal Museum, September 27, 2008. http://www.postalmuseum.si.edu/symposium2008/DeBlois-Harris-V_for_Victory-paper.pdf.
Debord, Guy. *The Society of the Spectacle*. Translated by Ken Knabb, http://www.bopsecrets.org/SI/debord/.
Debord, Guy, and Gil J. Wolman, "A User's Guide to Détournement." Translated by Ken Knabb, http://www.bopsecrets.org/SI/detourn.htm. (Originally in *Les Lèvres Nues*, no. 8 [May 1956].)
Del Mar, Norman. *Conducting Beethoven. Volume I: The Symphonies*. Oxford: Clarendon Press, 1992.
"Delta." "Home Correspondence: The Royal Commission and the Surplus." *The Journal of the Society of Arts*, vol. 2. London: George Bell, 1854, p. 343.
Dennis, David B. *Beethoven in German Politics, 1870–1989*. Yale University Press, 1996.
DeNora, Tia. *Beethoven and the Construction of Genius: Musical Politics in Vienna, 1792–1803*. University of California Press, 1995.
Derrida, Jacques. *The Truth in Painting*. Translated by Geoffrey Bennington and Ian Macleod. University of Chicago Press, 1987.

Dickinson, Goldsworthy Lowes. *Appearances*. New York: Doubleday, Page & Company, 1915.

DiMedeo, Annette Maria. *Frances McCollin: Her Life and Music*. Lanham, MD: Rowman & Littlefield, 1990.

DiOrio, Al. *Bobby Darin: The Incredible Story of an Amazing Life*. Philadelphia: Running Press, 2004.

Douglas, Susan J. *Listening In: Radio and the American Imagination*. University of Minnesota Press, 2004.

Duckworth, Alistair M., editor. *Howards End: Case Studies in Contemporary Criticism*. Basingstoke: Palgrave Macmillan, 1996.

Duncan, Malcolm C. *Duncan's Masonic Ritual and Monitor*. New York: Dick & Fitzgerald, 1866.

Dwight, John Sullivan. "Academy of Music—Beethoven's Symphonies." *The Pioneer* 1, no. 2 (January-February 1843): 56–60.

Dwight, John Sullivan. "Beethoven's Symphony in C Minor." *Dwight's Journal of Music* IV (October 8, 1853): 13.

[Dwight, John Sullivan.] "Musical Review: Music in Boston During the Last Winter." *The Harbinger* 1, no. 8 (August 2, 1845): 123–24.

Dwight, John Sullivan. "Musical Review: Music in Boston During the Last Winter.—No. III," *The Harbinger* 1, no. 10 (August 16, 1845): 154–57.

[Dwight, John Sullivan.] "Review: *Festus, a Poem*." *The Harbinger* 2, no. 2 (December 20, 1845): 25–27.

Dwight, John Sullivan. "The Sentiment of Various Musical Composers." *Sartain's Union Magazine of Literature and Art* VIII, no. 2 (February 1851): 132–33; Reprinted in *Dwight's Journal of Music* I (July 3, 1852): 98–99.

Dwight, John Sullivan. "Valedictory." *Dwight's Journal of Music* XLI (September 3, 1881): 122–24.

Dwight, John Sullivan. "What Lack We Yet?" *Dwight's Journal of Music* XL (September 11, 1880): 150.

Dyer, Richard. *Only Entertainment*. London: Routledge, 2002.

Ealy, George Thomas. "Of Ear Trumpets and a Resonance Plate: Early Hearing Aids and Beethoven's Hearing Perception." *19th Century Music* 17, no. 3 (Spring 1994): 262–73.

Eldridge, Richard. "Hegel on Music." In *Hegel and the Arts*, Stephen Houlgate, editor, pp. 119–45. Northwestern University Press, 2007.

Ellis, William Ashton. *Life of Richard Wagner*. London: Kegan Paul, Trench, Trübner & Co., Ltd., 1906.

Ellison, Ralph. *Invisible Man*. New York: Vintage Books, 1995.

Ellison, Ralph. *Shadow and Act*. New York: Random House, 1964.

Emerson, Ralph Waldo. *The Complete Works of Ralph Waldo Emerson*. Boston: Houghton, Mifflin and Company, 1903–04.

Emerson, Ralph Waldo. *Poems*. Boston and New York: Houghton, Mifflin and Company, 1884.

Emerson, Ralph Waldo. "Thoughts on Modern Literature," *The Dial* 1, no. 2 (October 1840): 137–58.

Engels, Friedrich. *Dialectics of Nature.* Translated by C. P. Dutt. New York: International Publishers, 1960.

Erlich, Cyril. *First Philharmonic: A History of the Royal Philharmonic Society.* Oxford University Press, 1995.

Evans, Richard J. *Rereading German History 1800–1996: From Unification to Reunification.* London: Routledge, 1997.

Eyries, Patrice, Mike Callahan, David Edwards, and Randy Watts. "Private Stock Album Discography," http://bsnpubs.com/nyc/privatestock/privatestock.html.

Federhofer, Hellmut. *Heinrich Schenker: Nach Tagebüchern und Briefen in der Oswald Jonas Memorial Collection, University of California, Riverside.* Hildesheim: Georg Olms Verlag, 1985.

Fetzer, John F. *Romantic Orpheus: Profiles of Clemens Brentano.* University of California Press, 1974.

Fillion, Michelle. "Edwardian Perspectives on Nineteenth-Century Music in E. M. Forster's *A Room with a View.*" *19th-Century Music* 25, no. 2/3 (Autumn 2001–Spring 2002): 266–95.

Finley, John H., Jr. *Four Stages of Greek Thought.* Stanford University Press, 1966.

Foata, Anne. "The Knocking at the Door. A Fantasy on Fate, Forster, and Beethoven's Fifth." *Cahiers victoriens et édouardiens* 44 (1996): 135–45.

Ford, Dennis. *The Search for Meaning: A Short History.* University of California Press, 2008.

Ford, John Lane. *Dower and Curse.* London: Tinsley Brothers, 1872.

Forster, E. M. *Goldsworthy Lowes Dickinson.* New York: Harcourt Brace Jovanovich, 1962.

Forster, E. M. *Howards End.* Mineola, NY: Dover Publications, 2002.

Forster, E. M. *Two Cheers for Democracy.* New York: Harcourt, Brace & World, Inc., 1951.

Forster, E. M. "A View Without a Room: Old Friends Fifty Years Later." *The New York Times Book Review,* July 27, 1958.

Forte, Allen. "Heinrich Schenker." In *The New Grove Dictionary of Music and Musicians,* Stanley Sadie, editor, vol. 16, pp. 627–28. London: Macmillan, 1980.

Franks, Henry. "Geist." In *Papers of the Manchester Literary Club,* vol. IV, pp. 95–106. London: Abel Heywood and Sons, 1878.

Frothingham, Octavius Brooks. *George Ripley.* Boston: Houghton, Mifflin and Company, 1886.

Fuller, Margaret. "Lives of the Great Composers, Haydn, Mozart, Handel, Bach, Beethoven." *The Dial* 2, no. 2 (October 1841): 148–203.

Fuller, Margaret. *Papers on Literature and Art.* New York: John Wiley, 1848.

Fuller, Samuel. *A Third Face: My Tale of Writing, Fighting, and Filmmaking.* New York: Alfred A. Knopf, 2002.

Fuller Maitland, J. A., editor. *Grove's Dictionary of Music and Musicians.* New York: Macmillan, 1911.

"Funds for Study with Schoenberg." *The New York Times,* September 26, 1933.

Gay, Peter. *Pleasure Wars: The Bourgeois Experience: Victoria to Freud*. New York: W. W. Norton & Co., 1998.

"George Jellinek." *The American Journal of International Law* 5, no. 3 (July 1911): 716–18.

"German Music? Maybe; Muck's Successor Undecided on Symphony Policy." *New York Tribune*, October 30, 1918: 9.

"German Opera Cut from List at Metropolitan." *New York Tribune*, November 2, 1917: 1.

Germana, Nicholas A. *The Orient of Europe: The Mythical Image of India and Competing Images of German National Identity*. Cambridge Scholars Press, 2009.

"Germans Honor War Dead: Hear Opera Singers and Orators at Carnegie Hall Meeting." *The New York Times*, May 30, 1916: 7.

Gifford, Peggy. *Moxy Maxwell Does Not Love Writing Thank-You Notes*. New York: Random House, 2008.

Gilbert, Martin. *The Churchill War Papers: The Ever-Widening War, 1941*. Vol. 3. New York: W. W. Norton & Co., 2001.

Gillen, Francis. "*Howards End* and the Neglected Narrator." *NOVEL: A Forum on Fiction* 3, no. 2 (Winter 1970): 139–52.

Glendinning, Victoria. *Leonard Woolf: A Biography*. New York: Free Press, 2006.

Goldbeck, Edward. "Beethoven." *Chicago Daily Tribune*, January 2, 1916: A5.

Goldman, William. *Adventures in the Screen Trade*. New York: Warner Books, 1983.

Goodman, Nelson. *Languages of Art: An Approach to a Theory of Symbols*. New York: Bobbs-Merrill, 1968.

Gordimer, Nadine. *Beethoven Was One-Sixteenth Black and Other Stories*. New York: Farrar, Straus and Giroux, 2007.

Gordon, Edwin E. *Tonal and Rhythm Patterns: An Objective Analysis*. Albany: State University of New York Press, 1976.

Gould, Stephen Jay. *The Flamingo's Smile: Reflections in Natural History*. New York: W. W. Norton & Co., 1985.

[Grace, Harvey.] "Interludes." *The Musical Times*, September 1, 1920: 594–97.

Graham, Maryemma, and Amritjit Singh, editors. *Conversations with Ralph Ellison*. University Press of Mississippi, 1995.

Graves, Charles L. *The Life & Letters of George Grove, C.B.* London: Macmillan and Co., 1903.

Great Exhibition of the Works of Industry of All Nations, 1851. Official Descriptive and Illustrated Catalogue. London: Spicer Brothers, Wholesale Stationers; W. Clowes and Sons, Printers, 1851.

"The Great Lower Rhine Music Festival at Düsseldorf, Whitsuntide 1830." In Senner et al., *The Critical Reception of Beethoven's Compositions by His German Contemporaries*, vol. 2, p. 132. Originally published in *Cäcilia* 12, no. 48 (1830): 3067.

Green, James F. "Beethoven's Fifth Symphony: A Forgotten Anecdote Discovered." *The Beethoven Journal* 25, no. 1 (Summer 2010): 36–37.

Grondin, Simon. "Timing and Time Perception: A Review of Recent Behavioral and Neuroscience Findings and Theoretical Directions." *Attention, Perception, & Psychophysics* 72 (2010): 561–82.

Grove, George. *Beethoven and His Nine Symphonies.* London and New York: Novello, Ewer and Co., 1896.

Grove, George, editor. *A Dictionary of Music and Musicians.* London: Macmillan & Co., 1880.

Haas, Frithjof. *Hans von Bülow: Leben und Wirken.* Wilhelmshaven: Florian Noetzel Verlag, 2002.

Hale, Philip. *Philip Hale's Boston Symphony Programme Notes.* Edited by John N. Burk. Garden City, NY: Doubleday, Doran, & Co., 1935.

Haley, Alex. "Playboy Interview: Malcolm X." *Playboy* (May 1963): 53–63.

Halliday, Jean. "Hyundai Push Not for Classical-Music Purists." *Advertising Age,* July 19, 2007. http://adage.com/article?article_id=119412.

Hallward, Peter. *Out of This World: Deleuze and the Philosophy of Creation.* London: Verso, 2006.

Hamann, J. G. "Aesthetica in nuce: A Rhapsody in Cabbalistic Prose." Translated by Joyce P. Crick. In *Classic and Romantic German Aesthetics,* edited by J. M. Bernstein, p. 124. Cambridge University Press, 2003.

Harbison, Beth. *Shoe Addicts Anonymous.* New York: Macmillan, 2008.

Harding, James M. "Adorno, Ellison, and the Critique of Jazz." *Cultural Critique* 31 (Autumn 1995): 129–58.

Harding, Walter, George Brenner, and Paul A. Doyle, editors. *Henry David Thoreau: Studies and Commentaries.* Fairleigh Dickinson University Press, 1972.

Hare, Nathan. "The Black Anglo-Saxons." *Negro Digest* 2, no. 7 (May 1962): 52–56.

Haweis, Hugh Reginald. *Music and Morals.* New York: Harper and Brothers, 1872.

Haweis, Hugh Reginald. *Travel and Talk: 1885–93–95.* London: Chatto & Windus, 1897.

Hawthorne, Nathaniel. *The Blithedale Romance and Fanshawe.* The Centenary Edition of the Works of Nathaniel Hawthorne, vol. 3. Ohio State University Press, 1964.

Hawthorne, Nathaniel. *The Letters, 1813–1843.* Edited by Thomas Woodson, L. Neal Smith, and Norman Holmes Pearson. The Centenary Edition of the Works of Nathaniel Hawthorne, vol. 15. Ohio State University Press, 1984.

Hegel, G. W. F. *Aesthetics: Lectures on Fine Art.* Translated by T. M. Knox. Oxford: Clarendon Press, 1975.

Hegel, G. W. F. *The Difference Between Fichte's and Schelling's System of Philosophy.* Translated by Walter Cerf and H. S. Harris. Albany: SUNY Press, 1977.

Hegel, G. W. F. *Hegel's Lectures on the History of Philosophy.* Translated by E. S. Haldane. London: Routledge & Kegan Paul Ltd., 1955.

Hegel, G. W. F. *Hegel's Philosophy of Mind.* Translated by William Wallace. Oxford: Clarendon Press, 1894.

Hegel, G. W. F. *Hegel's Philosophy of Right.* Translated by S. W. Dyde. London: George Bell and Sons, 1896.

Hegel, G. W. F. *Lectures on Logic.* Translated by Clark Butler. Indiana University Press, 2008.

Hegel, G. W. F. *Lectures on the Philosophy of History*. Translated by J. Sibree. London: George Bell and Sons, 1902.

Herrick, Robert. *The Poetical Works of Robert Herrick*. Edited by F. W. Moorman. Oxford: Clarendon Press, 1915.

Higginson, Thomas Wentworth. *Army Life in a Black Regiment*. Boston: Houghton, Mifflin and Company, 1900.

Higginson, Thomas Wentworth. *Part of a Man's Life*. Boston: Houghton, Mifflin and Company, 1905.

Hoffmann, E. T. A. *E. T. A. Hoffmanns Briefwechsel*. Edited by Friedrich Schnapp. München: Winkler-Verlag, 1967.

Hoffmann, E. T. A. *E. T. A. Hoffmann's Musical Writings: Kreisleriana; The Poet and the Composer; Music Criticism*. Edited by David Charlton; translated by Martyn Clarke. Cambridge University Press, 2004.

Hoffmann, E.T.A. "Review." In Senner et al., *The Critical Reception of Beethoven's Compositions by His German Contemporaries*, vol. 2, pp. 95–112. Originally published in *Allgemeine musikalische Zeitung* 12 (July 4 and 11, 1810): 630–42 and 652–59.

Hoffmann, Ralf. *"Der Grenzgänger"* (Interview with Rick van der Linden), *Okey!*, July-August 2001, http://www.okey-online.com/artikel/041_report/index .html.

Hölderlin, Friedrich. "Oldest Programme for a System of German Idealism" (1796). Translated by Stefan Bird-Pollan. In *Classic and Romantic German Aesthetics*, edited by J. M. Bernstein, pp. 185–87. Cambridge University Press, 2003.

Homer. *The Iliad of Homer*. Translated by Samuel Butler. London: Longmans, Green & Co., 1898.

Horace. *A Poetical Translation of the Works of Horace* (9th ed.). Translated by Philip Francis. Edinburgh: Alexander Donaldson, 1779.

Horace. *Horazens Oden*. Translated by Karl Wilhelm Ramler. Berlin: Sandersche Buchhandlung, 1818.

Horace. *The Works of Horace*. Translated by Christopher Smart. London: W. Flexney; Mess. Johnson and Co.; T. Caslon, 1767.

Horowitz, Joseph. *Understanding Toscanini*. University of California Press, 1994.

Houghton, Walter E. *The Victorian Frame of Mind, 1830–1870*. Yale University Press, 1957.

Howard, Michael. *The Franco-Prussian War: The German Invasion of France, 1870–1871*. London: Routledge, 2001.

Howell, Standley. "Beethoven's Maelzel Canon: Another Schindler Forgery?" *The Musical Times* (December 1979): 987–90.

Hullot-Kentor, Robert. *Things Beyond Resemblance: Collected Essays on Theodor W. Adorno*. Columbia University Press, 2006.

Hunt, Tristram. *Marx's General: The Revolutionary Life of Friedrich Engels*. New York: Metropolitan Books, 2009.

Hyde, Martha M. "The Format and Function of Schoenberg's Twelve-Tone Sketches." *Journal of the American Musicological Society* 36, no. 3 (Autumn 1983): 453–80.

"Hyundai's 'Big Duh' Campaign Snares Top Spots in Consumer Recall Study." Press release, March 31, 2008. http://www.hyundainews.com/Corporate_News/Corporate/03_31_2008_2774.asp.

Ives, Charles. *Charles E. Ives: Memos.* Edited by John Kirkpatrick. New York: W. W. Norton & Company, 1991.

Ives, Charles. *Essays Before a Sonata, The Majority, and Other Writings.* Edited by Howard Boatwright. New York: W. W. Norton & Co., 1970.

Jacques, Jeph. "Number 1336: Canathesia." *Questionable Content* #1336. http://questionablecontent.net/view.php?comic=1336.

Jander, Owen. "'Let Your Deafness No Longer Be a Secret—Even in Art': Self-Portraiture and the Third Movement of the C-Minor Symphony." *The Beethoven Journal* 8 (2000): 25–70.

Jander, Owen. "The Prophetic Conversation in Beethoven's 'Scene by the Brook.'" *The Musical Quarterly* 77, no. 3 (Autumn 1993): 508–59.

Jansen, F. Gustav, ed. *Robert Schumanns Briefe: Neue Folge.* Leipzig: Breitkopf und Härtel, 1904.

Jellinek, Georg. *Allgemeine Staatslehre.* Berlin: Verlag von O. Häring, 1905.

Jellinek, Georg. *The Declaration of the Rights of Man and of Citizens.* Translated by Max Farrand. New York: Henry Holt and Company, 1901.

Jellinek, Georg. *Introduction à la Doctrine de L'État.* Translated and annotated by Georges Fardis. Paris: Albert Fontemoing, 1904.

Jenkins, Roy. *Gladstone.* New York: Random House, 1997.

Johnson, Douglas, Alan Tyson, and Robert Winter. *The Beethoven Sketchbooks.* University of California Press, 1985.

Johnson, Eric. "A Composer's Vision: Photographs by Ernest Bloch." *Aperture* 16, no. 3 (November 1972).

Johnson, James H. *Listening in Paris: A Cultural History.* University of California Press, 1995.

Johnson, Paul. "When Daring Dons Sported Through the Unguarded Groves of Academe." *The Spectator* 282, no. 8914 (June 12, 1999): 29.

Jones, LeRoi. *Four Black Revolutionary Plays.* Indianapolis and New York: Bobbs-Merrill Company, 1969.

Julia, Emile-François. *Antoine Bourdelle: Maitre d'Œuvre.* Paris: Librairie de France, 1930.

Kant, Immanuel. *The Critique of Judgement.* Translated by James Creed Meredith. Oxford: Clarendon Press, 1952.

Kater, Michael H. *The Twisted Muse: Musicians and Their Music in the Third Reich.* Oxford University Press, 1997.

Kautsky, Karl. *Terrorism and Communism.* Translated by W. H. Kerridge. http://www.marxists.org/archive/kautsky/1919/terrcomm/index.htm.

Keating, Corey. "WEBeethoven: Advertimento." *The Beethoven Journal* 25, no. 1 (Summer 2010): 43–44.

Kedourie, Elie. *Nationalism,* 4th ed. Oxford: Blackwell Publishers, 1994.

Kellerman, Jonathan. *Rage.* New York: Ballantine Books, 2005.

Kemble, Fanny ("Mrs. Butler, late Fanny Kemble"). *A Year of Consolation.* New York: Wiley & Putnam, 1847.

Kenaan, Rodeina. "Staff Try to Save Battered Hotel That Was Journalist's Haven." Associated Press, February 25, 1987.

Kerr, Alfred. *Eintagsfliegen, oder Die Macht der Kritik, Die Welt im Drama IV.* Berlin: S. Fischer Verlag, 1917.

Kerst, Friedrich. *Der Erinnerungen an Beethoven.* Stuttgart: Julius Hoffmann, 1913.

Keyserling, Hermann. "A Philosopher's View of the War." *The Atlantic Monthly* CXVII, no. 2 (February 1916): 145–53.

King, Martin Luther, Jr. "Some Things We Must Do." In Clayborne Carson, Susan Carson, Adrienne Clay, Kieran Taylor, and Virginia Shadron, eds., *The Papers of Martin Luther King, Jr.: Volume IV: Symbol of the Movement, January 1957–December 1958,* pp. 328–43. University of California Press, 2000.

Kingsley, Charles. *Yeast: A Problem.* New York: Harper and Brothers, 1851.

[Kingsley, Frances.] *Charles Kingsley: His Letters and Memories of His Life.* London: Henry S. King & Co., 1877.

Kirwan, James. *The Aesthetic in Kant: A Critique.* London: Continuum, 2004.

Klemperer, Victor. *The Language of the Third Reich: LTI—Lingua Tertii Imperii: A Philologist's Notebook.* Translated by Martin Brady. London: Athlone Press, 2000.

Knapp, Raymond. "A Tale of Two Symphonies: Converging Narrative of Divine Reconciliation in Beethoven's Fifth and Sixth." *Journal of the American Musicological Society* 53, no. 2 (Summer 2000): 291–343.

Knittel, K. M. "Wagner, Deafness, and the Reception of Beethoven's Late Style." *Journal of the American Musicological Society* 51, no. 1 (Spring 1998): 49–82.

Köhler, Joachim. *Richard Wagner: Last of the Titans.* Translated by Stewart Spencer. Yale University Press, 2004.

Konrad, Ulrich. "Mozart's Sketches." *Early Music* 20, no. 1 (February 1992): 119–32.

Kopitz, Klaus Martin. *Beethoven, Elisabeth Röckel und das Albumblatt "Für Elise."* Köln: Verlag Dohr, 2010.

Der Koran: oder Das gesetz der Moslemen durch Muhammed den sohn Abdallahs. Translated by Friedrich Eberhard Boysen. Halle: *"in der Gebauerschen Buchhandlung,"* 1828.

The Koran. Translated by J. M. Rodwell. London: Williams and Norgate, 1861.

von Kotzebue, August. *Theater von August v. Kotzebue.* "Verlag von Ignaz Klang in Wien und Eduard Kummer in Leipzig," 1841.

Kowalska, Joanna, and Elzbieta Szelag. "The Effect of Congenital Deafness on Duration Judgment." *Journal of Child Psychology and Psychiatry* 47, no. 9 (September 2006): 946–53.

Kraus, Beate Angelika. "Beethoven and the Revolution: the view of the French musical press." In *Music and the French Revolution,* Malcolm Boyd, ed., pp. 300–12. Cambridge University Press, 1992.

Kraus, Beate Angelika. *Beethoven-Rezeption in Frankreich.* Bonn: Verlag Beethoven-Haus, 2001.

Kris, Ernst, and Hans Speier. *German Radio Propaganda: Report on Home Broadcasts During the War.* Oxford University Press, 1944.

Ladd, Linda. *Die Smiling.* New York: Pinnacle Books, 2008.

Langhans, Wilhelm. *Die Geschichte der Musik des 17. 18. und 19. Jahrhunderts.* Leipzig: Verlag von F. E. C. Leuckart, 1887.

Langland, Elizabeth. "Gesturing Toward an Open Space: Gender, Form and Language in E. M. Forster's *Howards End.*" In Laura Claridge and Elizabeth Langland, eds., *Out of Bounds: Male Writers and Gender(ed) Criticism,* 252–67. University of Massachusetts Press, 1990.

Lanier, Sidney. *Poems of Sidney Lanier.* New York: Charles Scribner's Sons, 1888.

Lavater, Johann Kasper. *Hundert Christliche Lieder.* Zurich: Orell, Gessner, Füßli und Comp., 1776.

Lawrence, D. H. *Studies in Classic American Literature.* New York: Penguin Classics, 1991.

Leaming, Barbara. *Orson Welles.* New York: Penguin Books, 1985.

Lehmann, W. P. "Decoding of the Martian Language." *The Graduate Journal* (University of Texas at Austin) 7, no. 1 (December 1965): 265–72.

Lejeune, Helga, and J. H. Wearden. "Vierordt's *The Experimental Study of the Time Sense* (1868) and Its Legacy." *European Journal of Cognitive Psychology* 21 (2009): 941–60.

Leslie, Esther. *Hollywood Flatlands: Animation, Critical Theory, and the Avant-Garde.* London and New York: Verso, 2004.

Le Sueur, Jean-François. "Chant du 1er Vendémiaire An IX." In Constant Pierre, *Musique des fêtes et cérémonies de la révolution française: Oeuvres de Gossec, Cherubini, Lesueur, Méhul, Catel, etc.* (Paris: Imprimerie Nationale), p. 167.

Levayer, Paul-Edouard, ed. *Chansonnier révolutionnaire.* Paris: Éditions Gallimard, 1989.

Liebknecht, Wilhelm. *Karl Marx: Biographical Memoirs.* Translated by Ernest Untermann. Chicago: Charles H. Kerr & Co., 1906.

Littlefield, Richard C. "The Silence of the Frames." *Music Theory Online* 2.1 (1996), http://mto.societymusictheory.org/issues/mto.96.2.1/mto.96.2.1.littlefield.html.

Lockwood, Lewis. *Beethoven: The Music and the Life.* New York: W. W. Norton & Co., 2005.

Lodge, Oliver. *The Substance of Faith Allied With Science: A Catechism for Parents and Teachers.* London: Methuen & Co., 1907.

Lorenz, Edmund S. *Practical Church Music: A Discussion of Purposes Methods and Plans.* New York: Fleming H. Revell Company, 1909.

Lossoff, Nicky. "Silent Music and the Eternal Silence." In *Silence, Music, Silent Music,* edited by Nicky Lossoff and Jenny Doctor, pp. 205–22. Aldershot: Ashgate, 2007.

Lucas, John. *Thomas Beecham: An Obsession With Music.* Woodbridge: Boydell Press, 2008.

Ludwig van Beethovens Konversationshefte, Band 9. Edited by Grita Herre. VEB Deutscher Verlag für Musik Leipzig, 1988.

Lunacharsky, Anatoly. *On Literature and Art.* Translated by Avril Pyman and Fainna Glagoleva. Moscow: Progress Publishers, 1965.

Macpherson, James. *Die Gedichte Ossians eines alten celtischen Dichters.* Translated by Michael Denis. Vienna: Johann Thomas Edlen v. Trattern, 1769.

Maeterlinck, Maurice. *The Life of the Bee.* Translated by Alfred Sutro. New York: Dodd, Mead, and Company, 1903.

Mah, Harold. *Enlightenment Phantasies: Cultural Identity in France and Germany 1750–1914.* Ithaca: Cornell University Press, 2003.

Malet, Lucas. *The Wages of Sin.* London: Swan Sonnenschein and Co., 1891.

Malloch, William. "Carl Czerny's Metronome Marks for Haydn and Mozart Symphonies." *Early Music* 16, no. 1 (February 1988): 72–82.

"Man Behind BET's 'Read a Book' Responds to Critics." *Tell Me More*, National Public Radio, September 17, 2007, http://www.npr.org/templates/story/story.php?storyId=14466377.

Mann, Thomas. *Doctor Faustus.* Translated by H. T. Lowe-Porter. New York: Alfred A. Knopf, 1948.

Marriner, Robin. "Derrida and the *Parergon*." In *A Companion to Art Theory* edited by Paul Smith and Carolyn Wilde, pp. 349–59. Oxford: Blackwell, 2002.

Martin, Theodore. *The Life of His Royal Highness the Prince Consort.* London: Smith, Elder & Co., 1875.

Marx, A. B. "A Few Words on the Symphony and Beethoven's Achievements in This Field." In Senner et al., *The Critical Reception of Beethoven's Compositions by His German Contemporaries.* University of Nebraska Press, 1999, vol. 1, pp. 59–77. Originally published in *Berliner allgemeine musikalische Zeitung* I (May 12, 1824): 165–68, 173–76, 181–84.

Marx, A. B. *Musical Form in the Age of Beethoven.* Edited and translated by Scott Burnham. Cambridge University Press, 1997.

Marx, Karl. *Capital.* "[T]ranslated from the third German edition by Samuel Moore and Edward Aveling; and edited by Frederick Engels; revised and amplified according to the Fourth German Edition by Ernest Untermann." Chicago: Charles H. Kerr & Co., 1909.

Marx, Karl. *Critique of Hegel's "Philosophy of Right."* Translated and edited by Joseph O'Malley. Cambridge University Press, 1977.

Marx, Karl. *A Contribution to the Critique of Political Economy.* Translated by Salo Ryazanskaya. New York: International Publishers, 1979.

Marx, Karl. *The Essential Marx: The Non-Economic Writings—a Selection.* Edited and translated by Saul K. Padover. New York: New American Library, 1978.

Marx, Karl, and Frederick Engels. *Karl Marx/Frederick Engels: Collected Works*, vol. 2. London: Lawrence & Wishart, 1975.

Marx, Karl, and Frederick Engels. *Karl Marx and Frederick Engels: Letters to Americans, 1848–1895.* Edited by Alexander Trachtenberg. New York: International Publishers, 1953.

Marx, Karl, and Frederick Engels. *Marx-Engels-Gesamtausgabe*, I. Abteilung, Band 1. Berlin: Dietz Verlag, 1975.

Mason, William. *Memories of a Musical Life.* New York: Century Co., 1902.

Mathew, Nicholas. "History Under Erasure: *Wellingtons Sieg*, the Congress of Vienna, and the Ruination of Beethoven's Heroic Style." *The Musical Quarterly* 89, no. 1 (Spring 2006): 17–61.

McCombe, A., et al. "Guidelines for the Grading of Tinnitus Severity: The Results of a Working Group Commissioned by the British Association of Otolaryngologists, Head and Neck Surgeons, 1999." *Clinical Otolaryngology & Applied Sciences* 26, no. 5 (October 2001): 388–96.

McGuffey, William. *McGuffey's Fifth Eclectic Reader.* American Book Co., 1879.

McGuire, Christine. *Until Judgment Day.* New York: Simon and Schuster, 2003.

McLeod, Ken. "'A Fifth of Beethoven': Disco, Classical Music, and the Politics of Inclusion." *American Music* 24, no. 3 (Autumn 2006): 347–63.

Mead, Darius, editor. *The American Literary Emporium, or Friendship's Gift.* New York: C. H. Camp, 1848.

Méhul, Étienne Nicolas. *Ariodant.* Libretto by François Hoffmann. New York and London: Garland Publishing, 1980 (facsimile of the first printed edition).

Méhul, Étienne Nicolas. *Euphrosine, ou Le Tyran Corrigé.* Libretto by François Hoffmann. New York and London: Garland Publishing, 1980 (facsimile of the first printed edition).

Méhul, Étienne Nicolas. *Symphony no. 1 in G minor.* Edited by David Charlton. Madison, WI: A-R Editions, 1985.

Méhul, Étienne Nicolas. *Three Symphonies.* Edited by David Charlton. New York and London: Garland Publishing, 1982.

Méhul, Étienne Nicolas. *Uthal.* Libretto by Jacques Benjamin Saint-Victor. New York and London: Garland Publishing, 1980 (facsimile of the first printed edition).

Melvin, Sheila, and Jindong Cai. *Rhapsody in Red: How Western Classical Music Became Chinese.* New York: Algora Publishing, 2004.

Michelet, Jules. *Historical View of the French Revolution.* Translated by Charles Cocks. London: George Bell and Sons, 1888.

Minor, Ryan. "Prophet and Populace in Liszt's 'Beethoven' Cantatas." In *Liszt and His World,* edited by Christopher H. Gibbs and Dana Cooley, pp. 113–66. Princeton University Press, 2006.

Mongrédien, Jean. *French Music from the Enlightenment to Romanticism 1789–1830.* Translated by Sylvain Frémaux. Portland, OR: Amadeus Press, 1996.

Morse, Samuel F. B. *Foreign Conspiracy Against the Liberties of the United States: The Numbers Under the Signature of Brutus, Originally Published in the New York Observer* ("Seventh Edition"). New York: American and Foreign Christian Union, 1855.

"Mrs. Jay Quits: Announces She Will Lead No More Uprisings Against German Art." *The New York Times,* July 3, 1919: 11.

Müller, Wilhelm Christian. "Something on Ludwig van Beethoven." In Senner et al., *The Critical Reception of Beethoven's Compositions by His German Contemporaries,* vol. 1, 101–11. Originally published in *Allgemeine musikalische Zeitung* 29 (May 23, 1827): 345–54.

Müller-Doohm, Stefan. *Adorno: A Biography.* Cambridge: Polity Press, 2005.

Münzer, Kurt. *Mademoiselle.* In *Die flammende Venus: Erotische Novellen,* Reinhold Eichacker, editor, pp. 119–32. Munich: Universal-Verlag, 1919.

Musgrave, Michael. *The Musical Life of the Crystal Palace.* Cambridge University Press, 1995.

Newman, William S. "Yet Another Major Beethoven Forgery by Schindler?" *The Journal of Musicology* 3, no. 4 (Autumn 1984): 397–422.

"News. Leipzig." In Senner et al., *The Critical Reception of Beethoven's Compositions by His German Contemporaries*, vol. 2, p. 92. Originally published in *Allgemeine musikalische Zeitung* 11 (February 1, 1809): 281.

Nelson, Amy. *Music for the Revolution: Musicians and Power in Early Soviet Russia.* Pennsylvania State University Press, 2004.

Nietzsche, Friedrich. *The Gay Science.* Translated by Walter Kaufmann. New York: Vintage Books, 1974.

Nietzsche, Friedrich. *Human, All Too Human.* Translated by R. J. Hollindale. Cambridge University Press, 1986.

Nietzsche, Friedrich. *On the Genealogy of Morals and Ecce Homo.* Translated by Walter Kaufmann and R. J. Hollingdale. New York: Vintage Books, 1989.

Nietzsche, Friedrich. *Thus Spoke Zarathustra.* Translated by R. J. Hollingdale. London: Penguin Books, 2003.

Nietzsche, Friedrich. *Twilight of the Idols and The Anti-Christ.* Translated by R. J. Hollingdale. London: Penguin Books, 1990.

Nietzsche, Friedrich. *Untimely Meditations.* Translated by R. J. Hollingdale, Edited by Daniel Breazeale. Cambridge University Press, 1997.

Nietzsche, Friedrich. *The Will to Power.* Translated by Walter Kaufmann and R. J. Hollingdale. New York: Vintage Books, 1968.

"No Power to Bar Papers: Court Enjoins Mount Vernon from Banning Hearst by Law." *The New York Times,* June 5, 1918: 22.

Nohl, Ludwig. *Life of Beethoven.* Translated by John J. Lalor. Chicago: Jansen, McClurg & Co., 1881; originally published in Germany by Ernst Julius Günther, Leipzig, 1867.

Nothnagle, Alan N. *Building the East German Myth: Historical Mythology and Youth Propaganda in the German Democratic Republic, 1945–1989.* University of Michigan Press, 1999.

Nottebohm, Gustav. *Beethoveniana. Aufsätze und Mittheilungen.* Leipzig: Verlag von C. F. Peters, 1872.

Nottebohm, Gustav. *Ein Skizzenbuch von Beethoven aus dem Jahre 1803.* Leipzig: Breitkopf und Härtel, 1880.

"Occasional Notes." *The Musical Times,* February 1, 1911: 87–88.

[Ossoli,] Margaret Fuller. *Memoirs of Margaret Fuller Ossoli.* Boston: Phillips, Sampson and Company, 1852.

Oulibicheff, Alexandre. *Beethoven, ses critiques et ses glossateurs.* Paris: Jules Gavelot, 1857.

"Our Representative Man." *Punch,* September 14, 1878: 117–18.

Owens, Thomas Clarke, ed. *Selected Correspondence of Charles Ives.* University of California Press, 2007.

Paddison, Max. *Adorno's Aesthetics of Music.* Cambridge University Press, 1997.

"The Parliamentary Committee on Proprietary Remedies. Evidence Regarding Beecham's Pills." *The British Medical Journal* 1, no. 2718 (February 1, 1913): 234.

Perlis, Vivian. *Charles Ives Remembered: An Oral History.* Yale University Press, 1974.

Pierre, Constant, ed. *Musique des fêtes et cérémonies de la révolution française*. Paris: Imprimerie Nationale, 1899.

Piggott, Jan. *Palace of the People: The Crystal Palace at Sydenham, 1854–1936*. University of Wisconsin Press, 2004.

Piper, Adrian. "Passing for White, Passing for Black." *Transition* 58 (1992): 4–32.

Pope, Franklin Leonard. "The American Inventors of the Telegraph." *The Century* 35, no. 6 (April 1888): 924–44.

Prod'homme, J.-G. "*La musique et les musiciens en 1848*." *Sammelbände der Internationalen Musikgesellschaft* 14, no. 1 (October-December 1912): 155–82.

Pynchon, Thomas. *Gravity's Rainbow*. New York: Viking Press, 1973.

Quintilian. *Quintilian's Institutes of Oratory*. Translated by John Selby Watson. London: George Bell and Sons, 1876.

Radiguier, Henri. "La Musique Française de 1789 à 1815." In *Encyclopédie de la musique et dictionnaire du conservatoire*, Albert Lavignac and Lionel de la Laurencie, eds., 1562–1660. Paris: Librairie Delagrave, 1921.

Rampersad, Arnold. *Ralph Ellison: A Biography*. New York: Alfred A. Knopf, 1997.

von Ranke, Leopold. *Fürsten und völker von Süd-Europa im sechszehnten und siebzehnten jahrhundert*. Berlin: Duncker und Humblot, 1834.

Reich, Christopher. *The First Billion*. New York: Random House, 2003.

Repp, Bruno H. "Sensorimotor synchronization and perception of timing: Effects of music training and task experience." *Human Movement Science* 29 (2010): 200–213.

"Reunion in San Francisco." *Billboard*, May 5, 1945: 9.

Richards, Thomas. *The Commodity Culture of Victorian England*. Stanford University Press, 1990.

Ringer, Alexander L. "A French Symphonist at the Time of Beethoven: Etienne Nicolas Méhul." *The Musical Quarterly* 37, no. 4 (October 1951): 543–65.

Ripley, George, and Charles A. Dana, editors. *The New American Cyclopaedia: A Popular Dictionary of General Knowledge*. New York: D. Appleton and Company, 1861.

Robertson, Priscilla. *Revolutions of 1848: A Social History*. Princeton University Press, 1952.

Rogers, J. A. *Sex and Race: Volume III: Why White and Black Mix in Spite of Opposition*. New York: J. A. Rogers, 1944.

Rosenbaum, Sandra P. *Performance Practices in Classic Piano Music*. Indiana University Press, 1991.

Roth, Colin. "Carl Nielsen and the Danish Tradition of Storytelling." *Carl Nielsen Studies*, vol. 4 (2009): 164–85.

Rubsamen, Walter H. "Schoenberg in America." *The Musical Quarterly* 37, no. 4 (October 1951): 469–89.

Ruchames, Louis. "Wendell Phillips' Lovejoy Address." *The New England Quarterly* 47, no. 1 (March 1974): 108–17.

Rudenstine, Angelica Zander. *Modern Painting, Drawing & Sculpture Collected by Emily and Joseph Pulitzer, Jr.*, vol. 4. Harvard University Art Museums, 1988.

Rudolf, Anthony. *Sage Eye: The Aesthetic Passion of Jonathan Griffin*. Berkeley, CA: Menard Press, 1992.

Rumph, Stephen. "A Kingdom Not of This World: The Political Context of E.T.A. Hoffmann's Beethoven Criticism." *19th-Century Music* 19, no. 1 (Summer 1995): 50–67.

Rush, Don. "Queen's Freddie Mercury: The Circus Magazine Tapes." *Circus,* March 17, 1977.

Sachs, Harvey. *Toscanini.* New York: Harper & Row, 1988.

Sagan, Carl, with F. D. Drake, Ann Druyan, Timothy Ferris, Jon Lomberg, and Linda Salzman Sagan. *Murmurs of Earth: The Voyager Interstellar Record.* New York: Random House, 1978.

Sargeant, Winthrop. "Musical Events." *The New Yorker* 47, no. 52 (February 12, 1972): 70–73.

Sartre, Jean-Paul. *Situations,* vol. 4. Translated by Benita Eisler. New York: G. Braziller, 1965.

Sartre, Jean-Paul. *War Diaries: Notebooks from a Phoney War 1939–40.* Translated by Quentin Hoare. London: Verso, 1999.

Saxe Wyndham, Henry. *August Manns and the Saturday Concerts: A Memoir and a Retrospect.* London: Walter Scott Publishing Co., Ltd., 1909.

Schauffler, Robert Haven. *Beethoven: The Man Who Freed Music.* New York: Tudor Publishing Co., 1944.

Schauffler, Robert Haven. *The Unknown Brahms.* New York: Dodd, Mead and Company, 1933.

Schenker, Heinrich. *Counterpoint.* Translated by John Rothgeb and Jürgen Thym. New York: Schirmer Books, 1987.

Schenker, Heinrich. *Free Composition (Der freie Satz): Volume III of New Musical Theories and Fantasies.* Translated by Ernst Oster. New York: Longman, 1979.

Schenker, Heinrich. *Harmony.* Edited by Oswald Jonas, translated by Elisabeth Mann Borgese. University of Chicago Press, 1954.

Schenker, Heinrich. *Der Tonwille: Pamphlets in Witness of the Immutable Laws of Music.* Translated by William Drabkin. Oxford University Press, 2004.

Schering, Arnold. *Beethoven und der deutsche Idealismus: rede gehalten beim Festakt zur feier der 150. Wiederkehr des Geburtstages Ludwig van Beethovens an der vereinigten Friedrichs-Universitat Halle-Wittenberg am 16. Dezember 1920.* Leipzig: Verlag von C. F. Kahnt, 1921.

Schickele, Peter. "New Horizons in Music Appreciation." *Report from Hoople: P.D.Q. Bach on the Air,* Vanguard 79268 (1967).

Schiller, Friedrich. *Schiller's Complete Works.* Edited and translated by C. J. Hempel. Philadelphia: I. Kohler, 1861.

Schiller, Friedrich. *On the Aesthetic Education of Man.* Translated by Elizabeth M. Wilkinson and L. A. Willoughby. Oxford University Press, 1983.

Schiller, Friedrich. *Schillers Werke. Nationalausgabe. Neunundzwanzigster Band: Schillers Briefe 1796–1798.* Edited by Norbert Oellers and Frithjof Stock. Weimar: Hermann Böhlaus Nachfolger, 1977.

Schindler, Anton. *Beethoven As I Knew Him.* Translated by Donald W. MacArdle. New York: Dover Publications, 1996. (Translation of Schindler, *Biographie von Ludwig van Beethoven* [1860].)

Schindler, Anton. *Biographie von Ludwig van Beethoven.* 3rd ed. Münster, 1860.

Schindler, Anton. *The Life of Beethoven.* Translated and edited by Ignace Moscheles. London: Henry Colburn, 1841.

Schlegel, A. W. *Kritische Schriften und Briefe.* Stuttgart: W. Kohlhammer Verlag, 1962.

Schmitz, Arnold. *Das romantische Beethovenbild.* Berlin und Bonn: Ferd. Dümmlers Verlag, 1927.

Schoenberg, Arnold. *Arnold Schoenberg: Letters.* Edited by Erwin Stein. University of California Press, 1987.

Schopenhauer, Arthur. *The World as Will and Representation.* Translated by E. F. Payne. New York: Dover Publications, 1969.

Schrade, Leo. *Beethoven in France.* Yale University Press, 1942.

Schuller, Gunther. *The Compleat Conductor.* Oxford University Press, 1998.

Schumann, Robert. *Music and Musicians: Essays and Criticisms.* Translated by Fanny Raymond Ritter. London: William Reeves, 1891.

Sears, Clara Endicott, "compiled by." *Bronson Alcott's Fruitlands.* Boston: Houghton Mifflin Company, 1915.

Senner, Wayne M., translator, and Robin Wallace and William Meredith, editors. *The Critical Reception of Beethoven's Compositions by His German Contemporaries,* 2 vols. University of Nebraska Press, 1999 (vol. 1); 2001 (vol. 2).

Shakespeare, William. *Shakespear Theatrikalische Werke,* VIItr. Band. Translated by Christoph Martin Wieland. Zürich: Orell, Geßner und Comp., 1766.

Shandler, Jeffrey. *While America Watches: Televising the Holocaust.* Oxford University Press, 1999.

Shaw, George Bernard. *Complete Plays with Prefaces.* New York: Dodd, Mead & Co., 1962.

[Sheppard, Elizabeth Sara.] *Rumour.* London: Hurst and Blackett, 1858.

Shirakawa, Sam H. *The Devil's Music Master: The Controversial Life and Career of Wilhelm Furtwängler.* Oxford University Press, 1992.

A Short History of Cheap Music as Exemplified in the Record of the House of Novello, Ewer & Co. with Especial Reference to the First Fifty Years of the Reign of Her Most Gracious Majesty Queen Victoria with Three Portraits and a Preface by Sir George Grove, D.C.L., &c. London and New York: Novello, Ewer and Co., 1887.

Sillitoe, Alan. *The General.* New York: Alfred A. Knopf, 1961.

Simms, Bryan R. "New Documents in the Schoenberg-Schenker Polemic." *Perspectives of New Music* 16, no. 1 (Autumn-Winter 1977): 110–24.

Sinclair, James B. *A Descriptive Catalogue of the Music of Charles Ives.* Yale University Press, 1999.

Slonimsky, Nicolas. *A Thing or Two About Music.* New York: Allen, Towne, & Heath, Inc., 1948.

Slonimsky, Nicolas. *Lexicon of Musical Invective.* New York: W. W. Norton & Co., 2000.

Smith, Steven C. *A Heart at Fire's Center: The Life and Music of Bernard Herrmann.* University of California Press, 1991.

Solomon, Maynard. *Beethoven.* 2nd rev. ed. New York: Schirmer Books, 1998.

Solomon, Maynard. *Beethoven Essays*. Harvard University Press, 1990.

Solomon, Maynard. "Beethoven, Freemasonry, and the *Tagebuch* of 1812–1818." *Beethoven Forum* 8 (2000): 101–46.

Solomon, Maynard. "Beethoven's Tagebuch of 1812–1818." In *Beethoven Studies 3*, edited by Alan Tyson, pp. 193–285. Cambridge University Press, 1982.

Solomon, Maynard. "Beethoven's '*Magazin der Kunst*.'" *19th-Century Music* 7, no. 3 (April 1984): 199–208.

Sonneck, Oscar. *Beethoven: Impressions by His Contemporaries*. New York: Dover Publications, 1967.

Spender, Stephen. *The Creative Element*. London: Hamish Hamilton, 1953.

"Spotlight Winners of the Week." *Billboard*, May 1, 1961: 21–23.

Stadlen, Peter. "Beethoven and the Metronome." *Soundings* 9 (1982): 38–73.

Stadlen, Peter. "Schindler's Beethoven Forgeries." *The Musical Times* (July 1977): 549–52.

Stearns, Frank Preston. *Sketches from Concord and Appledore*. New York: G. P. Putnam's Sons, 1895.

Steblin, Rita. *A History of Key Characteristics in the Eighteenth and Early Nineteenth Centuries*. 2nd ed. University of Rochester Press, 2002.

Stein, Leonard. "A Note on the Genesis of the *Ode to Napoleon*." *Journal of the Arnold Schoenberg Institute* II, no. 1 (October 1977): 52–54.

Steinberg, Michael P. *Listening to Reason: Culture, Subjectivity, and Nineteenth-Century Music*. Princeton University Press, 2004.

Sterba, Editha and Richard. *Beethoven and His Nephew: A Psychoanalytical Study of Their Relationship*. New York: Schocken Books, 1971.

Stern, Fritz. *The Varieties of History*. New York: Meridian Books, 1956.

Stevens, C. E. "Gildas Sapiens." *The English Historical Review* 56, no. 223 (July 1941): 353–73.

Stevenson, Robert Louis, and Lloyd Osbourne. *The Ebb-Tide: A Trio and Quartette*. New York: Charles Scribner's Sons, 1913.

Stewart, Donald Ogden. *Perfect Behavior*. New York: George H. Doran Company, 1922.

Stravinsky, Igor. *An Autobiography*. New York: W. W. Norton & Co., 1962.

Sturm, Christoph Christian. *Reflections on the Works of God in Nature and Providence, for Every Day in the Year*. Translated by Adam Clarke. New York: McElrath, Bangs, & Herbert, 1833.

Sutherland, Allan. *Famous Hymns of the World: Their Origin and Their Romance*. New York: Frederick A. Stokes Company, 1906.

Swedenborg, Emmanuel. *The True Christian Religion; Containing the Universal Theology of the New Church*. New York: American Swedenborg Printing and Publishing Society, 1855.

Swift, Lindsay. *Brook Farm: Its Members, Scholars, and Visitors*. New York: Macmillan Company, 1900.

"Tam-tam-tam-ta." *Der Spiegel*, September 3, 1970: 81–82.

Taruskin, Richard. "On Letting the Music Speak for Itself: Some Reflections on Musicology and Performance." *The Journal of Musicology* 1, no. 3 (July 1982): 338–49.

Taruskin, Richard. "Public Lies and Unspeakable Truth Interpreting Shostakovich's Fifth Symphony." In David Fanning, ed., *Shostakovich Studies*, pp. 17–56. Cambridge University Press, 1995.

Thackeray, William Makepeace. *Denis Duval: Lovel the Widower: and Other Stories*. London: Smith, Elder & Co., 1869.

[Thayer, Alexander Wheelock.] "From My Diary. No. XVI." *Dwight's Journal of Music* II, no. 19 (February 12, 1853): 149.

Thayer, Alexander Wheelock. *Ludwig van Beethovens Leben*, Dritter Band. Berlin: W. Weber, 1879.

Thayer, Alexander Wheelock. *Ludwig van Beethovens Leben*, Vierter Band. Completed from preliminary work and materials by Hermann Dieters. Leipzig: Breitkopf und Härtel, 1907.

Thayer, Alexander Wheelock. *Thayer's Life of Beethoven*, revised and edited by Elliot Forbes. Princeton University Press, 1967.

Thoreau, Henry David. *Civil Disobedience and Other Essays*. New York: Dover Publications, 1993.

Thoreau, Henry David. *The Journal of Henry D. Thoreau*. Boston: Houghton, Mifflin and Company, 1906.

Thoreau, Henry David. *Walden*. Boston: Houghton, Mifflin and Company, 1892.

Ticknor, George. *Life, Letters, and Journals of George Ticknor*. Boston and New York: Houghton Mifflin Company, 1909.

Tiersot, Julien. *Les fêtes et les chants de la révolution française*. Paris: Librairie Hachette et Cie., 1908.

Tischler, Barbara L. "One Hundred Percent Americanism and Music in Boston during World War I." *American Music* 4, no. 2 (Summer 1986): 164–76.

Trotsky, Leon. *Dictatorship vs. Democracy (Terrorism and Communism): A Reply to Karl Kautsky*. New York: Workers Party of America, 1922.

Trotsky, Leon. "In 'Socialist' Norway" (1936). http://www.marxists.org/archive/trotsky/1936/12/nor.htm.

Trotsky, Leon. *My Life: An Attempt at an Autobiography*. New York: Charles Scribner's Sons, 1930.

Tusa, Michael C. "Beethoven's 'C-minor Mood': Some Thoughts on the Structural Implications of Key Choice." *Beethoven Forum* 2 (1993): 1–28.

Upton, George P., editor. *Theodore Thomas: A Musical Autobiography*. Chicago: A. C. McClurg & Co., 1905.

Ustinov, Peter. *Beethoven's Tenth: A Comedy in Two Acts*. New York: Samuel French, Inc., 1985.

Van de Walle, Etienne, and Elisha P. Renne. *Regulating Menstruation: Beliefs, Practices, Interpretations*. University of Chicago Press, 2001.

Vaneigem, Raoul. *The Revolution of Everyday Life*. Translated by Donald Nicholson-Smith. Welcombe: Rebel Press, 2001.

Van Zile Belden, Jessie. *Fate at the Door*. Philadelphia: J. B. Lippincott Company, 1895.

Vermeil, Jean. *Conversations with Boulez*. Translated by Camille Naish. Portland: Amadeus Press, 1996.

Virilio, Paul. *Speed and Politics.* Translated by Mark Polizzotti. Los Angeles: Semiotext(e), 2006.

Wade, Rachel W. "Beethoven's *Eroica* Sketchbook." *Fontes artis musicae* XXIV, no. 4 (October-December 1977): 254–90.

[Wagner, Cosima.] *Cosima Wagner's Diaries: Volume I, 1869–1877.* Edited and annotated by Martin Gregor-Dellin and Dietrich Mack; translated by Geoffrey Skelton. New York and London: Harcourt Brace Jovanovich, 1978.

Wagner, Richard. "Beethoven." Translated by William Ashton Ellis. In *Richard Wagner's Prose Works*, vol. V, pp. 61–126. London: William Reeves, 1896.

Wagner, Richard. *My Life* ("authorized translation from the German"). New York: Dodd, Mead & Co., 1911.

Wagner, Richard. *On Conducting (Ueber das Dirigiren).* Translated by Edward Dannreuther. London: William Reeves, 1887.

Wagner, Richard. *On Conducting.* Translated by William Ashton Ellis. In *Richard Wagner's Prose Works*, vol. IV. London: Kegan Paul, Trench, Trübner & Co., Ltd., 1912.

Wagner, Richard. *Richard Wagner's Letters to His Dresden Friends.* Translated by J. S. Shedlock. New York: Scribner and Welford, 1890.

Wagner, Richard. *Sämtliche Briefe*, Band VI. Edited by Hans-Josef Bauer and Johannes Forner. VEB Deutscher Verlag für Musik Leipzig, 1986.

Walker, Alan. *Franz Liszt: The Virtuoso Years, 1811–1947.* Rev. ed. Ithaca: Cornell University Press, 1987.

Walker, Alan. *Hans von Bülow: A Life and Times.* Oxford University Press, 2009.

Wallace, Robin. *Beethoven's Critics.* Cambridge University Press, 1986.

Walter, William E. "Culled From the Mail Pouch: Miss Farrar Remembers Karl Muck's War Problem." *The New York Times*, March 10, 1940: 159.

Walton, Ortiz M. "A Comparative Analysis of the African and the Western Aesthetics." In *The Black Aesthetic*, edited by Addison Gayle, Jr., pp. 161–72. Garden City, NY: Doubleday & Company, 1971.

Watts, Jerry Gafio. *Heroism and the Black Intellectual: Ralph Ellison, Politics, and Afro-American Intellectual Life.* University of North Carolina Press, 1994.

Weatherhead, Andrea K. "*Howards End*: Beethoven's *Fifth*." *Twentieth Century Literature* 31, no. 2/3 (E. M. Forster Issue) (Summer-Autumn 1985): 247–64.

Webb, E. R. *Gemini's Cross.* Mustang, OK: Tate Publishing, 2007.

Wegeler, Franz, and Ferdinand Ries. *Beethoven Remembered: The Biographical Notes of Franz Wegeler and Ferdinand Ries.* Translated by Frederick Noonan. Arlington, VA: Great Ocean Publishers, 1987.

Wehr, Wesley. *The Eighth Lively Art: Conversations with Painters, Poets, Musicians, & the Wicked Witch of the West.* University of Washington Press, 2000.

Weingartner, Felix. *On Conducting.* Translated by Ernest Newman. London: Breitkopf und Härtel, 1906.

Weingartner, Felix. *On the Performance of Beethoven's Symphonies.* Translated by Jessie Crosland. London: Breitkopf und Härtel, 1907.

Wheelwright, Philip. *Heraclitus.* Princeton University Press, 1959.

Whitman, Walt. *Leaves of Grass.* New York: Modern Library, 1921.

Whorton, James C. *Inner Hygiene: Constipation and the Pursuit of Health in Modern Society.* Oxford University Press, 2000.

Winsor, Justin, editor. *The Memorial History of Boston, Including Suffolk County, Massachusetts, 1630–1880.* Boston: James R. Osgood and Company, 1883.

Woideck, Carl. *Charlie Parker: His Music and Life.* University of Michigan Press, 1998.

Wonke, Gundula, and Dieter Wallschläger. "Song Dialects in the Yellowhammer *Emberiza citrinella*: Bioacoustic Variation Between and Within Dialects." *Journal of Ornithology* 150, no. 1 (January 2009): 117–26.

"X.Y.Z." "The King of Saxony. (To the editor of the 'Spectator.')" *The Spectator* (London), no. 3861 (June 28, 1902): 1005–06.

Yang, Xiyun. "U.S. Orchestra Performs in China, in Echoes of 1973." *The New York Times*, May 7, 2010.

Yarrow, Kielan, et al. "Illusory Perceptions of Space and Time Preserve Cross-Saccadic Perceptual Continuity." *Nature* 414 (November 15, 2001): 302–5.

Young, Percy M. *Beethoven: A Victorian Tribute; based on the papers of Sir George Smart.* London: Dennis Dobson, 1976.

Žižek, Slavoj. *In Defense of Lost Causes.* London and New York: Verso, 2008.

Index

A NOTE ABOUT THE AUTHOR

Matthew Guerrieri writes on music for *The Boston Globe* and *NewMusicBox,* and his articles have also appeared in *Vanity Fair, Playbill, Musical America,* and *Slate* magazines. *The First Four Notes* is his first book.

A NOTE ON THE TYPE

This book was set in a type called Baskerville, a face made for John Baskerville (1706–1775) from his designs. Baskerville's original face was one of the forerunners of the type style known to printers as "modern face"—a "modern" of the period A.D. 1800.

Composed by North Market Street Graphics, Lancaster, Pennsylvania

Printed and bound by Berryville Graphics, Berryville, Virginia

Designed by Maggie Hinders